1ST ROW: US Air Force Sergeant David Fichter (b.1951); US Army Captain Dr. Alan Garfinkel (b.1942); US Army Specialist Leonardo H.G. Jarvis (1945–2003); US Army Specialist Marc Leepson (b.1945); US Army Warrant Officer Gerald "Jerry" McKinsey (1947–1968).
2ND ROW: US Army Staff Sergeant Michael Mann (b.1947); US Army Sergeant Tom Cavanaugh (b.1946); US Army Captain Christian Buehler (b.1941); US Navy, Thomas F. Brock (1947–2009); US Army 1st Lieutenant Jerome R. Watson (b.1944); US Army Warrant Officer Richard Deer (b.1947). **3RD ROW:** US Army Specialist David Lutz (1948–2016); (left) US Army Specialist David Patrick Dries (1945–1996); US Army Corporal Darrell Sterkel (b.1949) and Jim Shipley; US Army Staff Sergeant Janet Singer (1947–2015); US Navy Corpsman James Britt Clayton, Jr. (1947–2010). **4TH ROW:** Unidentified (image supplied by the US Army Quartermaster Museum); US Army Specialist Fernando Escalante (b.1945); US Army Major Florence Dunn; US Army Master Sergeant Edward Green (1926–1979). **5TH ROW:** US Army Captain John C Krizer (1941–2015); US Marine Corps Private Ivan Hiestand (b.1946) receiving a Purple Heart from General Westmoreland; US Air Force Staff Sergeant Daniel C. Berenz (1947–2009); Unidentified (image supplied by the US Army Quartermaster Museum); US Marine Corps Private Jim Prendergast (b.1947); US Marine Corps Corporal Robert "Bob" Raphael (b.1947). **6TH ROW:** US Army 1st Lieutenant Anthony Laurino (middle row, center) and his platoon (9th Infantry Division); US Army Specialist Dennis DeCarlo (b.1949);

DK SMITHSONIAN ☀

THE VIETNAM WAR

THE DEFINITIVE ILLUSTRATED HISTORY

DK UK
Project Editor Miezan van Zyl
Senior Art Editor Sharon Spencer
US Editors Karyn Gerhard, Margaret Parrish
Managing Editor Angeles Gavira Guerrero
Managing Art Editor Michael Duffy
Jacket Design Development Manager Sophia MTT
Jacket Editor Claire Gell
Jacket Designer Sean Ross
Pre-Production Producer Tony Phipps
Producer Anna Vallarino
Publisher Liz Wheeler
Art Director Karen Self
Publishing Director Jonathan Metcalf

DK DELHI
Senior Editor Dharini Ganesh
Project Art Editor Vaibhav Rastogi
Art Editors Sanjay Chauhan, Konica Juneja,
Debjyoti Mukherjee, Upasana Sharma
Assistant Editor Isha Sharma
Senior Editorial Manager Rohan Sinha
Deputy Managing Art Editor Anjana Nair
Jacket Designer Dhirendra Singh
Managing Jackets Editor Saloni Singh
Picture Researcher Aditya Katyal
Manager Picture Research Taiyaba Khatoon
DTP Designers Jaypal Chauhan,
Syed Md Farhan
Senior DTP Designers Harish Aggarwal, Jagtar Singh
Pre-Production Manager Balwant Singh
Production Manager Pankaj Sharma

TOUCAN BOOKS
Managing Editor Ellen Dupont
Senior Editor Dorothy Stannard
Senior Art Editor Thomas Keenes
Editor Abigail Mitchell
Additional Editing Cathy Meeus
Editorial Assistants Michael Clark, Joseph Persad
Cartography Ed Merritt
Proofreader Marion Dent
Indexer Marie Lorimer

SMITHSONIAN CONSULTANTS
Dr. F. Robert van der Linden Curator of Air Transportation and Special Purpose Aircraft, National Air and Space Museum; **Dr. Alex M. Spencer** Curator of British Military Aviation and Flight Materiál, National Air and Space Museum; **Jennifer L. Jones**, Chair, Armed Forces Division, National Museum of American History

First American Edition, 2017
Published in the United States by DK Publishing
345 Hudson Street, New York, New York 10014

A catalog record for this book is available from the Library of Congress.
ISBN 978-1-4654-5769-1

DK books are available at special discounts when purchased in bulk for sales promotions, premiums,
fund-raising, or educational use. For details, contact: DK Publishing Special Markets, 345 Hudson Street,
New York, New York 10014 or SpecialSales@dk.com

Printed and bound in Hong Kong

A WORLD OF IDEAS:
SEE ALL THERE IS TO KNOW
www.dk.com

CONTENTS

1

THE BACKGROUND
BEFORE MARCH 1959

2

AMERICA DRAWN INTO VIETNAM
MAR 1959– DEC 1964

A FRENCH AIRCRAFT DOWNED AT DIEN BIEN PHU

3
AMERICA GOES TO WAR
JAN 1965–SEP 1967

PLANNING US WAR STRATEGY

A US HELICOPTER GUNNER

THE TURNING POINT
SEP 1967–DEC 1968

5
NIXON'S WAR
JAN 1969–DEC 1971

US ANTIWAR PROTEST

SEARCH-AND-DESTROY MISSION

6

EASTER OFFENSIVE TO US EXIT
JAN 1972–JAN 1973

ARVN SOLDIERS DURING THE SIEGE OF AN LOC

7

ENDGAME AND AFTERMATH
AFTER JANUARY 1973

EVACUEES TAKE TO THE ROAD

Foreword

At the end of World War II, the United States emerged as a political and economic superpower in sole possession of nuclear weapons. While America prospered and its influence spread around the globe, it faced a daunting challenge. Despite suffering massive human and economic losses, the Soviet Union also sought to use its newly found power to extend its influence and to spread its contrasting tenets of communism abroad in a direct challenge to the United States.

By the late 1940s, communism was firmly entrenched in eastern Europe. In 1949, communist forces seized control of China while the Soviets exploded their first atomic bomb, ending America's nuclear monopoly. Fearful of mutually assured nuclear annihilation, both east and west settled into an uneasy Cold War. But that by no means meant an end to conflict.

Throughout the latter half of the 20th century the Cold War frequently erupted into indirect military combat, through the use of proxies. While the United States, communist China, and the Soviet Union parried to an uneasy truce in Korea in the early 1950s, revolutionaries in Indochina fought successfully for their independence from France. The peace was short-lived as Vietnam was divided between the communist north and the capitalist south. Tensions rose until open conflict once again broke out in the early 1960s, this time with the United States entering the fray to counter Soviet influence in the region.

America's involvement increased just as long-brewing social revolution erupted in the United States. As more advisers and then combat troops were sent to support South Vietnam, many American citizens began to openly question the nation's involvement in a foreign war when so many pressing social issues needed to take precedent. This tumultuous internal conflict was openly expressed as protests, all set against the backdrop of an increasingly unpopular war. Searing images of death and destruction filled television screens during the evening news, further fanning unrest and seismic social upheaval within America's diverse society.

This book takes the reader on a carefully crafted journey through the maze of events that became the war in Vietnam. Remarkably thorough, and extraordinarily well-illustrated, this engaging book provides a well-written analysis through an American lens but does not hesitate to tell the story, no matter how difficult or painful. It is an excellent and highly readable synopsis of a very complicated era and a very complicated war.

F. Robert van der Linden, Ph.D.

Curator of Aeronautics
Smithsonian National Air and Space Museum

A purple smoke flare marks the landing spot for an incoming medevac helicopter after a battle in A Shau Valley.

1
THE BACKGROUND
Before March 1959

Resistance to French rule grew in Indochina in the early 20th century, as communist thinkers encouraged criticism of colonialism. The First Indochina War would win Vietnam its freedom from colonial oppression, but also lead to a dangerous rift between North and South.

«Vive La France?
Soldiers of the Third Regiment of the French Foreign Legion stand to attention outside their headquarters in Lang Son in 1950. A decisive Viet Minh victory at the Battle of Route Coloniale 4—a highway to the French base at Cao Bang—saw French units abandon Lang Son later that year.

THE BACKGROUND
BEFORE MARCH 1959

I n the 19th century, France conquered Vietnam, Cambodia, and Laos, creating the colony of French Indochina. The French divided Vietnam into three parts: Tonkin, Annam, and Cochin China. Repressing nationalist revolts, the French maintained colonial rule in Vietnam until World War II, when Indochina was occupied by the Japanese. At the war's end, the communist-led Viet Minh declared Vietnam independent, but France strove to retake control of its colony. After prolonged fighting, Viet Minh guerrillas defeated the French in the First Indochina War, inflicting a final humiliation at the battle of Dien Bien Phu. After negotiations at the Geneva Conference, Vietnam became independent as two states, divided by a Demilitarized Zone (DMZ). North Vietnam was under communist rule, while South Vietnam was backed by the United States.

[1] The 12th-century temple complex of Angkor Wat in Cambodia displays the splendor of the medieval Khmer Empire. [2] French soldiers keep watch during the siege of Dien Bien Phu in 1954, which brought French rule in Indochina to an end. [3] Japanese troops enter Saigon during World War II.

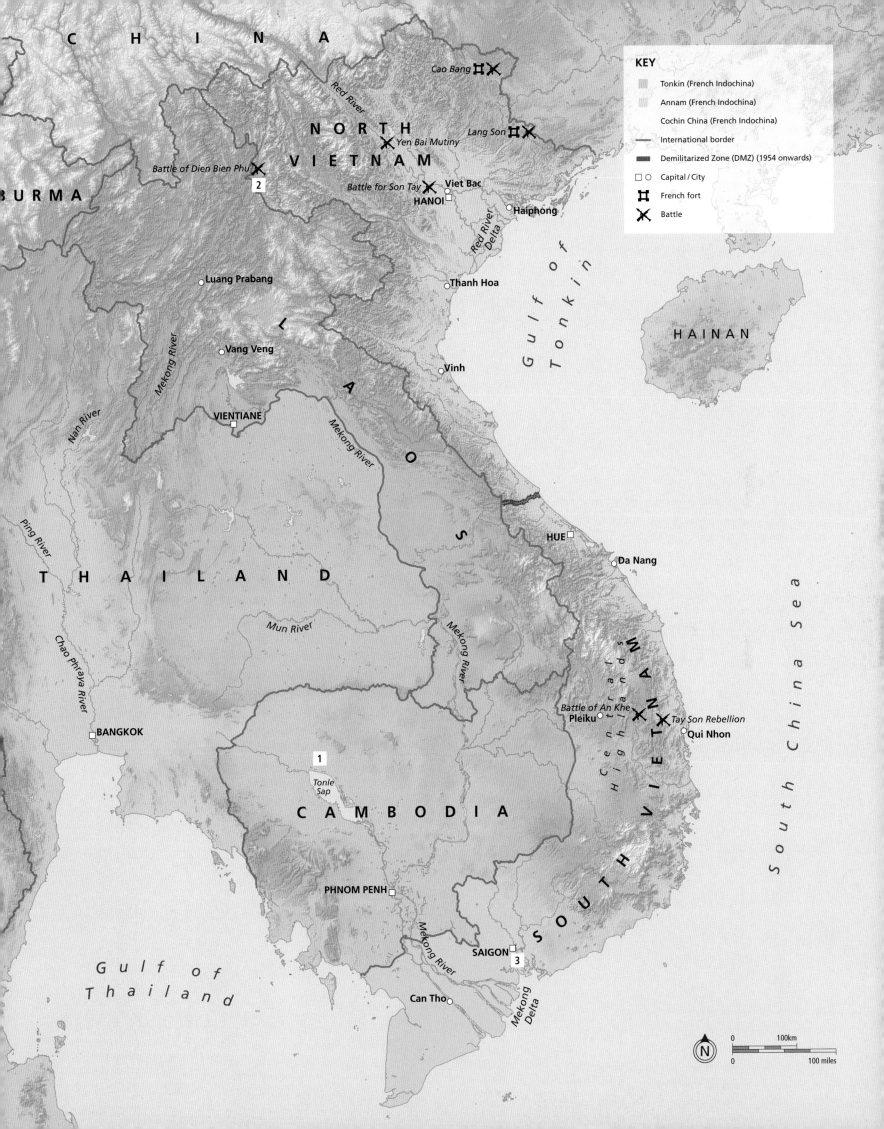

CHINA

Red River

NORTH
VIETNAM

Cao Bang ⌗✗

Lang Son ⌗✗

BURMA

✗ Yen Bai Mutiny

Battle of Dien Bien Phu ✗
2

Battle for Son Tay ✗ Viet Bac
HANOI □

Haiphong

Luang Prabang ○

Thanh Hoa ○

Mekong River

Vang Veng ○

Vinh ○

L A O S

Gulf of
Tonkin

HAINAN

Nan River

VIENTIANE □

Mekong River

Mun River

THAILAND

HUE □

Da Nang ○

Ping River

Mekong River

Central Highlands

Chao Phraya River

Battle of An Khe ✗
Pleiku ○ ✗ Tay Son Rebellion
Qui Nhon ○

BANGKOK □

1

Tonle
Sap

A N N A M

C A M B O D I A

S O U T H   V I E T N A M

South China Sea

PHNOM PENH □

Mekong River

SAIGON □
3

Gulf of
Thailand

Can Tho ○

Mekong Delta

N

0   100km
0   100 miles

TIMELINE BEFORE MARCH 1959

Dynastic Vietnam ▪ **Catholics persecuted** ▪ French colonialization ▪ **The First Indochina War** ▪ Battle of Dien Bien Phu ▪ **Rise of Ho Chi Minh** ▪ Independence won ▪ **The Geneva Accords** ▪ Operation Passage to Freedom ▪ **US support for South Vietnam**

1800–50	1851–1900	1901–20	1921–30	1931–40	1941–50
1802 Emperor Gia Long founds the Nguyen Dynasty, unifying Vietnam under a single ruler.	**1858** Responding to persecution of Catholics, France and Spain invade southern Vietnam. The French stay to create the colony of Cochin China in 1864.	**1905** Vietnamese nationalist Phan Boi Chau writes a history of the loss of Vietnam, in which he advocates independence from colonial rule.	**FEBRUARY 1930** Vietnamese troops opposed to French rule mutiny at Yen Bai, but the uprising is swiftly crushed.		
1835 Vietnamese Catholics and French Catholic missionaries are persecuted for their participation in a revolt against Emperor Minh Mang.	**DECEMBER 1883** A French expeditionary force invading Tonkin (northern Vietnam) defeats Chinese "Black Flag" irregulars at the Battle of Son Tay.	**MAY 1916** Emperor Duy Tan is deposed and exiled by the French after he attempts to lead an anticolonial revolt in Vietnam.	**OCTOBER 1930** Hi Chi Minh founds the Indochinese Communist Party at a meeting held in the British colony of Hong Kong.	**1933** Catholic nationalist Ngo Dinh Diem becomes interior minister of Annam under Emperor Bao Dai, but resigns when his proposals for administrative reform are rejected.	⌃ French troops land in Indochina, 1945 **MAY 19, 1941** Ho Chi Minh and his colleagues found the Viet Minh movement to fight against the French colonialists and the Japanese occupation of Vietnam.
				SEPTEMBER 1940 With France having been defeated by Nazi Germany in Europe, the French allow Japanese troops to use bases in northern Vietnam for their war against China.	**MARCH 9, 1945** Japanese troops take over Indochina from the French, declaring Vietnam, Cambodia, and Laos independent. Emperor Bao Dai officially rules Vietnam.
1847 Emperor Tu Duc comes to the Vietnamese throne. Determined to resist foreign influence, he persecutes Vietnamese Catholics.	⌃ Battle of Son Tay, 1883 **1885** After battling Vietnamese and Chinese forces, the French establish a protectorate over Tonkin and Annam (central Vietnam), which is ratified by the Treaty of Tientsin.	**1919** Vietnamese nationalists living in Paris, including Ho Chi Minh, petition for the right to self-determination at the Versailles Conference. They are ignored.			**SEPTEMBER 2, 1945** Ho Chi Minh declares an independent North Vietnam.
					DECEMBER 19, 1946 After French warships shell Viet Minh forces in Haiphong (November 23), the Viet Minh attack Hanoi, starting the First Indochina War.
	1887 French Indochina is created as an administrative union of Tonkin, Annam, Cochin China, and Cambodia. Laos is added to French Indochina in 1893.				**FEBRUARY 1950** Armed by Communist China, the Viet Minh take the offensive, attacking French outposts on Vietnam's northern border.

LE PETIT JOURNAL ILLUSTRÉ

L'EXÉCUTION DE TREIZE REBELLES TONKINOIS

≫ Yen Bai Revolt, 1930

"Our people have **broken the chains** that have **fettered** them for **nearly a century** and have won **independence** for **Vietnam.**"

HO CHI MINH, IN A SPEECH IN BA DINH SQUARE, HANOI, SEPTEMBER 2, 1945

1951–54

1955–59

JANUARY–JUNE 1951
The Viet Minh launch an offensive against French defenses in the Red River Delta, which is defeated with heavy losses.

OCTOBER–NOV 1952
France carries out an in-depth assault on Viet Minh-held areas of northern Vietnam in Operation Lorraine.

OCTOBER 1953
Cambodia and Laos are declared fully independent of French rule.

NOVEMBER 20, 1953
French airborne troops establish a base at Dien Bien Phu, near the border of Vietnam and Laos.

MARCH 13, 1954
The garrison at Dien Bien Phu comes under attack from Viet Minh infantry and artillery surrounding the base.

APRIL 24, 1954
The Geneva Conference opens with the goal of creating peace in Korea and Indochina.

JULY 21, 1954
The Geneva Accords divide Vietnam at the 17th parallel, with the Viet Minh controlling the North and the State of Vietnam controlling the South.

MAY 7, 1954
Dien Bien Phu falls to the Viet Minh after eight weeks of fighting—a shattering blow to French morale.

JUNE 16, 1954
Ngo Dinh Diem becomes prime minister of Vietnam, under the presidency of former emperor Bao Dai.

⌃ Indochina War Medal, first awarded in 1953

⌃ Refugees during Operation Passage to Freedom, 1954–55

MAY 18, 1955
The movement of about one million refugees—many of them Catholics—from North to South Vietnam is completed.

« Laos becomes independent, 1953

MARCH 3, 1955
In Cambodia, King Norodom Sihanouk abdicates his throne to stand for election as prime minister.

APRIL–MAY 1955
Prime Minister Diem crushes the powerful Binh Xuyen criminal organization in Saigon.

OCTOBER 27, 1955
After defeating Bao Dai in a referendum, Diem proclaims South Vietnam to be the Republic of Vietnam, and names himself as its president.

APRIL 28, 1956
The last French soldier leaves Vietnam.

JULY 1956
The deadline for nationwide elections to reunify Vietnam, one of the terms of the Geneva Accords, passes with no elections held.

AUGUST 1956
North Vietnamese leader Ho Chi Minh admits serious errors were made in a communist land reform program that provoked rural uprisings.

MAY 9, 1957
President Diem addresses the US Congress during a state visit to the United States.

⌃ Ho Chi Minh, leader of North Vietnam

JANUARY 1958
US officials in South Vietnam express concern about the repressive nature of Diem's regime and mounting opposition to the government in the countryside.

MARCH 1959
The North Vietnamese politburo decides to support and promote a guerrilla uprising in South Vietnam.

《 BEFORE

The Vietnamese formed their first kingdom in the Red River Valley some 3,000 years ago.

OUT OF CHINA'S SHADOW

The Vietnamese were ruled by China from 111 BCE, but acts of rebellion—including the uprising led by the Trung sisters in around 40 CE—would result in **Vietnamese independence** in 939. Further wars enabled the Vietnamese to expand southward and by the start of the 19th century, they occupied much the same territory as modern-day Vietnam.

Battle for Son Tay

In December 1883, at the town of Son Tay, Vietnamese and Chinese forces resisted the French takeover of Tonkin (northern Vietnam). Although ultimately victorious, the French suffered heavy casualties.

Indochina Colonized

In the 19th century, at the height of European imperialism, France seized control of Vietnam, Laos, and Cambodia to create French Indochina. However, the Vietnamese had a history of resistance to foreign domination and France found its rule fiercely contested.

French influence over Vietnam began with the introduction of French Catholic missionaries: in 1802, French bishop Pigneau de Béhaine helped Emperor Gia Long to defeat the Son Tay rebellion and ascend to the throne. However, the emperor's successors turned against the Catholics, and wanted to limit French involvement. In 1858, the persecution of Catholics gave a pretext for the French to invade Cochin China, an area of Vietnam that included Saigon and the Mekong Delta.

In the mid-19th century, the momentum of imperialism was unstoppable. The major European powers, utterly convinced of their cultural supremacy, carved up the world between them, taking advantage of their military and technological superiority. Once the French established themselves in Cochin China—officially declared a French colony in 1864—it was only a matter of time before France extended its "protection"

over the entire region. The nearby kingdom of Cambodia was weak, and accepted French control in exchange for defense against its neighbor, Siam (Thailand), as did Laos. Vietnam alone resisted French pressure for further concessions, eventually calling on China for aid.

Assault on Tonkin

In 1883, France launched a sea and land offensive in Tonkin, the northern heartland of Vietnam, to force the Vietnamese imperial government to accept a French protectorate. Assisted by Chinese

irregulars known as the Black Flags, as well as by Chinese regular troops, the Vietnamese inflicted heavy losses on the French Expeditionary Force. In 1885, however, China made peace with France at Tientsin, and although armed resistance continued in some parts of Tonkin, the Vietnamese government had no choice but to acknowledge French control.

French rule

The colonial system imposed by France did not even recognize the existence of "Vietnam." Instead, French Indochina—established in 1887—was a union of Tonkin, Annam (central Vietnam), Cochin China, and Cambodia, with Laos added in 1893. Vietnam, as it had been prior to the French takeover, was split into three. Imposed in order to make the territory easier for the French to control, this division of Vietnam also had historic justifications. Cochin China had only been settled by Vietnamese peasants relatively recently and had not come under the rule of a Vietnamese emperor until the 19th century. Nonetheless, the Vietnamese people had a strong sense of national identity, and many were unhappy with these divisions.

Administration of Indochina was headed by a governor-general who reported to the Colonial Office in Paris. Meanwhile, traditional rulers retained their thrones, yet had little real power and were readily dismissed if the French found them insufficiently subservient. The Vietnamese emperor still had his court at Hue

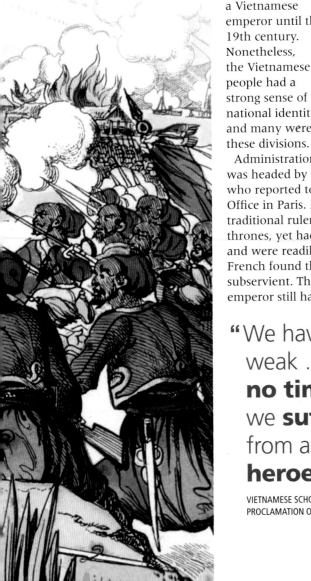

> "We have … been weak … but **at no time** have we **suffered** from a **lack of heroes.**"
>
> VIETNAMESE SCHOLAR NGUYEN TRAI, PROCLAMATION OF VICTORY, 1427

Stamp of approval

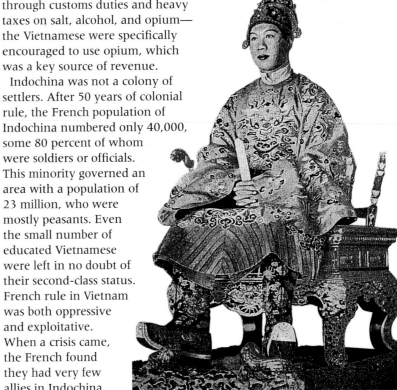

France introduced postage for Indochina from the 1890s. This stamp, issued in 1904, is inspired by France, but later stamps often depicted local scenes and people in traditional dress.

Colonial attitudes

The French had little contact with local people, except as servants. Despite living in Indochina, they maintained strictly Western lifestyles and customs—as shown by this photograph of officials and their wives from around 1900.

and his mandarins (high-level bureaucrats) exercised some authority in Annam, but even there the French ran the show.

Rubber economy

In line with their "civilizing mission," the French opened schools to educate the children of the Vietnamese elite in French culture, introduced new medical treatments, built roads and railroads, extended irrigation systems, and introduced new crops. However, the main function of the Vietnamese in the French imperial system was to work as exploited laborers on French-owned rubber plantations or in mines. The colonial system paid for itself through customs duties and heavy taxes on salt, alcohol, and opium— the Vietnamese were specifically encouraged to use opium, which was a key source of revenue.

Indochina was not a colony of settlers. After 50 years of colonial rule, the French population of Indochina numbered only 40,000, some 80 percent of whom were soldiers or officials. This minority governed an area with a population of 23 million, who were mostly peasants. Even the small number of educated Vietnamese were left in no doubt of their second-class status. French rule in Vietnam was both oppressive and exploitative. When a crisis came, the French found they had very few allies in Indochina.

AFTER

France ruled its Asian colonies with an iron fist, quickly quashing any nascent signs of nationalism.

NATIONALISTS IN WAITING

Vietnamese opposition to French rule showed itself in **sporadic revolts** through the early 20th century. The ruthless oppression by the French colonial police forced most nationalists to operate in exile, including the young revolutionary **Ho Chi Minh**.

POWER VACUUM

Nazi Germany **took control of France** in June 1940, thereby drastically transforming the situation in French Indochina. The colonial administration there was cut off from support or reinforcement from Paris. Japan, fighting a war across the border in China, took the opportunity to **send troops into Indochina 22–23 》**.

The last emperor

Bao Dai was crowned ruler of Annam (central Vietnam) in 1932. The French saw him, like all traditional rulers, as a figurehead for French colonial power, but Bao Dai harbored his own aspirations to lead Vietnam to independence.

Revolt and Resistance

Vietnamese nationalists strove time and again to organize uprisings in the face of French oppression. After the Japanese occupied French Indochina in 1941, the communist-led Viet Minh seized the chance to create a nationwide movement for independence.

« **BEFORE**

Formerly an independent country, Vietnam was colonized by France in the 1880s. Resistance to this foreign domination was initially organized by Vietnam's traditional governing elite.

IMPERIAL DREAMS

The Vietnamese scholar-mandarins who resisted French colonialism—such as Phan Dinh Phung, who led a guerrilla movement in the 1890s, and Phan Boi Chau, a revolutionary in the early 20th century—envisaged a restoration of **imperial rule « 16–17**.

However, the overthrow of the Qing Dynasty in China and its replacement by a republic in 1912 led many nationalists to abandon monarchism. The **Russian Revolution** of 1917 and the founding of the Moscow-based Communist International (Comintern) to encourage revolution worldwide brought a radical element to Vietnamese anticolonialism.

LONG LIVE THE THIRD COMMUNIST INTERNATIONAL!
EVVIVA IL TERZA INTERNAZIONALE COMMUNISTA!
VIVE LA TROISIÈME INTERNATIONALE COMMUNISTE!
ES LEBE DIE DRITTE KOMMUNISTISCHE INTERNATIONALE!

SOVIET PROPAGANDA

Rebels of Yen Bai

Vietnamese soldiers in the French colonial army staged a fruitless uprising at Yen Bai in February 1930. The June 1930 cover of this Parisian magazine shows the mutiny's leaders being led to the guillotine—where the rebels' last words were nationalistic cries of "Viet Nam!"

LE PETIT JOURNAL
ILLUSTRE
HEBDOMADAIRE - 41ᵉ Année
61, rue Lafayette, Paris
29 Juin 1930 - Nᵒ 2062
PRIX: 50 CENTIMES

L'EXÉCUTION DE TREIZE REBELLES TONKINOIS
Voir à l'intérieur l'explication des gravures.

French authorities imposed severe restrictions on their Vietnamese subjects, denying them freedom of speech and the right to form political parties or trade unions. With little scope for political action, nationalists such as future South Vietnamese president Ngo Dinh Diem expressed their desire for independence through movements whose leaders were based abroad.

In the 1920s, Nguyen Thai Hoc founded the Vietnamese nationalist party Vietnam Quoc Dan Dang (VNQDD) in China. VNQDD was a republican movement modeled on China's own nationalist party, the Kuomintang. In February 1930, the VNQDD encouraged colonial army troops at Yen Bai, in northern Vietnam, to mutiny against their French officers. The mutiny came to nothing. French repression was swift, and Nguyen Thai Hoc was among the rebels executed.

the Japanese effecting a military occupation of Vietnam that was barely resisted by France.

Nationalist strategy

The humiliation of the French, and of other Europeans in Asia at this time, encouraged Vietnamese nationalism. It also raised the possibility of new support. By offering to attack the Japanese in Indochina, nationalists could pitch for the backing of the Allies at war with Japan, including Kuomintang China and the United States. In 1941, in a remote area on the border with southern China, Ho Chi Minh and his communist colleagues founded the Viet Minh Doc Lap Dong Minh (League for the Independence of Vietnam), shortened to Viet Minh. Their intention was to create a broad-

New occupants
During World War II, the Japanese sent troops into Indochina—like these men, carrying Japan's "Rising Sun" flag. The occupying forces left Vietnam's colonial system in place, including its army and police.

based nationalist movement that would attract support from all strata of Vietnamese society. Their declared objectives were the defeat of the "fascist Japanese" and their "French accomplices" and, most importantly, the independence of a democratic, progressive Vietnam. Tactically, they avoided mentioning communism or revolution.

Rival Vietnamese nationalist groups enjoyed more support from the Kuomintang, but it was the Viet Minh that built a network of clandestine cells in Vietnam. In late 1944, Ho's colleague Vo Nguyen Giap began to form the Vietnam Armed Propaganda and Liberation Brigade: a fledgling guerrilla army, poorly armed and confined to the remotest areas of the country.

On March 9, 1945, fearing an Allied invasion of Indochina, the Japanese carried out a coup against the French authorities. Easily overcoming the French army, they announced an end to the colonial era. Cambodia and Laos were declared independent under their

monarchs, as were Annam and Tonkin under Vietnamese emperor Bao Dai. In the absence of French troops, Giap's Viet Minh guerrillas were now able to operate in the Viet Bac region, north of Hanoi. Wary of the Japanese, however, the Viet Minh bided their time, and made few raids upon the occupying forces. They eagerly anticipated a Japanese defeat, which would at last mean the possibility of Vietnam achieving genuine independence.

" [The French] do not treat us as **brothers ... they treat us as slaves** and ... as **dogs.**"

VIETNAMESE NATIONALIST PHAN BOI CHAU, 1931

Ho takes the lead

The Vietnamese communist movement, headed by Nguyen Ai Quoc, later known as Ho Chi Minh, was also based in China until the Chinese Kuomintang government turned against the communists in 1927. Three years later, Ho founded the Indochinese Communist Party in Hong Kong, then a British colony. The party patiently extended its clandestine influence among Vietnamese workers and peasants, but it was a small movement, in no position to challenge the French regime.

World War II transformed the situation in Vietnam. The German occupation of France in June 1940 shattered French prestige and left French Indochina exposed to pressure from Japan, which had been fighting a war in China since 1937. In September 1940, Japanese troops invaded French Indochina,

Revolutionary comrades
Vietnamese nationalists Vo Nguyen Giap (left) and Ho Chi Minh (right) were leading figures in the founding of the Viet Minh independence movement in 1941. They were both dedicated communists, loyal to the Soviet-run Comintern.

AFTER

The defeat of Japan by the Allies in August 1945 left a power vacuum in Indochina, enabling the Viet Minh to occupy Hanoi.

FIRST INDOCHINA WAR
Ho Chi Minh declared an **independent Democratic Republic of Vietnam 22–23 ≫** on September 2, 1945. His government enjoyed widespread support in Vietnam, but the French were determined to **reestablish their rule** in Indochina. The failure to negotiate an agreement between France and the Viet Minh led to the **First Indochina War 26–27 ≫** in December 1946.

REVOLUTIONARY LEADER Born 1890 Died 1969

Ho Chi Minh

"Nothing is more **precious** than **independence** and **liberty.**"

HO CHI MINH, IN A PERSONAL MEMOIR BY JEAN SAINTENY, 1972

A Vietnamese nationalist and passionate communist, Ho Chi Minh devoted his life to political struggle. Many details of his career are obscure, both because he lived the clandestine existence of a revolutionary activist for many years and because his actions have been mythologized for the purposes of propaganda. Yet there is no doubt that he deserves to be recognized as the father of modern Vietnam.

Born Nguyen Sinh Cung, he was known from the age of ten as Nguyen Tat Thanh, and then as a young man as Nguyen Ai Quoc (Nguyen the Patriot). His family lived in Annam, the area of central Vietnam where the Vietnamese emperor still exercised nominal authority under French protection. Like most members of Vietnam's traditional Confucian scholar-mandarin elite, his father deeply resented foreign domination.

Ho attended the Quoc Hoc lycée in Hue, which was designed to educate select Vietnamese children in French culture and civilization. Instead of joining the colonial administration as expected, at around the age of 21, Ho set off to see the world. Working his passage on ships as a kitchen hand and taking on casual menial jobs to support himself, he spent time in the US, Britain, and France. After World War I, he became politically active, joining a group of Vietnamese nationalists in Paris as they unsuccessfully petitioned the statesmen at the Versailles peace conference to apply their principles of self-determination and democracy to Vietnam.

Marxist training

The establishment of the world's first communist state in Russia split the international socialist movement. Left-wing activists everywhere faced a choice between social democracy and communism. In 1920, Ho made the fateful decision to opt for the latter. He wrote articles for the communist-backed anticolonial newspaper *Le Paria* and in 1923 traveled to the newly established Soviet Union, where he was taught to see the issue of Vietnamese independence in the wider perspective of the Marxist world revolution promoted by the Soviet-controlled Communist International (Comintern).

Ho's commitment to political struggle was absolute, with the only evidence for a personal life being his

Revolutionary hero

Sometimes known as "Uncle Ho," Ho Chi Minh led the Vietnamese struggle for independence from French colonial rule in the First Indochina War. By the time of America's war in Vietnam, weakened by age and illness, he had become largely a figurehead.

Cheering for their leader
Ho Chi Minh is feted by his colleagues at the congress that founded the Workers' Party of Vietnam in 1951, during the war against France. He frequently changed the name of the party organization in order to obscure his unswerving communist affiliation.

brief marriage to a Chinese woman in the mid-1920s. He was a faithful representative of Comintern, and it was in this role, in 1930, that he organized the various Vietnamese communist groups into a single Vietnamese Communist Party—which he renamed the Indochinese Communist Party after Comintern objected to the previous name's nationalist implications.

Leader reborn
After a period of obscurity, in 1940 he reemerged onto the stage of history as Ho Chi Minh—"bringer of light." This name represented

a deliberate decision to present himself as a national leader in the Vietnamese Confucian tradition, embodying the virtues of age and wisdom. The move bore fruit after Ho's opportunistic declaration of Vietnamese independence in 1945.

> ## "The storm is [an] opportunity for the **pine** and the **cypress** to show **strength** and **stability**."
>
> HO CHI MINH IN *FROM COLONIALISM TO COMMUNISM* BY VAN CHI HOANG, 1964

The majority of the Vietnamese people readily accepted Ho as their legitimate leader, while the French were confused by his apparent moderation when he traveled to France for negotiations. In reality, Ho was moderate only out of political calculation. His alliances with noncommunist nationalists

always ended in their exclusion from power and often their summary execution.

Police state
As leader of North Vietnam from 1955, Ho presided over a state that left no room for individual freedom and ruthlessly imposed its system on a reluctant peasantry. He was still leader in 1959, when the North Vietnamese politburo took the decision to resume war to achieve the goal of a united communist Vietnam, but was superseded by Le Duan in 1960. Ho continued to have some influence on the conduct of the war until 1965, after which he was largely a figurehead, though he played a part in advising North Vietnam's peace negotiators. The simplicity of his personal habits and his absolute lack of corruption sustained an image of purity and dignity that won respect among his people. His death in 1969 provoked a tremendous outpouring of grief.

HO CHI MINH'S HOUSE IN HANOI, WHERE HE LIVED FROM 1958 UNTIL HIS DEATH

Shrine to Ho
The Ho Chi Minh Museum at Kim Lien, near Ho's birthplace, celebrates the Vietnamese leader's life. Since his death in 1969, Ho has been glorified by the Vietnamese people, with his image appearing everywhere: as statues, in posters, and propaganda.

Ho Chi Minh in Paris
The Vietnamese leader visits the French capital in summer 1946 for talks on his country's independence. The French agreed on a path to limited self-government, but this was not enough to satisfy nationalist aspirations.

« BEFORE

The Japanese occupation of Indochina in World War II effectively ended French rule.

CHANGING STATUS
In March 1945, Japanese troops occupying Indochina declared **Vietnam, Laos, and Cambodia independent**. Despite this, Indochina remained under Japanese control. Then, in August 1945, **Japan was defeated by the Allies**, including the United States, Britain, China, and France.

JAPAN SIGNS THE INSTRUMENT OF SURRENDER, 1945

From **Independence** to **War**

In September 1945, Viet Minh leader Ho Chi Minh declared Vietnam independent, establishing a government with popular support. However, the French were not prepared to accept the loss of their colony and declared war on the Viet Minh.

By the time Japanese forces occupied Vietnam in March 1945, the Viet Minh movement was already solidly embedded in the Vietnamese population, with a network of cells in towns and villages. No longer threatened by the French colonial army, the Viet Minh's guerrilla force had increased its strength in the Viet Bac region north of Hanoi, aided by agents of the American OSS (Office of Strategic Services), the forerunner of the CIA, who had seen the Viet Minh as a useful ally in America's war against Japan. But Viet Minh commander Vo Nguyen Giap mostly avoided fighting the Japanese occupiers, keeping

Rallying symbol
The Viet Minh adopted the red flag with a gold star as its banner in 1940. It became the official flag of the Democratic Republic of Vietnam when Ho Chi Minh proclaimed the country's independence in 1945.

his limited forces intact for a future bid for power.
Japan's surrender to the Allies after the dropping of

Ho was accepted as the country's legitimate ruler by virtually all social groups, including the Catholic Church. His government immediately began organizing an administration and set about tackling starvation, which was rife in the countryside.

Searching for allies

The Viet Minh knew that the key to the future lay in the attitude of the wartime Allies. Ho Chi Minh modeled his independence declaration upon the American Declaration of Independence of 1776 in the hope of winning the backing of the United States. No mention was made of communism or social revolution.

The American government, although opposed to colonialism, was anxious to maintain good relations with France and declined to intervene on behalf of the Viet Minh. The Allies decided that, in order to accept the surrender of Japanese troops in Vietnam, the British army would occupy the country south of the 16th parallel and China would occupy the area to the north. No friends to French colonialism, the Chinese allowed Ho Chi Minh's government to remain in place; the British, however, saw it as their duty to facilitate the restoration of French rule.

Aided by the British, French administrators and troops returned to southern Vietnam in October 1945. Quashing Viet Minh resistance, they regained control of Saigon and other major towns, although guerrillas continued to dominate the countryside. After lengthy negotiations, the Chinese agreed to allow the French to return north of the 16th parallel,

The French return

French legionnaires land in Indochina in October 1945. After the defeat of Japan in World War II, the French expected to reestablish their prewar colonial role in Indochina, regardless of the rise of the Viet Minh.

and the first troops under General Philippe Leclerc landed at Haiphong in March 1946. Ho's government, lacking international support, decided to compromise with France, which was proposing self-government within a French–ruled Indochina Federation.

Ho Chi Minh traveled to France for negotiations at the Fontainebleau Conference in July 1946, in an attempt to seek an agreement, despite French determination to block full independence for a united Vietnam.

Empty handed

Ho returned to Vietnam without a satisfactory deal. Tension between the French and Vietnamese in northern Vietnam broke into open conflict in November 1946. After violent incidents in Haiphong, the French bombarded the city from sea and air, forcing the Viet Minh to withdraw from the port. Responsibility for the final breakdown of peace is disputed, but on December 19, on the orders of General Giap, the Viet Minh launched an attack on the French garrison in Hanoi. When this failed, Ho Chi Minh's government withdrew from the city to fight a guerrilla campaign. The First Indochina War had begun.

atom bombs on Hiroshima and Nagasaki had left Vietnam without any effective authority in place. The Viet Minh took advantage of this power vacuum, raising its flag from one end of the country to the other in a general insurrection. The Viet Minh leadership established itself in Hanoi.

Declaring independence

On September 2, 1945, Ho Chi Minh declared the independent Democratic Republic of Vietnam in Hanoi's Ba Dinh Square. Emperor Bao Dai, Vietnam's traditional ruler, bowed to the evident will of the people and abdicated, giving his blessing to the new government. Although almost unknown in Vietnam until then,

$450 MILLION The value of the military aid provided by the United States to the French in Indochina in 1951, rising to $785 million by 1953.

AFTER

The French were at first able to restrict the Viet Minh guerrillas to remote border areas, but the communist victory in China in 1949 gave the Viet Minh the support of a powerful neighbor.

COLD WAR DIMENSIONS
Better armed and trained, the Vietnamese guerrillas **took the offensive against the French 24–25 »**. At the same time, the Viet Minh leadership openly aligned itself with the communist side in the global Cold War.

US INTERVENTION
In June 1949, the French installed former emperor Bao Dai as head of the state of Vietnam, which was given a degree of independence within the French Union. From 1950, **France obtained American military aid 26–27 »** for its colonial war, which was rebranded as part of the Free World's defense against communist expansion.

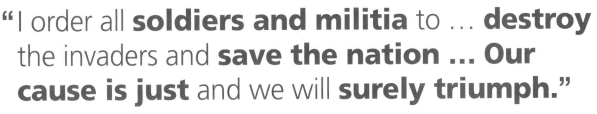

"I order all **soldiers and militia** to … **destroy** the invaders and **save the nation … Our cause is just** and we will **surely triumph.**"

VO NGUYEN GIAP, CALL TO ARMS, DECEMBER 19, 1946

Revolutionary Guerrilla Warfare

After World War II, guerrilla warfare of the kind practiced by the Viet Minh in Indochina came to be seen not just as a threat to European colonial powers but also as a major challenge to American interests worldwide.

In revolutionary guerrilla warfare, irregular forces use guerrilla tactics—ambushes, raids, hit-and-run attacks, concealment, and mobility—in pursuit of the goals of political and social revolution. When the Viet Minh embarked on a guerrilla war against the French in 1946, they were following a path already laid out in theory and practice by Mao Zedong's communists in China.

The Marxist theory, to which communists subscribed, had originally anticipated a revolution based on a revolt by industrial workers in urban areas. Mao envisaged a communist revolution resulting from a guerrilla war based in the countryside. According to Mao's theory, guerrillas would establish themselves in remote areas and use propaganda to win popular support among the peasantry. Their military tactics would progress from scattered raids, ambushes, and sabotage by small-scale forces to larger-scale operations exploiting the mobility of guerrilla forces. Finally, full-scale military operations with heavy weaponry would allow them to defeat the enemy in the field. This scenario was broadly enacted in the process that brought Mao to power in China in 1949.

Although Vo Nguyen Giap, the key organizer of the Viet Minh military rebellion, was reluctant to acknowledge his debt to the Chinese example, his conduct of the war against France and later against the United States clearly showed Mao's influence. The Viet Minh's strategic concept of *dau tranh* (struggle) envisaged a long-term conflict in which military and political pressure would combine to wear down the enemy.

Giap's strategy

The Viet Minh organized guerrilla forces at three levels. Village militia comprised part-time soldiers—peasants who used improvised weapons in clandestine attacks on enemy soldiers or officials in their locality. Regional forces operated in their own districts and provinces. The main-force guerrillas trained with the best available arms at remote bases in mountain and jungle areas, ready to be deployed for major operations.

The point of a guerrilla strategy was to allow a weaker military force to triumph over a stronger enemy by avoiding a direct trial of strength until conditions were advantageous. Despite some costly mistakes, Giap mostly chose his occasions for battle wisely, attacking exposed outposts or ambushing forces on the move. The great strength of the Viet Minh lay in its understanding of the importance of morale and political commitment in war. They aimed to demoralize the French and win the support of the Vietnamese people. This was relatively easy, as the vast majority of the population hated French rule. Viet Minh propaganda always stressed nationalism, with no mention of communism, of which most Vietnamese had no knowledge.

By the early 1950s, the Viet Minh had control of large areas of Vietnam, where they collected

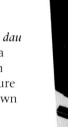

Clarifying aims

A Viet Minh propaganda poster asks soldiers fighting and dying for the French colonialists: "Why? And for whom?" The Viet Minh always tried to ensure that their own troops understood the reasons for fighting.

Planning an operation

General Vo Nguyen Giap briefs his officers on the details of a planned engagement at Dien Bien Phu in 1954. Despite an apparently relaxed style of command suitable to guerrilla forces, Giap demanded absolute discipline and obedience to orders.

taxes and rice. Even in areas supposedly under French control, the Viet Minh often operated freely at night, carrying out terror attacks against officials and soldiers.

Inspiration
The success of the Viet Minh campaign, culminating in the humiliation of French troops at Dien Bien Phu in 1954, encouraged other would-be revolutionaries to take up arms. Just as they were admitting defeat in Vietnam, the French faced a fresh guerrilla campaign mounted by nationalists in Algeria, which would lead to Algerian independence in 1962.

In Cuba, Fidel Castro's guerrillas overthrew President Fulgencio Batista in 1959, an

300,000 The approximate number of Viet Minh guerrillas in 1952.

90,000 The number of French troops operating in Vietnam that year.

achievement quickly followed by the resumption of guerrilla warfare in South Vietnam, this time against the regime of Ngo Dinh Diem. By 1965, Castro's erstwhile companion Ernesto "Che" Guevara had launched a call for further guerrilla uprisings as part of a worldwide campaign against American imperialism. The Viet Minh and their successors, the Viet Cong, had helped a military strategy turn into a hazy project for revolution across the world.

From the 1970s, urban guerrilla movements and international terrorism replaced rural guerrilla organizations as the focus for revolutionary aspirations.

NEW CAUSES
Left-wing groups such as the Red Brigades in Italy, the Baader-Meinhof gang in Germany, and the Tupamaros in Uruguay identified themselves as urban guerrillas, conducting armed campaigns in cities. In the 1980s, **the link between guerrilla tactics** of all kinds and **left-wing ideology** was broken. The United States backed Contras using guerrilla tactics against the left-wing Sandinista government in Nicaragua, and also armed and trained Muslim Mujahideen fighting the Soviet Union in Afghanistan. In the 21st century, guerrilla warfare has been primarily associated with Islamic jihadists operating in Iraq and Afghanistan.

MUJAHIDEEN FIGHTER

> " Communist[s] must **grasp the truth:** Political **power** grows out of the **barrel of a gun.**"

MAO ZEDONG, *PROBLEMS OF WAR AND STRATEGY*, 1938

Revolution in Cuba
Fidel Castro (left) led a successful guerrilla campaign to take power in Cuba in 1959. His adoption of the communist side in the Cold War convinced the United States of the urgent need to combat revolutionary guerrilla insurgencies.

The **First Indochina War**

The war fought between the French Expeditionary Force and Viet Minh guerrillas from 1946 to 1954 was a brutal attritional struggle. The French were able to hold the major cities but suffered heavy losses defending outposts in territory dominated by the guerrillas.

In the immediate aftermath of the fighting in Hanoi that opened the war in December 1946, French generals believed the Viet Minh could be eliminated in a single punitive action. Taking the offensive in 1947, they forced the guerrillas to take refuge in the remote northern border region, but failed to destroy them.

Until 1949, the Viet Minh remained a manageable problem for the French, but the communist victory in China that year changed the situation. Armed and trained by the Chinese, the Viet Minh went on the attack. In September and October 1950, General Vo Nguyen Giap ordered offensives against French fortified bases along the Chinese border, from Cao Bang to Lang Son. All the outposts were overrun or abandoned and the French withdrawal turned into a rout.

Attacks step up
Overconfident in the wake of this stunning victory, in the following year, Giap launched offensives in the Red River Delta, threatening Hanoi and Haiphong. Commanded by General Jean de Lattre de Tassigny, the French repulsed the attacks with artillery and air bombardment, including the use of napalm—an incendiary bomb. As many as 10,000 Viet Minh were killed. However, a series of French operations in 1952 showed their inability to inflict serious damage on Viet Minh areas. They could not block supply routes from China or stop the guerrillas from invading neighboring Laos.

US support
On the whole, the French Expeditionary Force fought well. It was a multinational army of professional soldiers in which the Foreign Legion and troops from France's African colonies figured prominently. From 1950 onward, the French received increasing military aid from the United States, which had identified the Viet Minh as a communist threat. They also expanded the Vietnamese National Army, serving the notionally independent state headed by Bao Dai. Its morale, however, was poor. In some areas, militias controlled by Catholic bishops or by the Cao Dai and Hoa Hao religious sects held off the Viet Minh.

By 1953 most of rural Vietnam was out of French control. Even in government-controlled areas guerrillas carried out terrorist attacks. With no prospect of victory, the French began to search for a way to withdraw from Indochina.

Indochina War medal
This was awarded to members of the French Expeditionary Force that served in Indochina, 75,000 of whom died. The force included French Legionnaires and colonial units in addition to regular troops.

> " There may be a **catastrophe;** there is **little chance of a miracle.**"
>
> GENERAL DE LATTRE DE TASSIGNY, REPORT ON INDOCHINA SITUATION, SEPTEMBER 1951

BEFORE

After World War II, the French hoped to reassert their great power status.

THE FRENCH UNION
In the **power vacuum** that existed in Indochina in the final stages of World War II, Ho Chi Minh declared **Vietnam independent ⟨⟨ 22–23**. However, after the war, France sought to regain its colonies, rebranding its empire as the French Union. They wanted to keep overall control while granting limited self-government. Ho Chi Minh rejected the proposal and in November 1946 launched a **guerrilla campaign ⟨⟨ 24–25** against the French.

French column on the move
An American-supplied tank leads motorized infantry along a dike in the Red River Delta. Restricted to roads, French columns—*Groupements Mobiles*—were vulnerable to ambush by more flexible Viet Minh infantry.

AFTER

The Geneva Conference, intended to negotiate peace in Korea and Indochina, opened in April 1954. By then, French troops were already under siege by the Viet Minh at Dien Bien Phu.

FRENCH WITHDRAWAL
The surrender at **Dien Bien Phu 30–31 ⟩⟩** in May 1954 ended any French ambitions to stay in Vietnam. At **Geneva 34–35 ⟩⟩**, the victorious Viet Minh leadership, under pressure from the Soviet Union and China, accepted an independence deal that **divided Vietnam 38–39 ⟩⟩**.

Vanquishing the French
A naïve Viet Minh poster of 1946 shows a Frenchman laid low by the Viet Minh and the French tricolor replaced by the flag of the Democratic Republic of Vietnam. The majority of Vietnamese people supported the Viet Minh.

« BEFORE

The Russian Revolution of 1917 created the Soviet Union, a communist state committed to fomenting world revolution.

RISE OF THE SUPERPOWERS
In World War II, the Soviet Union fought as an ally of the United States and Britain against Nazi Germany. After the war, **relations between the Soviet government** and its **former allies** deteriorated rapidly. Lines to mark **zones of occupation** by Soviet and Western forces became fortified borders between **communist and anti-communist blocs**.

The **Cold War**

From the late 1940s, the United States set out to block the spread of communism worldwide. In this Cold War context, the struggle between the French and the Viet Minh was transformed from a local colonial conflict into part of a global confrontation.

Addressing Congress in March 1947, US President Harry Truman announced the decision to support "free peoples" anywhere in the world menaced with "subjugation by armed minorities or by outside pressures." The aim was to prevent the spread of communism and Soviet influence, which were seen as a direct threat to American national security. The "Truman Doctrine" was followed by a series of events—including the communist seizure of power in Czechoslovakia and the Soviet blockade of Berlin in 1948–49—that brought the United States into the openly hostile confrontation with the Soviet Union known as the Cold War. The explosion of the first Soviet atom bomb, in a remote area of Kazakhstan in August 1949, made this a confrontation between nuclear-armed powers.

Nuclear deterrent
A Soviet nuclear device is tested in Novaya Zemlya on October 30, 1961. Fear of the destructive power of nuclear weapons forced America and the Soviet Union to avoid full-scale conflict with one another.

China embraces communism
A poster from 1950 shows the Chinese people welcoming the installation of a communist government in Beijing. China's membership of the communist bloc was a major setback for America in the Cold War.

The Korean War
While American fears about communism were turning into full-blown paranoia, Mao Zedong led the communists to victory in the Chinese Civil War. This dramatic development shifted the focus of American attention from Europe to Asia. At the end of World War II, China's neighbor Korea had been divided into Soviet and American zones of occupation. The Soviet zone had become communist North Korea, while a pro-American dictator ruled South Korea. When North Korean forces invaded the South in June 1950, the United States led a large-scale military intervention under the banner of the United Nations, repulsing the North Korean invaders.

The Korean War was to have an enduring effect on America's approach to the later Vietnam War. In Korea, after the defeat of the North Korean invasion, American General Douglas MacArthur ordered his troops to advance into North Korea. China responded by sending its army into Korea, massively escalating the conflict and driving the UN forces back again.

During the Vietnam War, the Americans would always rule out an invasion of North Vietnam,

fearing a similar response from the Chinese. Korea taught American strategists the principle of "limited war"—restricting operations in order to prevent the conflict widening into a world war. The United States did not use nuclear weapons and did not attack China, even though American and Chinese soldiers were fighting in Korea.

Weapons and training
The communist victories in China and the Korean War had an immediate impact upon American policy toward Indochina. Once Mao was in power in Beijing, an open connection was established between the Viet Minh in Vietnam and the communist

MALAYAN EMERGENCY

In 1948, ethnically Chinese communist insurgents launched a guerrilla campaign against British and Commonwealth troops in the British colony of Malaya. However, the Malayan communists lacked popular support and had no friendly neighbor to supply them with arms. Although the communist campaign continued until 1960, it was eventually defeated by counterinsurgency tactics—a strategy that the US later used, with less success, in Vietnam.

Meanwhile, France deliberately emphasized the communist threat in a search for desperately needed

"Every year **humanity** takes a **step toward communism.**"

SOVIET LEADER NIKITA KHRUSHCHEV TO SIR WILLIAM HAYTER, JUNE 1956

powers, with weapons and training for the guerrillas coming from the Soviet Union and China.

American troops in Korea
A guard of honor welcomes US troops to South Korea during the Korean War, fought at the same time as First Indochina War between the French and the Viet Minh. More than 35,000 US soldiers died in the Korean War.

military support from the United States. The first deliveries of American military equipment to the French in Indochina arrived in June 1950, shortly after the start of the Korean War.

In American eyes, the war in Indochina came to be seen as France's

contribution to the containment of communism in Asia. While other allies of the United States sent troops to fight in the Korean War, the French were allowed to concentrate upon their own anticommunist struggle.

America, however, could never be wholly comfortable with supporting a European colonial power trying to maintain its empire. It set up the Military Assistance Advisory Group (MAAG) in Vietnam, officially to observe French use of US military equipment, but in practice beginning a creeping US engagement in the country. By the early 1950s, commitment to the Cold War had begun inexorably to draw the Americans into Vietnam.

AFTER »

The Geneva Conference in 1954 tried to secure peace deals for Korea and Indochina.

VIETNAM DIVIDES
After their devastating defeat at **Dien Bien Phu 30–31 »**, the French agreed to negotiate Vietnam's independence. The **Geneva Accords 34–35 »** that ensued divided Vietnam. The United States backed Ngo Dinh Diem as ruler of South Vietnam while North Vietnam became a communist state under Ho Chi Minh.

After six years of fighting in the First Indochina War, the French realized that they could not defeat the Viet Minh.

TRUTH DAWNS
By 1953, the French government began to look for an **honorable way of withdrawing from Indochina**. General Henri Navarre, appointed French commander in Indochina in May 1953, had orders to preserve his forces rather than pursue a military victory. The **Viet Minh ≪ 18–19**, however, launched an invasion of Laos in early 1953, in support of rebels against the French-backed Laotian government. General Navarre felt compelled to respond to the threat.

French Defeat at Dien Bien Phu

Committed to a major set-piece battle under unfavorable circumstances, French forces besieged at Dien Bien Phu fought with outstanding courage but could not avoid defeat at the hands of a superior enemy. The Viet Minh triumph ended the colonial era in Indochina.

In the fall of 1953, French General Henri Navarre made the fateful decision to establish a base at remote Dien Bien Phu, inside Viet Minh-controlled territory, near Vietnam's Laotian border. His objective was to disrupt Viet Minh supply lines to their forces in Laos. On November 20, three French parachute battalions dropped into Dien Bien Phu and secured the area after some sharp fighting. Eager to escalate from guerrilla operations to full-scale battle, Viet Minh commander Vo Nguyen Giap ordered substantial infantry forces with artillery to move toward Dien Bien Phu.

Navarre was aware of this Viet Minh response from radio intercepts. Instead of withdrawing,

Parachute drop
In November 1953, the French parachuted troops into Dien Bien Phu to establish a fortified base. Called Operation Castor, the attack overwhelmed Viet Minh soldiers on the ground.

The Viet Minh advance
On March 13, 1954, the Viet Minh opened the fighting at Dien Bien Phu by capturing a key French hilltop outpost, codenamed Beatrice. Viet Minh infantry overwhelmed the French defenses.

increasingly short of munitions. Fresh reinforcements parachuted in, but antiaircraft fire rendered air operations perilous, as did the onset of the monsoon. In a classic siege technique, the Viet Minh dug trench systems toward the French perimeter, until close enough to overcome the defenses by infantry assault. Giap launched the final attack on May 1. There was no surrender. On May 7, the shattered remains of the French fortified camp fell to the Viet Minh in hand-to-hand combat.

In eight weeks of fighting, about 2,000 soldiers on the French side had been killed. The battle had been even costlier for the Viet Minh, with an estimated 8,000 killed and twice that number wounded. But Giap had inflicted such a humiliating defeat upon France that any continuation of its colonial rule in Indochina was unthinkable.

he poured thousands of troops into the Dien Bien Phu base, hoping to inflict a major defeat on the Viet Minh if they chose to attack.

Almost 190 miles (300 km) from their bases at Hanoi, and without usable roads, the French troops depended on supply by air. Navarre assumed the Viet Minh would have their own supply problems, but Giap had a vast army of laborers to move supplies across country.

Battle stations
The French base was on a plain ringed by hills. While the French dug trenches and built strongpoints to defend their vital airstrip, the Viet Minh occupied the high

10,000 The number of soldiers on the French side who were taken prisoner at Dien Bien Phu. Only one in three of them survived captivity.

ground, installing Chinese-supplied artillery and antiaircraft guns.

By February 1954, French aircraft flying in and out of the base were coming under heavy fire. Full-scale fighting began on March 13. By then, France had 11,000 troops in Dien Bien Phu, led by Colonel Christian de Castries. They included French paratroopers,

A well-oiled supply chain
The Viet Minh forces at Dien Bien Phu were supplied by some 15,000 porters who carried food and munitions over hundreds of miles of inhospitable terrain on bicycles or on their backs.

Foreign Legionnaires, colonial soldiers from North Africa, and elements of the Vietnamese National Army. Facing them were 50,000 Viet Minh supported by 105 mm and 155 mm artillery.

The first Viet Minh attacks rapidly overran two French forward positions, codenamed Beatrice and Gabrielle. The intensity of the Viet Minh artillery barrage astonished the defenders, whose counterfire proved ineffectual. By March 17, the airstrip was unusable and resupply had to be by parachute.

Besieged on all sides
Desperate to avoid disaster, the French government sought US assistance. A plan was devised for a fleet of 60 US B-29 bombers to attack Viet Minh positions. The use of atom bombs was even discussed. However, President Dwight D. Eisenhower ruled against intervention. The only Americans to take part were civilians flying transport aircraft.

The besieged garrison continued its heroic resistance, unable to evacuate its wounded and

> " [I] feel the **end is approaching** but we will **fight to the finish**."
>
> COLONEL CHRISTIAN DE CASTRIES, MESSAGE FROM DIEN BIEN PHU, MAY 7, 1954

AFTER »

On the day after the fall of Dien Bien Phu, political leaders at the Geneva Conference tried to solve the Indochina question.

PEACE ACCORDS
In **Geneva 34–35** », the French government reached an agreement with the Viet Minh. An independent Vietnam would be divided at the 17th parallel, with a **communist government** established in Hanoi in the northern portion. The Viet Minh's struggle for **a united Vietnam** resumed in 1959.

LESSONS LEARNED
After the US was sucked into war in Vietnam in the 1960s, American troops came under a similar siege at **Khe Sanh 200–03** » in 1968. Fearful of another Dien Bien Phu, the US deployed much greater airpower.

Dien Bien Phu

The Viet Minh siege of the French Expeditionary Force at Dien Bien Phu lasted from March 13 to May 7, 1954. The conditions within the besieged base, where shallow trenches provided little protection against constant enemy artillery fire, demanded exceptional powers of endurance. French doctor Major Paul-Henri Grauwin, head of the mobile surgical unit at Dien Bien Phu, tended to the injured and dying during the final week of the siege.

In his account he describes the relentless harassment of the French Expeditionary Force by the Viet Minh artillery—one attack following another, almost without stopping. The Viet Minh were taking hold of trenches in the north, one yard at a time, and the French were waiting for the final onslaught to take place.

During the final week of the siege, it rained all day with no respite and the passages were full of stretchers the entire time. Meanwhile, more wounded soldiers waited outside, under fire, in the pouring rain and the mud. The Viet Minh suddenly increased their numbers tenfold until they were everywhere. Rising out of the mud and water, they infiltrated passages, trenches, and shell holes.

"Around me I could see nothing but mud, mud everywhere...**"**
MAJOR PAUL-HENRI GRAUWIN, IN HIS MEMOIRS, *DOCTOR AT DIEN-BIEN-PHU*, 1955

French soldiers at Dien Bien Phu
Newly arrived paratroopers take up position in the trenches. About 4,000 airdropped volunteers reinforced the defenses during the siege, almost all of them eventually either killed or taken prisoner by the Viet Minh.

The **Geneva Accords**

The origin of America's Vietnam War lay in the agreements reached at the Geneva Conference in 1954. Negotiations ended the war between France and the Viet Minh, but divided Vietnam and left its future to be settled by a later, more destructive conflict.

<< BEFORE

Soviet dictator Joseph Stalin's death in March 1953 led to a temporary thaw in the Cold War.

PEACE WINDOW
Improved relations between Soviet leaders and the United States and its allies led to an armistice that halted the fighting in the Korean War in July 1953. French setbacks in the **First Indochina War << 26–27**, culminating in their defeat at **Dien Bien Phu << 30–31** in May 1954, then led France to seek a settlement with the Viet Minh.

JOSEPH STALIN LYING IN STATE

At a meeting held in Berlin in January and February 1954, representatives of the Soviet Union, Britain, the United States, and France agreed to convene an international conference in Geneva to negotiate peace settlements in Korea and Indochina. The United States consented to communist China's invitation to the conference, although they refused to recognize the legitimacy of Mao Zedong's regime. The State of Vietnam, set up by France in 1949, was represented, as was Ho Chi Minh's Democratic Republic of Vietnam, although it was not recognized as legitimate by the Western powers.

The Geneva Conference opened in April 1954. Negotiations on Korea achieved nothing, with the result that it continued to be regulated by the terms of the ceasefire agreed the previous year. The question of Indochina was more urgent.

> **The Accords were completed in the early hours of July 21, but the clocks had been stopped to give the impression that it was still July 20—the deadline given by French prime minister Pierre Mendès-France.**

Interested parties

A plenary session of the Geneva Conference assembles representatives of all the states with an interest in the Korean or Indochinese Wars. The most effective negotiations were those between France and the Viet Minh.

losses in the Korean War. Fearing American military intervention in Vietnam that might prolong the conflict indefinitely, China urged Ho Chi Minh to seek a compromise and postpone total victory. British Foreign Secretary Sir Anthony Eden also put his weight behind a compromise deal, having envisaged the division of Vietnam into North and South from an early stage.

secure a withdrawal of French forces resulted in fundamental issues being evaded or postponed.

Dividing line

The Geneva Accords, issued on July 21, 1954, separated the warring forces. All Viet Minh troops were to regroup north of the 17th parallel—an arbitrary line agreed to after much haggling—while the French withdrew to its south. A timetable was set for all French troops to quit Vietnam. The final declaration of the conference insisted that the 17th parallel was not to be seen as a political border. Elections were to be held within two years to unify Vietnam under a democratic government.

FRENCH TROOPS PAY THEIR RESPECTS TO FALLEN COMRADES IN INDOCHINA

The withdrawal of French troops, completed in 1956, ended the colonial era in Indochina and left Vietnam partitioned.

NORTH AND SOUTH
A **communist government** led by Ho Chi Minh took power north of the 17th parallel **38–39 »**. The South became the **American-backed Republic of Vietnam** under Ngo Dinh Diem, who became president in 1955 after defeating Bao Dai in a government-controlled referendum. The **nationwide elections** called for by the Geneva Accords and intended to create a democratic unified Vietnam never took place.

> " The **military demarcation line** is a temporary one and may in **no way** be seen as a **political or territorial border.**"

FINAL GENEVA DECLARATION, ON THE DIVISION OF VIETNAM, JULY 1954

Fighting continued even while the delegates convened. The French defeat at Dien Bien Phu in the first week of May was followed by another military disaster in June, when the Viet Minh annihilated Groupe Mobile 100 at An Khe.

France either had to find a peace deal or escalate the war by drafting high numbers of conscripted troops into Vietnam. The situation threw the French government into crisis. On June 18, Pierre Mendès-France, a politician who had long advocated a negotiated settlement with the Viet Minh, was appointed prime minister of France. He promised to achieve a peace deal within a month or resign.

External pressures

Despite their military successes, the Viet Minh were also under pressure to reach an agreement. The Soviet Union and China wanted an easing of relations with the West. The Chinese communists in particular needed a period of peace to consolidate their revolution and recover from their

The United States might have been expected to take a leading part in the negotiations, but it did not. The American Secretary of State, John Foster Dulles, more or less boycotted the conference because of his fierce dislike of communists. Dulles's deputy, Walter Bedell Smith, did take part, but to no great effect.

In the end, an agreement was reached through direct talks between Mendès-France and the Viet Minh representative Pham Van Dong. The French insisted on Cambodia and Laos becoming independent on French terms, which sidelined revolutionary movements allied to the Viet Minh. In Vietnam, the focus on an immediate deal to end the fighting and

Old allies
Conference delegates included (left to right) British Foreign Secretary Sir Anthony Eden, US Under Secretary of State Walter Bedell Smith, and French Foreign Minister Georges Bidault.

However, the United States was not a signatory of the Accords; nor was the State of Vietnam, where the nationalist Ngo Dinh Diem had just been appointed prime minister. The Geneva Accords left the future of Vietnam dangerously undecided.

Tent cities
Catholics who fled North Vietnam for South Vietnam after the country's partition in 1955 were initially housed in vast encampments. They survived on emergency aid from the United States.

Street battle in Saigon
Civilians flee as forces loyal to Ngo Dinh Diem take on Binh Xuyen paramilitaries in April 1955. Backed by the US, Diem suppressed militias of various armed movements in South Vietnam.

Vietnam Divided

By 1955, Vietnam had won its independence, but was divided. In South Vietnam, the Catholic nationalist Ngo Dinh Diem emerged as ruler with the backing of the United States, while in North Vietnam, Ho Chi Minh's regime imposed a communist system.

For 300 days after the signing of the Geneva Accords, the border between North and South Vietnam remained open. Around a million Vietnamese moved from North Vietnam to the South, primarily Catholics who feared the consequences of communist rule. Such qualms were encouraged by propaganda promulgated by the CIA, and justified by the hardline attitude of the communist authorities. About 90,000 people moved in the opposite direction, to the North—chiefly Viet Minh guerrillas who had fought against the French. However, many Viet Minh activists covertly remained in the South after partition.

American support

The United States, committed to opposing the spread of communist influence worldwide, began to assert its presence in the South well before the French completed their withdrawal. Although the

Americans did not consider their chances of saving South Vietnam from communism to be high, they took on the task of advising the South Vietnamese government and army. To their surprise, they found that the main politician they were backing, Ngo Dinh Diem, was capable of asserting his authority effectively.

As prime minister under President Bao Dai, Diem had crushed the Binh Xuyen, a mafia-like organization with the status of an independent army, and cracked down on the militias of the Cao Dai and Hoa Hao religious sects. These militias played an important role in politics and had long defied government control, although some members joined remnants of the Viet Minh.

No election

In October 1955, Diem staged a referendum in which he defeated Bao Dai, making himself president of the Republic of Vietnam. Diem had no intention of allowing the nationwide elections provided for in the Geneva Accords to take place—neither he nor the United States had ratified the accords. The United States was happy to supply money and equipment to a man who had shown he could use it effectively, to suppress troublesome factions and keep communism at bay.

Consolidating power

Diem's successful creation of a US-backed police state in the South was an uncomfortable surprise to Ho Chi Minh and his colleagues. They had counted on the weakness of South Vietnam to allow the

Mailing propaganda
A South Vietnamese postage stamp issued in 1955 shows refugees fleeing North Vietnam. The decision of many thousands of Vietnamese to move south rather than live under communism inspired anticommunist propaganda.

unification of Vietnam under communist rule, with or without elections being held.

At first, Ho Chi Minh was preoccupied with establishing a monopoly of power in North Vietnam. Noncommunist nationalists who had fought under the banner of the Viet Minh were

executed or sent to labor camps, and the communist party line was drilled into the entire population through propaganda and the use of terror against those who disagreed. In the countryside, revolt triggered by the introduction of a land reform program was crushed by force, leading to hundreds of thousands of deaths. Yet the North Vietnamese government had the advantage of being perceived as a Vietnamese regime. Diem, on the other hand, was seen as continuing the era of foreign influence in Vietnam by allowing the Americans to replace the French.

> **"[The] 50–50 chance** of saving South Vietnam is **worth trying."**
>
> GENERAL LAWTON COLLINS, US SPECIAL REPRESENTATIVE IN VIETNAM, 1955

AFTER »

North Vietnamese communists sought to take advantage of growing discontent in rural South Vietnam.

TENSIONS MOUNT
In May 1959, the North Vietnamese communist leadership sent activists to organize an **armed uprising 50–51** » in rural areas of South Vietnam, where Diem's rule was seen as corrupt and biased toward large landowners. **Buddhists also resented Diem 72–73** » for favoring Vietnam's Catholic minority. The number of **US advisers** in Vietnam exceeded 3,000 by early 1962.

BEFORE «

In 1954, France, facing defeat by Viet Minh guerrillas in the First Indochina War, signed the Geneva Accords.

PEACE TERMS
The French officially declared Vietnam independent under former emperor Bo Dai. The **Geneva Accords « 34–35** partitioned the country at the 17th parallel, leaving two Vietnamese governments in place—Ho Chi Minh's Democratic Republic of Vietnam in Hanoi and Bo Dai's State of Vietnam in Saigon. Democratic elections to reunite the country were timetabled for 1956.

KEY CONCEPT

RELIGION IN VIETNAM

Confucianism and Buddhism were the main belief systems in Vietnam, but Catholics constituted a large minority of about two million. The Hoa Hao, who followed their own strand of Buddhism, and the Cao Dai (shown right), who practiced a syncretist religion established in the 1920s, had their own militias, both suppressed by Diem in 1955.

SOUTH VIETNAMESE PRESIDENT Born 1901 Died 1963

Ngo Dinh Diem

"I had a high regard for the man. He was certainly an intense patriot."

AMERICAN GENERAL MAXWELL D. TAYLOR, TV INTERVIEW, 1979

A controversial figure in his lifetime and since, Ngo Dinh Diem became the prime minister of South Vietnam in the wake of the 1954 partition of the country. Supported by the United States, Diem was a Vietnamese nationalist with a staunchly anticommunist and pro-Catholic worldview. While his regime saw myriad challenges and instability, the United States would ultimately regret its decision to orchestrate his downfall in 1963.

Like his adversary Ho Chi Minh, Diem was born into the traditional mandarin elite of Annam in central Vietnam. The Ngo family combined Confucianism with Catholicism, a minority belief in Vietnam. Diem followed the path of chastity as if he were a Catholic priest—but instead of entering the Church he pursued a bureaucratic career under Bao Dai, the Vietnamese emperor, who ruled in Annam under French control. Soon enough, Diem achieved recognition for his outstanding abilities, and he rose quickly through the ranks of the imperial civil service.

Despite Diem's position, he was a committed opponent of French colonialism. In 1933—when Emperor Bao Dai appointed him minister of the interior in the Annamese government—Diem proposed the introduction of a representative assembly, which would be a significant step toward self-government. However, when the reforms were blocked, Diem resigned, denouncing Bao Dai as "nothing but an instrument in the hands of the French."

Biding his time

Even without formal office, Diem remained a key figure in nationalist politics over the next two decades and was recognized as a potential future leader. In 1945 and 1949, he turned down invitations to become prime minister under Bao Dai, in regimes that were compromised by association with the Japanese or the French. He also refused Ho Chi Minh's invitation to join the government of the Democratic Republic of Vietnam in 1946. Diem had personal reasons to distrust the Viet Minh, its activists had killed one of his brothers and once held Diem himself under duress.

After the outbreak of the First Indochina War, Diem sought to lead a "third force" in Vietnamese politics, made up of nationalists who also rejected communism. His activities antagonized both sides.

First president

In 1955, Ngo Dinh Diem founded the Republic of Vietnam and became its first president. A fiercely independent nationalist, Diem used US money and arms to build up and defend South Vietnam, but steadfastly resisted his allies' influence in matters of policy.

Feted in New York

President Diem enjoys a tickertape parade through New York City on a state visit to America in May 1957. The South Vietnamese leader was greeted with enthusiasm as the man who had saved his country from communism.

Threatened with assassination by the Viet Minh, Diem soon found that the French authorities were unwilling to provide him with protection. In 1950, he sought safety abroad, first in Europe and then in the United States. Partly exploiting his Catholic connections, he endeavored to establish links with important US political figures, including Senator John F. Kennedy, and with the CIA.

Nepotistic leader

When the French declared Vietnam independent in June 1954, Diem was able to dictate his own terms for accepting the post of prime minister from Bao Dai. Backed by the Can Lao party and its secret police—run by his brother Ngo Dinh Nhu—Diem was quick to oust Bao Dai and stamp his own authority on South Vietnam.

The United States provided plentiful support to a man who seemed capable of saving the South from communism, but their influence over his behavior was limited. Proclaiming an ideology of "personalism," Diem built his regime around family loyalty. His brother Ngo Dinh Nhu and Nhu's

wife—South Vietnam's de facto "First Lady"—joined Diem in the presidential palace. Another of his brothers, Ngo Dinh Thuc—the archbishop of Hue—also proved a powerful ally.

Diem also cultivated the support of the Catholic minority, swelled by refugees from the North. However, some 90 percent of South Vietnam's population was Buddhist.

Overthrow

Officers in the South Vietnamese forces (ARVN) loathed the rule of Diem's family and his secret police. He was lucky to survive an air attack on the presidential palace by his own air force in 1962. Diem's favoritism toward Catholics further destablized his regime, while the Buddhist Crisis had a catastrophic effect on US opinion—especially when Madame Nhu spoke out to mock the martyrdom of Buddhist protester Thich Quang Duc. The US had hoped that Diem would be a bulwark against communism. Now seeing him as a liability, they chose to support an ARVN coup. Diem was ousted on November 1, 1963. Captured as they fled, Diem and his brother Nhu were assassinated on November 2—bayoneted and shot in the back of an armored vehicle.

> "[I] want now to do what **duty and good sense** require. I believe in **duty above all**."
>
> NGO DINH DIEM'S LAST PHONE CALL TO US AMBASSADOR HENRY CABOT LODGE, NOVEMBER 1, 1963

Religious protest

Buddhist monks at a pagoda in Saigon lead a hunger strike to demonstrate against Diem in 1963. That May, anti-Buddhist laws prevented them from flying flags in Hue. During the gathering—a celebration of Buddha's birthday—nine Buddhists were killed by the police.

- **January 3, 1901** Born into the influential Ngo Catholic clan in Quang Binh province, Annam (central Vietnam).

- **1918** Enrolls at the prestigious School of Public Administration and Law in Hanoi.

- **1921** Becomes a mandarin in the imperial administration of Annam.

- **1933** Appointed interior minister in Emperor Bao Dai's government. Resigns after three months when his proposals for reforms are rejected.

- **1943** Forms a clandestine political party associated with exiled Prince Cuong De.

- **1946** Refuses to join the Viet Minh after discussion with Ho Chi Minh.

- **1949** Offered the position of prime minister of the State of Vietnam by Bao Dai, but declines.

- **1950** Goes into exile after the Viet Minh threaten to assassinate him; lobbies for support in the US and Europe.

- **1954** Returns from exile and is appointed prime minister under Bo Dai; his brother Ngo Dinh Nhu founds the Can Lao Party to support him.

DIEM'S BROTHER NGO DINH NHU MARRIED TRAN LE XUAN—MADAME NHU

- **October 1955** Declares himself President of the Republic of South Vietnam after winning a referendum rigged by the Can Lao Party.

- **May 1957** Visits the United States, where he addresses Congress.

- **November 1960** Survives an attempted coup by South Vietnamese army officers.

- **February 1962** Survives the bombing of the presidential palace.

- **May–August 1963** Faces the Buddhist Crisis, which discredits his rule.

- **November 1, 1963** Overthrown in a US-authorized military coup.

- **November 2, 1963** Brutally assassinated, along with Ngo Dinh Nhu.

Cambodia and Laos

Cambodia and Laos, Vietnam's neighbors in Indochina, followed their own paths to independence. In the 1950s, Cambodia maintained a precarious measure of stability, but Laos was sucked into the First Indochina War and quickly descended into chaos.

BEFORE

Sparsely populated and weakened by centuries of decline, Cambodia and Laos offered little resistance to the imposition of French colonial rule.

FORMER GLORIES

Whereas Vietnam was shaped by Chinese Confucianism, Cambodia and Laos belonged to the Indian Hindu-Buddhist cultural sphere. **Cambodia** had been the site of the **Khmer empire** in medieval times, but all that remained of such glories by the 19th century were the ruins of Angkor Wat. Preyed upon by its more powerful neighbors Vietnam and Siam (Thailand), **Cambodia welcomed a French protectorate** in 1863. The country was integrated into **French Indochina «16–17** in 1887, while remaining nominally under the rule of its traditional monarchy.

CAMBODIA'S ANGKOR WAT

EMBATTLED LAOS

By 1779, **Laos** was split between rival kingdoms that were dependencies of Siam. During the 19th century, **Vietnam and Siam fought for control of the region**. The French established a protectorate in Laos in 1893 and integrated it into French Indochina in 1898, although a Laotian king remained on the throne in the north at Luang Prabang.

In the spring of 1945, during their wartime occupation of French Indochina, the Japanese gave nominal independence to Cambodia and Laos under their traditional rulers. King Norodom Sihanouk declared Cambodia's independence from France in March 1945 and King Sisavang Vong followed suit in Laos in April.

Moves by nationalists

In October 1945, French troops, aided by the British, reoccupied the Cambodian capital, Phnom Penh, and arrested the pro-independence prime minister, Son Ngoc Thanh. Meanwhile, in Laos, the anticolonial Lao Issara (Free Laos) movement, headed by Prince Phetsarath, carried out a coup against King Sisavang Vong. It was not until April 1946 that French forces recovered control of Laos, forcing Prince Phetsarath to take refuge in Thailand.

In both countries, France pursued a policy of political modernization, turning their traditional rulers into constitutional monarchs with

KING OF CAMBODIA

NORODOM SIHANOUK

Sihanouk became Cambodia's king in 1941, aged 18. He abdicated after independence but continued to lead the country as prime minister and later as head of state. Observing strict neutrality during the Vietnam War, he was overthrown in a US-backed coup in 1970. Through the subsequent civil war he experienced arrest and exile, before returning to restore national unity in 1991. In 1993, the monarchy was revived and Sihanouk became king for a second time.

governments answerable to elected assemblies. In 1949, France, struggling to recover the base they had in Indochina prior to the war, granted the two countries greater self-government but continued to control defense and security.

Thailand provided a safe base both for the Lao Issara and for the Cambodian pro-independence groups of the Khmer Issarak movement. Although not strong enough to seize power, these

The three princes

Princes Boun Oum, Souvanna Phouma, and Souphanouvong celebrate an agreement at Geneva in 1962 that made Laos a neutral state under a coalition government. The smiles were shortlived, as the country's civil war and political chaos continued unabated.

organizations established a threatening armed presence in areas of Cambodia and Laos. From 1950, they became linked to the Viet Minh guerrillas. The Lao Issara mutated into the pro-communist Pathet Lao, led by a member of the Lao royal family, Prince Souphanouvong. The Pathet Lao leader's half-brother, Prince Souvanna Phouma was also originally a member of Lao Issara, but in 1951 took the post of prime minister in the royal Lao government.

The Viet Minh wades in

In 1953, the Viet Minh launched a major offensive in Laos in alliance with the Pathet Lao. It was partly in response to this that the French mounted their ill-fated operation at Dien Bien Phu in northwestern Vietnam. In the same year, King

Sihanouk tried to salvage a worsening political situation in Cambodia. Menaced by Viet Minh-backed Issarak guerrillas and by nationalist politicians opposed to his rule, he abandoned his palace in order to launch a campaign for full independence from France, successfully placing himself at the head of a popular anticolonial movement.

France bows out

By the end of 1953, France had ceded effective independence to the royal governments in Laos and Cambodia. Sihanouk proved an able politician. In 1955, he abdicated in order to become prime minister. Cambodia entered a period of fragile peace and mild prosperity, but Laos was not so fortunate. The Pathet Lao, backed by newly independent North Vietnam, were able to control large areas of the country, engaging in a civil war with the government. The government armed Hmong (Miao) mountain tribesmen as guerrillas to fight the Pathet Lao and received increasing military support from the United States.

> " The **king may be mad**, but it is a **brilliant** sort of **madness.**"
>
> FRENCH GENERAL PAUL GIROD DE LANGLADE ON CAMBODIAN KING NORODOM SIHANOUK, 1953

Cambodia and Laos were soon swept up in America's crusade against communism.

THE HO CHI MINH TRAIL

By 1960, Laos was in the frontline of the Cold War. North Vietnam occupied parts of Laos in order to create the **Ho Chi Minh Trail 56–57 »**, the supply route for communist forces in South Vietnam. It also supported the insurgency by Laotian communist Pathet Lao guerrillas.

The United States stepped up its intervention in Laos. A second Geneva Conference in 1961–62 declared Laos neutral but had no lasting effect. Civil war continued with covert American involvement. The US Air Force subjected eastern Laos, site of the Ho Chi Minh Trail, to the most sustained **bombing campaign in history**.

RISE OF THE KHMER ROUGE

In Cambodia, Norodom Sihanouk strove to maintain his country's **neutrality**, refusing American military aid. However, he could not stop Vietnamese communist forces from occupying base areas along the border with South Vietnam. In 1970, **a coup by General Lon Nol overthrew Sihanouk 248–49 »**. The United States poured in arms to the new government and bombed Cambodian border regions. The country became a battlefield, with Cambodian communist **Khmer Rouge guerrillas** dominating extensive areas.

Hmong fighters
The United States trained and armed Hmong mountain tribesmen in remote areas of Laos to fight against the North Vietnamese and Pathet Lao guerrillas. The Hmong were motivated by a traditional hostility to the Vietnamese.

2
AMERICA DRAWN INTO VIETNAM
March 1959–December 1964

Communist attacks on South Vietnam threaten its stability, prompting the US to send in Special Forces advisers to help. US support for President Diem's regime dwindles as it becomes obvious that he has alienated much of the South Vietnamese population.

« **Training the South Vietnamese**
US Ranger Lieutenant Bruce G. Smalley laughs as he teaches Corporal Y. Bhung how to use a bayonet in Buon Ki. The US Special Forces were sent to small towns and hamlets to recruit and train Montagnard tribesmen for the South Vietnamese Army.

AMERICA DRAWN INTO VIETNAM
MARCH 1959–DECEMBER 1964

From 1959, the North Vietnamese leadership decided to back a guerrilla uprising among the rural population of South Vietnam, who resented the rule of President Ngo Dinh Diem. The Ho Chi Minh Trail was created to carry military supplies from the North to guerrillas in the South. Fearing the spread of communism in Asia, the United States supported a South Vietnamese counterinsurgency campaign, sending in military advisers, including the Green Berets. In 1963, with Diem's regime losing the guerrilla war and facing protests by Vietnamese Buddhists and chaos on the streets, America backed a military coup in which Diem was killed. The following year, the Tonkin Gulf Incident, a naval clash off North Vietnam, won US Congressional authorization for an open-ended escalation of US military involvement in Vietnam.

1 An alleged attack on USS *Maddox* in 1964 led to the Tonkin Gulf Resolution, authorizing President Johnson to use all necessary force. 2 Viet Cong terrorist attacks in South Vietnam in 1964 culminated in the bombing of the American officers' quarters in Saigon. 3 The Green Berets forged an alliance with Montagnard tribespeople in the Central Highlands.

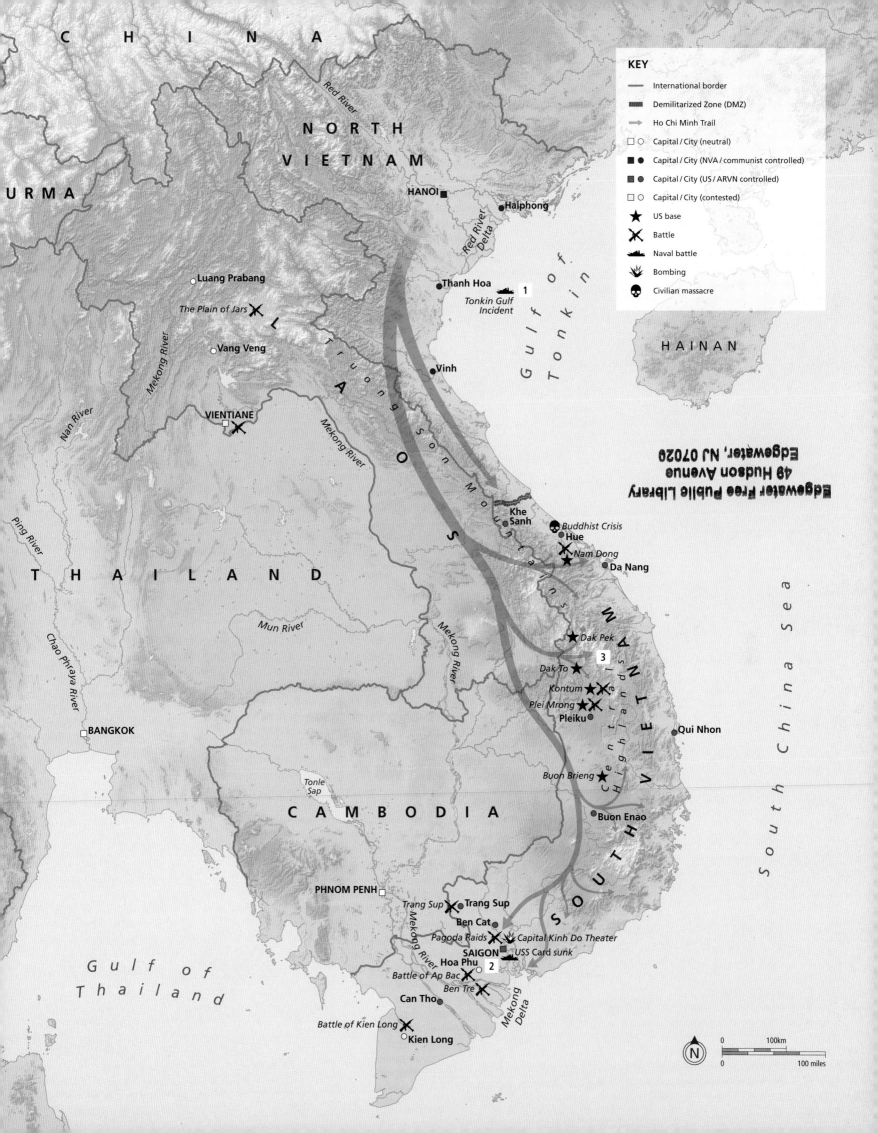

CHINA

NORTH
VIETNAM

BURMA

Red River

Mekong River

Luang Prabang

The Plain of Jars ✕

L A O S

Vang Veng

VIENTIANE ✕

THAILAND

Nan River

Ping River

Mekong River

Mun River

Chao Phraya River

BANGKOK

Mekong River

Tonle Sap

CAMBODIA

PHNOM PENH

Mekong River

Gulf of Thailand

HANOI ■   Haiphong

Red River Delta

Thanh Hoa   ⛴ **1**
Tonkin Gulf Incident

Vinh

Gulf of Tonkin

HAINAN

Truong Son Mountains

Khe Sanh
☠ *Buddhist Crisis*
Hue
✕ *Nam Dong*
★   ● Da Nang

Edgewater Free Public Library
49 Hudson Avenue
Edgewater, NJ 07020

Dak Pek ★

Dak To ★   **3**

Kontum ★★
Plei Mrong ★✕✕
Pleiku ✕

Central Highlands

Qui Nhon

Buon Brieng ★

Buon Enao

SOUTH VIETNAM

South China Sea

Trang Sup ✕ **Trang Sup**
Ben Cat ●
Pagoda Raids ✕✕💥 *Capital Kinh Do Theater*
SAIGON ■   ⛴ *USS Card sunk*
Hoa Phu ○   **2**
Battle of Ap Bac ✕
Ben Tre ✕

Can Tho

Battle of Kien Long ✕
Kien Long ○

Mekong Delta

KEY

— International border

▤ Demilitarized Zone (DMZ)

→ Ho Chi Minh Trail

□ ○ Capital / City (neutral)

■ ● Capital / City (NVA / communist controlled)

■ ● Capital / City (US / ARVN controlled)

□ ○ Capital / City (contested)

★ US base

✕ Battle

⛴ Naval battle

💥 Bombing

☠ Civilian massacre

N

0   100km

0   100 miles

TIMELINE MAR 1959–DEC 1964

Coups in Laos ▪ **Formation of the NLF** ▪ Kennedy becomes president ▪ **US Special Forces arrive in Vietnam**

▪ Agent Orange ▪ **Strategic Hamlets program** ▪ Buddhist Crisis ▪ **Removal of President Diem**

▪ Tonkin Gulf Incident ▪ **Tonkin Gulf Resolution** ▪ Viet Cong attack on Bien Hoa airbase

APRIL–DECEMBER 1959	1960	1961

MAY 9
North Vietnam establishes Military Transport Group 559 to build a supply route between North and South Vietnam. The route becomes known as the Ho Chi Minh Trail.

JANUARY 20
John F. Kennedy is inaugurated as 35th president of the United States.

JANUARY 28
Kennedy increases funding for South Vietnam to support a counterinsurgency strategy.

« Election ticket, 1960

JUNE 4
At a summit meeting in Vienna, President Kennedy and Soviet Leader Nikita Khrushchev approve a plan for a neutralist Laos.

JULY 1
General Maxwell Taylor is appointed as Kennedy's special military adviser on Vietnam.

⌄ Carrying supplies on the Ho Chi Minh Trail

JANUARY 26
The South Vietnamese 32nd regiment is defeated in an attack by Viet Cong guerrillas at the village of Trang Sup, northeast of Saigon.

NOVEMBER 11–12
President Diem survives an attempted military coup led by officers of the South Vietnamese Airborne Division.

AUGUST 9
In Laos, Captain Kong Le seizes power in a military coup and denounces American influence in his country. Laos increasingly becomes a focus of Cold War tension between the United States and the Soviet Union.

DECEMBER 12
With the backing of the North Vietnamese politburo, the National Liberation Front (NLF) is formed as the political wing of the antigovernment insurgency in South Vietnam.

⌃ Green Beret headgear

MAY 11
Kennedy dispatches 400 Special Forces personnel (Green Berets) to South Vietnam and authorizes covert operations.

NOVEMBER 22
Kennedy authorizes a major escalation of American involvement in South Vietnam, including the dispatch of military helicopters and aircrew to fly them into combat.

JULY 8
The first American soldiers are killed in South Vietnam in a guerrilla raid on their living quarters at Bien Hoa, near Saigon.

⌄ AK-47, used by the NVA and the Viet Cong

AUGUST 20
The first load of arms and other aid from North Vietnam is delivered to the Viet Cong.

DECEMBER 25
General Phoumi Nosavan takes power in a coup in Laos to counter the growth of Pathet Lao, a communist insurgency backed by North Vietnam.

NOVEMBER 8
Democrat candidate John F. Kennedy, with Lyndon B. Johnson as his running mate, narrowly defeats Republican Richard Nixon in the US presidential election.

DECEMBER 31
By the year's end, there are about 900 American military personnel in South Vietnam. Five American soldiers have been killed there during the course of the year.

DECEMBER 31
At the year's end, there are 3,200 US military personnel in South Vietnam. The American death toll for the year is 16.

We shall pay any price, bear any burden, meet any hardship, support any friend, oppose any foe, to ensure the survival and the success of liberty."

PRESIDENT JOHN F KENNEDY, INAUGURATION SPEECH, JANUARY 20, 1961

962

ANUARY 12
beration Ranch Hand begins. herican aircraft spray large eas of rural South Vietnam ch herbicides, chiefly Agent ange, to destroy vegetation d deprive guerrillas of cover d food.

⌃ The Strategic Hamlets program, implemented in 1962

MARCH 19
The South Vietnamese government launches its Strategic Hamlets Program, intended to defeat the rural insurgency by protecting peasants from communist influence.

EBRUARY 8
e United States sets up the ilitary Assistance Command, etnam (MACV) to support uth Vietnam against the et Cong. General Paul arkins is appointed MACV mmander.

1963

JANUARY 2
Viet Cong ambush South Vietnamese (ARVN) infantry and their American advisers at Ap Bac. It is the first major Viet Cong victory over American-supported troops.

MAY 8
South Vietnamese forces shoot nine unarmed Buddhist demonstrators in Hue, leading to widespread anti-Diem protests by Buddhists. South Vietnam is thrown into political crisis.

JUNE 11
In protest at Diem's policies, Buddhist monk Thich Quang Duc burns himself to death in central Saigon. International opinion of the Diem regime plummets.

NOVEMBER 2
President Diem is assassinated in the course of a military coup approved by the United States. General Duong Van Minh takes power at the head of a military junta.

DECEMBER 31
By the year's end, the number of US military personnel in Vietnam is 11,300. The American death toll for the year is 53.

⌄ JFK assassination headline

EXTRA
New York Post LATEST STOCK PRICES
WEATHER

JFK SHOT

NOVEMBER 22
President Kennedy is assassinated in Dallas, Texas. Lyndon B. Johnson is sworn in as president.

DECEMBER 31
At the year's end there are 16,300 American military personnel in Vietnam. The US death toll for the year is 122.

1964

JANUARY 20
The North Vietnamese leadership decides in favor of an all-out war to defeat the South Vietnamese government and its American allies.

JANUARY 30
General Nguyen Khanh overthrows General Minh in a bloodless coup and takes power in South Vietnam. Other South Vietnamese generals contest his rule.

JUNE 20
General William Westmoreland is appointed commander of American forces in Vietnam.

JULY 1
General Maxwell Taylor is appointed US Ambassador to South Vietnam.

AUGUST 2
In the Tonkin Gulf Incident, the destroyer USS *Maddox*, on a signals intelligence mission, is engaged by North Vietnamese torpedo boats.

AUGUST 4
The US Navy mistakenly reports a second naval encounter in the Gulf of Tonkin.

AUGUST 5
US aircraft strike targets in North Vietnam in retaliation for the alleged attacks in the Gulf of Tonkin.

AUGUST 7
US Congress passes the Tonkin Gulf Resolution authorizing the president to take any action he deems necessary to assist South Vietnam "in defense of its freedom."

NOVEMBER 1
The Viet Cong launch an attack on America's Bien Hoa airbase outside Saigon, killing four US personnel.

NOVEMBER 3
Johnson is reelected US president with a landslide victory over Barry Goldwater.

DECEMBER 31
At the year's end, there are 23,300 US troops in Vietnam. The American death toll for the year totals 216.

« ARVN and US troops under attack by the Viet Cong, 1964

Guerrilla Warfare Resumes

An undeclared war between the two Vietnams began in earnest in 1959. When it looked as though the Viet Cong guerrillas and North Vietnamese Army could become a serious threat, US presidents Eisenhower and Kennedy poured aid into South Vietnam to prop up the faltering regime.

At the end of the 1950s, South Vietnam appeared to be prosperous and stable—thanks to more than $200 million dollars worth of military and economic assistance from the US each year. By 1960, such aid made up as much as 70 percent of the country's total budget, and

Saigon was booming. The South Vietnamese capital, however, was not typical. Little, if anything, was being done to improve conditions in the villages where 90 percent of the population lived.

This meant that insurgency found a ready audience. The peasants, one guerrilla said after his capture,

were "like a mass of straw ready to be ignited." Even anticommunists living in South Vietnam agitated for change.

Use of force

As America poured resources into propping up the Diem regime in South Vietnam, Le Duan, a former

activist in South Vietnam, who had taken refuge in the North, pressed fellow members of North Vietnam's politburo to provide greater support for the insurgents in the South. As a result, in January 1959, the committee sanctioned the use of force in South Vietnam. While not wishing

« **BEFORE**

History showed how committed guerrilla fighters could beat a well-trained professional army.

PAST SUCCESS
The Viet Minh had fought a **guerrilla war « 24–25** against the French in Vietnam during the **First Indochina War « 26–27,** progressing from rural ambushes and raids to ambitious confrontations using sophisticated weapons. Their success had led to the **creation of communist North Vietnam « 38–39**.

BAS-RELIEF OF HO CHI MINH WITH VICTORIOUS VIET MINH IN QUANG TRI

THE TIME IS RIGHT
As President Diem hunted down insurgents in South Vietnam, the Central Committee in the North weighed its options. Should North Vietnam adhere to the "peaceful political action," favored by Ho Chi Minh in 1954, after the First Indochina War, or was it ready to renew armed struggle in the South?

to provoke their opponents, especially the Americans, by an outright invasion, it sought to build an effective guerrilla army in the South and supply it with weapons. It established Group 559 to organize supply lines.

Summoned by bells

The province of Ben Tre, in the southern Mekong Delta, was the scene for one of the first uprisings. As evening fell on January 17, 1960, gongs and bells summoned the locals to rise up against the ruling Diem regime and take control of their villages from the rapacious landlords and corrupt local officials. During the same month at Trang Sup,

A new culture
This guide to Vietnam was issued to US personnel serving in South Vietnam in 1962. Its aim was to lessen culture shock and help individuals win the hearts and minds of the Vietnamese people.

a village northeast of Saigon, insurgents fought their way into a South Vietnamese Army (ARVN) headquarters and made off with large numbers of weapons. That October, three crack paratroop battalions, hitherto presumed to be among the most loyal of the South Vietnamese units, surrounded Diem's presidential palace. The attempted coup was only narrowly thwarted by forces still faithful to the president.

The insurgents targeted local officials who had the power to imprison for life or put to death any communist opponent of the regime. By the end of 1960, more than 1,400 government officials had been assassinated.

Enter the Viet Cong

In December 1960, the National Liberation Front (NLF)—or the National Front for the Liberation of South Vietnam (NFLSV)—was founded at a conference in Tay Ninh province in South Vietnam. The US viewed the NLF as an arm of North Vietnam and called its military wing the Viet Cong—short for Vietnam communists.

By then, insurgents dominated large areas of the Mekong Delta, the Central Highlands, and the coastal plains. Their fighting strength had risen to an estimated 25,000 guerrillas, while the NLF's political wing had as many as 200,000 active sympathizers. Washington responded by sending in more weapons, training, and aid to support Diem.

Unpopular policies and corrupt practices aided recruitment to the Viet Cong.

RECRUITING GROUNDS
The **Strategic Hamlets Program 70–71 »** forced people living in rural areas prone to Viet Cong infiltration to move to specially fortified villages. This alienated the rural population, driving them into the arms of the Viet Cong.

SECRET NETWORK
The spread of the Viet Cong through South Vietnam, and infiltration of the country by the NVA, was facilitated by the expansion of the **Ho Chi Minh Trail 56–57 »**.

> "It is extremely difficult to **identify an enemy** unless he is **in uniform** or shooting at you."

KNOW YOUR ENEMY, ISSUED BY THE DEPARTMENT OF DEFENSE, 1966

Transporting the troops
South Vietnamese soldiers wait to be picked up by US helicopters in 1962. While North Vietnam armed and trained the communists, the US plowed resources into supporting the Diem regime and the ARVN.

A military art
An American military adviser shows South Vietnamese troops how to kill a communist guerrilla with a bayonet. The ARVN had to match their opponents' tactics and learn new combat skills.

‹‹ BEFORE

Resistance to the new regime in South Vietnam was inextricably linked to the previous resistance to French imperialism.

POLITICAL CONTINUITY
The forerunners of the Viet Cong were the **Viet Minh ‹‹ 24–25**, a guerrilla network founded by **Ho Chi Minh** to **fight against the French ‹‹ 26–27**. After the partition of the country in 1954, cells of Viet Minh stayed in South Vietnam, in particular in the Mekong Delta and along the Cambodian and Laotian borders.

VIET MINH POSTER CA. 1954

The **Viet Cong**

The National Liberation Front—known as the Viet Cong—aimed to overthrow the South Vietnamese regime and reunify North and South Vietnam. Despite its unconventional guerrilla tactics, it was a structured fighting force that amassed plenty of support.

It was the Diem regime that christened the forces of the National Liberation Front Viet Cong—short for "Vietnam Cong-san," meaning Vietnamese communists. The Americans called them "VC," "Victor Charlie"—a reference to the phonetic alphabet—and derivatives "Charlie," and "Chuck."

Early growth
The Viet Cong were divided into three operational forces—the main one being made up of full-time regulars. This was divided into battalions, regiments, and, from 1965, divisions, which had an operational strength of 7,350 men. There were also full-time regional forces under provincial command and part-time guerrilla units, which were used primarily for village defense.

What the Viet Cong termed cadres were another key element in the insurgents' political and military setup. More often than not, they were veterans of the war against the French with years of guerrilla experience behind them. At the start of the insurgency, the majority of cadres were so-called regroupees—South Vietnamese people who had moved to North Vietnam in 1954 and, following intensive military training and political indoctrination, moved back to the South.

Former Viet Minh members who had remained in South Vietnam often became active Viet Cong organizers as well, operating in small cells for greater security. Tran Van Bo was a typical example. He started off as a propagandist for the Viet Minh before quitting the movement to become a farmer in the Mekong Delta. He rejoined his former comrades some years later after Diem's troops had tried, but failed, to arrest him. Cadres like

Single short automatic selector switch

Ejection port

Charging handle to load rounds into firing chamber

Butt

Trigger

Trigger guard

Magazine release lever

30-round detachable magazine

Pistol grip

Weapon of choice
Soviet-manufactured AK-47 rifles—and Chinese variants, such as this Type 56—replaced the carbines with which the Viet Cong were first equipped. The AK-47, often called peasants' rifles, were reliable weapons and produced a tremendous amount of automatic firepower.

" For the **liberation** of our compatriots in the south, a situation of **boiling oil** and **burning fire** is necessary."

VIET CONG SOLDIER DU LIC, IN HIS DIARY, DECEMBER 1961

Lying in wait

A 1960s' Viet Cong poster boasts that US patrols, however well-armed, stand little chance of surviving ambush in the dense jungle. The propagandists targeted US ground forces in particular, hoping to lower morale.

him formed the nucleus of the National Liberation Front (NLF) when it was founded in 1960.

Viet Cong recruitment

The movement expanded rapidly. By late 1962, the NLF had around 300,000 active members and one million passive supporters in South Vietnam. The Viet Cong controlled at least a quarter of the villages in the Mekong Delta.

Initially, most new recruits were persuaded to join the Viet Cong voluntarily by the recruiting cadres who regularly visited rural hamlets. One of their arguments was that, once they turned 18, boys would be drafted into the South Vietnamese Army (ARVN) anyway. Recruiters assured their recruits

came to power. Others enlisted to get away from a dull village life. However, as time went on, and recruiting cadres were required to meet provincial targets, compulsion replaced persuasion and young men were pitchforked into joining.

with well-concealed staging areas from which to launch hit-and-run attacks. Following the example set by Chinese communists in guerrilla campaigns against Japan, these sanctuaries also served as training grounds and headquarters.

AFTER »

As the Viet Cong grew in strength, the US steadily increased its support for the Diem regime.

MULTIFACETED THREAT

On January 12, 1962, helicopters flown by US Army pilots ferried 1,000 ARVN troops to **attack a Viet Cong** stronghold near Saigon in Operation Chopper. The Viet Cong continued to pose both a military and ideological threat throughout the war, causing the US to put the **Phoenix Program 214–15 »** into action in 1967.

HIDDEN NO MORE

US tacticians believed they could make it harder for the guerrillas to conceal themselves by clearing the jungle. Over the course of the war, vast tracts of Vietnamese countryside were sprayed with **Agent Orange 146–47 »**, a herbicide containing the deadly chemical dioxin.

Rear sight | Front sight

Foregrip | Bayonet lug | Barrel

that, if they agreed to join the Viet Cong, they could serve close to their homes—in direct contrast to the ARVN policy of posting recruits as far away from their families as possible. There was also the promise of future gain after the war was won and the NLF

Safe havens

Viet Cong warfare was unlike anything their opponents had experienced. It was a war with no frontline in the accepted sense. The terrain also favored the insurgents and their tactics. South Vietnam's rainforests, mountains, and swamplands provided them

Training session

A Viet Cong woman demonstrates the use of an M1 carbine to a group of female recruits in September 1967. Only a few women in the Viet Cong were actual fighters—mainly in village defense forces where, like the male recruits, they were given some initial military training.

[1] RPG-2

[2] RPD MACHINE GUN AND
AMMUNITION DRUM

[3] HOMEMADE MACHINE GUN

[4] MACHETE

[5] HOMEMADE RIFLE

[6] PUNJI
STICKS

Viet Cong Gear and Weaponry

The Viet Cong fought a guerrilla war against US forces and the ARVN using a combination of homemade weapons, antique guns, and what arms could be spared by their North Vietnamese allies.

[1] **RPG-2** A Soviet-designed, shoulder-fired grenade launcher, this was effective against armored vehicles and helicopters. [2] **RPD machine gun and ammunition drum** This Soviet weapon with distinctive drum magazines was used to lay down fire during assaults and to cover retreats. [3] **Homemade machine gun** Based on the easily produced British Sten gun, this model is notable for its double-set triggers. [4] **Machete** Viet Cong forces used machetes to clear paths through dense jungle and for hand-to-hand combat when necessary. [5] **Homemade rifle** These weapons were extremely crude, highly inaccurate, and prone to fall apart after just a few shots. [6] **Punji sticks** Simple booby traps, these were made of bamboo or wood sharpened into spikes. [7] **Stick grenade** Viet Cong guerrillas were capable of producing their own grenades, although many were killed assembling

such weapons. [8] **RKG-3 antitank grenade** Easily held and thrown, this stick grenade could be conveniently transported in bundles. [9] **Floppy hat** Usually made of lightweight cotton, this style of hat has a camouflage pattern. [10] **Tunic** A wide array of simple tunics were worn by the Viet Cong. These enabled them to blend in with the Vietnamese peasantry. [11] **Ammunition belt** These held additional magazines or rounds. [12] **Rice carrier** This would have been filled with dry rice, tied at the ends, and carried across the back or shoulder. [13] **Backpack** Attached to this are a rice bowl and a camouflage ring. Bamboo and other foliage would have been pulled through the ring to provide camouflage. [14] **Pants** Black pajama-style pants were commonly worn. [15] **Sandals** Made from recycled rubber sourced from tire treads, these were dubbed Ho Chi Minh sandals by US troops.

[7] STICK GRENADE

[8] RKG-3 ANTITANK GRENADE

9 FLOPPY HAT

10 TUNIC

11 AMMUNITION BELT

12 RICE CARRIER

13 BACKPACK

14 PANTS

15 SANDALS

《 BEFORE

The men and women who built and used the Ho Chi Minh Trail followed in the footsteps of tribal hunters and the Viet Minh.

TRIBAL HUNTING PATHS

During the **First Indochina War 《 26–27** against the French, Ho Chi Minh dispatched an entire division along the tribal hunting paths that were later to become the backbone of the Ho Chi Minh Trail.

In 1954, General Vo Nguyen Giap, the Viet Minh's commander in the war, also used little-known tracks and trails to get his 55,000-strong army, plus its supporting artillery, into position for the **Battle of Dien Bien Phu 《 30–31**, which ended French colonialism in Southeast Asia.

Creating the Ho Chi Minh Trail

The North Vietnamese decided to create the Ho Chi Minh Trail as a means of infiltrating South Vietnam. It proved to be one of their greatest assets. During the course of the war more than one million Viet Cong and North Vietnamese soldiers used its network of tracks.

Colonel Vo Bam, a logistics expert working in the Ministry of Defense in Hanoi, masterminded the creation of the supply route known as the Ho Chi Minh Trail. His watchwords were "absolute secrecy, absolute security."

His initial plan was for North Vietnamese infiltrators to make their way stealthily through the narrow demilitarized zone (DMZ) between North and South Vietnam, and then follow Route Nine, the road linking the Vietnamese coastal plain with the Mekong Valley, to join Viet Cong detachments at jungle staging posts south of Khe Sanh.

The proposed route was practical, but also risky. When the South Vietnamese Army (ARVN), which regularly patrolled Route Nine, realized what was going on, it

sent reinforcements to Khe Sanh and began clearing the area. Bam was forced to reconsider his plan. He concluded that the DMZ could be avoided by rerouting the trail down the western side of the Truong Son mountains and through lower Laos. Both Hanoi and the Pathet Lao, the communist insurgents in Laos, approved the new route. The Royal Laotian Army put up little opposition.

Shouldering the load

South Vietnamese volunteers carry ammunition for the Viet Cong on the Ho Chi Minh Trail. Armies of women helped distribute ammunition and weapons shipped to Hanoi from the Soviet Union and China.

At the same time, a maritime infiltration route was established. Less well-known than the Ho Chi Minh Trail, it proved crucial to supplying Viet Cong insurgents in the far south of the country.

Life on the trail

In the early days of the war, the trail was rudimentary. A North Vietnamese colonel called Biu Tin, traveling the trail in December 1961, recorded a trek lasting three months, during which he had to hack or crawl through the jungle. On a later trek, he recorded that some soldiers had lost their way and died of starvation. Travelers also faced venomous snakes, leeches, and dysentery

As the war escalated, the demands made on the Ho Chi Minh Trail increased. In late 1963, Vo Bam's Group 559, which had been running the trail since its

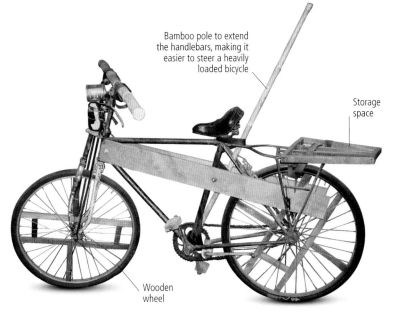

Bamboo pole to extend the handlebars, making it easier to steer a heavily loaded bicycle

Storage space

Wooden wheel

expand the trail. Equipped with modern Soviet and Chinese machinery, they carved out roads and built bridges that could handle heavy trucks and tanks. Convoys of vehicles, operating in relay, mostly at night, were soon transporting hundreds of tons of supplies southward.

Transport on the trail

The Viet Cong transported supplies by any means possible, including by bicycle. In 1967, *New York Times* war correspondent Harrison Salisbury told the US Senate that without bikes, the Viet Cong would be forced to get out of the war.

> " Had the Americans **cut the Ho Chi Minh Trail** the **outcome of the war** would have been far different."
>
> ANDREW R. FINLAYSON, *RICE PADDY RECON: A MARINE OFFICER'S SECOND TOUR IN VIETNAM*, 1968–1970

inception, investigated the feasibility of making it fit to transport large numbers of troops into South Vietnam. Five months later, Hanoi took the decision to transform the Trail into a sophisticated logistical network and put Colonel Dong Si Nguyen in charge of construction. Still underway a decade later, the trail became a spider's web of crisscrossing and intersecting tracks. Thousands of engineers toiled ceaselessly to widen and

> **TRUONG SON TRAIL The name given to the trail by the North Vietnamese, after the mountain range running through Central Vietnam. The Americans named it the Ho Chi Minh Trail.**

Defending the trail

Battalions of North Vietnamese regulars were assigned to defend the trail's flanks against possible ground attack. To protect it from bombing, elaborate antiaircraft defenses were set up at key points along the trail. Underground barracks, workshops, hospitals, fuel dumps, and storage facilities were also constructed.

The number of infiltrators rose, reaching an average of 4,500 soldiers a month by 1966 and 6,000 a month the year after that. As even the US government reluctantly came to realize, what the North Vietnamese had created was one of the great military engineering achievements of the 20th century.

AFTER

As the war went on, severing the Ho Chi Minh Trail became a priority for the US.

TRAIL OF DESTRUCTION
Beginning in 1964, Royal Laotian, South Vietnamese, and US **warplanes bombed the trail** around the clock, making some 500 sorties a day. By late 1968, the number had doubled. Nevertheless, the trail stayed open and the supplies kept rolling. After each attack, hordes of Viet Cong soldiers and volunteers raced to repair the damage. **By 1972, the trail had been supplemented by a new Secret Road 272–73 ≫**.

THE HO CHIN MINH TRAIL TODAY

Democratic team
A campaign button for the 1961 election campaign advertises the original dream ticket, combining the youthful energy of Kennedy and the experience of running mate Lyndon Johnson.

The **Kennedy Administration**

Convinced that countries such as South Vietnam were key arenas in an ideological war between communism and freedom, John F. Kennedy was determined to support Diem's regime in its fight against the Viet Cong.

BEFORE

Soviet rhetoric helped change Kennedy's mind about supporting a war in Vietnam.

CHANGE OF HEART
As a young senator, John F. Kennedy told the Senate in April 1954 that **no amount of military assistance** in Indochina could conquer an enemy that **had the sympathy and covert support of the people**. Kennedy later changed his mind. In particular, he was determined to counter Soviet leader Nikita Khrushchev's pledge to support communists across the globe in their wars of national liberation. The US, Kennedy promised, would ensure liberty prevailed. It would pay any price and oppose any foe to stop the spread of communism.

KEY CONCEPT

THE DOMINO THEORY

In the early 1950s, American foreign policymakers became firm believers in the Domino Theory: if communism was allowed to take hold in one nation, neighboring countries would also fall under its influence, each one knocking over the next, until they had all fallen. President Eisenhower referred to the theory as his rationale for intervening in Vietnam, while Presidents Kennedy and Johnson later used it to justify increasing US involvement in the conflict.

John F. Kennedy won the US presidency in 1960 partly on the strength of pledges to wage the Cold War more vigorously than Eisenhower, his Republican predecessor. This meant developing US capabilities to fight small-scale conflicts, known as brushfire wars, including the one in Vietnam.

As part of his bid to beef up US foreign policy, Kennedy recruited a remarkable team of advisers: Robert McNamara, the former president of Ford Motor Company, as secretary of defense; Dean Rusk, president of the Rockefeller Foundation, as the secretary of state; foreign policy expert McGeorge Bundy as Kennedy's national security adviser; and economist Walt Whitman Rostow, who became Bundy's deputy. At the suggestion of Kennedy's brother Robert, the recently retired General Maxwell Taylor became

Kennedy's personal military aide. Taylor was a military maverick, preferring "flexible response" to traditional US strategy that relied on overwhelming retaliation. He argued that it was "as necessary to deter or win quickly limited wars as to deter general wars." In his view, retaining a strong and flexible infantry was as important as possessing nuclear missiles.

A new kind of conflict

Improving America's ability to wage conventional war was only part of Kennedy's plan. He wanted specific initiatives devised to deal with guerrilla activity, insurgency, and subversion. Kennedy believed the Army needed to come up with a new strategy, a wholly different kind of force, and a new kind of military training to meet what he considered to be the preeminent threat of the day. His answer was to double the size of US

Special Forces. This was only the beginning. Over the next three years, Kennedy issued 23 National Security Action Memorandums with counterinsurgency as their common subject.

Test case

South Vietnam was to be the proving ground for the new strategy. Having seen a clandestine attempt to overthrow Fidel Castro end in disaster at the Bay of Pigs and having backed down from confronting communism in Laos in the interests of US–Soviet cooperation, Kennedy decided that he had to make a stand in Vietnam. Vice President Lyndon Johnson

Lay of the land
In September 1963, General Maxwell Taylor (second right) went to Vietnam to assess the war effort. He met with MACV commander General Paul Harkins (carrying briefcase), whose reports had painted a favorable picture of US progress.

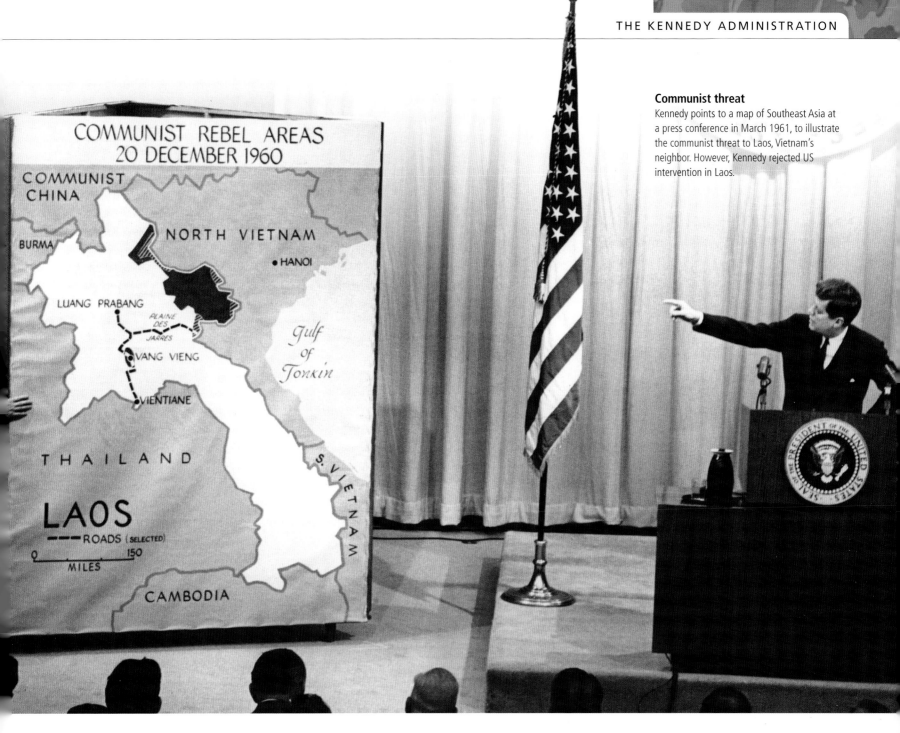

COMMUNIST REBEL AREAS
20 DECEMBER 1960

COMMUNIST CHINA

BURMA

NORTH VIETNAM

• HANOI

LUANG PRABANG

PLAINE DES JARRES

VANG VIENG

Gulf of Tonkin

VIENTIANE

THAILAND

S. VIETNAM

LAOS
---- ROADS (SELECTED)
0   150
MILES

CAMBODIA

Communist threat
Kennedy points to a map of Southeast Asia at a press conference in March 1961, to illustrate the communist threat to Laos, Vietnam's neighbor. However, Kennedy rejected US intervention in Laos.

> " We are neither **warmongers** nor **appeasers ... We are Americans.** "

JOHN F. KENNEDY, SPEECH AT THE UNIVERSITY OF WASHINGTON, NOVEMBER 16, 1961

concurred. After visiting Saigon in May 1961, Johnson told the president that he faced a stark choice: meet the challenge of communist expansion or prepare to give up on Southeast Asia.

Project Beef Up
Although Kennedy balked at sending US ground forces into action—a course urged by the Joint Chiefs of Staff—he authorized the implementation of Project Beef Up, which more than doubled American military assistance and economic support to the South Vietnamese. The dispatch of US helicopters and Special Forces contingents to support the training of the South Vietnamese Army

(ARVN) turned the tide for a while, at least according to the reports reaching Washington.

Hopes dashed
Believing that the US was well on its way to achieving stability in South Vietnam, in the fall of 1962 Kennedy instructed McNamara to prepare to wind down the number

of US military advisers there to 1,500 by the end of 1965. The plan was never implemented. With the resurgence of the Viet Cong in 1963 and the growth of popular protest against President Ngo Dinh Diem, Kennedy's response was to increase US military assistance. By the end of 1963, there were 16,000 US personnel in Vietnam.

AFTER

Kennedy and his advisers came to believe that the authoritarianism of President Diem was part of the problem, not the solution, in South Vietnam.

CHANGES AT THE TOP
In November 1963, Kennedy and his advisers covertly backed an **ARVN coup 76–77 》** and the installation of a military junta in South Vietnam.

Within three weeks, Kennedy had been **assassinated** in Dallas, Texas. Lyndon Johnson was immediately sworn in as president.

US PRESIDENT Born 1917 Died 1963

John F. Kennedy

"Peace need not be impracticable, and war need not be inevitable."

PRESIDENT J. F. KENNEDY, SPEECH AT AMERICAN UNIVERSITY, JUNE 10, 1963

Taking office in 1961, John Fitzgerald Kennedy presented himself as the leader of a new generation inspired by idealism and infused with optimism. To this day, his image endures as a symbol of hope for a better world, and his assassination in 1963 is often seen as the moment when America lost its innocence. His murder in the back of an open-top car during a visit to Dallas was the first step toward the bitter disillusionment that reached full flood during the Vietnam War.

Personal charisma
Age 43 at his inauguration, John F. Kennedy was the youngest person to win election to the presidency. He projected an image of youthful optimism and energy at a time of Cold War tension and social conflict.

Political ambition
Kennedy was born into an Irish-Catholic family in Brookline, Massachusetts. His father, Joseph, an ambitious businessman and diplomat, intended that his eldest son, Joe Kennedy Jr., would translate the family's wealth into political power. When Joe Jr. was killed in World War II that role passed to John.

A Harvard graduate and a hero of the naval war in the Pacific, Kennedy entered Congress as a Democrat in 1946 and became a senator at the age of 35. His marriage to the glamorous Jacqueline Bouvier confirmed the image of unstoppable success. However, the young senator had severe back pain and a hormonal disorder known as Addison's disease. The state of his health, which required operations and treatment

On the home front
In August 1963, African Americans marched on Washington, D.C., and demanded an end to discrimination. Kennedy advanced cautiously on civil rights but laid the foundation for legislative changes that took place after his death.

KENNEDY WITH DAUGHTER CAROLINE, WIFE JACKIE, AND SON JOHN JR.

with steroids, was successfully kept secret from the public, as were his extramarital affairs.

World view

Kennedy's narrow victory over the far more experienced Republican candidate Richard Nixon in the 1960 presidential election was a triumph of image over substance. However, Kennedy's performance as president in troubled times earned him enduring respect. As well as facing pressing domestic issues, notably the Civil Rights Movement and the activities of organized crime, Kennedy confronted challenges on the world stage. Having criticized the previous Republican administration for allowing the Soviet Union to gain the advantage in the Cold War, he was committed to taking a tough line on the containment of communism. On the other hand, he understood the risks of nuclear war and hoped to combat communism in the Third World by counterinsurgency support for anticommunist regimes.

The Bay of Pigs fiasco, a CIA-backed invasion of Cuba planned by the previous administration, was a major setback. Kennedy authorized the invasion in the first 100 days of his presidency, but then refused to give it his full support. Sensing that the new president was inexperienced and irresolute, Soviet leader Nikita Khrushchev took the offensive, building the Berlin Wall in summer 1961 and then agreeing to Cuban president Fidel Castro's request to station nuclear missiles in Cuba.

The resulting Cuban Missile Crisis in October 1962 was Kennedy's finest hour. Resisting pressure for an attack on Cuba, he negotiated the withdrawal of Soviet weaponry, a diplomatic victory that led to progress in reducing nuclear tensions between the superpowers.

Policy in Vietnam

In Southeast Asia, Kennedy backed a counterinsurgency strategy spearheaded by the Green Berets, a policy that expressed his desire to halt the spread of communism

Funeral of a president
President Kennedy's flag-draped casket lies in state in the central rotunda of the US Capitol on November 25, 1963. His burial plot in Arlington National Cemetery became a place of pilgrimage for Americans.

while also avoiding outright warfare. He was initially in favor of fellow Catholic Ngo Dinh Diem's presidency of South Vietnam, but became disillusioned with Diem's failure to win the hearts and minds of his people. By 1963, America faced a stark choice: lose Vietnam to communism or reinforce its military presence there. Neither option was attractive to Kennedy. His hesitations were evident by the time of the US-backed assassination of Diem. Whether the war in Vietnam would have been radically different but for Kennedy's own assassination cannot be known.

"Freedom is indivisible, and when one man is enslaved, all are not free."

PRESIDENT JOHN F. KENNEDY, SPEECH IN WEST BERLIN, JUNE 26, 1963

American Intervention in **Laos**

By 1960, Laos was in the throes of a civil war, with various factions vying for control. Both the US and North Vietnam intervened—North Vietnam to access the Ho Chi Minh Trail, and the US to build a secret army to fight the communist Pathet Lao.

The US had been pumping resources into Vietnam's neighbor, Laos, in an attempt to establish a pro-Western government, but the country was a political quagmire. Eisenhower's response was to send in small

« BEFORE

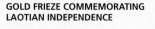

GOLD FRIEZE COMMEMORATING LAOTIAN INDEPENDENCE

Laos gained independence from France in 1953, leading to an internal power struggle. Laos soon learned that freedom from the French did not mean freedom from Western intervention.

BROTHERS AT ODDS
Since gaining its independence, Laos had been torn by internal divisions exacerbated by outside interference. Prince Souvanna Phouma's attempts to **unify the nation** under a coalition government had failed, while the communist **Pathet Lao « 42–43**, led by Prince Souphanouvong, had gained control over the northeast of the country. To US President Eisenhower, keeping Laos out of communist hands was even more important than supporting the Diem regime in Vietnam, but providing **US financial assistance** had done nothing to stabilize the situation.

Special Forces detachments as military advisers. The first of them, initially posing as contract civilian specialists, arrived in July 1959, just as the rainy season started.

The teams were drawn from the Seventh Special Forces Group stationed at Fort Bragg in North Carolina. There were 12 of them, plus a control team, which was posted to Vientiane, the Laotian capital. The others were sent to four rear-area training sites. Each team consisted of a team leader and his assistant, two light weapons specialists, a medical expert and an aidman, a radio operator, and a motor maintenance engineer. Each team's tour of duty lasted six months.

9,000 Number of hill tribesmen in the CIA's *Armée Clandestine* by summer 1961.

Special Forces in action
Initially, the teams were restricted to working simply as instructors, but in August 1960 they found

themselves caught up in the civil war between neutralists—who backed a neutral foreign policy— and pro-Westerners, with the communist Pathet Lao waiting in the wings.

That November, Special Forces detachments went into action as combat advisers to pro-Western General Phoumi Nosavan's forces as they advanced on Vientiane, which the neutralists had seized in a coup d'etat led by Captain Kong Le.

Phoumi's men occupied Vientiane, causing Kong Le to enter into a new alliance. In early 1961, the coalition of Kong Le's neutralists, Pathet Lao, and North Vietnamese (NVA) troops fought Phoumi and the Special Forces at the Plain of Jars, a strategically critical area of grassy hills. In subsequent fighting, the Special Forces suffered their first casualties. Sergeant First Class John Bischoff

and Sergeant Gerald Biber, members of Captain Walter Moon's four-man-strong Field Tracking Team, were killed in action on April 22. Moon himself was taken prisoner—as was Sergeant Orville Ballenger a week later.

Kennedy seeks neutrality
Deciding what to do about Laos was the first foreign policy dilemma that President Kennedy would face. Eisenhower had advised the new president that the

Passing the torch
Kennedy discusses matters of state with Eisenhower on January 19, 1973, the day before his inauguration. This was an informal meeting to discuss continuing problems, especially the situation in Indochina.

Secret soldiers
These Hmong guerrillas in Laos' "Secret War" are armed with weapons dropped by Air America, the CIA's clandestine airline. The guerrillas were trained by Special Forces advisers and Thai Police Aerial Reinforcement Unit teams.

"The **security of all Southeast Asia** will be **endangered** if Laos loses its **neutral independence.**"

PRESIDENT JOHN F. KENNEDY, TELEVISION ADDRESS TO THE NATION, MARCH 23, 1961

AFTER

Laos continued to be a target during the Vietnam War as a result of North Vietnamese incursions there.

FREQUENT TARGET
When the American **war in Vietnam began 90–91 》**, US ground troops stayed out of Laos. American aircraft did not. From 1964 until the 1975 **ceasefire 324–25 》**, US aircraft flew 580,944 missions over Laos, dropping a staggering 2,093,100 tons of bombs on the country to combat the communist threat. This made Laos the **most heavily bombed place** in the history of the Earth.

situation in Laos was so grave that it might be necessary to deploy ground forces. Laos, he said, was the key to all of Southeast Asia. If it fell to communism, then South Vietnam, Cambodia, Burma, and Thailand would follow.

However, Kennedy did not send US ground troops into action. In April, he concluded that a negotiated settlement was the best he could hope for and agreed to participate in a peace conference. More than a year of talks followed.

In July 1962, an agreement was finally made to establish a neutral and independent Laos.

Operation Momentum
In spite of this, Laos remained divided by factions determined to continue the battle for power. The North Vietnamese needed to control the eastern corridor that formed an integral part of the Ho Chi Minh Trail. Meanwhile, the US was determined to block the North Vietnamese incursions.

It was a task Kennedy gave to the CIA, which had already set its own secret plan in motion. Operation Momentum, as it was codenamed, recruited a Hmong guerrilla army—the *Armée Clandestine*— to fight for the CIA by proxy. It was soon a match for the Pathet Lao. By the end of 1963, around 20,000 Hmong had been recruited. The "Secret War," which lasted for more than 13 years, was the largest paramilitary operation the CIA had ever undertaken.

Green Berets

Championed by President Kennedy, the US Special Forces, known as the Green Berets, began their service in Vietnam by training the hilltribe people in guerrilla warfare.

Regimental badge with the motto "de oppresso liber"—to free the oppressed

Counterinsurgency was a key policy for the Kennedy administration, and the expansion of US Special Forces to implement the strategy became a top military priority. At the time of Kennedy's inauguration in January 1961, there were three Special Forces groups in existence—the

« BEFORE

President Kennedy valued the Green Berets for the flexibility of their response.

SMALL BEGINNINGS
The elite fighting force known as the Green Berets developed from the **Tenth Special Forces Group** established in June 1952. The unit consisted of just 10 soldiers, all, as now, volunteers.

NEW TYPES OF CONFLICT
Kennedy's belief in the efficacy of Special Forces predated his presidency. He believed Eisenhower had focused too heavily on **nuclear arms**, leaving the US ill-equipped to fight conventional conflicts of the kind Kennedy expected to face in Asia. Kennedy especially praised the Special Forces' "flexible response."

" The Green Beret is … a symbol of **excellence,** a badge of **courage,** a mark of **distinction.** "

PRESIDENT JOHN. F. KENNEDY, MEMORANDUM TO THE US NAVY, APRIL 11, 1962

Tenth, the Seventh, and the First. These were joined by the Fifth, activated in September 1961, and the Eighth and the Third in 1963.

The right recruits
Special Forces soldiers were highly trained. In addition to satisfying tough physical demands and being qualified parachutists, potential recruits had to show they were independent thinkers with the potential to fight and survive in harsh combat conditions. The first phase of the assessment and selection procedure lasted 24 days and included a week-long field training exercise. Round-the-clock land navigation exercises, reconnaissance patrols, ambushes, raids, and an escape and evasion exercise pushed the recruits to the limits of their physical and mental endurance. In the second phase of the training, recruits received instruction in one of five specialty areas—operations and intelligence, weapons, engineering, medicine, and communications. In the third phase, they learned the basics of guerrilla warfare.

> The Green Berets were not the only US special operations forces in Vietnam. The Navy Seals (Sea–Air–Land) specialized in riverine missions from 1962.

Green Berets in Vietnam
In April 1961, President Kennedy ordered the dispatch of 400 Green Berets to South Vietnam from the First Special Forces Group based on Okinawa island, Japan. Captain Ron Shackleton and half of Detachment A-113 were tasked with setting up the Civil Irregular Defense Group (CIDG) program designed to protect the Montagnards, the mountain tribespeople, from infiltration by the Viet Cong. Kennedy also authorized the launch of a

clandestine campaign against North Vietnam by South Vietnamese troops trained and directed by Special Forces advisers.

The Special Forces presence expanded rapidly, commanded from the fall of 1962 by Colonel George C. Morton. Their presence did not go unnoticed by the insurgents. In January 1963, the border surveillance camp at Plei Mrong became the first Special Forces camp to be assaulted by the Viet Cong.

By October 1964, there were 44 Special Forces Operational Detachments Alpha, also known as A-Teams, in South Vietnam, of which 28 were deployed on border surveillance, with the aim of preventing Viet

Badge of pride
This beret was worn by a member of the Seventh Special Forces Group Airborne, which trained the South Vietnamese army. In combat, caps or helmets replaced berets.

Cong infiltration from Laos or across the Demilitarized Zone (DMZ). The results were mixed. Most infiltrators sought alternative routes, or simply avoided the Special Forces' patrols. In addition, the camps were hard to maintain and mostly only accessible by air. Ninety percent of the troops assigned to them had to be flown in or dropped by parachute, along with their supplies. The CIDGs that the Green Berets organized were more successful. The American hope was that these would prevent infiltration by the Viet Cong across the Central Highlands.

AFTER »

ADDRESSING THE MONTAGNARDS

From 1968, the CIA enlisted the support of the Green Berets in counterterrorism operations.

PHOENIX PROGRAM
The Green Berets gradually relinquished their role in the CIDG program to the ARVN and became more involved in reconnaissance and intelligence gathering, particularly for the CIA's

Phoenix Program 214–15 ».
Special Forces ceased all operations in Vietnam in March 1971, though continued to perform an advisory role.

NEW INSURGENCIES
The Green Berets have operated in many war zones since Vietnam, including Iraq, Somalia, Bosnia, Afghanistan, and Syria.

Mission accomplished
Special Forces commander Captain Vernon Gillespie contacts his base camp by radio while the South Vietnamese soldiers he is leading burn down a Viet Cong hideout in 1964.

The Green Berets in Vietnam

The Green Berets spent their early days in Vietnam dissuading the Montagnards from joining the communist cause. It often took a while for Americans to win the trust of the mountain people. Keeping that trust was also difficult—as 31-year-old Special Forces Captain Vernon Gillespie Jr. found in 1964, when five of the six Montagnard camps in his region staged a mutiny.

The primary mission at the Green Beret camp was twofold: to run reconnaissance missions to interdict the North Vietnamese Army infiltration routes and to rescue captive Montagnards that the Viet Cong were using as laborers and porters at their way stations. The Green Berets brought these people back to a camp at Buon Brieng to deprive the Viet Cong of this labor source.

Tension had been building among the Montagnards at Buon Brieng in late July and early August 1964. On the night before September 19, a rebellion broke out in the camp and the Green Berets were prepared for it. However, the next morning, they discovered rebellion was occurring over a far wider area. Green Beret Captain Vernon Gillespie Jr. told the Montagnards battalion commander that he was taking command of the camp, which meant the Vietnamese Special Forces in the camp were under US protection.

❝Any move against the Vietnamese would be considered a move against the US government, and we would fight.**❞**
GREEN BERET CAPTAIN VERNON GILLESPIE JR., FROM *WAR STORIES OF THE GREEN BERETS* BY HANS HALBERSTADT, ZENITH PRESS, 1994

Bringing them in
Gillespie questions two Viet Cong (in black) captured at Buon Brieng. He convinced the younger boy—a Montagnard in a Vietnamese copy of a US Army cap—to defect and betray the location of the guerrillas' jungle camp.

«

BEFORE

Collectively called the
Montagnards (Mountain People)
by the French, the hilltribes of
Vietnam yearned for a homeland
of their own.

HISTORICAL ENMITY

Vietnamese distrust of the Montagnards
predated French colonialism. The
Montagnards, who were labeled *moi*
(savages) by the Vietnamese, sided with
France in the **First Indochina War**
« 26–27 in the hope of being rewarded
with an autonomous homeland. However,
the **Geneva Accords « 34–35** made no
provisions for them, and they continued to
face discrimination during the Diem regime.

Mountain People

**Both the US and North Vietnam tried to enlist the support of the Montagnards, the
indigenous people of South Vietnam's rugged highlands. The Green Berets spent the early
part of the war wooing, training, and arming the tribesmen, whom they nicknamed Yards.**

I t was the CIA, not the Diem
government, that came up
with the idea of enlisting the
Montagnards as allies in the fight
against the Viet Cong. In late 1961,
Colonel Gilbert B. Layton, a

Marine officer on loan to the CIA
in Saigon, and David Nuttle, an
International Voluntary Services
official working with the Rhade
tribe in the Central Highlands,
jointly conceived what they called
the Civilian Irregular Defense
Group (CIDG) program as a means

of blocking Viet Cong infiltration.
William E. Colby, the CIA station
chief in Saigon, backed the scheme.

Pilot project

They chose Buon Enao, just to the
northeast of Buon Ma Thuot, in
the heart of Rhade country, to test

Trigger

Bamboo
bowstring

Montagnard crossbow
Usually used for hunting, crossbows were also employed as weapons during the war. They were carved from tropical timber and fired bamboo arrows.

the plan, and in November 1961, Nuttle, a CIA officer, and a Special Forces medical specialist visited the village to confer with the local elders. After more than two weeks of negotiations, the elders agreed to collaborate with the Americans, and in February 1962, a Green Beret team arrived in Buon Enao to train the village defenders. They planned to extend their operations to neighboring villages once a secure base had been established.

By the summer, five Green Beret A-Detachments were operating in the Rhade tribal area. Camps were established to serve as bases for the so-called trail watchers—specially formed and trained groups of Montagnards

Cong shot down Captain Terry D. Cordell's aircraft in full view of the CIDG strike force he was advising in Buon Enao, the Rhade were so enraged by his loss that they turned on the Viet Cong and drove them off in disorder.

With help from the US Navy's Seabees, the Green Berets constructed dams, roads, bridges, and schools for the Montagnards. They also dug wells and provided basic healthcare. The results confirmed the success of the cooperation. By December 1963, some 19,000 Montagnards had enrolled in part-time village militias, while 6,000 more were serving in CIDG strike forces, which stood ready to be airlifted to trouble spots.

Organized rebellion
Not all Montagnards supported the US against the communists. The relationship was complicated by the Montagnards' hatred of the

The war devastated the lives and villages of the Montagnards, forcing many into exile.

SIEGE OF KHE SANH
Around a quarter of the prewar population of one million Montagnards died during the war. Many were killed in action, including around half of the 900 Montagnards who assisted in the defense of the Special Forces camp of Lang Vei during the **Siege of Khe Sanh 200–03 》**.

POSTWAR
After the war, Montagnards fled Vietnam for Thailand or Cambodia but **pockets of resistance** survived in the Highlands until the 1980s.

ever-more repressive policies against the Montagnards, rebellion ensued, spearheaded by an ethnonationalist movement—the United Front for the Liberation of Oppressed Races (FULRO).

In September 1964, some 3,000 Montagnards in five Special Forces camps in the Central Highlands killed 80 South Vietnamese troops and took 20 Americans hostage. Eventually, Special Forces officers persuaded the rebels to lay down their arms. The FULRO militants and their main supporters fled over the border to Cambodia.

" [They] are the **bravest,** most **loyal and fiercest** fighters."

FIFTH SPECIAL FORCES STAFF SERGEANT GEORGE CLARK, *THE YEAR IN SPECIAL OPERATIONS*, 2009

tasked with reconnaissance on South Vietnam's jungle frontier, including along the Ho Chi Minh Trail. Khe Sanh, in the Bru tribal area, became operational in July 1962, and Dak To and Dak Pek, both in the Sedang tribal area, were set up in August.

Special qualities
The Green Berets established good relationships with their new allies. The collaboration became a bright spot in what was often a confusing and frustrating war. "The Yards," one Green Beret was reported as saying, "are easy to get along with."

The Montagnards were quick to demonstrate their bravery. In June 1962, for example, village defenders in the Sedang tribal area repelled a Viet Cong attack armed only with knives and bows and arrows. That October, when Viet

South Vietnamese regime. The Special Forces therefore spent a large proportion of their time in the early days winning the Montagnards' trust and dissuading them from defecting to the Viet Cong. When the military junta that replaced Diem in 1963 pursued

Green Beret advisers
Members of the Green Berets show Montagnard tribesmen how to operate a 57 mm recoilless rifle so that they can defend their village against Viet Cong attack.

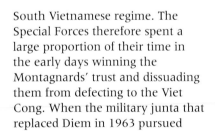

Friendly visit
A Green Beret laughs with Montagnards in the Central Highlands. Special Forces visited villages to forge relationships—drinking rice wine and learning about the tribes' music, traditions, and weapons.

Hilltop fortress
This aerial view of a strategic hamlet shows four lines of defense. These usually consisted of trenches strewn with traps and mines and mounted by barbed wire. Some hamlets also had a watchtower.

« BEFORE

The Viet Cong's influence in rural areas had long been a problem for the Diem regime.

THE AGROVILLES
As early as 1959, Diem began moving South Vietnam's rural population from their ancestral homes to **fortified villages**, called agrovilles, to isolate them from the influence of communists and protect them from attack. The villagers resented the move, especially since the regime forced them to buy the land. No more than **20 agrovilles were ever completed** and the South Vietnamese government had abandoned the scheme by 1961.

Strategic Hamlets

After two years of growing insurrection in the South Vietnamese countryside, pressure mounted on Diem to devise an effective counterinsurgency strategy. His answer was the Strategic Hamlets Program.

The idea of moving villagers to specially fortified hamlets to protect them from the Viet Cong was promoted by Sir Robert Thompson, the leader of a British advisory mission to Vietnam. The British had contained a rebellion in their colony, Malaya, by employing a similar scheme. In Vietnam, it was envisaged that ARVN troops would provide protection for the hamlets until locally trained self-defense militias could take over. At the same time, economic and social reforms would also help to win the villagers' trust.

Thompson had misread the Vietnamese situation. In Malaya, the majority of insurgents were of Chinese origin, not Malayan. The Vietnamese were being asked to take up arms against their fellow countrymen. Furthermore, in Malaya, the British had fortified existing villages, not constructed new ones. The Vietnamese version of the plan entailed a large-scale displacement of villagers that only added to the prevailing discontent with Diem's government.

Rural idyll

It was not only South Vietnam that tried to win over the rural population. This North Vietnamese scroll, entitled *Nong* (Peasants), from 1960, depicts an idealized scene of farming under communism.

NONG

First settlements

Operation Sunrise, the program's pilot project, launched in Binh Duong province, north of Saigon, in March 1962. The plan, administered by Diem's brother, Ngo Dinh Nhu, was to construct five fortified settlements in the Ben Cat district, an area with a strong Viet Cong presence. The project was doomed from the beginning. One of the settlements was so far from the nearest market that only 70 of the 200 families earmarked to move there went. In addition, people were unwilling to take up arms to defend their new homes.

Myths and realities

In September 1962, the regime announced that 4,322,034 people—33.39 percent of South Vietnam's population—were living in fortified settlements. By the end of the year, more than 6,000 such settlements were said to be in operation, with hundreds more under construction.

Some Americans high up in the Kennedy administration swallowed what Diem and Nhu were telling them. Roger Hilsman, the State Department's intelligence director, initially described the scheme as an effective strategic concept. Defense Secretary Robert McNamara believed the program showed that Diem was at last making progress in countering subversion.

The reality was very different. Many villagers bitterly resented being forced to labor unpaid, digging defensive moats, implanting bamboo stakes, and erecting fences to protect themselves against people who were not threatening them directly. The ones who agreed to join local self-defense groups became embittered when the modern weapons promised by the government failed to arrive in any quantity. Even Hilsman grew disillusioned when he visited South Vietnam on a fact-finding mission in 1963.

Corruption was endemic among the officials appointed to administer the program. Instead of distributing the money that had been earmarked to buy seed and fertilizer, and pay for irrigation schemes, schools, and medical care among the communities, they frequently embezzled it.

Viet Cong response

For their part, though initially alarmed by the program, the Viet Cong soon became fully aware of its shortcomings. Their response was to launch a systematic campaign that targeted the most important hamlets. Specially trained Viet Cong units were organized to destroy them, either by direct attack or infiltration.

At Hoa Phu, in the Long An province in the Mekong Delta, an area particularly resistant to the program, villagers urged on by Viet Cong guerrillas who had infiltrated the settlement, tore down its defenses and returned to their native villages. In total, 200 of the strategic hamlets in the province were similarly destroyed or simply abandoned.

Photo opportunity

Madame Ngo Dinh Nhu, South Vietnam's "First Lady," inspects the defenses of a hamlet with her husband Ngo Dinh Nhu (second left), who administered the program. He promoted it as a "movement of solidarity and self-sufficiency."

"A few old men .... [had] swords, a flintlock, and half a dozen American **carbines."**

US STATE DEPARTMENT DIRECTOR OF INTELLIGENCE ROGER HILSMAN, 1963

By the beginning of 1964, the Strategic Hamlets Program was in chaos.

FALL AND RISE
Following **Diem's assassination 76–77 ≫**, the program was abandoned. In 1967, pacification policies were revived by Civil Operations and Revolutionary Development Support **(CORDS) 212–13 ≫**.

SPY REVELATIONS
After the Vietnam War ended, it was revealed that Nhu's chief lieutenant, Colonel Pham Ngoc Thao, was a communist agent. He had **sabotaged the Strategic Hamlets Program** by deliberately implementing it so quickly that it drove the alienated villagers into the camp of the Viet Cong.

The **Buddhist Crisis**

Relations between Diem, a devout Catholic, and South Vietnam's Buddhists had always been strained. When government troops opened fire on a crowd of Buddhist protesters in Hue on May 8, 1963, the incident precipitated a nationwide crisis.

Addressing the crowd
A Buddhist leader speaks from atop a car on June 16, 1963. Buddhists protested in different ways: some made speeches, others mutilated themselves or committed suicide.

<< **BEFORE**

Diem's pro-Catholic policies only continued the discrimination that South Vietnam's 10.5 million Buddhists had endured under French colonial rule.

HISTORY OF RESILIENCE
Buddhism had been practiced in Vietnam since at least the second century, occasionally falling out of favor with royal rulers and their courts. During their **rule of Indochina** << 16–17, the French encouraged the spread of Christianity. Seeing Buddhism as a threat, they passed laws to prevent its spread and growth. Diem, a Catholic, **refused to repeal** these French laws.

FIFTEENTH-CENTURY BUDDHA STATUE

Diem clearly favored fellow Catholics: he appointed them to key civil service and military jobs and gave them free choice of the land distributed by the government. This favoritism, however, caused deepening resentment among the nation's Buddhists, who made up more than 70 percent of the population. Buddhist hostility to the regime remained latent until an incident in Hue propelled them into open opposition to the Diem regime.

Buddhist protest
Hue was the spiritual center of South Vietnamese Buddhism. On May 8, 1963, thousands assembled there to celebrate the Buddha's 2,587th birthday. The local administration, however, forbade the flying of the Buddhist flag to commemorate the occasion. Many Buddhists gathered outside the radio station in protest, to listen to a speech by Buddhist leader Thich (venerable) Tri Quang.

Claiming that the speech had not been authorized by the censors, the station director refused to allow Quang to broadcast. He also summoned Major Dang Xi, a Catholic and the deputy province chief, to the scene. Xi ordered the crowd to disperse and, when the Buddhists failed to do so, told his men to open fire. As the crowd stampeded, 14 people, two of whom were children, were shot or trampled to death. The Buddhists were outraged. They demanded that Diem lift the ban on religious flags, compensate the families of the victims, and punish the officials responsible for the killings. Diem claimed instead that the deaths had been caused by a Viet Cong agent throwing a hand grenade into the crowd, and rejected the Buddhists' demands even as demonstrations in Hue against the regime became an almost daily occurrence. Diem imposed martial law on Hue and instituted a dusk-to-dawn curfew.

When news of the initial incident at Hue reached Washington, Dean Rusk, the secretary of state, was quick to respond. In a telegram to the US embassy in Saigon, he told

Ambassador Nolting to urge Diem "to take no repressive measures against Buddhists" and to "make ... gestures towards restoration of order and amity." Nolting did his best, but to little avail. Diem grudgingly assured him that the repression would cease, but it soon became clear that he had no intention of keeping his word. He and his brother, Nhu, stalled for time, hoping to ride out the crisis.

Pagoda raids

The unrest continued. It spread to Saigon, where, on May 30, 500 Buddhist monks staged a sit-down street demonstration against the regime. Four days later another

protest was forcibly dispersed by Diem's security police. Then, on June 11, Thich Quang Duc, a 73-year-old monk, publicly burned himself to death at a major city intersection. Over the coming weeks, six other monks and nuns

followed his example. The protests gathered momentum, with high school and university students taking a leading role.

On August 21, Nhu acted. Shortly after midnight, truckloads of his personal security police, disguised as

soldiers, surrounded the Xa Loi Pagoda, Saigon's principal Buddhist shrine. They ransacked the building and arrested some 400 monks and nuns. In Hue, monks barricaded themselves inside the Dieude Temple for eight hours before surrendering. More than 1,400 were arrested across the country.

Dire consequences

The events of August 21 were the last straw. Henry Cabot Lodge, who arrived in Saigon to take over from Nolting, was convinced that Diem had to go. The Buddhists were more than prepared for that eventuality. Tri Quang had already secretly met with US Embassy officials and encouraged the US to take action, noting that they were partly responsible for the situation in South Vietnam. US leaders, however, blamed Diem and Nhu.

" The US must either make Diem reform or **get rid of him.**"

BUDDHIST MONK TRI QUANG, 1963

Mass protest

Protesters try to tear down a barbed wire barricade with their bare hands as they are confronted by the police at Giac Minh pagoda on July 17, 1963. Hundreds of monks, nuns, and laypeople were kicked, punched, and clubbed by police in the Cholon district of Saigon.

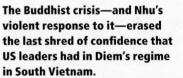

AFTER ⟫

The Buddhist crisis—and Nhu's violent response to it—erased the last shred of confidence that US leaders had in Diem's regime in South Vietnam.

SANCTIONED REMOVAL

South Vietnamese generals began plotting the **overthrow of Diem** and his brother **76–77 ⟫**. President Kennedy and US Ambassador Lodge concurred. Kennedy authorized Lodge to let the generals know that, while the US would not assist them in mounting a coup, it would support them afterward.

Despite the generals' hopes, Diem's removal **did not bring order** to South Vietnam. The generals' military junta was weak, and more **coups would follow 78–79 ⟫**. The Viet Cong continued to make inroads in South Vietnam, eager to take advantage of this political instability.

Buddhist martyr
Thich Quang Duc sits silent and still as he is engulfed by flames. The monk set himself on fire in protest in June 1963, leading other Buddhists to follow suit. Provoking worldwide horror, his action was a catalyst in the fall of Diem's regime.

Diem Assassinated

As 1963 dawned, the situation in South Vietnam was rapidly worsening, and it was not helped by the ARVN's performance near Ap Bac. As popular discontent with Diem and his despotic regime mounted, his generals began plotting his overthrow.

A s 1962 drew to a close, the opinion in both Saigon and Washington was that US military aid to South Vietnam was starting to tip the scales against the Viet Cong. What the US military advisers wanted was a chance to demonstrate how the ARVN, with US weaponry, could defeat the guerrillas. On January 1, 1963, they got their chance.

16 The number of factions plotting to kill Diem during the lead-up to his assassination.

Fiasco at Ap Bac

During the previous week, South Vietnamese intelligence had reported that three companies of Viet Cong—plus local auxiliaries— were concentrating near Ap Bac, a village in the Mekong Delta. Lieutenant Colonel John Paul Vann, the top US adviser with the

« **BEFORE**

Diem was on shaky ground, but had survived two previous attempts to overthrow him.

HOLDING ON BY A THREAD
Diem's **Strategic Hamlets Program** « **70–71**, intended to win him support, alienated the rural population. Meanwhile, the **Buddhist crisis** « **72–73** had led to protests on the streets and the public martyrdom of a Buddhist monk.

In November 1960, Lieutenant Colonel Vuong Van Dong led an **attempted military coup** but failed to overthrow the president. In February 1962, a second attempt was made: Diem and his family just managed to escape death when two renegade air force fighter pilots bombed and strafed the presidential palace.

ARVN Seventh Division, urged its commander Colonel Biu Dinh Dam to attack. The idea was to launch a three-pronged pincer attack.

One infantry regiment, landed by helicopters, would move in from the north. Two battalions of troops would advance from the south, and a rifle squadron on board armored personnel carriers would approach from the west. The ARVN had plenty of artillery and air support.

On the face of it, the Viet Cong looked doomed. The reality was different. In the first place, despite Vann's urgings, Dam delayed the attack for a crucial 24 hours. This gave the Viet Cong time to dig in behind prepared defenses. They patiently waited until the first three waves of helicopters had dropped troops, then, as the fourth wave came in to land, opened fire. The result was carnage. By noon, five US helicopters had been forced down and their crews were in

danger. It took Vann three hours to persuade the South Vietnamese to make a rescue attempt. When he did, the vehicles advanced so slowly that they became sitting ducks.

Elsewhere, things were also going badly. The two battalions supposed to advance from the south refused to move forward. Finally, the South Vietnamese deployed the paratroopers Vann had proposed to block a Viet Cong retreat—but deployed them to the west, not in the east as Vann had requested. In the deepening twilight, they were mistaken for Viet Cong by their own side. In the confusion, the Viet Cong simply slipped away.

Crisis point

Diem's other problems were mounting. The Strategic Hamlets Program was proving a failure and the Buddhists called for political reform. Diem's American allies were increasingly concerned.

Diem's generals were also disaffected. On August 23, just two days after Nhu's security police had raided Buddhist temples in Saigon and Hue, ARVN Chief of Staff Tran Van Don told Lucien Conein, a veteran CIA officer operating

The Assassination of JFK

When news of Diem's assassination reached President Kennedy, he was profoundly shocked. Three weeks later, on November 22, Kennedy himself was shot in Dallas, Texas, when Lee Harvey Oswald opened fire on the presidential limousine.

Unsafe haven
Evading their pursuers, Diem and Nhu sought refuge at St. Francis Xavier Church in Cholon's Chinese district on November 1. They received holy communion before their capture and murder.

under cover, that a coup d'etat was being planned. The generals would not act without US approval.

Opinion in the White House was divided, but on August 26, Kennedy acted. The new US ambassador in Saigon, Henry Cabot Lodge, was authorized to inform the generals that, while the US would not actively help them to mount their coup, it would support a new government, once formed.

The generals pounce

This was not the unequivocal pledge the South Vietnamese had been seeking from the US, but on November 1, the generals took action. Airborne and army troops backed up by some 40 tanks surrounded the presidential palace. While 150 presidential guards prepared to defend the palace, Diem called first Don and then Lodge. Neither gave him any comfort. Rejecting the generals' demands for his surrender, Diem escaped with his brother, Nhu, but they were soon captured. Despite promises of safe passage, they were brutally killed in the back of an armored car on November 2.

Diem and Nhu were buried in unmarked graves in Saigon's main Catholic cemetery.

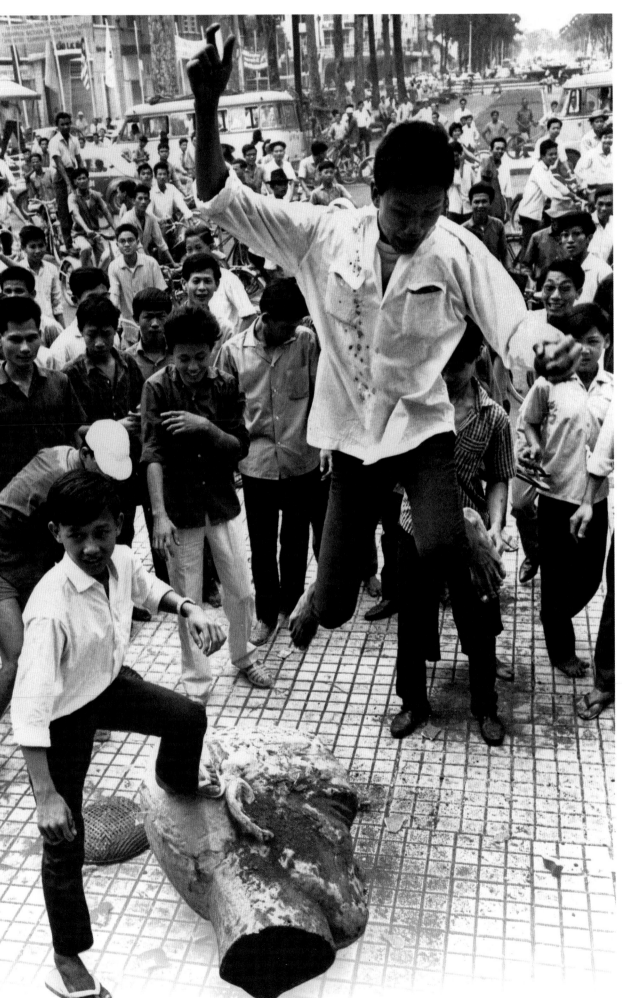

Celebrating the fall
Two South Vietnamese boys jump on the dismembered head of a statue in Saigon on November 5, 1963. Symbolic of Diem's fallen regime, the head bore the face of Diem's powerful and much-hated sister-in-law, Madame Nhu.

> "If … [he] remains **obdurate,** we must **face the possibility** that **Diem** himself cannot be **preserved.**"
>
> ASSISTANT SECRETARY OF STATE ROGER HILSMAN IN THE "HILSMAN CABLE," AUGUST 24, 1963

AFTER

Diem's assassination left South Vietnam's future more uncertain. In many ways, his removal only made the situation worse.

REVOLVING DOOR
Between 1963 and 1965, there were 12 different governments in the South as coup followed coup. The Viet Cong was quick to take advantage of this **and mounted a series of attacks 78–79 »**. In June 1965, ARVN General Nguyen Van Thieu became **president of South Vietnam** and remained so for the next 10 years.

DETERMINED LEADER
Lyndon B. Johnson took over as President of the United States. One of his first acts was to **reaffirm US commitment 90–91 »** to South Vietnam. He told a group of his closest advisers that he was not going to lose Vietnam and would not be the president who saw Southeast Asia go the same way as China.

South Vietnam on the Brink

President Johnson was anxious to avoid committing US ground troops to Vietnam, but while he prevaricated, Hanoi acted. In November 1964, North Vietnamese regulars began infiltrating South Vietnam along the Ho Chi Minh Trail to support the Viet Cong.

≪ BEFORE

The assassinations of South Vietnam's President Diem and President Kennedy three weeks later changed the situation in Vietnam and the US response to it.

MILITARY JUNTA
The increasingly repressive regime of President Diem, culminating in the **Buddhist crisis ≪ 72–73** through the summer and fall of 1963, led Kennedy and his advisers to back **a coup d'etat in South Vietnam ≪ 76–77**, during which **Diem was assassinated**. He was replaced by a **military junta**.

NEW PRESIDENT
Lyndon Johnson, who became president following **Kennedy's assassination ≪ 76–77** in November 1963, was a hardliner. He and his advisers expected that Diem's removal would dramatically improve the situation in South Vietnam, but this proved to be misguided.

US VICE PRESIDENT LYNDON B. JOHNSON IS SWORN IN AS PRESIDENT

While President Johnson was busy reaffirming US commitments to South Vietnam, the news from the country kept getting worse. In the view of US Secretary of Defense Robert McNamara, the 12 army officers who formed the Military Revolutionary Council governing the country were so preoccupied with political affairs that they were failing to give their troops or government officials outside Saigon any direction. Nor were they supported by the various other factions who had opposed Diem.

The key question for President Johnson was not whether, but how, to prop up South Vietnam. Although opinion polls showed him to have a huge lead over Senator Barry Goldwater, his chief Republican challenger in the 1964 election, Johnson worried about his prospects. At a White House reception on Christmas Eve 1963, he told the Joint Chiefs of Staff: "Just let me get elected and then you can have your war."

Verge of anarchy
In South Vietnam, the situation continued to deteriorate. On January 30, 1964, another coup, led by General Nguyen Khanh, overthrew the divided junta. Johnson believed Khanh's promise to step up the South Vietnamese war effort, but, as McNamara noted after a March 1964 visit, ARVN losses and

Jungle attack
South Vietnamese forces and American soldiers come under attack by Viet Cong guerrillas while unloading supplies sent by the United States in 1964. At this point in the war, American casualties numbered a few hundred.

desertions were high and increasing while the Viet Cong was recruiting energetically.

Viet Cong activity intensified. On February 3, fighters mounted an attack on the US advisory compound in Kontum as part of a major offensive against the South Vietnamese in the Tay Ninh province and the Mekong Delta. Three days later, they exploded a bomb in Saigon's crowded Capital Kinh Do Theater, killing three Americans and wounding 50 more.

In early April, the Viet Cong captured Kien Long, a district capital in the Mekong Delta. Three hundred ARVN troops were killed. The following month, North Vietnamese commandos from the

65th Special Operations Group sank the aircraft carrier USNS *Card* in Saigon harbor. Although salvage crews managed to raise the stricken ship 17 days later, the attack was a major blow to US prestige. So, too, was a Viet Cong assault on the US Special Forces camp at Nam Dong in the Northern Highlands on July 4. The Viet Cong overran the camp's defenses, killing 50 South Vietnamese and two US military advisers before withdrawing.

Decisive action
Johnson had to respond. The president agreed to a massive expansion of counterinsurgency operations, a substantial increase in the size of the ARVN, and to

> " [The] **atmosphere** fairly **smelled of discontent,** with workers **on strike,** students demonstrating."
>
> GENERAL WILLIAM WESTMORELAND, MARCH 1964

dispatch more US aircraft and other military equipment. Yet he still shrunk from sending US combat troops into action. Nor would he authorize the bombing of North Vietnam as advocated by Air Force General Curtis LeMay. Khanh pressurized Johnson into taking further action. "The United States must take a firm course," he told a Saigon press conference in August 1964, "so that North Vietnam knows it is not a "paper tiger."

Christmas in Saigon
At approximately 6 p.m. on Christmas Eve 1964, an explosion in the parking area of the Brinks Hotel on Hai Ba Trung Street in Saigon tore a hole through two floors of the building, killing one man and injuring more than 70 others.

Strategy in the North
While Johnson and his advisers debated what to do, the North Vietnamese leadership was also making major policy decisions. They concluded that Johnson had no intention of abandoning the US commitment to South Vietnam or of negotiating a settlement that

40 PERCENT of the South Vietnamese population was estimated to be under the control or predominant influence of the Viet Cong in March 1964.

would be acceptable to them. Accordingly, they decided to escalate the war by building up the insurgent forces in South Vietnam until they were strong enough to annihilate ARVN regulars. In November 1964, North Vietnamese troops started infiltrating South Vietnam via the Ho Chi Minh Trail.

AFTER

Johnson's reluctance to escalate the war evaporated after direct attacks on US interests.

TONKIN RESOLUTION
In the summer of 1964, the Viet Cong launched attacks on two US destroyers in the Gulf of Tonkin. Within days of the second attack, the US House of Representatives passed the **Tonkin Resolution 80–81 »**, authorizing use of armed force in Vietnam.

BOMBING NORTH VIETNAM
After an attack on Pleiku, a US air base, in February 1965, Johnson authorized **retaliatory airstrikes 94–95 »**.

The Tonkin Gulf Incident

In August 1964, the war escalated dramatically when North Vietnamese PT boats attacked two US destroyers in the Gulf of Tonkin. The first attack went unpunished, but claims of a second attack sparked the first US bombing of North Vietnam.

« BEFORE

Tensions in the Gulf of Tonkin mounted after the US authorized covert naval operations against North Vietnam.

GULF MISSIONS

In 1961, a reconnaissance and sabotage operation codenamed OPLAN 34-A was implemented by South Vietnamese commandos in high-speed patrol boats based at Da Nang. They were trained by **US Navy Seals** under CIA direction.

Meanwhile, the **DeSoto patrols**—secret missions carried out by US destroyers—began in 1962. They gathered intelligence on new Soviet radar and antiaircraft missile systems in the Tonkin Gulf.

The Joint Chiefs of Staff ordered Admiral Ulysses Grant Sharp Jr., US naval commander in the Pacific, to reactivate the DeSoto patrols in the Gulf of Tonkin in July 1964.

The USS *Maddox*, commanded by Captain John J. Herrick, was the first destroyer to be assigned to the task. One of its major objectives was to learn more about North Vietnam's coastal defenses. By August 1, Herrick's vessel was cruising in zigzags about 8 miles

The president speaks out

The *New York Times* on August 5, 1964, printed Johnson's TV and radio address to the nation from the previous day. Johnson promised that repeated attacks on US armed forces would lead to retaliation, but sought to reassure the nation that he was not calling for a wider war.

(13 km) from the North Vietnamese mainland and 4 miles (6 km) from Hon Me, one of the larger islands off the coast.

The first attack

The *Maddox* was not the only vessel active in the Gulf. Two days before its arrival, four South Vietnamese patrol boats sailed from Da Nang on a covert mission to raid the

Soviet radar installations on two of the islands in the Gulf. Two of them shelled Hon Me on July 30 before withdrawing, while the others bombarded Hon Ngu. Herrick spotted the boats in the distance as they retired. He also picked up North Vietnamese radio traffic indicating that their naval forces were being put on high alert.

By mid-morning on August 2, the *Maddox* was nearing the mouth of the Red River Delta when Herrick observed three North Vietnamese patrol torpedo (PT) boats headed straight for the destroyer. Once they got to within 10,000 yards, Herrick ordered his gun crews to open fire. He also radioed the aircraft carrier USS *Ticonderoga* for

assistance. Four jet fighters arrived overhead just as the PT boats launched their torpedoes. They all missed. Herrick's gunners badly damaged one of the PT boats, while the jets sank the second and damaged the third. The entire skirmish lasted exactly 37 minutes.

Johnson reacted immediately. The *Maddox* and the USS *Turner Joy*, another destroyer, were ordered to resume patrolling the Gulf and to attack any force that attacked them. The following evening, *Maddox* intercepted North Vietnamese radio messages, which gave Herrick the impression that another attack was imminent. He called for air support, but in the darkness neither the pilots nor the ships' crews could spot any enemy craft. Then *Maddox*'s sonar operators reported approaching torpedoes. Both destroyers opened fire in the direction of the sonar contacts, but were firing blind.

Swift retaliation

Johnson lost no time in declaring that the two destroyers had been subjected to unprovoked attacks. He sanctioned retaliatory air strikes on four North Vietnamese patrol boat bases and a major oil storage depot. Operation Pierce Arrow, as it was codenamed, sunk eight North Vietnamese PT boats and

severely damaged 21 more. Two US aircraft were shot down; the pilot of one of them, Lieutenant Everett Alvarez Jr., became the first US airman taken as a prisoner of war by North Vietnam.

Tonkin Gulf Resolution

On August 5, a special session of the Senate debated the Tonkin Gulf Resolution, giving Johnson the authority to "take all necessary measures, including the use of armed force" against any aggressor. It took less than two hours to pass the resolution, with only two senators, Ernest Gruening (D-Alaska) and Wayne Morse (D-Oregon), voting against. The House of Representatives passed it unanimously.

The allegation that the North Vietnamese had attacked the destroyers a second time was less convincing upon closer examination. Herrick, for one, was unsure whether any such attack had taken place. He later said that neither destroyer had made any "actual visual sightings" of PT boats. Commander James Stockdale, who led the jets from the *Ticonderoga*, was certain that no North Vietnamese vessels had been present. Such doubts were discounted by Johnson and his advisers, even though the

president privately seemed to share them, postulating that the sailors had seen not torpedoes, but flying fish. His doubts mattered little. The resolution gave him what he wanted—a free hand to take whatever actions he deemed necessary in Vietnam.

Johnson would use the authority of the Tonkin Gulf Resolution to increase US involvement in Vietnam.

BOMBS AT THE READY

Contingency planning for a bombing campaign in North Vietnam was already underway, but it took another **Viet Cong attack** to precipitate further US reprisal. A raid on the airfield at Pleiku—and the nearby helicopter base at Camp Holloway—on February 7, 1965, triggered the massive bombing campaign codenamed **Operation Rolling Thunder 94–95 »**.

Signing the resolution

President Johnson signs the Tonkin Gulf Resolution—the "Joint resolution to promote the maintenance of international peace and security in Southeast Asia"—on August 10, 1964, in the White House East Room.

> "Our **destroyers** were just shooting at **phantom targets** —there were **no PT boats.**"

SQUADRON COMMANDER JAMES STOCKDALE, IN THE *CHICAGO TRIBUNE*, 1990

US PRESIDENT Born 1908 Died 1973

Lyndon B. Johnson

> "I will do **my best;** that is **all I can do.** I ask for your help and God's."
>
> LYNDON B. JOHNSON, STATEMENT AFTER THE ASSASSINATION OF PRESIDENT JOHN F. KENNEDY, NOVEMBER 22, 1963

Lyndon Baines Johnson rose to the presidency in the wake of President Kennedy's death in 1963, and was confirmed in power by a landslide election victory the following year. In office, Johnson initiated an idealistic program of domestic reforms designed to tackle poverty and racial injustice. However, mounting involvement in Vietnam and violence on the streets of American cities undermined support for his presidency—ranked, by the end, as one of the most unpopular in US history.

Political powerhouse

Johnson was a product of the Texas Hill Country. His father, a farmer and businessman, had sat in the Texas state legislature. Johnson embarked on a career in politics, rising through a combination of hard work and a talent for ruthless political maneuvering. Aged 28, he entered Congress as a New Deal Democrat and 10 years later was elected a Senator, albeit amid accusations of vote rigging. The Senate provided an ideal arena for his talents as a political fixer; he was an outstandingly successful leader of the Democratic majority from 1955, driving controversial legislation through Congress.

Texan president

A boisterous career politician committed to improving the lives of disadvantaged Americans, Johnson had his reputation destroyed by the Vietnam War, which he could neither win nor bring to an honorably peaceful conclusion.

Johnson on civil rights

President Johnson meets civil rights leaders at the White House on August 6, 1965, the day the Voting Rights Act, prohibiting racial discrimination in voting, was signed into law.

His ability to induce politicians to change their votes—by a mixture of brow-beating, arm-twisting, and favors—became legendary. Johnson aspired to be the Democratic presidential candidate in 1960, but his hopes were flattened by the tidal wave of support for John F. Kennedy. Although the sophisticates of the Kennedy camp were inclined to disparage Johnson, with his blunt Texan manner and his reputation for unscrupulous wheeler-dealing, he was nonetheless invited to run as vice-president to secure the Southern vote. Once in office, however, the Kennedy inner circle was reluctant to allow Johnson any significant role. Instead, he carved out areas in which his drive could express itself, notably civil rights and the fledgling space program.

Taking the reins

Johnson was two cars behind Kennedy in Dallas when the president was shot. Sworn in aboard Air Force One that afternoon, he assumed the reins of power with confidence and dignity. Johnson's swift

appointment of the Warren Commission—a week after the event—to investigate Kennedy's assassination was a strong political maneuver, designed to hold the lid firmly down on a dangerous issue.

In domestic affairs, Johnson committed himself even more firmly than Kennedy to the cause of civil rights. Johnson's utopian vision of the "Great Society"—upon which

his 1964 election campaign was based—ushered in antipoverty and antidiscrimination programs, designed to defend America's least privileged citizens.

Vietnamese nightmare

Foreign affairs were not Johnson's forte. He had none of Kennedy's background in diplomacy or broad international outlook. Faced with the worsening crisis in Vietnam, Johnson was heavily dependent on advisers inherited from Kennedy's administration. More pugnacious than his predecessor, Johnson treated the North Vietnamese politburo like recalcitrant congressmen, who might be bullied or bribed into doing what he wished. Far from wanting a war in Vietnam, he loathed it as a distraction from his real concerns and a nightmare from which he could not escape.

By the end of his presidency, Johnson was a tragic figure. His vision of the Great Society had proved a mirage as black rioters took to the streets and the cost of

" I do not find it easy to send the **flower of our youth,** our finest young men, **into battle.** "

LYNDON B. JOHNSON, NEWS CONFERENCE, JULY 28, 1965

war undermined federal finances. His decision not to seek the Democratic nomination for a second term in 1968 was based on the knowledge that he could not have secured it. Johnson lived only four years after leaving office— he died one day before the signing of the peace deal that ended America's Vietnam War.

Antiwar protests

Protesters prepare an unfriendly welcome for President Johnson on a visit to Sydney, Australia, in October 1966. Johnson was plagued by similarly hostile demonstrations wherever he traveled, whether in the United States or abroad.

JOHNSON'S CAMPAIGN FOR PRESIDENCY

83

3

AMERICA GOES TO WAR

January 1965–September 1967

By 1965, Viet Cong guerrillas are making inroads in South Vietnam. America responds by expanding its role in the war, sending the first US ground troops there in March. Direct conflict between America and North Vietnam soon follows.

« Into the fray
Enemy fire greets American soldiers of the Seventh Marines as they wade ashore at Cape Batangan, Quang Ngai province, in 1965. The Seventh Marines wiped out the First Viet Cong Regiment, which had retreated to the peninsula, during Operation Piranha.

AMERICA GOES TO WAR
JANUARY 1965–SEPTEMBER 1967

F rom early 1965, American military involvement in Vietnam rapidly escalated with the launch of Operation Rolling Thunder, a bombing campaign against North Vietnam and the Ho Chi Minh Trail, and the large-scale engagement of combat troops in the South. Under General William Westmoreland, the US Army and Marines employed a combination of firepower and mobility to find and destroy insurgents, a strategy that placed a heavy

responsibility on ground troops. Yet sustained bombing failed to dent North Vietnam's will to fight and it proved frustratingly difficult to demonstrate that any decisive advantage had been gained from the strategy of attrition in the South. As American casualties increased at an alarming rate and rising troop levels required the extension of the draft, an initially small antiwar movement in the United States gathered momentum.

1 The US Navy patrolled the Mekong Delta in search of insurgents. 2 Vietnamese beach resorts provided respite from combat for American troops and their allies. 3 As General Westmoreland pursued a strategy of attrition, the number of US troops escalated.

CHINA

NORTH VIETNAM

Red River

Luang Prabang

L A

Vang Veng

Mekong River

VIENTIANE

Nan River

T H A I L A N D

Udorn ✈
Nakhon Phanom ✈

Takhli ✈

Mun River
Ubon ✈

Korat ✈

Chao Phraya River

Ping River

BANGKOK

C A M B O D I A

Tonle Sap

PHNOM PENH

Sihanoukville

Mekong River

Gulf of Thailand

Can Tho

Ca Mau Peninsula

ORT 🕱 HANOI

ORT 🕱 ● Haiphong

Red River Delta

● Thanh Hoa

ORT 🕱

ORT 🕱

● Vinh

ORT 🕱

ORT 🕱

Operation Flaming Dart 🕱

ORT 🕱 ● Vinh Moc

★ *Quang Tri*
Firebase Evans ★ ● Hue

Gulf of Tonkin

HAINAN

― *Yankee Station*

● Da Nang
● China Beach

● Chu Lai ✕
Cape Batangan (Operation Piranha)

ORT 🕱

ORT 🕱

Camp Holloway ★
ORT 🕱 ● Pleiku
Plei Me ★
Battle of Ia Drang Valley ✕★

ORT 🕱

ORT 🕱

ORT 🕱

★ *Katum*

● Tay Ninh
Ben Suc ○
Trung Lap ○● Cu Chi
Tan Son Nhut ✈
SAIGON ■

ORT 🕱
★ *Ap Bau Bang*

★ *Long Binh Post*

Nui Dat ★✕ *Battle of Long Tan*
● Vung Tau

Mekong River

Mekong Delta

C e n t r a l   H i g h l a n d s

● Qui Nhon

● Nha Trang
Cam Ranh Bay ★

― *Dixie Station*

S O U T H   V I E T N A M

South China Sea

1

2

3

KEY

— International border
▦ Demilitarized Zone (DMZ)
➤ Ho Chi Minh Trail
□ ○ Capital / City (neutral)
■ ● Capital / City (NVA / communist controlled)
■ ● Capital / City (US / ARVN controlled)
□ ○ Capital / City (contested)
★ US base
― US carrier station
✈ US air base
✕ Battle
🕱 Bombing
▨ Iron Triangle
▨ Rung Sat Special Zone

N

0 ————— 100km
0 ————— 100 miles

TIMELINE JAN 1965–SEP 1967

Allied operations ▪ **Elections in South Vietnam** ▪ Protests in the United States
▪ **Operation Rolling Thunder** ▪ First battle for US ground troops ▪ **Helicopters and aircraft** ▪ Search-and-destroy tactics ▪ **The Iron Triangle** ▪ Pacification in South Vietnam

1965

FEBRUARY 7
In response to an attack by the Viet Cong on the US base at Pleiku, air strikes are launched against targets in North Vietnam in Operation Flaming Dart.

MARCH 8
US Marines go ashore at Da Nang, the first American combat troops to enter Vietnam.

JUNE 14
General Nguyen Van Thieu is elected president of South Vietnam. His running mate, Air Marshal Nguyen Cao Ky becomes prime minister.

≫ Badge supporting US troops

FEBRUARY 26
The first South Korean troops arrive in South Vietnam.

APRIL 4
Two US F-105 Thunderchiefs are shot down by North Vietnamese MiG-17 fighters over North Vietnam.

JULY 24
North Vietnamese antiaircraft defenses make their first use of Soviet-supplied surface-to-air missiles (SAMs).

JULY 28
President Johnson announces that 50,000 more ground troops are to be sent to Vietnam—requiring an increase in the draft to 35,000 per month.

NOVEMBER 2
American Quaker Norman Morrison burns himself to death in front of the Pentagon in protest of the Vietnam War.

≪ US tunic

NOVEMBER 14–17
US Air Cavalry fight North Vietnamese troops in the Battle of Ia Drang. A battalion of the Cavalry is ambushed by the NVA at landing zone X-Ray.

MARCH 2
The sustained bombing of North Vietnam by US Air Force and Navy aircraft begins, in Operation Rolling Thunder (ORT), launched mainly from bases in Thailand.

APRIL 17
Student antiwar protesters demonstrate outside the White House.

AUGUST 18–24
US Marines launch a strike against the Viet Cong in Operation Starlite: the first major offensive operation by US ground forces in Vietnam.

1966

≫ Spooky being armed, Saigon, 1966

MAY 12–13
Students in Chicago and New York City occupy university buildings to protest against the Vietnam draft.

JUNE 1
Buddhist demonstrators, opposed to South Vietnam's military government, storm the US consulate in Hue.

JANUARY 8–14
US and Australian troops penetrate the Viet Cong's Cu Chi tunnel network in the "Iron Triangle."

JAN 28–MAR 6
US, Korean, and ARVN troops carry out a "search-and-destroy" operation in Binh Dinh province.

JUNE 29–30
American aircraft attack targets in Hanoi and Haiphong—cities previously off limits for bombing raids.

JANUARY 31
US bombing of North Vietnam in Operation Rolling Thunder resumes after a 37-day pause.

JULY 15–AUGUST 3
In Operation Hastings, US Marines repel a substantial incursion by NVA troops across the DMZ into Quang Tri province.

DECEMBER 31
At the year's end there are 184,000 American troops in Vietnam. The American death toll for the year totals 1,928.

≫ Bush hat adopted by US pilots based in Thailand

"[Now] **enemy forces are larger;** attacks, terrorism and sabotage have **increased** in scope and intensity ... **we control little,** if any, more of the population ..."

DEFENSE SECRETARY ROBERT MCNAMARA, MEMORANDUM, OCTOBER 14, 1966

1967

AUGUST 18
Australian troops fight the Viet Cong in the Battle of Long Tan, the most famous Australian engagement of the war.

❯ First MiG 21-s arrive in Vietnam, August 1966

OCTOBER 14
US Defense Secretary Robert McNamara makes a damningly pessimistic assessment of lack of progress toward winning the war.

JANUARY 6–15
US and South Vietnamese Marines carry out a major amphibious operation in the Mekong Delta.

AUG 1966–MAR 1967
US Third Marine Division repels NVA attempts to cross the DMZ into Quang Tri province during Operation Prairie.

❯ Operation Prairie, August 1966–March 1967

OCTOBER 24–25
President Johnson meets Asian leaders, including President Thieu, at the Manila Conference, where they discuss a way to end the war in Vietnam.

JANUARY 8–26
In Operation Cedar Falls, the US carries out a large-scale search-and-destroy action to clear the Viet Cong from their "Iron Triangle" stronghold north of Saigon.

⌃ Cedar Falls, January 1967

MAY 9
The US launches the Civil Operations and Revolutionary Development Support (CORDS) program to coordinate efforts to pacify the South Vietnamese. countryside.

MAY 14
Operation Junction City ends after 82 days without achieving its prime objective of locating the Viet Cong headquarters in South Vietnam (COSVN).

FEBRUARY 22
Operation Junction City, the largest US military offensive of the war, is launched.

APRIL 15
Large-scale marches take place in New York City and San Francisco, attracting hundreds of thousands of antiwar protesters.

JULY 6
The North Vietnamese politburo adopts a plan for a "General Offensive and Uprising" in South Vietnam, with attacks on border areas to be followed by attacks in cities—which will become the Tet Offensive.

SEPT 14–NOV 24
In Operation Attleboro, the US 196th Light Infantry Brigade spearheads search-and-destroy sweeps through Viet Cong base areas in Tay Ninh province, bordering Cambodia.

DECEMBER 31
At the year end there are 389,000 US troops in Vietnam. The US death toll for 1966 is 6,350.

APRIL 20–24
US aircraft target Haiphong Harbor and attack North Vietnamese airfields for the first time in a significant escalation of the air war.

APRIL 24–MAY 11
US Marines repulse North Vietnamese troops in a series of actions around the Marine combat base at Khe Sanh.

⌃ First Bell Huey Cobras arrive in Vietnam, 1967

JULY 29
An accidental fire aboard the carrier USS *Forrestal* in the Gulf of Tonkin kills 134 US crewmen.

Decision for War

In early 1965, elected president in his own right, and with authority to escalate the war as he saw fit, President Johnson committed US forces to combat in Southeast Asia in the hope of preserving an independent, noncommunist South Vietnam.

President Johnson's decision to scale up American military involvement coalesced over time. Plans for massive troop increases were laid in the early 1960s, as the United States invested heavily in military and logistical infrastructure for South Vietnam. When economic aid, diplomatic measures, and military advising failed to quell support for the insurgency, Johnson embraced a more aggressive, military approach. First, though, he needed public support to escalate a conflict he had promised the American people he would not ask their sons to fight.

A convenient pretext

On February 7, 1965, a Viet Cong attack on Camp Holloway, a US base near the city of Pleiku, in the Central Highlands, gave Johnson a valid pretext for just such an escalation. With eight Americans killed, dozens more wounded, and several helicopters destroyed, the Johnson administration used the attack to garner public support for deeper involvement. In response, on the same day President Johnson authorized Operation Flaming Dart, a campaign of reprisal airstrikes. Initially, 49 sorties were flown by US and South Vietnamese pilots. Significantly, the targets for their attack included Viet Cong strongholds near the demilitarized zone (DMZ) on the border of the two countries, and also struck North Vietnamese military installations, hinting at the air war to come.

Following Viet Cong reprisals, US fighter-bombers, launched from US aircraft carriers in the Gulf of Tonkin, undertook further strikes against North Vietnamese and Viet Cong targets. On March 2, in a massive further commitment to the conflict, the United States launched Operation Rolling Thunder. This sustained bombing campaign was intended to drive North Vietnam out of the war entirely.

Landing at Da Nang

The escalation of the air war required more American military personnel on the ground in South Vietnam for security and support. On March 8, 1965, elements of the Ninth Marine Expeditionary Brigade landed near the city of Da Nang, where they were met on the beach by city officials and a welcoming crowd. Charged with securing American bases to free up South Vietnamese soldiers for

Welcomed with flowers
American Marines of the Ninth Expeditionary Brigade land with their weapons and equipment at Da Nang on March 8, 1965. They were greeted with flowers by crowds of local people who gathered on the beach.

« **BEFORE**

When he became president, Johnson inherited a volatile situation in South Vietnam.

WINNING A MANDATE
Johnson ran for the presidency in 1964 as a peace candidate. A landslide victory provided him with a mandate to chart his own course, and the **Tonkin Gulf Resolution «80–81** provided congressional authorization to commit US forces to war against the North Vietnamese Army and Viet Cong guerrillas, who were attacking throughout the South.

VIET CONG BADGE

POLITICIAN 1916–2009

ROBERT McNAMARA

Defense secretary from 1960 until 1968 for presidents Kennedy and Johnson, Robert McNamara had previously been president of the Ford Motor Company and had served in World War II in the US Army Air Forces. As defense secretary, McNamara used statistics such as body counts to measure the success of combat operations. The reasons for his departure from office remain unclear. After leaving government, he became head of the World Bank (1968–81).

combat operations, these Marines were the first official American combat troops in South Vietnam. By the end of the year, more than 180,000 American service personnel were stationed in bases throughout South Vietnam.

Meeting of allies
From left to right, Henry Cabot Lodge, reappointed in 1965 as ambassador to South Vietnam, Defense Secretary Robert McNamara, South Vietnam's president Nguyen Van Thieu, and prime minister Nguyen Cao Ky at a meeting in Saigon, in July 1965.

"You have a phrase ... 'riding the tiger.' You rode the tiger. We shall."

LYNDON JOHNSON ON THE US COMMITMENT TO SOUTH VIETNAM, OCTOBER 1967

From defense to offense

Over the summer of 1965, the defensive mission of US forces morphed into an offensive one, as ground patrols near US bases ventured further and further afield in active search of the enemy. The shift took place without public debate or even any significant announcement, leaving the vast majority of Americans unaware that a war was coming until it was already well underway.

Johnson administration officials were divided on the issue of escalation, with most arguing that only military force could achieve political results. Others urged caution, saying that President Johnson could choose to "ride the tiger" by going to war against a determined Vietnamese foe, but he could not be certain of being able to choose the place to dismount. Ultimately, the tenacity of the North Vietnamese and Viet Cong would be a deciding factor in the war's outcome.

AFTER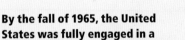

By the fall of 1965, the United States was fully engaged in a ground war in South Vietnam and an air war over North Vietnam.

POLITICAL STABILITY
The deepening involvement of US forces provided a measure of political stability in the South, as it finally **elected a president**—Nguyen Van Thieu, an ARVN general who had supported the overthrow of Diem. He would remain in office for the war's duration.

EFFECTS ON THE POPULATION
The US presence also dramatically altered life for the South Vietnamese people as the war engulfed ever-increasing areas of the country. Moreover, the war failed to stem growing **communist insurgency** or to counter North Vietnam's continuing attempts to claim South Vietnam.

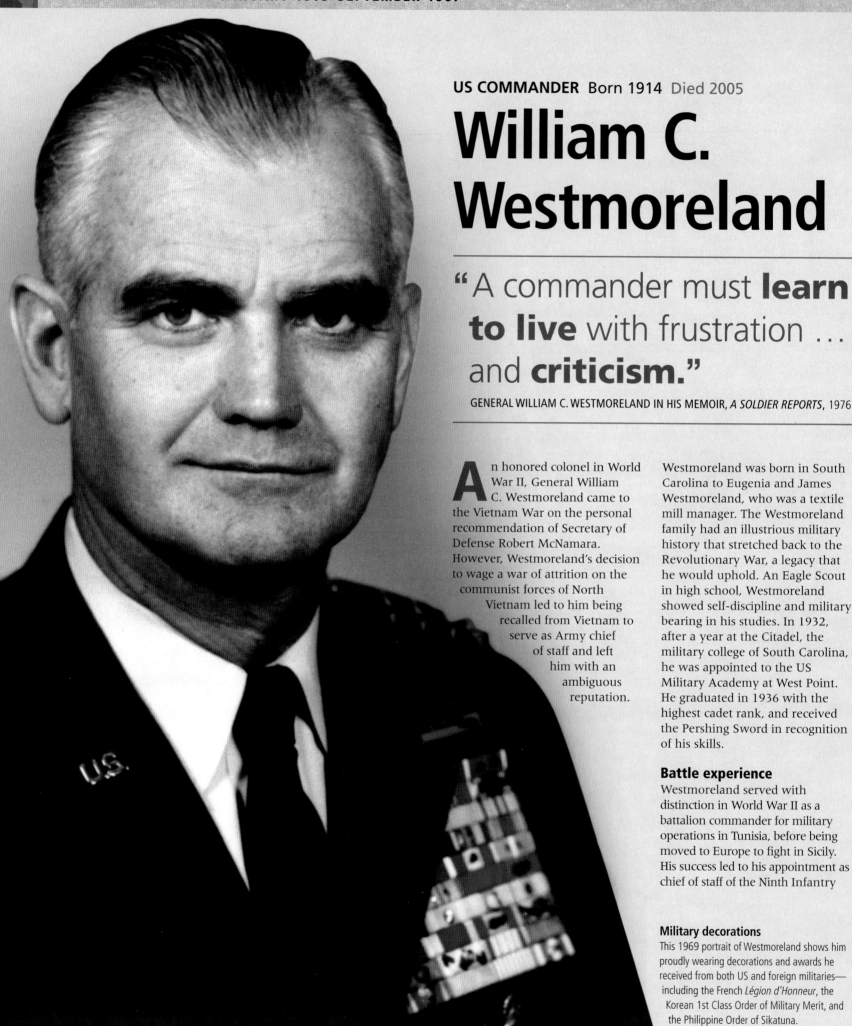

US COMMANDER Born 1914 Died 2005

William C. Westmoreland

> " A commander must **learn to live** with frustration … and **criticism.**"
>
> GENERAL WILLIAM C. WESTMORELAND IN HIS MEMOIR, *A SOLDIER REPORTS*, 1976

An honored colonel in World War II, General William C. Westmoreland came to the Vietnam War on the personal recommendation of Secretary of Defense Robert McNamara. However, Westmoreland's decision to wage a war of attrition on the communist forces of North Vietnam led to him being recalled from Vietnam to serve as Army chief of staff and left him with an ambiguous reputation.

Westmoreland was born in South Carolina to Eugenia and James Westmoreland, who was a textile mill manager. The Westmoreland family had an illustrious military history that stretched back to the Revolutionary War, a legacy that he would uphold. An Eagle Scout in high school, Westmoreland showed self-discipline and military bearing in his studies. In 1932, after a year at the Citadel, the military college of South Carolina, he was appointed to the US Military Academy at West Point. He graduated in 1936 with the highest cadet rank, and received the Pershing Sword in recognition of his skills.

Battle experience

Westmoreland served with distinction in World War II as a battalion commander for military operations in Tunisia, before being moved to Europe to fight in Sicily. His success led to his appointment as chief of staff of the Ninth Infantry

Military decorations

This 1969 portrait of Westmoreland shows him proudly wearing decorations and awards he received from both US and foreign militaries—including the French *Légion d'Honneur*, the Korean 1st Class Order of Military Merit, and the Philippine Order of Sikatuna.

Division in the final assault on Germany, and later as commander of a postwar occupation regiment. Over the next decades, he distinguished himself in several important positions, including commanding officer of the 101st Airborne Division. He progressed quickly through the officer ranks to lieutenant general by 1963, with seemingly limitless career potential. In January 1964, he arrived in Vietnam, and in June took charge of Military Assistance Command, Vietnam (MACV).

Search and destroy

Westmoreland arrived skeptical about the war and the chance of US victory. Although his public stance was invariably positive, in private he was candid in his view that without the ability to go into Laos, the war would be long, difficult, and problematic.

The successful defense of Vietnam's Central Highlands led *Time* magazine to name Westmoreland its Man of the Year in 1965. However, this good

Serious message

Westmoreland's engraved lighters, presented to select soldiers and visitors to his Pentagon office, show the pride Westmoreland took in military order—a stark contrast to the darkly humorous lighters that circulated among troops.

fortune would soon change. Limited by political and resource constraints, Westmoreland's war strategy settled on attrition. The NVA and Viet Cong were able to sustain a high body count, which meant that the number of US troops sent to fight them rose to more than 500,000. Public support for the war plummeted.

Wanting to start removing US forces from Vietnam, President Johnson moved Westmoreland back to the US to become the Army's chief of staff. While this was framed as a promotion, many

interpreted it as a repudiation of Westmoreland's leadership. For the next four years, he focused on global army readiness, tackling racism in the Army, and creating an all-volunteer military.

Twilight years

Westmoreland retired from the Army in July 1972. His campaign for the Republican nomination for governor of South Carolina in 1974 was unsuccessful. In January 1982, CBS aired a documentary that accused Westmoreland and his staff of manipulating enemy counts to gain support for attrition. Westmoreland sued for libel in response. The long case brought renewed attention to the ethics of Westmoreland's leadership, and was eventualy settled out of court.

Westmoreland devoted his retirement years to speaking opportunities and supporting veterans until Alzheimer's brought an end to his public life. He died in 2005, aged 91, and was buried at West Point Cemetery, New York.

> ## " It was **difficult war** against an unorthodox enemy. "
>
> GENERAL WILLIAM C. WESTMORELAND, REFLECTING ON THE VIETNAM WAR, 1976

- **1914** Born on March 26 in Saxon, South Carolina.
- **1936** Named first captain in his final year of studies. Graduates from the US Military Academy and is commissioned as a second lieutenant.
- **1936–39** Trains at Fort Sill, Oklahoma.
- **1939** Commands his first unit in Hawaii.
- **1942–45** During World War II, serves as battalion commander in North Africa, Sicily, France, and Germany.
- **1946** Takes command of 504th Parachute Infantry Regiment, 82nd Airborne Division.
- **1947–50** Serves as chief of staff for the 82nd Airborne Division.
- **1952** Joins the Korean War effort as a brigadier general.
- **1955–58** Promoted to secretary of the Army chief of staff.
- **1958–60** Promoted to commanding officer, 101st Airborne.
- **1960–63** Becomes superintendent at the US Military Academy.
- **January 1964** Made deputy commander of Military Assistance Command Vietnam (MACV). Becomes commanding officer of MACV in June of the same year.
- **1965** Appointed general; named *Time* magazine's Man of the Year.
- **1968** Returns to the US; promoted to US Army chief of staff.
- **1972** Retires from the US Army after 36 years of service.
- **1974** Leads an unsuccessful campaign for the Republican nomination to be governor of South Carolina.
- **1976** Publishes a memoir about his life entitled *A Soldier Reports*.
- **1985** Pursues a libel suit against a damning 1982 CBS documentary, which is settled out of court.
- **2005** Dies on July 18 in Charleston, South Carolina; buried at West Point.

Liked by his men

Westmoreland inspects the First Infantry Division in 1966. He was liked by troops, and aimed to be "respected" but not "loved" as he performed his duty of care. In retirement, he tried to ensure that veterans were not criticized for their service in Vietnam.

ATTENDING A VETERANS' PARADE

≪ BEFORE

When Lyndon Johnson took office in November 1963, his national security advisers explained the conflict in Vietnam as a war of aggression rather than a civil war.

NSAM 273

National Security Action Memorandum 273 characterized the conflict not as a civil war between citizens of a single country, but as **a war of aggression** by one country (North Vietnam) against another (South Vietnam) involving an "externally directed and supported communist conspiracy."

COLD WAR CONTEXT

This understanding of Vietnamese politics was formed in the **context of the Cold War ≪ 28–29** and laid the ground for future US policy toward Vietnam, determining the nature of America's involvement.

Bombing North Vietnam

In the spring of 1965, the US Navy and Air Force shifted their efforts from narrowly focused, reprisal air strikes to the sustained bombing of military and civilian targets in North Vietnam in Operation Rolling Thunder.

Operation Rolling Thunder, the heavy bombing of North Vietnam by the United States Air Force and Navy and the ARVN Air Force, lasted from March 2, 1965, until November 1968. The bombing gradually increased in intensity, focusing first on military targets, then on transportation systems, petroleum storage, and industrial targets, as well as the civilian population centers of Hanoi and Haiphong.

Operational aims

Rolling Thunder had several goals: to disrupt the movement of men and war materiel from North Vietnam into the South via the Ho Chi Minh Trail; to damage North Vietnamese war-making ability; to undermine North Vietnamese civilian morale; and to incentivize North Vietnamese participation in diplomatic talks with South Vietnam. The US strategists hoped that sustained bombing of North

Vietnam might precipitate its forces' withdrawal from the South, thereby causing the Viet Cong insurgency to collapse and the South Vietnamese government to stabilize. None of that came to pass.

Political interference

Several factors limited the effectiveness of Rolling Thunder. First, Johnson insisted on micromanaging the air war, bragging that American pilots

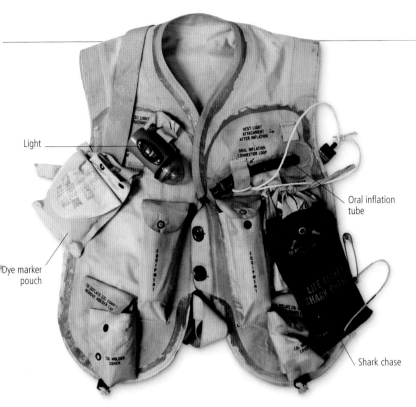

Light

Dye marker pouch

Oral inflation tube

Shark chase

Life saver
The US Navy Mark 2 pneumatic life vest was standard issue for naval aviators and aircrews throughout the Vietnam War. It is not known how many US pilots shot down over water owe their lives to this kit.

North Vietnamese air defenses consisted of Soviet-made fighter aircraft, radar, antiaircraft artillery, and surface-to-air missile sites, but also a highly organized civil defense program. With air raid sirens, frequent drills, and extensive underground shelters, North Vietnamese civilians soon learned to clear busy streets and squares in a matter of seconds, further limiting the human cost of the bombing.

Massive costs
During the course of the operation, the United States dropped more than 900,000 tons of bombs on North Vietnam, an effort that resulted in the loss of some 950 American aircraft and more than

AFTER »

Although it caused tens of thousands of civilian deaths, Rolling Thunder failed to damage North Vietnam sufficiently to trigger meaningful negotiations.

POLITICAL PLOY
The **halt to Rolling Thunder** just prior to the 1968 presidential election was called by Johnson to encourage votes for fellow Democrat Hubert Humphrey. The strategy **failed** to win the election, which went to the Republican candidate.

VICTORY FOR PEACE
Richard Nixon won the presidency in 1968 by promising "peace with honor." Following the election, North Vietnam enjoyed a respite from bombing until President Nixon authorized **further punishing airstrikes 292–93 »**, initially in response to the 1972 Easter Offensive, and subsequently to bring the North Vietnamese back to the **negotiating table 300–01 »**.

"could not hit an outhouse without [his] permission." Johnson was legitimately concerned about the risk of triggering war with China or the Soviet Union if their supply lines into North Vietnam and advisers on the ground were targeted. Strict rules of engagement prevented American aircraft from

pursuing fleeing North Vietnamese fighter aircraft or flying into airspace near the Chinese border.

Furthermore, Johnson's involvement in the selection of bombing targets prevented long-range planning, while also disrupting the ability to respond with air strikes to actionable intelligence in a timely fashion. Johnson's micromanagement engendered frustration within the US military, leading to persistent accusations that civilian leadership had undermined an American victory. Johnson also periodically implemented "bombing pauses," designed to incentivize diplomatic talks in an attempt to appease the American antiwar movement. Instead, North Vietnam used the pauses to reorganize its defenses.

Northern resilience
Traffic along the Ho Chi Minh Trail proved an elusive target. Indeed, North Vietnamese infiltration of South Vietnam accelerated in spite of the bombing. US intelligence estimated that there were fewer than 100 viable military targets in the whole of North Vietnam prior to Rolling Thunder, and virtually all of those targets were damaged or destroyed by 1966. The people of North Vietnam, a largely nonindustrialized country, simply found ways of adapting to the destruction that surrounded them.

Ready to strike
A US Navy F-4 Phantom aboard the USS *Independence* aircraft carrier is readied for an air strike against North Vietnam on July 18, 1965.

> " I can't ask our American soldiers out there to **continue to fight** with **one hand tied** behind their backs."
>
> PRESIDENT JOHNSON TO HIS ADVISERS, FEBRUARY 1965

a thousand American airmen killed, captured, or wounded. Despite civilian casualties in excess of 1,000 per month, North Vietnam's morale held and its claim on the South never wavered.

Soviet SAM
SA-2 surface-to-air missiles (SAMs) were supplied to the North Vietnamese. The USSR also provided technicians and trainers to operate these advanced missile systems, which were highly effective against enemy aircraft.

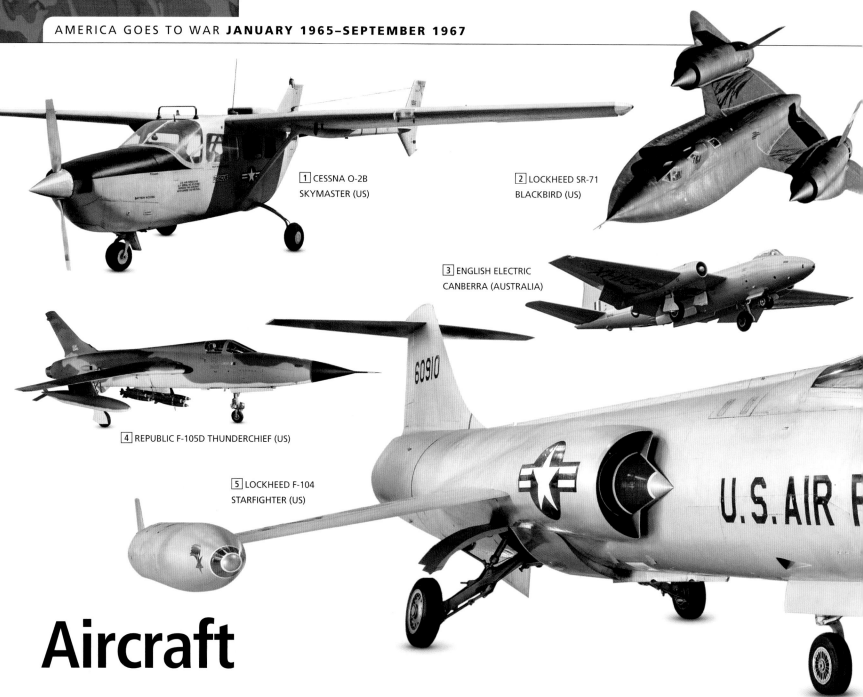

1 CESSNA O-2B SKYMASTER (US)

2 LOCKHEED SR-71 BLACKBIRD (US)

3 ENGLISH ELECTRIC CANBERRA (AUSTRALIA)

4 REPUBLIC F-105D THUNDERCHIEF (US)

5 LOCKHEED F-104 STARFIGHTER (US)

Aircraft

The US Air Force and Marines deployed the very latest aircraft, built using state-of-the-art materials and technology. North Vietnam's pilots flew modern fighter jets supplied by their Chinese and Soviet allies.

1 **Cessna O-2B Skymaster (US)** Equipped with loudspeakers and a leaflet dispenser, this plane was used to conduct psychological warfare operations. 2 **Lockheed SR-71 Blackbird (US)** Flight speeds of over Mach 3 (three times the speed of sound) made it near impossible for North Vietnam to stop this reconnaissance jet. 3 **English Electric Canberra (Australia)** The Royal Australian Air Force used this medium bomber for low-level attacks. 4 **Republic F-105D Thunderchief (US)** A versatile fighter-bomber, the Thunderchief was used extensively in the early years of the conflict. 5 **Lockheed F-104 Starfighter (US)** This interceptor primarily conducted air-superiority missions. 6 **F-100 Super Sabre (US)** The Super Sabre was the longest-serving US jet fighter-bomber in Vietnam. 7 **McDonnell F-4S Phantom II (US)** A two-seater fighter-bomber, the F-4 was used by the US Navy and Marines. 8 **MiG-19 (North Vietnam)** This Soviet-designed fighter jet saw combat in the Linebacker operations of 1972. 9 **MiG-21 (North Vietnam)** The North Vietnamese Air Force claimed 56 aerial combat victories with this speedy interceptor. 10 **MiG-17 (North Vietnam)** Pilots trained to fly this aircraft in China and the USSR. 11 **Grumman A-6E Intruder (US)** In use since 1963, this jet could conduct strikes in all weather conditions. 12 **LTV A-7 Corsair II (US)** These bombers were used to destroy the Thanh Hoa Bridge in 1972. 13 **Chance-Vought RF-8G Crusader (US)** Designed to take off from ships, this aircraft was used in air-to-air combat. 14 **Grumman HU16C Albatross (US)** This flying boat undertook search-and-rescue operations. 15 **Boeing B-52D Stratofortress (US)** A strategic bomber, this B-52 carried around 60,000 pounds of bombs.

6 F-100 SUPER SABRE (US)

7 MCDONNELL F-4S PHANTOM II (US)

8 MIG-19 (NORTH VIETNAM)

9 MIG-21 (NORTH VIETNAM)

10 MIG-17
(NORTH VIETNAM)

11 GRUMMAN A-6E
INTRUDER (US)

12 LTV A-7
CORSAIR II (US)

13 CHANCE-VOUGHT
RF-8G CRUSADER (US)

14 GRUMMAN HU16C ALBATROSS (US)

15 BOEING B-52D STRATOFORTRESS (US)

Air-to-Air Combat

At the beginning of the war, North Vietnam had virtually no planes and no airforce. With Soviet and Chinese assistance, however, it quickly developed air defenses capable of challenging US air attacks.

Eye of the storm
This sequence from gun camera footage shows US Major Ralph L. Kluster shooting down a MiG-17 over North Vietnam from his F-105D Thunderchief in June 1968.

To defend against Operation Rolling Thunder, North Vietnam acquired more than 100 fighter jets from China and the Soviet Union, including the Russian high-performance MiG-21, which became North Vietnam's main interceptor. It also put in place an integrated air defense system, with early-warning radar and radar-directed antiaircraft artillery (AAA). This accounted for about 80 percent of the US planes downed over North Vietnam. Although Soviet-supplied surface-to-air missiles (SAMs) struck their targets just 2 percent of the time, they were a threat to high-altitude missions, such as B-52 sorties.

North Vietnam's air defenses became extremely effective. Although US flights could bomb

‹‹ BEFORE

US and Soviet jet aircraft entered into aerial combat for the first time during the Korean War.

BATTLE OVER KOREA
The US F-86 Sabre and the Soviet MiG-15 went toe to toe in **aerial dogfights** during the **Korean War**. The United States also used **helicopters** in Korea, especially for search-and-rescue (SAR) of pilots downed behind enemy lines.

PREPARING FOR CONFLICT
In the early stages of the Vietnam War, before the **Tonkin Gulf Incident ‹‹ 80–81**, US Air Force pilots **trained South Vietnamese crews** to fly propeller-driven T-28 fighters. After US air raids on North Vietnam in August 1964, the People's Republic of **China** provided Hanoi with a small number of MiG-15 and MiG-17 fighter jets.

AAA and SAM sites and counter (but not eliminate) that part of North Vietnam's defenses, it could not destroy its fleet of MiGs other than through air-to-air combat. Hanoi stationed its MiGs at airfields in southern China, which was beyond the area of combat permitted by Washington.

Phantoms and Thunderchiefs

The US answer to the MiG-21 was the F-4 Phantom, the USAF's most successful interceptor and the Navy's main fleet-defense fighter. It was also a ground attack jet, although the F-105 Thunderchief was the primary plane used in

28 The number of MiGs destroyed by Sidewinder missiles from F-4 Phantoms between 1965 and 1968.

Operation Rolling Thunder. Designed to deliver nuclear weapons into the Soviet Union, the F-105 was also an effective

Morale patch
This aviator patch, from 1964, shows a bird holding a bomb or shell. Fun patches like this one, known as morale patches, were designed by artistic service personnel, who had them made in tailor shops in Saigon.

Thunderchiefs from the rear, forcing them to dump their ordnance before reaching their target. Against F-4s, the MiG pilots would delay their attack until late in the bombing run, when the Americans' fuel was low.

To counter these hit-and-run guerrilla tactics, the Seventh Air Force designed a ruse known as Operation Bolo. A flight of F-4s armed with Sidewinder missiles

flew in a way to mimic on radar an F-105 squadron. When the MiGs took the bait, they found themselves in a dogfight. On January 7, 1967, a disguised F-4 formation led by Colonel Robin Olds shot down seven MiGs in 15 minutes. Two days later another mission downed two more. In the wake of the attacks, the MiG force stood down for four months, after which Olds shot down another MiG in May.

Rescue and recovery

Airmen faced extreme risks on every mission. The possibility of rescue boosted morale. By 1966, the USAF had four Aerospace Rescue and Recovery Group squadrons in South Vietnam and one in Thailand, with numerous ground bases on constant alert and airborne orbits over Laos. The SAR task forces usually consisted of two HH-3 Jolly Green Giant helicopters, two A-1 Skyraider escorts, and an HC-130 control aircraft. Rescuing downed airmen was hazardous. Crewmen earned more than 9,000 medals for valor in 2,800 rescues.

Helping hands
A downed pilot in a steep ravine reaches for a helicopter's rescue cable in this painting by Pierre Mion, printed in *National Geographic* in 1968. A former soldier himself, Mion was a war artist for the US Marine Corps during the Vietnam conflict.

> "The **MiGs reacted as we hoped.** To make a wonderfully long story short, **they lost.**"
> COLONEL ROBIN OLDS, SAIGON NEWS CONFERENCE, 1967

conventional fighter-bomber. Its performance at low altitude made it ideal for going "Downtown," as pilots called the heavily defended airspace around Hanoi.

The principal air-to-air weapon of the F-4 and the F-105 was the AIM-9 Sidewinder infrared-guided or heat-seeking missile. Developed in the 1950s, the sidewinder saw its first extended use in Vietnam.

Air duels

North Vietnamese commanders hesitated to risk MiG-21s against the F-4s in air-to-air combat. They preferred to take on the slower Thunderchiefs and would often use ground-control radar guidance to attack the

Leader of the pack
Colonel Robin Olds paints a victory star on the McDonnell F-4 Phantom in which he shot down a MiG-21 on May 4, 1967. Olds led the USAF's 8th Tactical Fighter Wing, which downed 24 NVA planes in total.

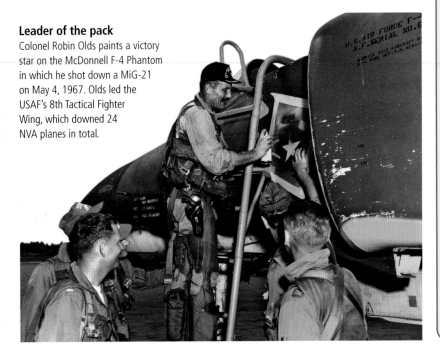

AFTER »

Under President Nixon, the air war mainly focused on Laos and Cambodia.

THE AIR WAR SHIFTS
After Operation Rolling Thunder, the intensity of air-to-air and SAR actions decreased in Vietnam. Instead, the USAF bombed NVA and Viet Cong bases in **Laos 264–65 »** and **Cambodia 248–49 »**. Bombing in Vietnam flared up again during **Operation Linebacker II 292–93 »** in 1972.

THE ARVN AIR FORCE
The Nixon administration restricted ARVN aircraft to helicopters and short-range planes to prevent Saigon from expanding the war to North Vietnam. This meant that it was poorly prepared for a conventional attack such as the **Easter Offensive 276–77 »** in 1972.

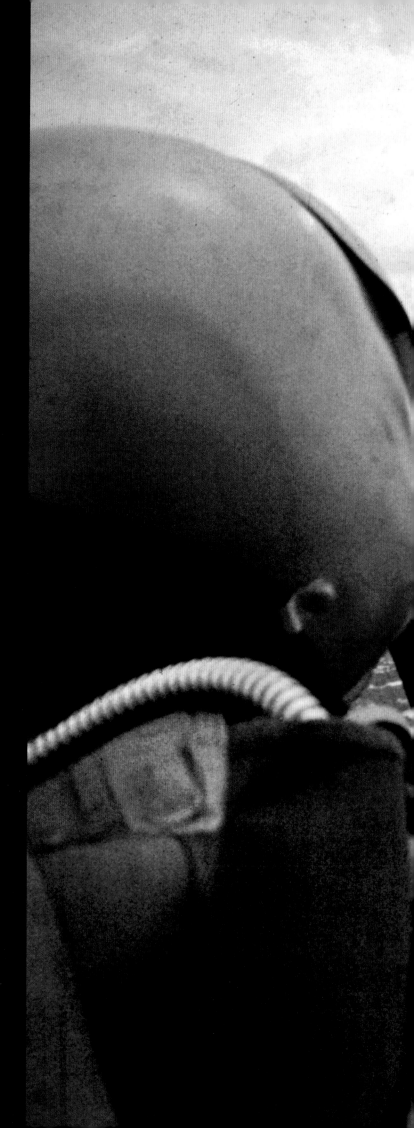

A Pilot's View

Pilots in Vietnam faced dangers from the ground when flying into a landing zone (LZ) in North Vietnamese territory. Captain Thomas A. Pienta was flying a trail helicopter—tasked with waiting and reporting once the LZ became clear—with his "Rat Pack" gunship platoon when he came under fire from a North Vietnamese unit.

"All hell was breaking loose around us … because the LZ was filled with 10- to 15-foot-tall baby rubber trees, which were hard to see until I was right on top of them. I had to pick my spot and could not come directly to the ground as I normally did. Snaring a tail rotor in the trees could kill you just as easily as a machine gun.

We were just coming out of translational lift—the point at which a helicopter stops flying and starts hovering—when a rocket-propelled grenade (RPG) slammed into our Huey. It apparently hit in the left fuel cell just above Brady's gun well. I believe he died instantly. PFC Hoppe, on the right door gun, was blown out of the ship.

We were completely engulfed in flames. The JP-4 fuel and magnesium combined to make a lethal fire. The cliché about not hearing the one that gets you was true in my case. I first thought that a fragmentation grenade had inadvertently been dropped in our ship … It seemed as if there was a big whoosh, similar to the effect a Zippo lighter has after being freshly overfilled and lit, or the whoosh of a propane grill lighting after the gas has been left on too long before the igniter is applied. All the oxygen in the Huey was immediately sucked up by the flames, and we were on fire."

CAPTAIN THOMAS A. PIENTA DESCRIBING HIS EXPERIENCE AS A HELICOPTER PILOT TO *VIETNAM* MAGAZINE, DECEMBER 1996

Destruction from the skies
An American pilot watches as a South Vietnamese T-28 aircraft drops napalm bombs on Viet Cong positions. Even when not directly involved in the action, pilots had a front-row seat to view the danger and destruction of the air war.

Search-and-Destroy

South Vietnam's volatile political situation required a flexible strategy to target enemy combatants, minimize civilian casualties, and keep American troops safe. Search-and-destroy was General Westmoreland's solution.

Despite the complexity of the war's political dimensions, US military authorities settled on a relatively simple strategy to accomplish the US goal of preserving an independent, noncommunist South Vietnam. Ground operations focused on protecting US military installations, destroying the Ho Chi Minh Trail and other supply routes, and wearing down the strength of the enemy through a strategy known as search-and-destroy.

Key objectives
This strategy of attrition involved locating and killing enemy combatants, discovering and destroying material intended to support the enemy (including food), and identifying and neutralizing people who supported the enemy and their efforts.

The helicopter was essential to such operations. Its unprecedented mobility allowed the delivery of combat troops to remote areas in the jungle and mountains.

An archipelago of fire support bases built throughout South Vietnam provided security to US military installations and delivered

1,369 The number of American combat deaths in Vietnam in 1965.

9,378 The number of American combat deaths in Vietnam in 1967.

devastating firepower to search-and-destroy missions. Such firebases could be fairly elaborate and semipermanent, or could be more rudimentary, built and dismantled as the company moved on. Either way, they would always have a landing zone (LZ) for helicopters, medical and communication areas, and a tactical operations center. Soldiers would hunker down in hootches (improvised shelters) or dugouts fortified with sandbags.

Measuring success
Military Assistance Command Vietnam (MACV) evaluated search-and-destroy operations by the statistical analysis of data—pounds of rice seized, the quantity

PHOTOJOURNALIST (1919–65)
DICKEY CHAPELLE

Born Georgette Louise Meyer, photojournalist Dickey Chapelle had covered battles in Japan in World War II, as well as revolutions in Hungary, Cuba, and Algeria before her assignment in Vietnam. Chapelle was outspoken in her dislike of communism and support for US advisers in South Vietnam. In November 1965, she became the first female journalist to die in the war, while on patrol with Marines on a search-and-destroy mission. She was killed by shrapnel from a tripwire boobytrap near Chu Lai.

BEFORE

Search-and-destroy tactics, previously used by the British, were designed for guerrilla warfare.

BRITISH PRECEDENT
The British had used search-and-destroy methods against **communist guerrillas in Malaya** in the 1950s, a conflict known as the Malayan Emergency.

MISSION CHANGE
President Johnson's **escalation of America's role** in Vietnam in 1965 led to a change in mission. In addition to providing security for airbases engaged in **Operation Rolling Thunder** ‹‹ 94–95, ground troops assumed an ever-greater share of combat against the Viet Cong in South Vietnam

" [I]t wasn't nothing unusual about **burning them hootches down ...** It's just a normal procedure we do. "

VETERAN JACK HILL, RECALLING A SEARCH-AND-DESTROY OPERATION IN 1967

of weapons captured, and the number of combatants killed. The body count became search-and-destroy's main measure of success, with combat units rewarded by commendations, bragging rights, and even prizes such as "stand-down R&R"—a period spent in a base with superior amenities.

Civilian casualties
The indiscriminate nature of the violence generated by search-and-destroy was ripe for tragedy. Combat efforts against NVA regulars resulted in battles between

well-prepared foes, but operations against Viet Cong insurgents yielded frequent civilian casualties. It was difficult to distinguish ordinary civilians from insurgents, whose family homes were often in contested areas. The creation of "free fire zones"—from which all friendly forces had ostensibly been cleared—enabled US commanders to bomb and shell areas thought to contain enemy combatants with impunity.

Command emphasis on the body count, as well as concern for American casualties, led to

THE MALAYAN EMERGENCY

indiscriminate violence against Vietnamese people. Even when villagers suspected of having Viet Cong sympathies survived a search-and-destroy attack, they often endured forced relocation or watched helplessly as their livestock, rice stores, and homes were destroyed. These encounters encouraged support for the insurgency among those affected. They also left many American soldiers questioning the efficacy and ethics of the war they were charged with fighting.

Flaming arrow

Lieutenant Commander Donald D. Sheppard aims a flaming arrow at a bamboo hut believed to conceal a Viet Cong bunker on the banks of the Bassac River, in December 1967.

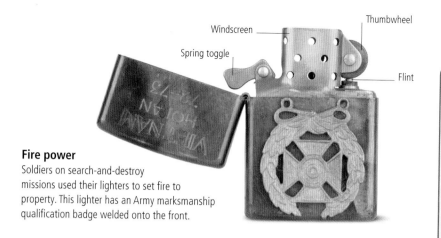

Windscreen

Spring toggle

Thumbwheel

Flint

Fire power

Soldiers on search-and-destroy missions used their lighters to set fire to property. This lighter has an Army marksmanship qualification badge welded onto the front.

Search-and-destroy proved controversial over time. While US forces succeeded again and again in seizing territory and inflicting higher casualties on the enemy than they endured themselves, American strategy failed to yield political results. The morale of the insurgents withstood such attacks,

and the infiltration of North Vietnamese soldiers and supplies increased. American efforts to support the South Vietnamese military and take the war to the enemy also encouraged ARVN dependency on the United States, making American withdrawal more difficult.

AFTER

Search-and-destroy dominated American ground war strategy until the withdrawal of US troops under President Nixon.

WESTMORELAND IS REPLACED
General Creighton Abrams replaced General Westmoreland, the chief advocate of attrition, as MACV commander in June 1968.

PUBLIC OPINION
Combat operations in the spring of 1969 resulted in heavy US casualties and **increased scrutiny** of the war by **antiwar activists 162–63 》**. As a result, Nixon ended large-scale search-and-destroy operations.

« BEFORE

Battle of Ia Drang Valley

In November 1965, American and North Vietnamese troops fought their first large-scale battle, in the Ia Drang Valley of South Vietnam's Central Highlands. Five days of brutal fighting established a pattern for Vietnam War battles that would repeat again and again.

Dramatically higher troop levels in the fall of 1965 provided US commanders with enough resources to take on the NVA.

TAKING UP POSITION
North Vietnamese Army (NVA) forces had already infiltrated South Vietnam via the **Ho Chi Minh Trail « 56–57**.

GEARING UP
President Johnson's **escalation of the war « 90–91** increased the number of US ground troops, providing enough manpower for major battles as well as counterinsurgency patrols.

The Battle of Ia Drang Valley was part of the second phase of a month-long operation known as the Pleiku Campaign. The first phase provided relief for the US Special Forces camp at Plei Me, which was besieged by the North Vietnamese Army (NVA) for a week in October 1965.

In the second phase, elements of the American First Air Cavalry Division were deployed to draw the NVA away from Plei Me.

Battle begins
The operation, which was known as Silver Bayonet I, was an early demonstration of the air mobility

concept, in which ground troops were dropped onto and withdrawn from the battlefield by helicopter. After a brief artillery bombardment to clear the initial landing zone (LZ X-Ray), helicopters began landing eight at a time, and the men of the First Air Cavalry took up defensive positions.

The battalion was dropped into the Ia Drang Valley on November 14, to engage with North Vietnamese units operating in the area. They were quickly confronted by a large force at a well-defended base camp. The battalion came under fire almost immediately, and within two hours the battle was on: multiple American companies came under heavy attack, and one platoon was cut off from the rest of the battalion entirely.

On the move

The fighting at LZ X-Ray lasted for two days and nights, as US forces repulsed attack after attack by NVA infantry advancing in waves. Eventually, enough reinforcements

First wounded

Men of the First Air Cavalry Division rest and receive medical care 3 miles (5 km) north of the Ia Drang Valley in November 1965. The weary men had survived an ambush, and had spent all day and night in intense firefights.

Men who had already endured three days of combat now found themselves fighting in close quarters, sometimes hand to hand, for 16 hours. The tide finally turned on November 19, thanks to reinforcements and artillery and air strikes—so close to US lines that they caused friendly fire casualties.

Both sides bore heavy losses in the battle: nearly 300 Americans were killed and hundreds more

with American units so that airstrikes could only be used at the risk of friendly fire.

Both sides declared victory—the US for suffering fewer casualties and achieving a territorial objective, and the NVA for standing up to US forces and surviving to fight again US forces eventually withdrew from the area and returned to their bases, allowing the NVA to resume operations.

Measuring attacks

This graphical firing table, made in Chicago in 1960, was used to position a 155 mm howitzer armed with M107 shells. It allowed soldiers in the field to calibrate the range, angle, and fuse setting of artillery pieces to hit the enemy target.

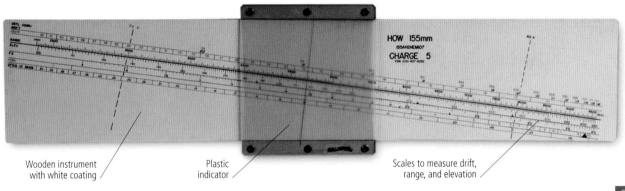

HOW 155mm
ISSAHCHEMI07
CHARGE 5

Wooden instrument with white coating

Plastic indicator

Scales to measure drift, range, and elevation

arrived to even up the numbers of soldiers on each side, and LZ X-Ray was secured on day three—but at heavy cost. The remaining US units abandoned the area to make way for a B-52 strike, then marched toward a new landing zone,

were wounded, while the NVA had perhaps 500 to 1,000 dead and as many wounded.

Drawing conclusions

The battle was significant for many other reasons. It was also the first

AFTER

The Battle of Ia Drang Valley was just the first of many such conflicts between US and NVA forces over South Vietnam.

CHANGE OF HEART

The US continued to increase its number of troops in Vietnam even as the war became **less popular 162–63 »**. After the war, however, memoirs by those who had served softened public opinion. *We Were Soldiers Once … and Young*, a true account of the Battle of Ia Drang Valley by Lt. Gen. Harold Moore was later made into a movie.

> " Even a tank we 'destroyed' … might be repaired to **fight again** another day. "

LIEUTENANT COLONEL THOMAS P. MCKENNA, *KONTUM: THE BATTLE TO SAVE SOUTH VIETNAM*, 2011

LZ Albany, just over 2 miles (3 km) away. NVA forces ambushed the column en route, resulting in a new round of vicious combat.

Lighting the way home

Four days into the battle, wounded soldiers of the First Cavalry watch flares from planes light up a field in the Ia Drang Valley. Bodies of wounded and fallen soldiers alike were taken to this clearing to await evacuation by helicopter.

major encounter between US and NVA regular forces, and the battle established a template for the remainder of the war. The US would rely on superior technology and firepower to inflict heavy losses on their foe, who would withdraw when fighting was no longer prudent. The North Vietnamese also learned that the best way to blunt the effectiveness of US artillery and airpower during battle was to keep close contact

MOVIE POSTER

MEL GIBSON

WE WERE SOLDIERS

Air Mobility

Helicopters enabled American commanders to move large numbers of troops over rugged terrain in a short amount of time. They also provided air artillery, medevac supply, and other vital support functions.

Airmobile Blue Max
This report relates to an action by the Second Battalion of the 20th Artillery, First Air Cavalry Division, known as Blue Max, one of two aerial artillery units operating during the Vietnam War. Their main air-to-ground weapons were Folding-Fin Aerial Rockets (FFARs) and M60 machine guns.

« BEFORE

Igor Sikorsky invented the first practical helicopter in 1939, but helicopters were not used in general combat until after World War II.

KOREAN WAR HELICOPTERS
The US Army acquired its first helicopters in 1947. The versatile **Bell H-13 Sioux** proved its worth in the **Korean War** (1950–53) for fire support, resupply, transportation, and medical evacuation (medevac). In 1954, General James Gavin published an influential article, "Cavalry, and I Don't Mean Horses," praising the **maneuverability that helicopters offered ground forces**.

The value of airmobility emerged during the 1950s. During the Cold War, the ability to disperse and move troops quickly provided greater force security than having large, slow formations of troops exposed to nuclear attack. Despite some rivalry between the US Army and Air Force, and some old-guard concern that helicopters were too vulnerable to attack, Secretary of Defense Robert McNamara had the airmobile concept tested at Fort Benning, Georgia. The results were encouraging, and in 1965 the Army created the First Cavalry Division (Airmobile) and deployed it to Vietnam.

4,000 The number of rounds per minute that the miniguns on the AH-1 Cobra gunship could fire.

The helicopter war
When the First Cavalry arrived in Vietnam, helicopters were already in use. Army and Marine advisers had begun transporting and positioning ARVN troops with helicopters in 1962. Also in that year, testing in the field of armed UH-1 Iroquois helicopters was underway. The UH-1, known as the Huey or Slick by the troops, became the workhorse of Army and Marine Corps aviation in Vietnam. Its uses were broad: troop

transport, gunship, supply, medevac, command and control, reconnaissance, and search-and-rescue. Armed with rockets, it also served as airborne artillery.

In 1967, the Huey was supplemented by the AH-1 Cobra gunship attack helicopter, which, when fully loaded with rockets, had the same firepower as a ground artillery battalion. The Cobra also carried 7.62 mm miniguns for close air support. Both the First Cavalry and the 101st Airborne Division (Airmobile)—fully converted to airmobile in 1969—had their own aircraft. Airmobility was so popular, however, that over time many other divisions and corps added their own aviation units.

The effectiveness of airmobility was apparent in the First Cavalry's tactics in the Battle of Ia Drang in the fall of 1965. The engagement was a prototype of airmobile doctrine that became standard throughout the theater of the war. Reconnaissance helicopters located the enemy and possible landing zones (LZs); Hueys and larger capacity CH-47 Chinooks ferried entire companies of infantry to the landing zones with gunship cover;

Staying connected
Captain William E. Taylor, company commander of the First Cavalry Division, Airmobile, uses an AN/ARC-122 radio to coordinate ground and air actions during an operation in June 1966.

Ground cover
US Army helicopters provide machine gun cover for South Vietnamese ground troops as they prepare to attack a Viet Cong base north of Tay Ninh, near the Cambodian border, in March 1965.

medevac choppers (called Dust-offs) carried out dead or wounded soldiers, while other helicopters resupplied equipment and rations. Throughout the battle, artillery observers and commanders could direct ground operations from light observation helicopters.

Airmobile limitations
Although helicopters allowed generals to insert troops quickly, and without the fatigue that a long march entailed, their noisy approach forewarned the enemy. Not only could the element of surprise be lost, but also the

landing zone could be "hot"—under enemy fire. In addition, much of the terrain in Vietnam was steep and covered in jungle, making it difficult for helicopters to land, and even for ground troops already in place to create a landing zone of sufficient size. Although bombing sorties could open a patch of ground to create a landing zone, they could also telegraph an assault.

The airmobile units trained soldiers to rappel by ropes or ladders into dense vegetation that prevented aircraft from landing, but that maneuver also exposed the men to enemy fire. Despite these dangers, the suppressing fire from gunners in the Hueys and Cobras reduced the threat to the landing zone and to the helicopters themselves.

Airmobile tactics also had a strategic implication. The rapid insertion and extraction of troops was ideal for search-and-destroy operations in which US technology inflicted severe losses on the enemy quickly, but air mobility was less useful when it came to clear-and-hold tactics. It placed US units in remote places that were difficult to defend and sustain.

AFTER »

After Vietnam, vertical takeoff and landing (VTOL) became key to positioning ground troops in all wars in difficult terrain.

EVACUATING VIETNAM
During the **evacuation of Saigon 322–23 »** in 1975, helicopters ferried US military personnel and civilians and some South Vietnamese refugees from the roof of the US Embassy to waiting ships and aircraft.

AIRMOBILE TO AIR ASSAULT
In subsequent US wars in **Grenada**, **Panama**, the **Persian Gulf**, **Somalia**, **Bosnia**, **Iraq**, and **Afghanistan**, helicopters—including innovations such as the UH-60 Blackhawk and AH-64 Apache—and the new V-22 Osprey **tilt-wing aircraft** remained the foundation of the airmobile concept. The strategy is now known as air combat by the First Cavalry and air assault by the 101st Airborne and Marine Corps.

Serving their country
Young men from western Pennsylvania are sworn in to the Army after being drafted for military service in 1967. Scenes like this were commonplace during the war years.

 BEFORE

Americans viewed compulsory military service as a necessity during World War II and in the years that followed.

THE PEACETIME DRAFT
The Selective Training and Service Act of 1940 authorized the **first peacetime draft in US history**. After World War II, this was was replaced by the Selective Service Act of 1948. As manpower needs in the 1950s and early 1960s were low, the system aroused **little opposition** among the public.

The **Call** to **Service**

In the United States, the rights and obligations of citizenship have long engendered argument, and Vietnam was no different. Many Americans questioned the necessity of the war, and millions of young men chose to avoid military service.

When President Johnson quietly escalated the war in the summer of 1965, he chose to rely on the draft to meet rising manpower needs rather than calling upon the National Guard and reserves. Johnson's reliance on conscription was intended to avoid a divisive public debate about the war, but instead it provoked one. When monthly draft calls more than doubled, young Americans who had never imagined joining the military were suddenly forced to contemplate combat in the remote jungles of South Vietnam. The draft cast a long shadow over America's youth.

Military service was not the experience of the majority of young men of the era. Of the

27 million men eligible to serve, only 11 million did so, and of these 2.5 million were deployed to Vietnam. Roughly one-third of those in Vietnam were volunteers motivated by patriotism, a hatred of communism, or the desire for a military career. Another third were draft-motivated volunteers who enlisted to have some control over their futures when conscription seemed imminent. The remaining third were draftees, often unable to invoke one of the lawful means of avoiding the draft, such as family hardship, infirmity, certain types of labor, conscientious objection, or student status.

Draft resisters

Of the 16 million who avoided military service during the period of US military involvement in Vietnam, only 600,000 actually

Souvenir of service
This combat jacket belonged to US Army Sergeant Charles E Morris. As noncommissioned officers, sergeants rose through the ranks to fill training and mentoring roles. In Vietnam, sergeants sometimes also led combat missions.

Sergeant's stripes

" Hell no, we won't go!"

POPULAR ANTIWAR, ANTI-DRAFT SLOGAN OF THE 1960S AND 1970S

broke the law by failing to report or fleeing abroad, most commonly to Canada. These draft resisters risked jail for refusing to fight a war they did not support.

By the late 1960s, a majority of Americans regarded the draft system as unfair. Local draft boards, usually composed of white men, often veterans themselves, adjudicated on requests for deferments while trying to meet their quotas. Men of means who could provide documentation of physical infirmity from doctors or long-standing moral pacifism from clergymen had an advantage in this process. Poor men and men of color were least likely to avoid military service, because draft boards tended to defer white, middle-class men whose futures were deemed more valuable than those unable to afford college. The unfairness of this led to incremental changes

to the system that eventually ended graduate school and teaching deferments.

The draft lottery

As a result of the public discontent, Congress passed legislation in 1970, authorizing a lottery system

to make draft selection fairer. Young men watched with bated breath as Selective Service officials drew tiles—366 of them, one for each day of the year—from a hopper on national television. Eligible men with birthdays drawn in the first third or so of the process received induction notices, while those whose birthdays were drawn last did not. The process was more rational, but hardly felt fair to those who were called up and did not want to go to Vietnam.

Length of service

For those who did go, cycling in and out of the war could be a solitary experience. Unlike in World War II, when soldiers served for the duration of the conflict, during the Vietnam War individuals were deployed for a one-year tour of duty. This policy was intended to blunt public hostility to the war by avoiding unit call-ups that could generate opposition within a community. As a result, Vietnam veterans returned home as

Code of conduct

A card entitled Nine Rules was first issued to US soldiers in Vietnam in 1967. It summarized the US government's view of the reason for the US presence and gave guidelines for the conduct of troops serving in the country.

individuals aboard commercial flights they nicknamed the Freedom Bird, often without fanfare except from their own friends and family.

AFTER »

Opposition to the draft formed a big part of antiwar protest. Ending the draft was a long-standing promise of the Nixon administration.

A PROMISE FULFILLED
In 1973, President Nixon made good on his 1968 **campaign promise 216–17** » to end the draft and shift to an all-volunteer force. Nixon's advisers believed that market forces would ensure a steady supply of suitable volunteers, but the unpopularity of the war contributed to a **loss of respect** for military service that affected military recruitment for the remainder of the 1970s and later.

NEW INVESTMENT
Difficulty meeting military manpower needs remained an unfortunate **legacy of the war** until the 1980s, when massive defense spending finally improved the quality and popularity of the armed forces as a career option.

Life on Base

The comfort and stability of permanent bases stood in stark contrast to the horrors and deprivations of combat. Similar to small towns, the larger bases were slices of Middle America in the jungles of Vietnam.

« BEFORE

The construction boom in South Vietnam was unprecedented in American military history.

MOVING CAMPS
Previous foreign wars had emphasized **troop mobility** rather than long-term occupation, and conflicts simply did not last long enough to result in sophisticated construction projects. Vietnam was different. Even before the **commitment of US ground troops « 90–91** escalated the war, the US had built large bases to house troops and provide support to the air and ground wars.

Over the course of the war, the United States built hundreds of bases across South Vietnam. Some were rugged outposts perched on mountaintops or hidden deep in the jungle, while others were just as well developed as any stateside base. One—Long Binh Post—was so large that it had a commuter bus service. All of these bases supported the US war effort, but the contrasts between the different types led to disparate experiences for the Americans who lived on them. Between soldiers in makeshift camps eating C-rations, and men in catered brick mess halls, there could be no one typical experience of life in Vietnam.

Building infrastructure
Constructing the US base network took time and money. Navy construction battalions and troop

Military money
The Vietnam War was the last war to use the Military Payment Certificate program, which tried to prevent local economies from being destabilized by an influx of US dollars.

labor built some of the military infrastructure, but private American construction firms employing Vietnamese workers were responsible for most of it.

Holiday spirit
US Marines sit down to celebrate their first Tet holiday (Vietnamese New Year) on base in January 1965. Their meal, which included fresh fruits and cold beer, was prepared by local women.

Collectively, they built more than 100 airfields, permanent billets for 350,000 troops, and hospitals with 8,000 beds to treat the wounded.

In order to ensure that life for US soldiers was as comfortable as the tactical situation would allow, and that every corner of the war effort was properly supplied, they also built seven deep-draft ports, storage for three billion barrels of oil, 600 miles (966 km) of roads, and 5 miles (8 km) of bridges. Some 56 million square feet of storage areas were built, as well as cold storage—which facilitated fresh food for 90 percent of the meals served to American troops during the war.

Fun and games

As the years passed, bases became ever more elaborate, necessitating all the services—water treatment, garbage collection, fire protection—

Religious ceremonies

Making the most of the Christmas ceasefire, on December 25, 1969, troops of the 25th Infantry Division take part in a carol service at Fire Base Evans. As well as the Christian holiday, the festival of Passover was acknowledged, with an organized annual seder for Jewish troops.

of modern US cities. Construction priorities shifted from housing and services to recreational facilities intended to boost troop morale.

Support personnel on larger bases often did regular shifts in offices, in warehouses, or on flight lines, leaving hours of off-duty time to fill. To provide entertainment—and also prevent mischief such as drug use or going absent without leave (AWOL)—commanders authorized

enabled military personnel to acquire souvenirs of their war experience—handicrafts, watches, cameras, jewelry, and even American-made cars—that helped to balance the negatives of spending a year in a war zone.

Out of danger

The majority of US personnel in Vietnam served in support capacities, as mechanics, drivers,

passing through these installations recognized that support troops risked little—yet received the same combat pay—and enjoyed far superior living conditions.

The abundance on display in American PXs, open mess clubs, and even individual soldiers' quarters did not only upset other US personnel. The largess was particularly shocking to displaced Vietnamese people nearby—many of whom worked menial jobs on base, and fashioned their homes and meals from American garbage.

AFTER »

TECHNOLOGY

TRANSISTOR RADIO

Developed in 1954, transistor radios were a must-have device in Vietnam, with 99 percent of American soldiers owning or having access to one. They used them to tune in to sanitized transmissions on the US Armed Forces Radio, but they also listened to rock music and defiant political commentary. North Vietnamese radio programs, with hosts such as "Hanoi Hannah," played music for US troops, interspersed with anti-American propaganda and sometimes disturbingly accurate reports of battles and troop movements.

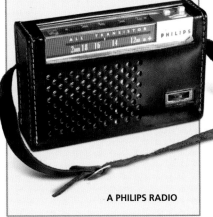

A PHILIPS RADIO

"**Most of the time** you didn't know you were **in a war.**"

WILLIAM R. UPTON, IN *PIZZA AND MORTARS: BA-MUOI-BA AND BODY BAGS*, 2003

the construction of theaters, craft shops, education centers, libraries, athletics courts, and swimming pools. Alcohol consumption was rampant among American troops, with more than 2,000 open mess clubs (unit-run bars) in South Vietnam at the system's peak.

Meanwhile, the expansion of electricity and broadcast media across the country enabled men to improve their barracks with simple pleasures such as electric fans, hot plates, and radios. Shopping at the local post exchange (PX), or placing an order in the Pacific Mail-Order System (PACEX) catalog for delivery back home,

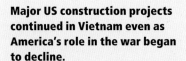

BEER eased tension and quenched thirst. Budweiser was the No. 1 seller on base but soldiers also drank the local "33" (Ba Muoi Ba).

cooks, and clerks. For those stationed on large rearward bases, their war was a far cry from the mud, dust, and constant danger of fire support bases, remote radio outposts, and especially combat patrols. Poor morale among the troops was a persistent problem, and commanders often addressed it by trying to make life on base more comfortable. These efforts had the opposite effect: soldiers furthest in the rear, where life was more comfortable, had lower morale than soldiers in forward areas, where combat provided a sense of urgency and purpose. The disparity between bases also engendered resentments. Combat troops

Major US construction projects continued in Vietnam even as America's role in the war began to decline.

BUILDING MORALE

Commanders at Long Binh Post—which already had a golf course, massage parlor, nightclubs, and more—planned to build a 1,690-acre (7 square km) recreational lake for swimming and fishing in 1970. They were forced to scrap the $110,000 project due to negative media coverage, as public opinion in the United States railed **against the war 162–63 »**.

The gradual **withdrawal of US forces 234–35 »** would change the landscape of the war, as US bases were **turned over** to ARVN units—as Long Binh Post was in 1972—or abandoned to become **ghost towns**.

Recuperation and Entertainment

For US troops with only letters from loved ones to remind them of home, the long months and often tough conditions in Vietnam took a toll on morale. Periods of relaxation, especially out of the country, were therefore eagerly anticipated.

BEFORE

During World War II and the Korean War, a combination of censorship, propaganda, movies, and entertainment tours kept up troop morale.

THE USO

Prior to the Vietnam War, logistical restrictions meant that travel outside the war zone for **rest and relaxation** (R&R) was rare. The nonprofit United Service Organization (USO) arranged **troop entertainment**, including live appearances by top stars such as Rita Hayworth (World War II) and Marilyn Monroe (Korea).

Music therapy

Singer and dancer Lola Falana performs for American servicemen in Da Nang as part of the Bob Hope Christmas tour in 1970. Hope entertained the troops in Vietnam every Christmas from 1964 to 1972.

Life in the war zone meant acute hardships that over time dampened soldier morale. High heat and humidity, endless rain and mud, biting insects, and, for combat troops, the anxieties and danger of battle all took their toll. There were also long working hours, relentless military discipline, and limited opportunities for privacy or individuality. Mail provided the only contact with friends and family back home, and loneliness and homesickness were rife. Like antiwar demonstrators back in the United States, many service personnel questioned the war's ethics and necessity, and whether it could even be won.

Leisure facilities

Low morale could lead to indiscipline, absenteeism, drug abuse, and other subversive behavior that threatened discipline and mission readiness. To counter the problem, the US military equipped bases with an array of leisure amenities to occupy the troops. Most bases within the war zone had ball courts, while larger bases had swimming pools, and a few even had golf courses, go-cart tracks, and bowling alleys. Some bases had education centers, arts and crafts workshops, libraries, movie theaters, and performance spaces.

Celebrity visits

Live entertainment was also provided. Although the United Service Organization (USO) arranged celebrity-studded tours from time to time, most of the civilian acts that toured the military bases were unknown entertainers flown in from Asia and Australia. For bases that were too dangerous for civilian entertainers to visit, the Army's Special Services Division dispatched Command Military Touring Shows composed of GI musicians on temporary duty. A few bases even had their own theater companies.

By the late 1960s, there were hundreds of acts touring the war zone at any given time, and the US Army in South Vietnam was effectively the largest promoter of live entertainment in the world.

3,200 The number of performers, from 26 countries, touring the Vietnam circuit in 1970.

R&R centers

The military also provided US troops with respite from the war through a robust R&R program. It built dozens of stand-down R&R centers across South Vietnam. These were standard bases with extra amenities into which combat units rotated while on break from combat. They included the "Tay Ninh Holiday Inn" and "Waikiki East." The military also built two in-country R&R centers at China Beach and Vung Tau, resorts with long sandy beaches, offering hotel services such as clean sheets and towels, and ceiling fans. The most popular R&R option, however, was out-of-country R&R, which

Reunion in Hawaii

US airman Patrick Nugent poses for the cameras with his son and his wife Luci, the daughter of President Johnson, in Honolulu, Hawaii, after his arrival on leave from Vietnam.

provided the greatest contrast with the war. Soldiers were able to indulge themselves with food, drink, prostitutes, and shopping for five days. At the peak of the R&R program, troops on leave could visit one of nine destinations on the Pacific Rim, including Bangkok, Hong Kong, and Sydney. Hawaii was the most popular out-of-country option, providing home comforts plus the chance to spend time with family.

AFTER

Advances in technology meant that US soldiers in subsequent foreign wars did not suffer the same degree of isolation.

R&R SINCE VIETNAM

US military authorities continue to believe in the importance of maintaining troop morale. **MWR (morale, welfare, and recreation)** centers were provided in Iraq and Afghanistan to provide units with leisure facilities, such as pool tables, video games, and swimming pools. R&R in countries such as Qatar was also offered, but most troops chose to visit home instead.

Catching the rays
An aircraft crew on board the USS *Constellation*, in the Gulf of Tonkin, take advantage of a lull in combat operations to relax and enjoy the sunshine on the aircraft carrier's flight deck.

Mementos and Memorabilia

Many veterans returned home from Vietnam with small tokens to remind them of their experience. These war souvenirs most often commemorated the friendships they had made and the people they had fought alongside.

1 FRIENDSHIP BRACELET

[1] **Friendship bracelet** This bracelet was given to Jerry Harlowe by Montagnard tribespeople in 1969. [2] **Peace plate** This craft was made in a Vietnam craftshop, run by a member of the Women's Army Corps. [3] **Hand-carved statue** Sixteen inches (41 cm) tall, this statue was purchased in Pleiku in 1969. [4] **Short timer cane** Short timers—those with only a few weeks left on their tour—were given carved sticks by their unit. [5] **Short timer cane** This is engraved with the owner's name and service details: Cu Chi, 1966–67. [6] **Woodcut** A South Vietnamese aircraft maintenance officer made this woodcut during downtime with Lieutenant Colonel Robert Liotta, of the US Air Force. Liotta was given this copy to take home. [7] **Short timer calendar** Colored-in calendars were also used to count down to the end of a tour. Some featured popular cartoon characters—such as Snoopy—while others were more crude. [8] **Teddy bear** Belonging to a soldier killed in the war, this memento was left at the Vietnam Veterans Memorial. [9] **Scrapbook made by Albert E. Short** The veteran created this book in the 1980s as a way to process his memories of the war. [10] **Scrapbook made by Albert E. Short** Many servicemen took photographs, such as these from 1965, that later went into scrapbooks or on veterans' websites. [11] **Zippo cigarette lighter box** Zippo lighters were a common memento. [12] **Cigarette lighter in box** This bears an enamel badge with the insignia of an armed helicopter unit. [13] **Cigarette lighter** With its clear protest symbol, this was likely inscribed after its owner had finished his tour. [14] **Plastic cigarette lighter** This lighter commemorates the partnership of the First Battalion RAR, from Australia and New Zealand, and US 173rd Airborne Brigade.

2 PEACE PLATE

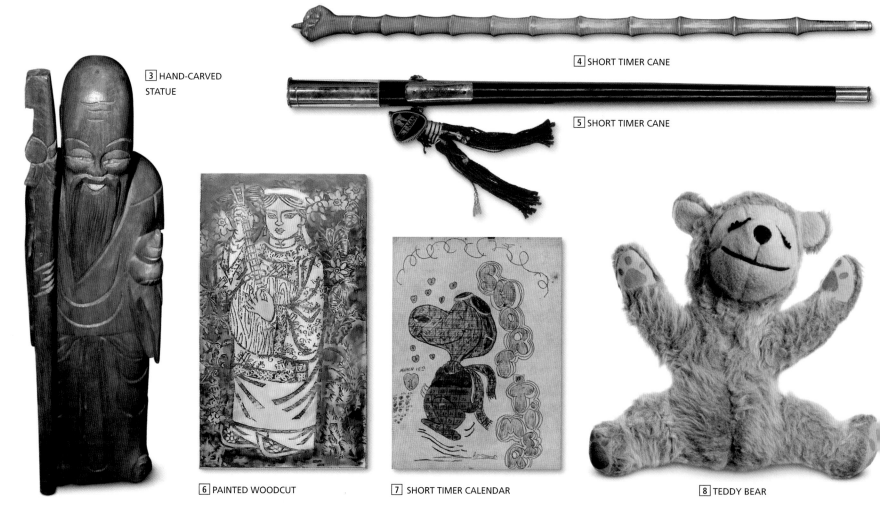

3 HAND-CARVED STATUE

4 SHORT TIMER CANE

5 SHORT TIMER CANE

6 PAINTED WOODCUT

7 SHORT TIMER CALENDAR

8 TEDDY BEAR

9 SCRAPBOOK MADE BY ALBERT E. SHORT

10 SCRAPBOOK MADE BY ALBERT E. SHORT

11 ZIPPO CIGARETTE
LIGHTER BOX

12 CIGARETTE
LIGHTER IN BOX

13 CIGARETTE LIGHTER

14 PLASTIC CIGARETTE
LIGHTER

A Place to Party

For those stationed at big, permanent bases, life was often a far cry from the typical image of being in a war zone. Many young men took advantage of the facilities to enjoy their time on base—as was the case for Pete Whalon of Redondo Beach, California, who extended his tour to serve as a lifeguard at one of the 12 pools on Long Binh Post.

With its cold beer, loud music, absence of lifers (career soldiers), and lack of rules, the pool (nicknamed the Bayou) soon became the coolest place to party. In his account, Whalon describes a typical evening at the Bayou with up to thirty drunks in and around the pool as music blasted from the Sugar Shack. Marathon sessions of Monopoly would take place in the Shack and there were rowdy water-football games. The smell of marijuana was heavy in the air and four maverick military policemen (MPs) had assured them that they would never get busted for smoking marijuana while the four MPs were in country. Empty beer cans and wine bottles were strewn across the ground. There were very few restrictions and every night was an open-pool party.

"I often felt as though I was hosting a perpetual, out-of-control frat party—seven nights a week."

PETE WHALON, IN HIS MEMOIR, *THE SAIGON ZOO: VIETNAM'S OTHER WAR: SEX, DRUGS, ROCK 'N ROLL: A VERY DIFFERENT VIETNAM MEMOIR*, 2006

The high life
GIs pass around a joint in their living quarters on base in Quang Tri. With walls plastered with posters, and a transistor radio blaring music, the scene could easily be confused for young men relaxing at home in the US.

America's Allies

To allay public concerns about the US "going in alone," President Johnson engineered a multinational coalition to fight in South Vietnam. When allied support for the war began to wane, US and South Vietnamese soldiers ended up providing most of the manpower.

Aussie support
Servicemen of the Royal Australian Air Force arrive at Tan Son Nhut airbase near Saigon on August 10, 1964. More than 60,000 Australian soldiers fought in the Vietnam War from 1962 through the end of 1972.

« BEFORE

The formation of the United Nations (UN) in 1945 offered the promise of world peace by enabling nations to resolve their differences without violence.

COLLABORATIVE FAILURE
Since 1948, the UN's peacekeeping force, composed of **troops volunteered by member nations**, have been been used to suppress noncompliant armed forces in conflicts around the world.

The biggest obstacle to the UN stepping in to prevent the Vietnam War was that the Soviet Union and the United States, both members of the UN Security Council, with the power to veto resolutions, **supported opposing sides** in the war. Attempts by the United Nations to resolve the conflict through negotiation failed.

G eneral Westmoreland's strategy of attrition required steady increases in troop strength. Believing that other countries should contribute to the war effort, in the summer of 1965 President Johnson pressed US allies around the world to support the war effort.

France objected to foreign intervention in Vietnam. Great Britain and Canada offered only rhetorical support, and Spain sent about 50 soldiers; other nations provided economic, technical, and medical aid to South Vietnam.

91 PERCENT **of South Vietnam's regional allies came from South Korea.**

6 PERCENT **came from the Philippines and Thailand.**

The Johnson administration fared better with regional allies, who feared communism's international advance. The mutual defense provisions of the Southeast Asia Treaty Organization provided formal justification for Australia, New Zealand, Thailand, and the Philippines to send troops to South Vietnam, while general support of US regional interests led the Republic of Korea (the ROK) to support American efforts.

Soldiers from these nations were known collectively as "Free World Military Forces" (FWMF) and they fought in support of both US and ARVN efforts in South Vietnam.

Australian troops
The Australian government was fully committed to Johnson's policy. Australia's first commitment of military advisers to train the ARVN in 1962 was escalated in 1965 to include combat troops, namely the First Battalion, Royal Australian Regiment, and logistics personnel attached to the United States' 173rd Airborne Brigade. This collaboration revealed major differences in US and Australian operational methods, so later deployments of Australian forces involved only independent operations. Australian troops relied less on heavy firepower and more on small patrols,

setting ambushes, and cultivating positive relations with local civilians through civic action. Some 60,000 Australians fought in Vietnam, with about 500 killed and 3,000 wounded by war's end.

ROK Forces
The Republic of Korea (South Korea) provided considerable support to its US ally, in return for

Giggle hat
This boonie hat, worn by Australian forces in Vietnam, was intended to protect the wearer in hot and humid climates. Officially called "hats utility, jungle green," such hats were nicknamed giggle hats (as well as "hats ridiculous-for-the-use-of") by troops due to their appearance.

Civilian support

This badge was worn by civilian nurse Dorothy Angell, who was part of an Australian Surgery Team at Bien Hoa in 1967. Her team, from Melbourne's Alfred Hospital, performed hundreds of life-saving operations on Vietnamese civilians.

ĐOÀN GIẢI PHẪU ÚC ĐẠI

DOT ANGELL

Public resentment toward the war in Vietnam caused problems for the governments fighting under the FWMF banner.

BOWING OUT

Antiwar protests 216–17 ≫ had a major impact in the United States, but they also affected America's allies. In Australia, they forced reductions in troop strength and **eventual withdrawal**, while intense protests in New Zealand ultimately **altered its relationship** with the US for decades. In South Korea, the Vietnam War remains a bitter subject, but keeping faith with its US ally has proved **economically fruitful** in the long run.

---

aid commitments to South Korea. About 300,000 ROK troops served in South Vietnam, 5,000 of whom were killed. The ROK was the third largest force to combat North Vietnamese infiltration and the Viet Cong insurgency. They conducted search-and-clear operations, usually in battalion-sized units, and excelled at setting ambushes and discovering weapons caches. In

their careful sweeps of Vietnamese villages, ROK troops earned a reputation for ruthlessness. Their actions led to accusations of war crimes in several villages where hundreds of civilians were killed.

Thailand and the Philippines

In addition to deploying soldiers to Laos and South Vietnam to fight North Vietnamese infiltration,

Thailand also hosted several large US Air Force bases on Thai soil. Bases in Thailand supported Rolling Thunder bombings and provided tactical air support to US ground operations in South Vietnam. Thai forces also undermined North Vietnamese efforts to extend Hanoi's influence into Laos, and about 40,000 Thai soldiers served in South Vietnam itself, as volunteers.

The Philippines provided similar support to US air operations via the US naval base at Subic Bay, which serviced the ships of the US Navy's Seventh Fleet. It also responded to President Johnson's call for "more flags" in South Vietnam by sending 1,500 troops to assist with civic action programs.

> "Have we **wrung every soldier** out of **every country** we can?"
>
> PRESIDENT JOHNSON IN A MEETING WITH HIS ADVISERS, JULY 21, 1965

Allies attack

ROK soldiers advance on an enemy position near Nha Trang, on the South Central Coast of Vietnam, in 1972. The South Korean Ninth Infantry (White Horse) Division was based at Nha Trang.

Rear sight

Carrying handle

Ejector port

Stock

Pistol grip

Trigger, protected
by a ring guard

Rear sling swivel

20-round detachable
box magazine

Battle of **Long Tan**

The 60,000 Australians who fought alongside US and ARVN troops in the war displayed resilience and courage in many operations. Nowhere was this more true than at Long Tan, where they were victorious despite being outnumbered twenty to one.

The First Australian Task Force's (1ATF) mission in Vietnam was to win control of Phuoc Tuy province. The bulk of 1ATF was made up of two infantry battalions, a squadron of armored personnel carriers (APCs), and two artillery batteries. They were joined by a New Zealand artillery battery that had been in Vietnam since 1965, and supported by US artillery and air support.

In June 1966, 1ATF established a base at Nui Dat, in the center of the province. They improved the village defenses and mounted a series of patrols, without major engagements. On July 29, however, Australian intelligence discovered a large force of Viet Cong and NVA troops, totaling some 2,500 men, in the surrounding area. The communists' mission was to show their strength to the local villagers by striking at the Australians and perhaps overrunning the base. Hanoi believed that a defeat of 1ATF would force the Australian government to scale back its role in the war.

The battle builds

At 2:43 a.m. on August 17, a bombardment rocked Nui Dat. Three infantry companies were sent out to locate the communist forces but the rest of the day passed without significant incident. On August 18, 105 infantrymen from D Company of the Sixth Battalion, Royal Australian Regiment, were sent out on patrol, joined by three New Zealanders, forward observers from the artillery battery. The commander of the patrol was Major Harry Smith. His men were carrying light loads of ammunition—120 rounds per rifle and 1,000 rounds for each machine gun.

Coincidentally, August 18 was the date when two rock 'n' roll acts were due to give the first-ever concert at Nui Dat. Many in D Company were annoyed to miss out. As they left base at 11 a.m., they could hear the musicians rehearsing.

« BEFORE

Over time, Australia's advisory role in Vietnam changed to direct combat.

JUNGLE BASE
In 1962, the Australian government sent 30 military advisers to South Vietnam. Three years later it sent a battalion, which would operate under American command. In 1966, the **First Australian Task Force** (1ATF), an independent unit of 4,500 men, was sent to **Phuoc Tuy province**, southeast of Saigon, an area covered in dense vegetation, with a long tradition of resistance to foreigners.

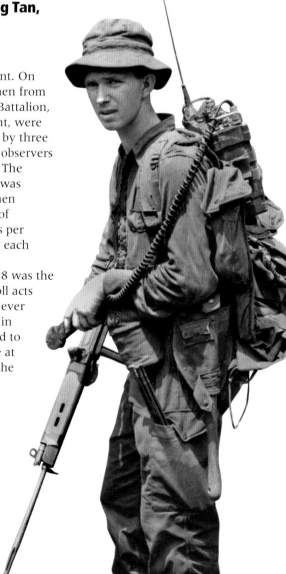

Australian signalman
Private Ken Meredith, with a radio on his back, waits for the order to return to base after the Battle of Long Tan. The signals team was vital to the coordination and conduct of battle.

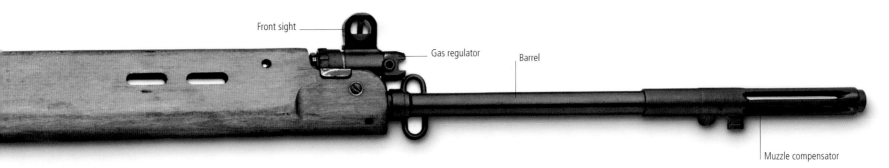

Front sight

Gas regulator

Barrel

Muzzle compensator

Self-loading rifle

The British-made L1A1 self-loading rifle was the standard rifle of the Australian Army from 1960 to 1992. The term self-loading referred to its repeat-fire action. Gas-operated, it ejected spent cartridges and loaded new ones automatically.

" Being **mortared** ... want **all artillery possible** ... Enemy left flank. **Could be serious.**"

RADIO MESSAGES FROM D COMPANY, AT 4:26 AND 4:31 P.M., AUGUST 18, 1966

Waves of attacks

D Company advanced toward Long Tan, 3 miles (5 km) from Nui Dat. They were unaware that there was an enemy regiment massed in a rubber plantation near the village. At 3:40 p.m., a platoon from D Company clashed with forward troops of the Viet Cong and forced them to withdraw. Returning in greater numbers half an hour later, the Viet Cong launched waves of attacks, hoping to encircle and destroy the Australians.

The situation looked bleak for the Australians. D Company was spread out, leaving some elements isolated. Monsoon rains decreased visibility, preventing the American jets called in to provide support from launching an airstrike. The beleaguered company relied on artillery batteries at Nui Dat, which bombarded within 50 yards of their position and fired nearly nonstop, even though their position was twice struck by lightning. To make the situation worse, a relief force was not immediately dispatched due to concern about leaving Nui Dat undefended. Reinforcements in the form of 10 armored personnel carriers and some 100 men eventually left at 6 p.m.

Holding out

Meanwhile, the Australians at Long Tan began to run out of ammunition. At 6:08 p.m., two Australian helicopters dropped fresh supplies. Smith reformed his company into a consolidated defensive position. Shortly afterward, the Viet Cong launched a massed assault, attacking on three sides. A combination of determined resistance and artillery

Long Tan Action
This commemorative artwork was painted by Australian war artist Bruce Fletcher in 1970. Some of the details—such as the headlamps on the APCs and the resupply by cargo hook—are embellishments. Supplies were dropped rather than lowered, and headlamps were turned off.

fire held them off until the arrival of the relief force as darkness fell at 7 p.m. This forced the enemy to withdraw, and within 15 minutes all firing had ceased.

The Australians had lost 18 and 24 were wounded. Sweeps of the area the next day showed that at least 245 Viet Cong had been killed (although the number may have been as high as 800). Australian dominance of Phuoc Tuy was not seriously challenged again.

AFTER »

After Long Tan, the Australian presence increased, peaking at 7,672 soldiers in 1968.

CORAL–BALMORAL
In the wake of the communist offensive known as **Mini Tet 210–11** » in May 1968, much of the First Australian Task Force was sent to Lai Khe to block enemy movement out of Saigon. Its main fire support bases in the area, Coral and Balmoral,

were attacked for 26 days, making **Coral–Balmoral** the Australians' bloodiest battle of the war, with 25 deaths. Australian involvement declined in 1970 as part of **Vietnamization 228–29** ».
The last Australian military personnel left in December 1972.

COMMEMORATION
Australia suffered 521 deaths during the the war. It holds Vietnam Veterans' Day on August 18, the day of the Battle of Long Tan.

LONG TAN MEDALLION

Firepower
US soldiers on a "Zippo track"— an armored personnel carrier equipped with a flame thrower— incinerate an area of the Iron Triangle during Operation Cedar Falls in January 1967.

« BEFORE

Binh Duong province had been a stronghold for insurgents since the days of French rule in Vietnam.

SECRET CHANNELS
The Viet Minh built a tunnel network in Binh Duong province during the **First Indochina War** « **26–27**. After the partition of the country at the end of that war « **38–39** North Vietnam began sending men and supplies along the **Ho Chi Minh Trail** « **56–57** to insurgents building a stronghold there.

SEARCH-AND-DESTROY
In 1966, General Westmoreland, commander of US forces in Vietnam since June 1964, introduced a strategy known as **search-and-destroy** « **102–03**.

War in the Iron Triangle

In 1967, US forces attacked North Vietnamese and Viet Cong strongholds in the border region northwest of Saigon. General Westmoreland's plan was to push enemy fighters into less populated areas, where US air power could demolish them.

The Iron Triangle was an area of approximately 120 square miles (310 sq. km) in the Binh Duong province, just a few hours' drive from Saigon. North Vietnamese forces and Viet Cong insurgents enjoyed strong support from local villagers in the area, and the Viet Cong had invested heavily in a fortified tunnel complex in the area of Cu Chi. The tunnels, like the Iron Triangle as a whole, provided a staging area for North Vietnamese and Viet Cong attacks on US and South Vietnamese units in the region and also on Saigon itself.

American forces made three major assaults on the Iron Triangle over a nine-month period between the fall of 1966 and May 1967. Operation Attleboro began in September 1966, Operation Cedar Falls in January 1967, and Operation Junction City lasted from February to May 1967.

Operation Attleboro

The main aim of Operation Attleboro was to destroy NVA and Viet Cong supply lines in the Iron Triangle. It developed into a major confrontation between a force of around 6,000 Viet Cong and NVA regulars and 22,000 US and ARVN troops. A series of intense battles over nearly three weeks resulted in heavy Viet Cong and NVA casualties (more than 1,000) and the seizure of oil stores, weapons, communication equipment, documents, and 2 million pounds (907,000 kg) of rice. However, as proved to be the case in most search-and-destroy operations, the Viet Cong chose to disengage from the fight when it was expedient to do so—in this case fleeing to sanctuaries across the Cambodian border. Once American forces had withdrawn from the area, Viet Cong and North Vietnamese forces simply returned.

Cedar Falls

Operation Cedar Falls was one of the largest American operations of the Vietnam War, involving some 30,000 US and ARVN troops. It relied on a "hammer-and-anvil"

Forced removal
A US Army Chinook helicopter arrives to evacuate civilians from the village of Ben Suc during Operation Cedar Falls in January 1967. Possessions were limited to what could be carried.

A month after Cedar Falls, US forces embarked upon the largest search-and-destroy operation of the war.

JUNCTION CITY
In February 1967, US forces embarked on **Operation Junction City 144–45 »**, the United States' only major airborne operation in South Vietnam. Its aim was to destroy COSVN, the communist command center.

PACIFICATION EFFORTS
Shortly after Cedar Falls, the US Marines stepped up their **Combined Action Program 140–41 »** to pacify villages cleared of Viet Cong. Similar efforts were made by the **Civilian Operations and Revolutionary Development Support (CORDS) 212–13 »**.

"The villages were just dust— ashes and dust."

COLONEL HARRY SUMMERS, ESSAY IN *VIETNAM MAGAZINE*, 1988

maneuver, in which some American forces were stealthily positioned to block an enemy retreat (the anvil) while others (the hammer) effectively drove the enemy through the jungle toward them. The battle plan also reversed the usual search-and-destroy methods by using American units to destroy suspected enemy villages, and then employing South Vietnamese units to detain and interrogate survivors. At the same time, Cedar Falls targeted the terrain with defoliants and Rome Plows (armored bulldozers) to destroy vegetation that could conceal insurgent activity.

In terms of casualties, territory, and war materiel captured, the operation was a resounding victory for the United States. However, the long-term goal of driving North Vietnamese and Viet Cong forces into unpopulated areas, where they could be destroyed from the air, was not met. They did retreat into an unpopulated area, but, as in Operation Attleboro, it was across the Cambodian border, beyond the reach of bombing authorized by Washington at this point in the war.

Cedar Falls also resulted in the demolition of an entire village, Ben Suc, which the Viet Cong used as a supply station on the Saigon River. Some 6,000 Vietnamese civilians, two-thirds of them children, were taken to "New Life Villages" by the ARVN. These were essentially refugee camps run by the South Vietnamese government. Families that once sustained themselves through farming suddenly struggled to find food. Meanwhile, US forces burned, then plowed under and bombed, Ben Suc, ensuring that the refugees could not return to their village.

Reaction in the US
To the American public, the military successes of war in the Iron Triangle began to pale beside the disturbing human dimensions of the refugee crisis it created. The American writer and

journalist Jonathan Schell, visiting Ben Suc for *The New Yorker* in the summer of 1967, reported on the US destruction of the village. The reports, which took up almost the entire July 15 edition of the magazine, highlighted problems with the ethics of the American approach in Vietnam, providing arguments for the growing antiwar movement in America.

Ready and waiting
Viet Cong guerrillas pose for a photograph as they track US movements in a jungle clearing of the Iron Triangle during Operation Cedar Falls.

« BEFORE

A century after the Civil War, African Americans still did not enjoy equal access to education, opportunities, or franchise in the United States.

FIGHT FOR THEIR RIGHTS
Historically, African Americans viewed military service positively, because it provided job skills and conferred respect that could result in better employment opportunities in civilian life. In World War II, African Americans embraced a **"Double V" strategy** that supported victory abroad while also demanding race equality in the United States. However, the pace of change remained slow after the war, leading to the modern **Civil Rights Movement** of the 1950s and 1960s.

Honoring Dr. King
On January 15, 1971, African American soldiers raise their fists in black power salutes for the birthday of the late Dr. Martin Luther King Jr. His assassination in 1968 caused some black troops to reevaluate their participation in the war.

The **African American** Experience

Race relations were tense in the early 1960s, even before the war drew hundreds of thousands of men of color into military service. Questions about the war reached a fever pitch as African Americans confronted a war many deemed exploitative and imperialist.

The Vietnam War was the first US conflict fought with a fully racially integrated military. However, while the Armed Forces were formally desegregated by 1954, discrimination remained, often preventing black soldiers from rising in the ranks. Racial tensions also continued to boil on the home front, especially as the Civil Rights Movement gained momentum. Dr. Martin Luther King Jr. remarked in 1967 that it was a cruel irony to watch black and white men kill and die together in Vietnam, all for a nation unable to seat them together in the same room.

Changing attitudes
During the Vietnam War, African Americans' traditional support for military service began to wane, and by 1969, 56 percent of African Americans opposed the war. Many of those already fighting for civil rights turned their voices against the draft, with organizations such as the Black Panthers and the Student Nonviolent Coordinating Committee (SNCC) denouncing the war. One black man evaded the draft by fleeing to Canada—calling himself not a draft dodger but a runaway slave. Generally, people

In Honor OF Dr. Martin Luther King Jr.

Pride in their culture

Troops often had tour jackets personalized with images and dates of service. This jacket, now in the National Museum of African American History and Culture in Washington, D.C., declared support for the black power movement.

of color were more likely than white Americans to oppose the war in Vietnam, because they saw it as exploitative.

Unfair draft

The Selective Service system was rife with inequality. An individual's draft status was determined at the local level, where young black men had to plead their cases to all-white draft boards that tended to bestow exemptions and deferrals onto more "promising" white college students. There were no black Americans on draft boards in Alabama, Arkansas, Mississippi, or Louisiana, and one member of a Louisiana draft board was even a Grand Wizard of the Ku Klux Klan.

Tensions grow

The assassination of civil rights leader Martin Luther King Jr. in 1968 was a turning point for

areas and bases such as Long Binh, where life was quieter, racial tensions rose to the surface.

Black power

As a result of President Johnson's so-called Project 100,000, from 1966 to 1969, thousands more African American soldiers were recruited for the war effort. Forty-one percent of the recruits under this program were African American, and many were not career soldiers—they hailed from poor urban areas. The majority were assigned to combat roles.

> " The only thing keeping … white GIs alive is us **soul brothers.** "
>
> GI CHARLES PORTER, FROM JAMES WESTHEIDER, *FIGHTING IN VIETNAM*…, 2007.

African Americans, inciting many to violence out of anger and grief. In Vietnam, some white soldiers openly celebrated Dr. King's death: a group dressed as Klansmen paraded around the base at Cam Ranh Bay, and Confederate flags were hoisted with pride.

In contested areas, where the potential for violence made unity and brotherhood an operational necessity, race relations were mostly good, and some men found that the experience of battle had caused deeply held prejudices to be cast aside. However, in rearward

KEY CONCEPT

THE DAP

African American soldiers in Vietnam often greeted one another with an elaborate handshake called the dap. Customized by unit or hometown, it had political overtones as a display of racial solidarity between black men, even those who had never met before. The dap could bring activities to a halt, as black soldiers dapped with every other black soldier in a club or chow line. Some commanders and white soldiers resented the practice, and black soldiers risked punishment for engaging in it.

Many of these recruits were more radicalized than those in earlier years. Some called themselves "bloods," and were influenced by the teachings of men such as Malcolm X in the black power movement. They objected to poor treatment and demanded the right to express their culture with hairstyles, jewelry, music, and the dap handshake. One black sailor described watching a man being forcibly shaved and then thrown into a cell for sporting a "short afro," while white men got away with hair "as long as a girl's."

Tensions sometimes erupted into violence, prompting the military to enact reforms in 1969. Military commanders began to name facilities for fallen black soldiers, include black entertainers on celebrity tours, play soul music on military-run radio, and make black grooming products available in the post

Support role

A soldier moves cases of ammo in 1967. The black recruits who arrived through Project 100,000 saw two extremes: dangerous combat missions or menial tasks.

AFTER

Despite receiving 20 of the 200 Medals of Honor awarded for valor in Vietnam, many black veterans found that military service did not improve their prospects upon returning home.

VETERANS' STRUGGLE

Many **black veterans 344–45 »** struggled to find jobs—one commented that a friend who had served time in prison had found work easier to come by than he had. However, some African Americans **remained in the military** after the war, and many black officers who served in Vietnam went on to have distinguished military careers.

VETERANS MARION EDMONDS JR. (RIGHT) AND JOSEPH MCLEAN JR. AT THE VIETNAM WOMEN'S MEMORIAL

exchange (PX). Reforms, however, could not eradicate racism in the military. African American soldiers often came together in solidarity to form groups such as the Unsatisfied Black Soldier to support each other, study their history, and lobby for the small comforts that white men took for granted.

An **African American Soldier**

Racial discrimination was deeply ingrained in American society. As a result, life for black soldiers differed greatly from their white counterparts—in terms of experience, opportunities, and dangers. Haywood T. Kirkland, a GI, described how black soldiers banded together in the face of racism, both in Vietnam and upon returning home.

Racialism was apparent in the base-camp area. Kirkland described rebel flags flying from jeeps and how it made him feel insulted and intimidated. He noted that, often branded troublemakers, black soldiers were sent to the fields, even those who had supply clerk or cook military specialties, while the white soldiers usually got jobs as supply clerks or in the mess hall.

This led the black soldiers at the base camp to close ranks and become more organized as a group. They began to discuss being part of the struggle of black people and how Vietnam was doing nothing for it. When Kirkland returned home, the reaction of his peers who questioned why he had gone to war led to him developing a more revolutionary, militant attitude, the seeds of which had been laid back in Vietnam.

" They killed Dr. King just before I came home. I felt used.**"**

HAYWOOD T. "THE KID" KIRKLAND, INTERVIEWED IN *BLOODS: AN ORAL HISTORY OF THE VIETNAM WAR BY BLACK VETERANS,* 1984

Out in the field
An African American soldier and his fellow men, members of the 173rd Airborne Brigade, continue their search-and-destroy mission after a helicopter drops supplies in Phuoc Tuy province, Vietnam, in June 1966.

Airpower over South Vietnam

American airpower was highly effective, in terms of supporting troops in the field, minimizing US casualties, and delivering injured people—sometimes including Vietnamese civilians and enemy combatants—to safety.

BEFORE

While the Viet Cong ruled the jungle of South Vietnam, US forces dominated the skies.

NEW PHASE
As **Operation Rolling Thunder** **《 94–95** intensified in the skies over North Vietnam, more ground troops were required in the South to **provide security for American bases**.

SUPPORTING OPERATIONS
The success of operations such as **Cedar Falls 《 122–23** depended on air support to bomb Viet Cong forces flushed into the open by US ground troops.

Transporting helicopters
Bell UH-1 helicopters are loaded onto a Douglas C-133 Cargomaster for delivery to Vietnam after being repaired in Texas. Logistics operators found that by dismantling the tails, they could transport five helicopters instead of three.

As American troop levels climbed over the course of 1965, and the US began to engage in offensive rather than defensive operations, more airpower was needed to support and protect these ground troops, deepening American investment in the war.

Supplying the troops
The vast majority of the millions of fixed-wing and helicopter sorties flown over South Vietnam were for flying cargo, known in the war's vernacular as trash hauling. Some of the crews flew a set schedule each day, making regular deliveries or providing a shuttle service on a predictable route. Others flew ad hoc supply missions that often took them into treacherous weather conditions or onto dangerous runways.

Helicopter pilots often struggled to identify landing zones (LZs) from the air, especially in remote areas. They relied on radar guidance, nearby features in the landscape, and smoke grenades released by troops on the ground. To ensure the grenades were not released by enemy combatants seeking to lure the pilot into a trap, the smoke was color coded.

Hauling cargo in South Vietnam might mean delivering hot meals to exhausted GIs on patrol in the jungle, or water and ammunition to a landing zone under fire, or perhaps flying a Conex

Dropping supplies
Supplies landed by helicopter are loaded onto a truck for distribution. Empty supply boxes were often filled with sand and used as defense against mortars.

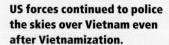

Danger zone
A First Air Cavalry Skycrane helicopter delivers ammunition and supplies to US Marines during the 77-day Siege of Khe Sanh, in February 1968. The aptly named Skycranes were also used to deliver heavy artillery.

AFTER

US forces continued to police the skies over Vietnam even after Vietnamization.

ONGOING DEPENDENCE
The process of **Vietnamization 228–29 》》**—turning the war over to South Vietnamese forces—facilitated American withdrawal from Vietnam. However, US airpower still played an important role. It prevented a rout during the ARVN's **Laotian incursion 264–65 》》** in 1971, then blunted North Vietnam's **Easter Offensive 276–87 》》** in 1972.

("container express") shipping crate of consumer goods, suspended in a net that could be easily dropped, to a mountaintop firebase. It could also mean flying combat troops into action, collecting the wounded and delivering them to hospitals, or removing the dead from the battlefield, a traumatic process that brought crews insulated to some degree by altitude directly into contact with the shooting war on the ground.

Whatever the mission, many US and ARVN Air Force aircraft risked small arms fire when taking off, landing, or flying just above treetops. Along the Ho Chi Minh Trail and in other hotspots along American bombing routes, airmen also faced antiaircraft artillery from the NVA and Viet Cong.

> US air superiority ensured that not a single American soldier in South Vietnam was killed on the ground by enemy aircraft during the Vietnam War.

Air strikes
The air war over South Vietnam also involved the tactical support of American ground troops, who could call for fixed-wing air strikes from Air Force or Navy bombers and covering fire from helicopter gunships. The range and power of such air strikes was much greater than that of conventional artillery and formed an important component of search-and-destroy strategy. Spooky, the modified Douglas AC-47, for example, could direct a curtain of machine gun fire onto a target for an hour or more. Weapons, houses, people—everything under fire from Spooky was turned to mulch.

Forward air controllers tried to exercise discretion over calling in air strikes when civilians were present. However, like the ground war strategy of search-and-destroy, the air war over South Vietnam often involved indiscriminate violence. American use of "free fire zones"— areas targeted by bombing and artillery in which all Vietnamese people who had not evacuated were assumed to be enemy combatants—resulted in unknown civilian casualties and contributed to South Vietnam's refugee crisis. Antipersonnel chemical weapons, such as napalm and white phosphorus, which caused untreatable wounds, resulted in further suffering.

American airpower directed at North Vietnamese forces proved a decisive advantage that kept North Vietnamese operations in check. Conversely, American bombing in populated areas undermined efforts to win the support of the South Vietnamese people, driving families and even whole villages to support the Viet Cong. Ultimately, perhaps, the indiscriminate nature of violence designed to protect American soldiers made them less safe.

" You almost **wanted things to happen** to see how good you were. **We were good.** That was really it."

JOHN NELSON, C-130 PILOT, INTERVIEW BY KIM SAWYER, DECEMBER 13, 2000. THE VIETNAM ARCHIVE, TEXAS TECH UNIVERSITY

Spooky in action
The crew of this Douglas AC-47 plane fire 7.62 mm rounds at an enemy target. These converted cargo aircraft, codenamed "spooky," provided support for ground operations at night.

US Helicopters

Allowing an unparalleled degree of maneuverability, helicopters had multiple uses, from delivering troops to combat zones to fire support, search-and-rescue, and reconnaissance. They came in many shapes and sizes.

1 **Hughes OH-6 Cayuse** This was deployed by the US Army for artillery observation and reconnaissance missions. 2 **Bell OH-58 Kiowa** Arriving in Vietnam in 1969, the OH-58 was frequently used for direct fire support, often equipped with a M134 7.62mm Minigun. 3 **Bell UH-1 Iroquois** Commonly known as the Huey, this workhorse performed diverse roles including air mobility, fire support, and medical evacuations. 4 **Sikorsky CH-53 Sea Stallion** The US Navy and the Marines used this heavy-lift transport helicopter, which was adept at recovering downed aircraft. 5 **Kaman HH-43 Huskie** Notable for its intermeshed rotors, the Huskie was a dedicated search-and-rescue helicopter. From 1966 to 1970, it completed 888 successful recoveries of servicemen. 6 **Boeing CH-47 Chinook** With its distinctive twin rotors, the Chinook was used to insert artillery batteries into difficult terrain and keep them supplied. 7 **Sikorsky CH-54 Tarhe** This unusual-looking helicopter was used for transporting awkward freight, such as armored vehicles and artillery. 8 **Sikorsky UH-34D Seahorse** The Marines liked the simplicity of this transport helicopter and adapted it to assault and evacuation. 9 **Bell AH-1G Cobra** This heavily armed attack helicopter was used to provide fire support to ground forces.

1 HUGHES OH-6 CAYUSE

2 BELL OH-58 KIOWA

3 BELL UH-1 IROQUOIS

4 SIKORSKY CH-53 SEA STALLION

5 KAMAN HH-43 HUSKIE

6 BOEING CH-47 CHINOOK

7 SIKORSKY CH-54 TARHE

8 SIKORSKY UH-34D SEAHORSE

9 BELL AH-1G COBRA

Digging In

Confronted with a much more powerful adversary, the Viet Cong leveled their odds on the battlefield by taking the war underground.

Vietnamese civilians and combatants—North and South—created thousands of miles of subterranean passageways and bunkers. Vietnam's limestone and clay soil was relatively easy to excavate, but also stable enough to support large, permanent underground dwellings.

Bunkers became a standard part of Vietnamese homes, particularly in contested areas where bombs and artillery were a constant threat. For South Vietnamese civilians who actively supported the insurgency, home bunkers also served a military purpose: hiding rice, ammunition, and other supplies, and sheltering guerrilla fighters.

17 The number of babies born in the tunnels of Vinh Moc during the course of the war.

‹‹ BEFORE

The Viet Cong drew upon their experience of fighting the French in the First Indochina War to help them confront US forces and the Saigon regime.

GOING UNDERGROUND
During the **First Indochina War** **‹‹ 26–27**, the Viet Minh relied on unconventional tactics and strategies to beat the French, also a more powerful opponent. These included building a complex network of **tunnels and bunkers** to conceal political and military operations, store weapons and supplies, and to shelter from bombs.

BOMBING THE TRAIL
South Vietnamese villages in the vicinity of the **Ho Chi Minh Trail** **‹‹ 56–57** supply lines were particularly vulnerable to American bombing.

Underground community

In Vinh Moc, a village in the heavily fortified DMZ, local people took the bunker concept a stage further. Starting in 1966, they began building permanent underground quarters. Eventually, 60 families relocated underground, living in a network of tunnels more than a mile long, safe from US bombs and artillery. The village tunnels included rooms for every family, a larger room for community meetings and school lessons, kitchens with special stoves to vent the smoke, an infirmary, and several secret entrances, including some that opened onto the beach. Villagers lived this way for five years, going into the open only at night to farm their land or to ferry food and other supplies to Viet Cong guerrillas on Con Co island, a communist base about 15 miles (24 km) offshore.

The villagers of Vinh Moc claimed that they did not lose a single life to American bombs after they relocated underground. However, life in tunnels was very difficult. Inhabitants endured stinging insects, venomous snakes, malaria, intestinal parasites, food shortages, and vitamin D deficiency. Rats and cassava, a nutritious root vegetable that grew wild, were mainstays of the villagers' diet. Tunnel dwellers

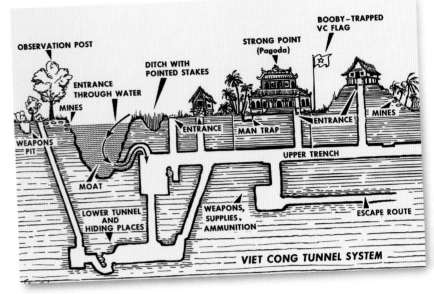

VIET CONG TUNNEL SYSTEM

Mapping the tunnels
This diagram, dating from 1966, is an American representation of a tunnel network. US training bases built tunnel systems to help prepare their troops. In reality, the tunnels were more complex, with many entrances and booby traps.

also risked tunnel collapse, oxygen deprivation, and death or injury from bombs.

The tunnel rats

Mapping and clearing the tunnels were lethal for the American, South Vietnamese, and Australian

Colored filters were sometimes used to send coded messages between tunnel rats

A compartment in the base stored a spare bulb and filters

soldiers who braved darkness, the danger of getting lost, and booby traps, especially when they ventured into a tunnel for the first time or dropped through a trap door between two levels of a tunnel system. They might be impaled by punji sticks—sharpened lengths of bamboo—stung by scorpions, or bitten by snakes tied to stakes in the roof. Early attempts to use dogs instead of people were soon abandoned, as dogs could not detect traps. Other precautions, such as using smoke to detect openings, or clearing tunnels with grenades had the drawback of alerting the enemy or destroying valuable intelligence.

An Australian combat engineer, Sandy MacGregor, is credited with being the first to discover the extent of the Cu Chi tunnels, an underground warren that spread for miles in the Iron Triangle northwest of Saigon. He coined the term "tunnel ferret" to refer to Australian soldiers charged with clearing tunnels, while Americans with the same duties were "tunnel rats."

MX-991/U flashlight
Tunnel rats, charged with investigating tunnel networks, were equipped with a flashlight, a pistol, and a knife. The angle-headed flashlights were waterproof and could be clipped to or suspended from the soldier's belt.

> " The Americans [would] **block** one or **two exits,** but there was **always some way out.** "
>
> FORMER VIET CONG INSURGENT TRAN THI GUNG, QUOTED IN *PATRIOTS: THE VIETNAM WAR REMEMBERED FROM ALL SIDES*, CHRISTIAN APPY, 2004

Some American tunnel rats were members of the First Infantry and 25th Infantry divisions who operated in teams of up to 13 men; others were ad hoc volunteers; they all had to be small, as the tunnels were tight. Two men went into a tunnel at one time; the job of the second man was to radio coordinates to the surface so that the tunnels could be mapped.

Worn down

Eventually, the cumulative effect of bombing, Rome Plows (armored bulldozers), and search-and- destroy infantry operations such as Cedar Falls and Junction City blunted the effectiveness of the Cu Chi tunnels. However, like the other tunnel networks in South Vietnam, Cu Chi was never eradicated. Where possible, tunnels were repaired and new ones built.

INSIDE A VIET CONG TUNNEL TODAY

The NVA and Viet Cong used the tunnel systems to help launch several major offensives, feats that are today celebrated in tours of the main tunnel systems.

LAUNCHING OFFENSIVES

Bombing limited the usefulness of the tunnel systems at Cu Chi and Vinh Moc, but US and South Vietnamese forces never succeeded in destroying the tunnels entirely. The tunnels of Cu Chi were used by Viet Cong guerrillas in the 1968 **Tet Offensive 176–93 》** and also in the **final offensive 316–17 》** of the war.

TOURIST ATTRACTIONS

Today, Cu Chi and Vinh Moc are important historical sites and open to tourists. **Tours of the tunnel systems** stress the ingenuity and fortitude of the Vietnamese people.

Captured guerrilla
A US infantryman trains his rifle on a Viet Cong guerrilla as he emerges from a tunnel entrance in the Trung Lap, about 25 miles (40 km) west of Saigon, in January 1966.

Tunnel Rat

Ruben Dominguez was trained to be a special electronic devices technician, but upon arrival in Vietnam, was given a new mission. Along with seven other "thin, small men" from his company, he was selected to infiltrate the elaborate underground networks of the Viet Cong as a tunnel rat. Dominguez was known as Ghost for his ability to explore the tunnels undetected.

Many tunnels were rigged with explosives and trip wires, but Dominguez claims the worst thing about the tunnels was the bugs, which would eat you alive. On one occasion he was sent down into a deep, complex hole, with very little room to move. Inside it was dark and smelled like urine and feces. He crawled along until he had almost reached the end and he was able to straighten up a little. He though he was walking through water—the flashlights tunnel rats were given were such poor quality it was difficult to see. There was the sound of digging up ahead and, as the light improved, a medical facility of some sort came into view.

"It wasn't water, it was what was left of the bodies … I got out of there."
US ARMY TUNNEL RAT RUBEN "GHOST" DOMINGUEZ, INTERVIEWED BY *VIETNAM VETERAN NEWS*, SEPTEMBER 2015

Rat in the hole
Pistol in hand, Sergeant Ronald Payne emerges from a Viet Cong tunnel in the so-called Hobo Woods, South Vietnam, on January 21, 1967. During his mission underground, Payne discovered detailed maps and plans belonging to Viet Cong guerrillas.

BEFORE

Past experience had taught the North Vietnamese and Viet Cong the importance of an effective supply line.

DEVELOPING THE TRAIL
During the war against the French, Viet Minh leaders in the mountains of the Laotian and Chinese border regions struggled to maintain contact with forces further south. To do so, they relied on a **network of footpaths** through the Truong Son Mountains. A generation later, when North Vietnam moved to a war footing, Colonel Vo Bam developed **a trail system ≪ 56–57** to supply the southern insurgents with war materiel and move fighters into the South.

B-52 strikes
From December 1965, the US stepped up its attacks on the trail by authorizing B-52 bombing. It is estimated that some 2 million tons of bombs were dropped on the Trail during the course of the war.

War on the Ho Chi Minh Trail

The United States waged war on the Ho Chi Minh Trail for years, without success. For every high-tech method it deployed, the Vietnamese people maintaining and using the trail found an effective and often ingenious workaround—albeit at tremendous human cost.

The Ho Chi Minh Trail was not a single trail, but rather a network of trails and roads that eventually reached 12,000 miles (19,300 km) in length. The trail varied in condition and sophistication over the years. Rustic paths, treacherous bamboo staircases, and rope bridges traversed by porters pushing bicycles gave way, by the early 1970s, to one-lane roads and bridges able to carry truck traffic.

1,000 MILES **(1,609 km)** The distance some North Vietnamese soldiers marched to reach South Vietnam before the introduction of trucks.

deep in the jungle, generally sleeping by day, in hammocks or in underground bunkers, and coming out at night to work. The threat of bombing was constant and living conditions were harsh. When food was scarce, they foraged for cassava or even moss. Malaria, dysentery, and trench foot were rampant, and medical care was rudimentary or nonexistent. When the workers returned home at war's end, they were pale, hairless, and frail, with health problems that would plague them for the rest of their lives.

Working the trail
North Vietnam deployed about 75,000 civilians to maintain the trail, including boys and girls in their teens. These Youth Volunteers could expect to spend time filling bomb craters, repairing bridges, and even detonating unexploded ordnance. They lived on the trail,

Repair and maintenance
A cave on the trail serves as an auto repair shop in 1968. In addition to underground storage areas and barracks, there were workshops for making and repairing military equipment and weapons.

"We are going to keep attacking you. Get smart ... Rally to the Government.**"**

LEAFLET DROPPED ON THE TRAIL, 1970

The US military tried to locate the trail more precisely by planting motion and sound sensors to detect traffic, and also developed "people sniffers," sensors designed to detect the smell of human urine and sweat. Army and Air Force pilots dropped leaflets in Vietnamese on the Trail, threatening more devastating bombing and urging workers and soldiers to desert.

Vietnamese trail workers found ingenious ways to undermine these efforts. They drove cattle down false trails to trigger motion and sound detectors, luring US bombers away from actual trail traffic. They hung bags of urine in trees far from the trail to fool the people sniffers. But mostly they worked diligently to repair by hand (or occasionally with heavy machinery) the damage wrought by bombs.

The Ho Chi Minh Trail played a role in all major offensives until the end of the war.

THE TRAIL GOES ON
The Ho Chi Minh Trail was used to position men and equipment for the 1968 **Tet Offensive 178–81 »**, North Vietnam's 1972 **Easter Offensive 276–87 »**, and the **Spring Offensive 316–17 »** of 1975. In 1971, South Vietnamese forces tried but failed to sever the trail in **Operation Lam Son 719 264–65 »**. Today, the modern vestiges of the trail provide an interior highway for Vietnam, bringing economic development.

Battle of wits
US Air Force and Navy planes bombed the trail heavily, hunting trail workers and North Vietnamese troops going south to fight. It is estimated that some 30,000 people died on the trail over the course of the war, though some put the figure as high as 100,000. However, because much of the trail was hidden under jungle canopy, American pilots grew frustrated that they were risking their lives to bomb what was often just trees.

To address this, US planes sprayed defoliants over the jungle to rid the trees of foliage. They even engaged in cloud seeding—spraying clouds with silver iodide and lead iodide to create rain—in order to slow truck traffic by reducing visibility or washing out roads and bridges. Project Popeye, a top-secret cloud-seeding operation over the Trail between March 1967 and July 1972, sought to extend the monsoon season each year by a month or more.

Lost cause
Despite their efforts, US forces failed to slow, let alone stop, traffic down the Ho Chi Minh Trail. Infiltration accelerated over the years, reaching 20,000 tons of war materiel per month by the late 1960s. At one point, US aerial surveillance detected 15,000 vehicles on the trail in a single day. Thousands of American and South Vietnamese soldiers and airmen were killed or injured trying to interdict the trail, an effort akin to holding back the tide.

Low-tech solution
Viet Cong guerrillas steer elephants through a high plateau forest in 1969. The elephants' ability to carry heavy loads and force their way through jungle made them a useful addition to a range of transportation methods.

Combined Action Program

With the Viet Cong taking refuge in remote villages of South Vietnam, the US Marine Corps turned to a new counterinsurgency method. The Combined Action Program sent Marines into towns and hamlets to forge positive relationships with the locals.

Despite General William Westmoreland's use of the attrition strategy and search-and-destroy tactics, the war remained a political struggle in need of political solutions. American units throughout South Vietnam embraced civic action as a means of winning hearts and minds, but the Marines built an entire program around it.

◀◀ BEFORE

Before America's role in the war escalated, US Special Forces made efforts to endear themselves to local civilian populations.

PRECEDENTS FOR CAP
The **Green Berets ‹‹ 64–65** had trained the Montagnards in counterinsurgency, but it was the Army's **Strategic Hamlet Program ‹‹ 70–71** that was the precursor of the Combined Action Program. Under the program, the Army **relocated** villagers to specially fortified hamlets and declared their former homes to be free-fire zones for rooting out insurgents in search-and-destroy operations.

GREEN BERET WITH VILLAGE CHILDREN

The US Army's primary strategy was one of attrition. It sought to prove to the North Vietnamese and Viet Cong that they could not win the war and should therefore seek a settlement. This strategy ensured a great deal of destruction, but it did little to stop NVA or Viet Cong fighters from receiving sanctuary at the village level. When the Army did engage in civic action to improve civil-military relations, it did so in addition to—not in lieu of—search-and-destroy operations. This shooting war was at odds with the Army's efforts to win hearts and minds.

Marine methods
The Marine Corps, operating primarily in the northernmost part of South Vietnam (called I Corps), offered an alternative model for conducting the war. Marine initiatives to improve villagers' standard of living included providing school supplies for children, tools for tradesmen, and equipment such as rice threshers for villages; sharing farming expertise to improve livestock and crop yields; and building dams and digging wells to provide clean drinking water and irrigation. They also provided medical care and distributed emergency food and clothing.

Patch of honor
The seal of the Combined Action Program shows a South Vietnamese flag joined with the Star Spangled Banner, in reference to the program's collaboration between US Marines and South Vietnamese militiamen.

The Marine Corps in Vietnam integrated civic action into doctrine through the creation of the Combined Action Program (CAP). It began as an improvised solution to a manpower shortage in 1965, when a junior officer suggested using South Vietnamese militia units to augment Marine strength. Formalized in 1967, CAP facilitated the creation of Combined Action Platoons, which consisted of a Marine rifle squad (comprised of 13–15 men), a Navy corpsman, and a local militia unit. Participation was voluntary on both sides, and only CAP Marines with Vietnam combat experience were eligible. They received about 10 days of training in Vietnamese language and customs before they were sent to live in a village to forge bonds with local people.

Working together
The platoons were strengthened by the complementary skills each side brought to the unit. The CAP Marines, who were on average about 20 years old, brought firepower, training, and also access to American resources such as medevac, artillery, and air support. The local militia, on the other hand, had varying degrees of military prowess—some were veterans of the First Indochina War—but also contributed key

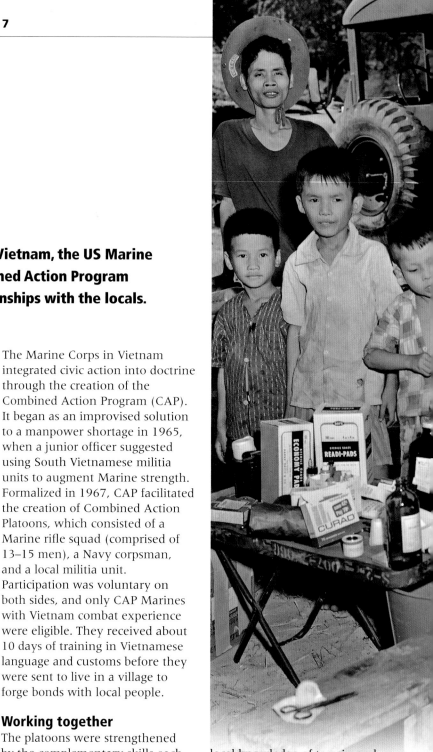

local knowledge of terrain and customs, as well as a fierce desire to defend their homes.

An effective model?
Ultimately, the Marine Corps declared the program a success, although the evidence is largely anecdotal. At its peak in 1970, the CAP had four Groups and more than 100 companies spread throughout I Corps. CAP platoons generally experienced lower casualty rates than units engaged in search-and-destroy operations, but they produced a higher body count relative to unit size. They also yielded positive results at lower cost. The Marine Corps boasted that no villages reverted

In 1971, the Combined Action Program was disbanded. The Phoenix Program became the main counterinsurgency tool.

SHIFTING RESPONSIBILITY
Nixon's policy of **Vietnamization 228–29 »**, which handed primary responsibility for combat operations over to the South Vietnamese Army (ARVN), led to the decline of the CAP program.

UNPOPULAR PROGRAM
In the final years of the war in Vietnam, counterinsurgency operations consisted mainly of those under the auspices of the **Phoenix Program 214–15 »**, a countrywide effort of American special forces units, CIA operatives, and the South Vietnamese military to "neutralize" suspected Viet Cong insurgents through incarceration or assassination. The fact that innocent civilians were caught in the dragnets of Phoenix caused **public support 254–55 »** for the Saigon government and the US presence in South Vietnam to wane.

Caring for the children
As other young patients look on, hospital corpsman Ronald L. Williams treats a boy with an infected leg in An Tan, during a medical civic action (MEDCAP) visit in June 1966. Williams served with the First Hospital Company, First Marine Division.

"[We got] information about VC activities **whispered through windows** in broken English."

MARINE CAPTAIN BING WEST, IN HIS MEMOIR, *THE VILLAGE*, 2003

to Viet Cong control, although that assertion might be rooted as much in Viet Cong pragmatism—why invest resources where public support is weak?—as it was in CAP platoons' ability to intimidate and persuade. Ultimately, the CAP platoons were too small, few, and unevenly distributed to have much impact on the war's outcome.

However, CAP Marines often made friends among the families in the villages to which they were assigned, and were invited to eat meals in civilians' homes. Friendships between CAP platoon members and South Vietnamese villagers who came to rely on them for security were remembered long after the war's end.

KEY CONCEPT

PSYCHOLOGICAL OPERATIONS

The United States also used psychological persuasion, known as PSYOPS, to win over the populace—and to threaten the NVA and Viet Cong. General Westmoreland claimed that PSYOPS and civic action were at the heart of counterinsurgency. A key tactic of PSYOPS was to drop leaflets from aircraft. Typically, these would urge people to reject the Viet Cong and support the South Vietnamese government.

« BEFORE

The US Navy had been a source of support for the South Vietnamese government since the 1950s.

ADVISORY ROLE

In the 1950s, the US Navy provided guidance to South Vietnam's Navy and advised the government on infrastructure projects and civic action programs. These **advisory and nation-building missions** continued throughout the war.

FIRST COMBAT ACTION

The US Navy's airstrikes against North Vietnam after the **Tonkin Gulf incident « 80–81** in 1964 marked the United States' first overt combat operations of the war.

The **Naval War**

The US Navy launched airstrikes, engaged in search-and-destroy operations, and transported aircraft and artillery. It was the first service to go into formal combat operations in 1965 and it was the last one to leave Vietnam a decade later.

Although the US Navy did not have to contend with serious threats from North Vietnamese naval forces on the high seas, the Seventh Fleet provided critical support to the war effort in a broad range of capacities. At Yankee Station, a point off the central coast of South Vietnam, multiple aircraft carriers launched airstrikes against North Vietnam and the Ho Chi Minh Trail as part of operations Flaming Dart, Rolling Thunder, and Linebacker, among others. Warships at Yankee Station also shelled the coast of North Vietnam and provided artillery support to American units operating in South Vietnam. At Dixie Station, much farther south, a single-carrier group provided close air support for US troops engaged in combat operations. Other Navy missions included advising the Republic of Vietnam Navy, transporting troops to Vietnam, building US bases,

Aircraft carrier
The USS *Enterprise*, here loaded with helicopters and planes during the evacuation of Saigon in April 1975, was used to launch airstrikes at various points in the war.

Harassing communist targets
The USS *New Jersey* fires shells into North Vietnam from the Gulf of Tonkin. The *New Jersey* was a heavy bombardment battleship, equipped with 16-inch guns.

Fatal accidents

Navy personnel engaged in riverine operations faced many of the same hardships and threats suffered by ground troops engaged in search-and-destroy operations farther north. However, for sailors in the Seventh Fleet, the threat of accident—fires, helicopter crashes, collisions, explosions, and errors

> " They are **tigers in every respect ...** Tales of their courage are **legendary.**"

REAR ADMIRAL ELMO R. ZUMWALT, DESCRIBING THE BROWN WATER NAVY, 1969

constructing and maintaining South Vietnamese port facilities, providing medical support in shipboard surgical hospitals, and coastal defense.

Intercepting supply lines

One of the Navy's most important roles was disrupting the so-called Sihanouk Trail—the North Vietnamese supply route into South Vietnam via the port of Sihanoukville in Cambodia. Weapons and supplies were smuggled on sampans and fishing trawlers. Initially, the Republic of Vietnam Navy addressed such smuggling, but its efforts were ineffective and prone to corruption. In 1965, the US Navy and Coast Guard launched Operation Market Time to intercept and search thousands of vessels. The Brown Water Navy, which patrolled inland waterways, performed a similar function in the Mekong Delta and the Ca Mau Peninsula, where transportation routes largely consisted of rivers and canals.

Search-and-destroy

The Brown Water Navy also conducted search-and-destroy missions against the Viet Cong, which had long operated in areas that infantry equipped with tanks and heavy artillery could not reach. In 1965, the Seventh Fleet's

70,000 The number of junks, sampans, and fishing boats, inspected by the Coastal Surveillance Force in 1966–67.

River Patrol Force launched Operation Game Warden, an attack on Viet Cong capabilities in the Mekong Delta. Consisting of small patrol boats and attack helicopters, it imposed a curfew on the local population and limited Viet Cong movements, securing waterways and preventing attacks on regional cities.

In 1967, the newly formed Mobile Riverine Force (MRF) extended the Navy's capabilities by pairing Army infantry with Navy armored assault boats. The initial operation in the Rung Sat Special Zone—a vast area of mangrove forest south of Saigon— involved a "hammer-and-anvil" attack in which riverine infantry landed to drive Viet Cong forces toward a second attack force delivered by helicopter. The operation helped secure provincial capitals and prevented the Viet Cong from mining water approaches to Saigon.

launching aircraft—exceeded the risk of injury from attack. The heaviest Navy casualties due to enemy action occurred in 1968, when Viet Cong divers detonated two mines alongside the USS *Westchester County*, killing 25 sailors. In 1967, the Navy's deadliest accident of the war resulted from the discharge of a Zuni rocket on the USS *Forrestal* that caused a chain of explosions that killed 131 sailors and injured 160 more.

AFTER ⟫

The US Navy played a vital role in US retaliatory action following North Vietnam's Easter Offensive in 1972.

LINEBACKER RAIDS
The US Navy took part in the **Linebacker bombing campaign, 292–93 ⟫**, unleashed on North Vietnam after the Easter Offensive in 1972. This and the Navy's mining of **Haiphong Harbor 290–91 ⟫** increased pressure on North Vietnam to accept a negotiated peace settlement.

LAST FORCE OUT
Long after most US ground units had withdrawn from Vietnam, the US Navy continued to provide **advisory, logistical**, and even **combat support** to the South Vietnamese. Navy ships stationed off shore provided the last hope to civilians seeking refuge during the **fall of Saigon 324–25 ⟫**.

Riverine operation
The crew aboard an inshore patrol craft (PCF), known as a swift boat, fire at Viet Cong positions in a search-and-destroy mission along the Duong Keo River on the Ca Mau Peninsula in April 1969. Riverine assault craft were heavily armed and armored.

BEFORE

Previous efforts to clear the area northwest of Saigon had had mixed results.

LIMITED RESULTS

Operation **Cedar Falls ≪ 122–23** in the Iron Triangle a month before Operation Junction City resulted in heavy enemy casualties and the seizure of weapons and rice stockpiles. But US forces and the ARVN **lacked the resources to occupy and patrol the area**, and the population soon moved back in. This showed the limitations of such operations.

TECHNOLOGY

M18 CLAYMORE MINE

Triggered remotely by an electric detonator wire, the Claymore was an antipersonnel mine. Highly lethal, it was used in ambush, often placed alongside Viet Cong trails, and to guard defensive positions such as fighting holes, ready to deliver a fan of 700 spherical steel balls to any enemy combatant who came within 50 yards (46 meters). Scissor-like legs secured it into the ground. In Vietnam, the Claymore was carried by all infantry units. To prevent accidents, "Front toward enemy" was always embossed on the side.

Intelligence gathering

Members of a US Army Long Range Reconnaissance Patrol (LRRP) prepare to set out on patrol during Operation Junction City. LRRP teams collected intelligence on the movement of communist fighters and coordinated artillery and air strikes.

Operation Junction City

A classic search-and-destroy operation, Junction City was intended to deal a deathblow to the insurgents' infrastructure in South Vietnam. However, Viet Cong and NVA forces recognized the folly of trying to combat the US war machine and sought to outlast it instead.

Operation Junction City was the largest joint US–ARVN operation of the war. Launched on February 22, 1967, it lasted 82 days and involved 45,000 US troops, including the war's only significant combat parachute assault. The primary area of operations, War Zone C in Tay Ninh province northwest of Saigon, was relatively flat and dry compared to the saturated paddies of the Mekong Delta and the steep hillsides of the Central Highlands. As a result,

Operation Junction City saw the heaviest use of armored vehicles during the war.

The objective

As with other search-and-destroy operations, the objective of Junction City was to clear the region of North Vietnamese and Viet Cong fighters. This time, however, the operation also involved a specific target: the

Central Office South Vietnam (COSVN), the mobile headquarters of the 2,000 or so staff who coordinated operations between North Vietnamese and Viet Cong fighters. Like

Armored personnel carrier
The relatively flat terrain of War Zone C was ideal for the US Army's M113 armored personnel carrier, nicknamed the Green Dragon by the Viet Cong. Made of aluminum, it offered its two-man crew protection, yet was lighter than a tank and had an off-road speed of 29 mph (47 km/h).

AFTER »

Operation Cedar Falls, Junction City employed a "hammer-and-anvil" technique to drive enemy forces overland toward destruction.

Taking position
Under the guise of conducting routine combat patrols, US forces were placed in position for the assault. Then, on the morning of February 22, eight infantry battalions under the control of the 25th Infantry Division helicoptered into landing zones, where they met little to no resistance. At the same time, 16 Lockheed C-130 aircraft dropped 845 airborne infantry into position. Collectively, these forces then extended their lines almost to the Cambodian border, creating a horseshoe-shaped cordon designed to trap the Viet Cong so that US forces could hunt them down. In fact, for the next month, American forces had only light contact with the Viet Cong, who were content to remain hidden.

> **249** The number of US helicopers used to drop eight infantry battallions into position on February 22.

Battle phase
The second stage of Junction City began in mid-March, when US forces set up Katum Special Forces camp and fire support bases to establish a more permanent American presence in the region. During this phase of the operation, Viet Cong forces mounted substantial resistance, especially on the grounds of a former rubber plantation. These battles forged a pattern, in which the Viet Cong launched deadly assaults against US forces, who beat them back with overwhelming firepower, inflicting heavy casualties. For example, fighting at the fire support base near Ap Bau Bang resulted in three Americans killed and 60 wounded, while 227 Viet Cong fighters were found on the battlefield when dawn broke.

Boosting morale
Overall, Junction City had mixed success. The airborne assault was spectacular, making for dramatic headlines on the home front and boosting the morale of US troops in Vietnam. However, the Viet Cong did not behave as anticipated. For the most part, the guerrilla fighters hid or retreated across the border into Cambodia, whose neutrality prohibited US forces from following. Although US forces discovered a cache of enemy propaganda suggesting that a component of COSVN was active in the region, the organization as a whole was neither discovered nor seriously compromised by the operation.

Junction City's most significant contribution to the American war effort was its body count. While US forces lost 282 dead in 11 weeks of fighting, the Viet Cong lost perhaps 10 times as many fighters. And yet, it made little difference in their ability to wage war against the South Vietnamese government and the American and South Vietnamese soldiers charged with defending it.

AFTER »

Junction City was ultimately ineffective. The COSVN remained elusive and retaining control of the Iron Triangle proved impossible for the US and its allies.

RETURN OF THE VIET CONG
ARVN forces charged with maintaining security in the Iron Triangle after the initial US assault proved either too small for the task or were simply not up to it, allowing **North Vietnamese and Viet Cong fighters to filter back**. US forces continued to hunt for the COSVN, whose staff increasingly took sanctuary across the border in Cambodia, beyond the reach of American troops.

Junction City jump
US paratroopers parachute into the drop zone, a flat and clear area west of Katum Special Forces camp, in their only major combat assault of the war. In general, Vietnam's rugged terrain made parachute assaults impractical.

Chemical Warfare

The US military's technological superiority was particularly evident in the activities of the Army's Chemical Corps, which brought the products of American laboratory research straight to the battlefields of Vietnam.

« B E F O R E

Chemical weapons, in the form of poisonous gas, were developed and used in World War I.

CHEMICAL R&D
The US Army's Chemical Warfare Service (CWS), founded in 1918, continued to develop gas weapons, but never used them during World War II. The CWS did, however, perfect the use of **incendiary devices** such as bombs and flamethrowers. Rebranded as the Chemical Corps in 1946, it also developed biological weapons.

Improvised explosives
A US soldier lies wounded by a Viet Cong booby trap made from white phosphorus scavenged from unexploded American ordnance. White phosphorus grenades were widely used to hit Viet Cong tunnel networks.

Chemical warfare in Vietnam was mostly one-sided: the US was the only combatant capable of regularly deploying such weapons. The use of chemical weapons opened another front for the antiwar movement, which targeted chemical manufacturers such as Monsanto and Dow Chemical for their support of the war. Activists launched boycotts, disrupted job fairs, picketed chemical plants, and lobbied elected officials to regulate the chemical industry and rein in its ability to profit from the misery and horror of war.

Operation Ranch Hand
In the 1960s, the Army Chemical Corps was charged with protecting US personnel from chemical attack, but also with perfecting and deploying chemical weapons. In Vietnam, the Chemical Corps partnered with the Air Force to conduct Operation Ranch Hand— the aerial spraying of chemical defoliants on forests and farmland from 1961 to 1971, with the stated aim of killing roadside vegetation, defoliating jungle hiding enemy troops, and destroying civilian crops suspected of being grown for enemy use.

Agent Orange
The most widely used herbicide in South Vietnam was Agent Orange, named for the orange band on the barrels in which it was stored. It consisted of two chemical herbicides mixed with diesel fuel or kerosene, but also a manufacturing byproduct, Dioxin, considered to be the most toxic molecule synthesized by man. Agent Orange was sprayed liberally by US planes.

The use of herbicides had profound consequences for the Vietnamese. Within two weeks of spraying, leaves would fall from trees or plants, remaining bare until at least the next rainy season. Destroyed crops exacerbated poverty and drove people from their land, contributing to the refugee crisis. The effect of multiple sprayings permanently destroyed vegetation and disrupted animal populations. Dioxin, which is associated with birth defects and diseases, also filtered into the soil. While international law prohibits chemical warfare against people, US courts ruled that Ranch Hand targeted plants, indemnifying the US from liability.

> **500,000** **ACRES The combined** area of South Vietnamese farmland sprayed with herbicide to destroy crops that could support the Viet Cong.

Incendiary substances
US chemical warfare in Vietnam also involved incendiary devices— ostensibly designed to burn structures but also highly effective against people. Essentially jellied

Jungle in flames
A US soldier clears a path through Vietnamese jungle with a flamethrower. In 1978, the US banned the use of flamethrowers in future combat, due to their "indiscriminate" and "excessively injurious" effects.

gasoline, napalm is chemically engineered to stick to its target; it burns incredibly hot and rapidly deoxygenates the air, suffocating people caught in confined spaces.

In Vietnam, the US Air Force dropped napalm bombs over villages or forests sheltering enemy combatants, resulting in massive orange fireballs. Soldiers also used napalm in flamethrowers to target bunkers and tunnels. White phosphorus, an incendiary and smoke-producing agent, was also used in Vietnam. Its distinctive white plumes were useful as markers and smokescreens. Like herbicides, incendiaries were effective but controversial, because they led to untreatable wounds. White phosphorus would continue to burn until it was completely deprived of oxygen, resulting in horrific burns and lethal poisoning.

Incendiaries did not discriminate between civilians and insurgents hiding in their midst. This resulted in thousands of civilian casualties, who overwhelmed the South Vietnamese health service. Both napalm and white phosphorus resulted in wounds that the human body was not equipped to heal, so their victims were usually left to die, untreated, in order for scarce medical resources to be directed toward those with a better chance of survival.

Deathly spray
American UC-123K aircraft spray Agent Orange on a Mekong Delta mangrove forest in 1970. The converted gliders had jet engines fitted and dispensers on their wings and tails, optimized to spray three gallons of pesticide per acre.

" Beautiful shade **trees** along the streets in … Da Nang are **dead or dying.**"

LIEUTENANT COLONEL JIM COREY, DEPUTY CHIEF OF CORDS, TO HIS SUPERIORS, MARCH 1969

AFTER

Criticism of America's use of napalm and defoliants in Vietnam continues, as the side effects of Agent Orange linger.

CONTROVERSY CONTINUES
Generations after the war, Agent Orange is believed to cause **birth defects** and many serious ailments, feeding continued public outrage. This opposition, and a string of accidents in the 1960s, led to the **disbanding** of the Chemical Corps from 1973 to about 1980. Now **active again**, Chemical Corps' new role includes preparing for chemical attack and mass decontamination.

THE WAR CATASTROPHE

AUSTRALIAN POSTER CRITICIZING AGENT ORANGE

147

Rain of fire
Huts in the South Vietnamese hamlet of Ban De burst into flames under a fall of phosphorus explosives, dropped by an American A-1 Skyraider aircraft during a 1966 strike against Viet Cong positions.

‹‹ BEFORE

When Ho Chi Minh declared the Democratic Republic of Vietnam independent from French control in 1945, he understood this to include all of Vietnam.

DREAM DENIED
The **Geneva Accords ‹‹ 34–35** promised to make that understanding a political reality through countrywide elections to be held in 1956, but the United States and southern Vietnamese people who did not want to live under communism had other ideas: the creation of an **independent Republic of Vietnam below the 17th parallel**. The vision of an independent, communist Vietnam, which Ho Chi Minh and his followers had been **fighting for**, slipped out of reach.

The North Vietnamese Army

For the North Vietnamese, the war was part of a decades-long struggle to defend their homeland from foreign aggressors—Japanese, French, and American alike—to depose the regime in Saigon, and to unify the nation under the communist leadership of Ho Chi Minh.

The Viet Minh agreed to the terms of the 1954 Geneva Accords because they had promised to reunify Vietnam under leadership determined by national elections in 1956, which virtually guaranteed victory for Ho Chi Minh and his movement. Ngo Dinh Diem, president of the newly formed Republic of Vietnam (South Vietnam), refused to hold these elections. The politburo of the Democratic Republic of Vietnam (North Vietnam) believed that they had no alternative but to return to war to unify the country.

Patriotic society
However, after eight years of war against France, North Vietnam knew it was not yet strong enough to win against the South. "Build up the north, look to the south" was a key North Vietnamese slogan during this time as they worked to modernize and professionalize the People's Army of Vietnam (North Vietnamese Army, or NVA). New ranks and a formal order of command were created, making the NVA more reflective of modern Western armies, and the NVA also acquired weapons from China and the Soviet Union. Tanks and aircraft from these allies allowed the NVA to form artillery and air

Ready to fire
North Vietnamese forces line up, ready to fire, during a training exercize in Bach Dang in July 1966. The NVA practiced tactical maneuvers and field exercises, hoping to make up for its lack of firepower by keeping its men well-prepared and well-disciplined.

Joining the fight

During the 1950s and 1960s, artists often created works that served a propaganda purpose. This 1954 poster shows women and families saying goodbye to men leaving to fight in the NVA.

force units, but the army continued to use the majority of its men in infantry units.

Patriotic society

In the 1960s and 1970s, war was all many North Vietnamese youth had ever known—against Japan, France, and now the United States. North Vietnam's one-party government ensured that the communists had no opposition. Northerners received information about the world—and the war—exclusively through state-controlled media that reinforced the patriotic necessity of compliant support.

All of North Vietnam was mobilized for war. Primary school children were inculcated in a love for "Uncle Ho" and loyalty to the

communist party; teenage Youth Volunteers cleared the Ho Chi Minh Trail of mines for years on end; elderly men served in village civil defense units that assisted with the aftermath of US bombing raids. The picture North Vietnam presented to the world was of

LÀM GẠO TIẾP TẾ BỘ ĐỘI

"Nothing is more **precious** than **independence** and freedom."

HO CHI MINH, AS FREQUENTLY QUOTED IN NORTH VIETNAMESE PROPAGANDA

unity and determination, even as its people endured grief, frustration, and exhaustion.

A tough fight

North Vietnam began to send NVA units southward in earnest in 1959. They also encouraged insurgent activity by the National Liberation Front (Viet Cong) in South Vietnam; and coordinated the war effort between the two. Like their American counterparts, soldiers in the NVA served a long way from home, but their tours of duty were indefinite. The journey into South Vietnam was occasionally

undertaken by truck but more often, especially during the early years, involved long marches over rugged terrain. Although trail workers deferred to soldiers for rations and shelter, conditions were still extremely harsh. After surviving months on the trail, NVA soldiers often lived exposed to the elements in temporary encampments, dark tunnels, and cramped bunkers.

Supply lines were also tenuous. NVA units foraged on the march, procuring rice voluntarily from sympathetic peasants and taking it by force from those in opposition. Rations were meager and, compared to US infantry, North Vietnamese soldiers traveled light:

a change of clothes, nylon tent and poncho, hammock, canteen, bowl and spoon, first-aid kit, ammunition pouch, and perhaps a week's worth of rice, as well as personal items such as photographs of family. They also carried machetes, shovels, flashlights, medical supplies, and

700 BILLION DOLLARS
The sum given to the NVA by the Soviet Union in 1967 alone, far surpassing China's contributions.

weapons, though these were often in short supply. Injured and ill soldiers received treatment in jungle hospitals before returning to duty. For those too gravely wounded to fight any longer, the journey home—on stretchers carried by porters back up the Ho Chi Minh Trail—took several months and could prove fatal.

AFTER »

As American support for the war declined, the North Vietnamese politburo knew that it merely had to survive, not defeat US forces.

SEEING IT THROUGH
US forces would eventually **withdraw 228–29 »** from Vietnam, leaving the South Vietnamese Army (ARVN) alone to fight. The ARVN time and again **proved itself weak**, while the NVA only became stronger.

After US withdrawal in 1973, North Vietnam set its sights on defeating the ARVN and deposing the Saigon regime in order to reunify the country. **Vicious fighting** led to hundreds of thousands of deaths on both sides, before Vietnam was formally **reunified 332–33 »** as the Socialist Republic of Vietnam in 1975, a communist regime.

Celebrating success

This enamelled aluminum badge commemorates the "5-8" victory of August 5, 1964—Operation Pierce Arrow, during which the first US planes were shot down—and was later awarded to NVA soldiers who shot down US aircraft.

1 DEGTYAREV LIGHT MACHINE GUN

2 MAT-49

3 TYPE 56 LIGHT MACHINE GUN

4 TYPE 56 ASSAULT RIFLE

5 SKS RIFLE

6 AMMUNITION BELT

7 7.62×39MM AMMUNITION CLIP

8 7.62×54MM CARTRIDGES

9 TOKAREV TT PISTOL

10 LUGER P.08

11 WALTHER P38

12 RPG-7

13 COMPASS

14 WATER BOTTLE

15 TROPICAL CORK HELMET

16 TUBULAR SCARF

17 NVA UNIFORM

NVA Gear and **Weaponry**

The North Vietnamese Army's main ground forces launched sustained, comprehensive, and successful offensives using modern weaponry supplied by their Chinese and Soviet allies.

1 **Degtyarev light machine gun** NVA infantry used this Soviet-designed weapon. 2 **MAT-49** This French submachine gun was seized in large numbers after French withdrawal from Vietnam. 3 **Type 56 light machine gun** A copy of the Russian RPD machine gun, the Type 56 was made in China. 4 **Type 56 assault rifle** Simple, reliable, and accurate, this Chinese copy of the AK-47 was the NVA's main infantry weapon. 5 **SKS rifle** The Russians exported this semiautomatic carbine to the NVA. 6 **Ammunition belt** This fed into the drum of the RDP/Type 56 light machine gun. 7 **7.62×39 mm ammunition clip** Stripper clips of bullets like this were used for AK-47 and Type 56 rifles. 8 **7.62×54 mm**

cartridges Sniper rifles such as the Moisin-Nagant used these. 9 **Tokarev TT pistol** Reliable and powerful, this was a popular semiautomatic. 10 **Luger P.08 pistol** Lugers, captured in previous wars, were supplied by the Russians and the Chinese. 11 **Walther P38** Small numbers of these German handguns were supplied by the Soviets. 12 **RPG-7** This Russian grenade launcher was a crucial antitank weapon. 13 **Compass** Navigating dense forests depended on having a compass. 14 **Water bottle** China supplied water bottles in large numbers. 15 **Tropical cork helmet** Helmets were also made from pressed paper or plastic. 16 **Tubular scarf** This was used to carry rice. 17 **NVA Uniform** Green, wool uniforms were worn from 1966.

Vietnamese Women at War

The war profoundly altered life for Vietnamese women on both sides of the conflict. Even those who did not actively participate in the war effort experienced terrible hardships, including the violent deaths of loved ones, homelessness, and hunger.

DOCTOR (1942–70)

DANG THUY TRAM

Born in Hue in 1942, Dang Thuy Tram volunteered for service in North Vietnam fresh out of medical school in 1966. For four years, she worked as a battlefield surgeon, providing care to communist combatants and civilians from a mobile clinic hidden in the jungle, until she was killed in 1970. Tram's diary, found by an American GI, was returned to her family in 2005 and published, to great acclaim.

The wars of the 20th century created opportunities for Vietnamese women, because their labor and skills were too valuable not to be utilized in the fight for national independence. Traditional Vietnamese culture offered women few options beyond being wives and mothers, but in wartime, they often assumed more public roles.

A wider family

Family was—and remains—of paramount importance to the Vietnamese people, and the communists were quick to exploit the power of family to mobilize political support. They argued that one's family did not just consist of blood relations but of the entire Vietnamese nation, and that service to the nation was therefore also service to one's family. By framing political struggle in this way, the communists encouraged many women to step into roles previously reserved for men.

North Vietnam

In North Vietnam, women worked to produce uniforms and supplies for the North Vietnamese Army (NVA). They also served in local militias, providing security to their communities and even capturing downed US airmen. Thousands of teenage girls volunteered for service maintaining the Ho Chi Minh Trail, including disarming

"Our **resentment** will be changed into silk."

POEM BY AN ANONYMOUS NORTH VIETNAMESE SEAMSTRESS, 1966

unexploded artillery shells and mines. Women also worked as porters on the trail, pushing heavy bicycles or carrying boxes on their backs for hundreds of miles.

Women were among the North Vietnamese support personnel who went south to provide medical care, organize logistics, and serve as spies in support of the NVA and the Viet Cong. They lived in danger and deprivation, returning home to North Vietnam only at war's end. Conditions were difficult, especially for women. They lacked sanitary supplies to care for themselves, and many were rendered unable to bear children due to poor diet and constant stress.

South Vietnam

The political situation in South Vietnam demanded that women choose sides, with some supporting the Saigon government, others supporting the Viet Cong, and most just trying to survive. Many soldiers in the South Vietnamese Army (ARVN) kept their families with them in the field, and thousands of women therefore acted as "soldiers without serial numbers," even defending camps against Viet Cong attack.

Starting in 1965, women could also serve in the Women's Armed Forces Corps, an ARVN auxiliary that relegated women to support roles. In the Viet Cong, on the other hand, women provided logistic support, medical care, and intelligence but also fought in the "long-haired army."

« **BEFORE**

Vietnamese history and legend feature several female warriors, but the lives of most Vietnamese women before the war revolved around the home.

LIFE VERSUS LEGEND

The **Trung Sisters** led a rebellion against China in the first century CE. Two hundred years later, **Trieu Au**, a "Vietnamese Joan of Arc," reputedly rode into battle against the Chinese on an elephant. Despite such examples, women **struggled to assert their place** in society—religious beliefs, Confucian principles, and custom often limited their influence to family and home.

Adopting the new

US Major Kathleen Wilkes and Sergeant First Class Betty Adams look on as new recruits to South Vietnam's Women's Army Corps trade their *ao dai* (a traditional dress that fell out of favor in North Vietnam) for ARVN uniforms.

Staying on guard
Two female workers talk in a factory serving the North Vietnamese Army in Hanoi in 1965. As US air attacks on North Vietnam increased, workers took to keeping rifles close by as a precaution.

Civilian women

Due to the ARVN draft on the one hand, and the appeal of fighting for the insurgency on the other, the men left in villages and refugee camps tended to be very old or very young. It was not unusual, in contested areas, for young women to be widowed many times as their husbands were killed in combat. This left women and girls to support entire families. Some found work on American bases: digging ditches, peeling potatoes, or as "hootch maids" cleaning up after American servicemen. Lacking other options, many women also worked as prostitutes in the nightclubs and massage parlors that sprang up around the bases, or offered themselves directly to US soldiers, sometimes in exchange for food. Whatever choices these women made, they were usually driven by their commitment to family.

Vietnamese women continued to assert their influence on the war until its final days. Notably, Nguyen Thi Binh served as the foreign minister of the Provisional Revolutionary Government (Viet Cong) and was one of the signers of the 1972 Paris Accords.

Appealing image
This communist propaganda poster reading "She made a determined attack on enemy positions" encourages women to serve as combatants. Others took a different approach, showing women harvesting rice or holding children.

LÊ THỊ HỒNG GẤM

TẤN CÔNG KIÊN QUYẾT QUẢ CẢM BÁM TRỤ VỮNG CHẮC KIÊN CƯỜNG

A F T E R

After the war, most Vietnamese women returned to traditional roles in the domestic sphere.

HOPE FOR CHANGE
Many South Vietnamese women who had supported the regime in the South fled the country **by boat 334–35 ≫** after 1975. Those who remained have not had it easy. Some areas still have issues with women being kidnapped, forced into prostitution, or sold as brides. Economic reforms have limited female-headed households' access to loans. The Vietnam Women's Union is currently working alone to push for increased **gender equality**.

A **Woman** in the **NVA**

Most women in the NVA joined in support capacities, accompanying the army as medics, supply personnel, or on bomb disposal teams. Whatever the role, life in the army was one of unrelenting hardship, shown by the experience of NVA servicewoman Phan Ngoc.

In all the companies, there were women between seventeen and eighteen years of age who had joined the army hoping to fight. When Phan Ngoc joined, she was initially assigned to cook and she describes her sense of anger and disappointment. However, a month later she became a sapper, working with dynamite, filling craters, and rebuilding bridges. As head of the company, she had twelve people working under her and was in charge of explosives.

A typical day for these women involved waking up at 5 a.m., but they worked during the day or at night depending on the bombs. They ate out of tins with branches because they had no chopsticks, cleaned the tins with leaves, and drank out of streams. At the same time, they tried to retain some elements of a normal life by carrying books with them and at night they would read or write home. Sometimes they put flowers in their hair.

❝We sang a lot, because we believed that songs are louder than the bombs.**❞**
PHAN NGOC, IN *EVEN THE WOMEN MUST FIGHT: MEMORIES OF WAR FROM NORTH VIETNAM BY* KAREN GOTTSCHANG TURNER AND PHAN THANH HAO, 2008

Called to arms
A group of young North Vietnamese women watch as one trains with a rifle. All women in North Vietnam were taught to fight with weapons and in hand-to-hand combat, but few chose to join the NVA—those who did were often young, single, and childless.

« B E F O R E

The hardships of ground combat in Vietnam were similar to those experienced in previous wars.

IN THEIR FOOTSTEPS
The **hunger, exhaustion, fear, and loneliness** endured by foot soldiers in Vietnam would have been familiar to veterans of **World War II**, **Korea**, the **American Civil War**, and conflicts long before that. However, infantry in Vietnam tended to see more war than their counterparts in earlier conflicts—an average of 240 days, compared to just 40 days for infantrymen in World War II. The fact that individuals in Vietnam **served for a fixed term « 108–09** and knew exactly when their tour of duty would end often turned the war into personal struggles for survival.

Chest deep
Private First Class Fred Greenleaf, with other soldiers and members of an ARVN Ranger Group, wade through an irrigation canal on the way to a Viet Cong-controlled village during Operation Rang Dong in 1967.

The **Challenges** of **Ground Combat**

No corner of the war zone was entirely safe in Vietnam, and no role was without risk, but some places and duties were more dangerous than others. Army and Marine Corps infantry—the ground troops—suffered most of the casualties.

Between moments of violence and terror, American ground troops faced many physical hardships, especially out in the bush. On patrols that might last hours, days, or even weeks, they "humped" through difficult terrain, hacking trails through lacerating elephant grass and vicious thorns. Vietnam's climate exacerbated soldiers' discomfort, guaranteeing oppressive heat and humidity most of the year, but also drenching rain at temperatures cool enough to cause hypothermia at higher elevations, such as in the Central Highlands.

There was also the weight. An infantryman's kit was easily 100 lbs (45 kg) or more. Fighting gear might consist of a web belt with ammunition pouches, hand grenades, smoke grenades, first-aid kit, and canteen. Packs contained a poncho and liner, extra socks and clothes, a gun-cleaning kit, and C-rations—cans of meat or chopped ham and eggs, cans of fruit, and pound cake. There might also be small luxuries such as candy, cameras, and cigarettes.

Soldiers with particular functions would also pack mines, a specialist radio, or other equipment, and all of them would carry as much weaponry as possible: extra grenades, a spare rifle bolt, sometimes a handgun, and usually a knife. A rifle, helmet, and flak jacket rounded out the kit. The gear was so heavy that soldiers often discarded items on the march to lighten the load.

Friend or foe?
Frustration was perhaps the infantrymen's primary state of mind—frustration caused by all the

physical discomforts, but also because of the confusing cultural and political climate in which they fought. The US Army and Marine Corps infantry are trained for combat, and they generally excelled in this role in Vietnam, but they were not prepared for the uncertainties of this particular combat zone. While North Vietnamese regulars were easy to identify, the insurgents were often indistinguishable from the civilian population of South Vietnam. Soldiers frequently

"The **national flower** ... should be an **immense thorn.**"

GEORGE OLSEN, DESCRIBING VIETNAM IN A LETTER TO A FRIEND, NOVEMBER 1969

Hard moments

Lance Corporal James C. Farley breaks down over the death of fellow Marines in March 1965. Farley himself survived the war and was awarded the Silver Star, the third-highest US military decoration for valor.

AFTER

The number of US ground troops in Vietnam continued to rise until 1969, as did the number of US casualties.

MORE TROOPS

General Westmoreland asked for **more US troops** to be sent to Vietnam. Troop numbers peaked at 543,000 in the spring of 1969. Despite US, South Vietnamese, and Australian action in 1965, 1966, and 1967, the enemy's back was far from broken, and the 1968 **Tet Offensive 176–93 »** brought the heaviest fighting of the war for the United States. At the same time, US casualties—some 14,000 killed and almost twice that number wounded in 1968—fueled **opposition to the war at home 216–17 »**.

described villagers as duplicitous, smiling and selling sodas to them during the day, then facilitating Viet Cong sabotage and sniping at night. The language barrier—most American soldiers knew only a few phrases of pidgin Vietnamese—and racial and cultural prejudices exacerbated tensions between South Vietnamese villagers and exhausted American infantrymen.

Psychological impact

Enemy mines and booby traps caused tens of thousands of American casualties, second only to small arms fire. The psychological consequences of these weapons were perhaps worse, because soldiers in the bush understood that any step could be their last. On any patrol, the danger was particularly acute for the "point man"—the first man in a column of troops—whose every sense strained to catch sight, sound, or scent of the enemy. To ensure the point man was mentally and physically fresh, point duty was normally rotated.

While all Americans who served in Vietnam suffered homesickness, loneliness, and resentment that life at home was moving on without them, combat troops also had the responsibility of taking lives, and to hesitate to do so could prove fatal. Some struggled to reconcile the killing with religious prohibitions on violence, but a few reveled in it; most, however, recognized it as an operational necessity. They had a job to do, and they owed it to each other to do it well. The loss and maiming of colleagues during combat also took a mental toll.

The vast majority of combat troops approached the challenges they faced stoically and with a high degree of professionalism, even though most of them were draftees or draft-motivated volunteers who never wanted to be soldiers.

ANTICHAP

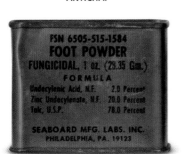

ANTIFUNGAL POWDER

LOUSE REPELLENT

SUNSCREEN

Bare essentials

Ground troops had to contend with natural hazards as well as the perils of combat. Sun, humidity, insects, and leeches led to a host of serious ailments, including foot rot, leading to gangrene, and malaria.

The **War** at **Home**

As American involvement in South Vietnam grew, so too did the size and intensity of the antiwar movement. Although white, middle-class college students became the face of the movement, Americans from all walks of life opposed the war in Vietnam.

« BEFORE

CIVIL RIGHTS LEADER MARTIN LUTHER KING JR., 1963

The growing Vietnam antiwar movement in the United States had deep roots and broad appeal.

WINDS OF CHANGE
The antiwar protesters had links to supporters among other mass social justice movements of the time, such as the antinuclear movement, the African American **Civil Rights Movement**, and the Berkeley Free Speech Movement, which advocated for campus reform.

OPPOSING DIEM
Early antiwar demonstrations in the United States opposed US support for the **Diem regime « 72–73** in South Vietnam, and coincided with commemorations for the victims of **atomic bombs** dropped on Japan.

Millions of Americans objected to the war in Vietnam, but only a small percentage of them participated in protests against it. Reasons for opposition to US involvement in the war varied dramatically, undermining the strength and solidarity of the antiwar movement as a whole. Pacifists opposed the war on principle, but many more Americans specifically opposed the war in Vietnam out of concern for civilian casualties and doubts about whether the cost —in dollars and American lives— was justified.

Many young men opposed the war out of self-interest; they did not want to fight. Others supported the aim of halting the spread of communism in South Vietnam, but disagreed on how to do so. Some in this group, while supporting the escalation of America's role in the war, advocated withdrawal if the US was not prepared to fight to win.

20,000 The number of people marching at an antiwar rally in Washington, D.C., in 1965.

300,000 The number of people at an antiwar rally in the city in 1971.

Early protests
Many antiwar activists had participated in the Civil Rights Movement, in which nonviolent tactics, such as marching and sit-ins, swayed public opinion and lent the movement its moral authority. In the early 1960s, small antiwar demonstrations led by fringe groups, including communists, pacifists, and antinuclear activists, gave way in 1965 to the first mass protest: a march in Washington, D.C. In October 1967, 100,000 demonstrators gathered at the Lincoln Memorial, with more than a third of them also marching on the Pentagon. By this time, protests consisting of tens

BOXER (1942–2016)

MUHAMMAD ALI

Boxing champion Muhammad Ali became one of the antiwar movement's strongest voices when he refused induction into the army in 1967. Ali, a conscientious objector due to his Muslim faith, declared that his enemy was not the Viet Cong, but racism in the United States. Ali was arrested, and could not box for three years until his conviction was overturned.

and even hundreds of thousands of people were taking place in cities around the country, commanding national media attention.

Meanwhile, mass and individual acts of civil disobedience—draft card burnings, induction dissent, and the refusal of those already on active military service to go to

Flames of protest
Demonstrators wave flaming draft cards at an antiwar protest in New York. This form of protest became more organized and widespread after 22-year-old David Miller was sent to prison for publicly burning his draft card in October 1965.

Marching on the Pentagon

On October 21, 1967, around 100,000 antiwar protesters gathered at the Lincoln Memorial, Washington, D.C. When some proceeded to march on the Pentagon, the demonstration turned into a riot, leading to 682 arrests.

Vietnam—led to a spate of legal trials that ensured antiwar protests remained in the headlines.

Students and hippies

In the mid-1960s, the antiwar movement gained a particular momentum on college campuses, largely provoked by the increase in draft calls. Some students conflated resistance to university authority and challenges to government authority. Demonstrations on campuses voiced opposition to military recruitment, private-sector recruitment for government contractors such as Dow Chemical (the manufacturer of napalm), and university research on behalf of the military. Police brutality against these student protesters often became the antiwar movement's most effective recruiting tool, as hitherto apolitical bystanders became radicalized at the sight of violence against their classmates.

Many observers characterized antiwar protestors as "drop outs" or "hippies"—followers of the 1960s' counterculture. Although there was overlap between these groups, especially among white, middle-class youth, the antiwar movement also included working-class people and people of color who objected to the draft.

Due to its links to other such movements, antiwar activism became associated with radical political and social ideas. The seemingly radical tactics, methods, and language of many of those who spoke out against the war could also dissuade some groups—such as older people and political conservatives—from engaging with protesters, even if these groups shared many of the protesters' concerns about the war.

AFTER ⟫

As US troop commitments and casualties rose, increasing numbers of Americans from all walks of life began to question US involvement in Vietnam.

TIDE OF OPINION

The American antiwar movement gained further momentum after the **Tet Offensive 186–87** ⟫, as disturbing accounts and images of combat in Vietnam—especially photographs of Vietnamese civilian casualties—increasingly dominated the news.

While most of these protests were peaceful, **violent confrontations** also took place between protesters and the police—for example, in **Chicago 216–17** ⟫ in 1968—as anger among those opposed to the war heightened.

"**You've got to put your bodies upon the gears ... and you've got to make it stop.**"

MARIO SAVIO, STUDENT AND POLITICAL ACTIVIST, 1964

Peaceful protest
Seventeen-year-old Jan Rose Kasmir presents a flower to National Guardsmen during a protest at the Pentagon on December 22, 1967. She hoped to convince the Guardsmen to put down their arms and join her cause.

4

THE TURNING POINT

September 1967–December 1968

In the fall of 1967, North Vietnam makes ambitious plans to retake Saigon. One of the war's largest campaigns, the Tet Offensive sees a series of coordinated attacks across South Vietnam, resulting in fierce fighting, heavy casualties, and civilian displacement.

« Fighting the offensive
US Marines take cover behind a tank as it fires rounds over an outer wall of the Hue citadel on February 13, 1968. The ancient city of Hue saw the longest, bloodiest battle of the Tet Offensive, with some of the worst devastation of the war.

THE TURNING POINT
SEPTEMBER 1967–DECEMBER 1968

In the fall of 1967, North Vietnam and the Viet Cong began to prepare for an offensive they hoped would win the war. After diversionary attacks on American bases in border areas, they delivered the main thrust of their offensive during the Tet (New Year) holiday in early 1968. The Viet Cong fought for control of towns and cities across South Vietnam, while the North Vietnamese Army seized the city of Hue. In spite of the scale of the attack, the Tet Offensive was a military failure for the communists, and Viet Cong forces were weakened substantially by the campaign. US and South Vietnamese (ARVN) troops retook urban areas, and US Marines successfully defeated a siege of their base at Khe Sanh. Later in 1968, a second phase of the Tet Offensive, "Mini Tet," also failed to win significant military gains for the North Vietnamese and Viet Cong.

1 GIs regularly patrolled the paddy fields near the US base at Da Nang. 2 American aircraft launched strikes against Viet Cong guerrillas in Dak To, in the Central Highlands. 3 US Marines were besieged at Khe Sanh in early 1968. The US media painted an increasingly negative picture of the offensive.

CHINA

NORTH
VIETNAM

BURMA

Red River

HANOI ■

● **Haiphong**

L

● Thanh Hoa

● Luang Prabang

Mekong River

A

Gulf
of
Tonkin

HAINAN

● Vang Veng

● Vinh

Nan River

O

VIENTIANE □

S

Mekong River

━ Yankee Station

THAILAND

Mun River

Mekong River

Operation Niagara ✹ ★ Con Thien
Lang Vei ★ ● ☠ Ca Lu
Khe ○ ★ ✕
Sanh ○ ✕ ● Hue ○ ● Phu Bai
3 ★ ✈
★ MACV

✕ ● **Da Nang**
1

Ping River

Kham Duc ✕

☠ **My Lai**

C
e
n
t
r
a
l

2

Hill 875 ✕ ★ Dak To
Kontum ✕

H
i
g
h
l
a
n
d
s

Chao Phraya River

BANGKOK □

Pleiku ●

S
O
U
T
H

● Qui Nhon ✕

South China Sea

*Tonle
Sap*

CAMBODIA

✕ Buon Ma Thuot

V
I
E
T
N
A
M

✕ Nha Trang

PHNOM PENH □

Kien ●
Dien

Bien Hoa
Tan Son Nhut ✈ ✕ ★ Long Binh
SAIGON ■ ✕

━ Dixie Station

Mekong River

Gulf of
Thailand

Can Tho ● ✕

*Mekong
Delta*

N
0   100km
0   100 miles

TIMELINE SEP 1967–DEC 1968

Nguyen Van Thieu elected president of South Vietnam ▪ **Attacks on US combat bases in DMZ** ▪ Antiwar protests in the US ▪ **Siege of Khe Sanh** ▪ Tet Offensive ▪ **My Lai Massacre** ▪ "Mini-Tet" Offensive ▪ **Phoenix Program** ▪ Peace negotiations start ▪ **Antiwar violence in the US** ▪ Richard Nixon becomes US president

1967

SEPTEMBER 3
Nguyen Van Thieu wins a presidential election to become constitutional ruler of South Vietnam.

OCTOBER 21–23
More than 30,000 antiwar protesters march on the Pentagon in Washington, D.C.

NOVEMBER 29
Defense Secretary Robert McNamara resigns after his proposals to scale down American involvement in the war are rejected.

DECEMBER 4
Police arrest hundreds of antiwar protesters as they attempt to block an armed forces draft induction center in New York.

≫ NVA 122 mm M1938 Howitzer

DECEMBER 31
By the year's end, there are 495,000 US troops in Vietnam. The American death toll for the year is 11,363.

SEPT 11– OCT 31
The US Marine base at Con Thien, near the DMZ, successfully resists a siege by NVA forces and prolonged heavy artillery bombardment.

SEPTEMBER 29
Speaking in San Antonio, Texas, President Johnson offers to end the bombing of North Vietnam if the North Vietnamese will enter peace negotiations.

OCT 29–NOV 7
An attack by the Viet Cong against a military outpost at Loc Ninh near the Cambodian border is repelled with heavy losses.

OCTOBER–DECEMBER
After targeting restrictions on US bombing of North Vietnam are dropped, the US conducts widespread raids on bridges and other transportation links, power plants, and factories.

NOVEMBER 3–22
In the Battle of Dak To, US and South Vietnamese troops repel an offensive by communist forces in the Central Highlands. The battle costs the United States 1,800 casualties.

≫ Hill 875, Dak To, November 1967

1968

JANUARY 5
Operation Niagara I begins, seeking intelligence about the movement of NVA forces threatening the Khe Sanh Marine base in northern South Vietnam.

JANUARY 21
The NVA besieges the Khe Sanh Marine base. The US responds with an aerial resupply of the base and bombardment of NVA positions.

JANUARY 30–31
North Vietnam launches the Tet Offensive. Viet Cong guerrillas and NVA troops carry out attacks in cities and towns across South Vietnam, including Hue and Saigon, where they penetrate the US Embassy compound.

⌃ Marine Corps patch

FEBRUARY 1
US and ARVN counterattacks begin, retaking Tan Son Nhut airbase in Saigon.

≫ Tet Offensive, Hue, February 1968

FEBRUARY 11–17
In the highest week's death toll of the war, 543 American soldiers are killed.

FEBRUARY 24
After more than three weeks' fighting in the city of Hue, US Marines succeed in retaking the imperial palace.

FEBRUARY 28
The US Joint Chiefs of Staff tell the president that 200,000 more soldiers are needed to win the war in Vietnam.

MARCH 2
The battle for Hue ends in a victory for American and ARVN forces.

MARCH 7
The battle for Saigon ends with the clearing of Viet Cong guerrillas from the city.

MARCH 12
The strong performance of antiwar Democrat Senator Eugene McCarthy in the New Hampshire primary casts doubt on President Johnson's chances of re-election.

"We are **mired in stalemate** ... the only **rational way out** then **will be to negotiate,** not as victors, but as an **honorable people** who ... did the best they could."

WALTER CRONKITE, TV BROADCAST, FEBRUARY 27, 1968

APRIL 30–MAY 3
US Marines repulse a major incursion by North Vietnamese troops across the DMZ in the Battle of Dai Do (or Dong Ha).

JULY 3
General Creighton Abrams replaces General Westmoreland as commander of US forces in Vietnam.

OCTOBER 8
Operation Sealords is launched, a long-term campaign by US and South Vietnamese naval and riverine forces against Viet Cong supply lines and bases in the Mekong Delta.

MAY 5–27
In the "Mini Tet" Offensive, the Viet Cong carries out attacks against 119 targets across South Vietnam, including the Cholon district of Saigon and Tan Son Nhut airbase.

MARCH 16
As extensive search-and-destroy operations are carried out in the wake of the Tet Offensive, American soldiers massacre hundreds of Vietnamese civilians at My Lai.

≫ Route 9, April 1968

APRIL 1
Operation Pegasus begins, an advance by US troops along Route 9 to relieve the siege of the Marine base at Khe Sanh.

APRIL 11
Defense Secretary Clark Clifford tells General Westmoreland he will not be given the extra troops he has stated he needs to win the war.

MAY 13
Preliminary peace talks open in Paris but they immediately stall over issues of procedure and representation.

JULY 5
US troops evacuate Khe Sanh. A few days later, the Viet Cong raises the North Vietnamese flag over the combat base.

≫ Battle of Michigan Avenue, August 1968

OCTOBER 31
Rolling Thunder, the American bombing campaign against North Vietnam, is terminated, reopening the peace talks.

≪ Peace negotiations

JULY 1
The controversial Phoenix Program is initiated to identify and eliminate Viet Cong political activists in South Vietnam.

AUGUST 26–29
Antiwar protests disrupt the Democratic National Convention at Chicago, leading to violent confrontations between demonstrators and police.

NOVEMBER 5
Republican candidate Richard Nixon wins the US presidential election, claiming to have a plan to end the war.

MARCH 31
President Johnson announces a halt to most bombings of North Vietnam to facilitate the opening of peace negotiations, and his decision not to seek another term in the White House.

APRIL 8
The Operation Pegasus relief force joins up with the Marines at Khe Sanh, ending the siege after 77 days.

≪ Fleeing "Mini Tet," May 1968

DECEMBER 1
By the year's end, there are 495,000 US military personnel in Vietnam; American deaths for the year total 16,899.

171

Going for Victory

Aware of the deteriorating political situation in South Vietnam, the communist leadership in the North decided to launch an ambitious military offensive against the South in the hope of rousing a general revolt and causing the US-backed government to collapse.

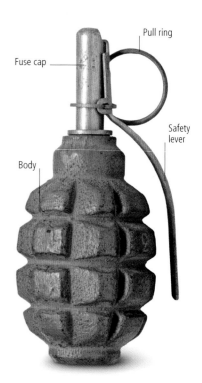

Russian firearms
The Viet Cong were often poorly equipped and outgunned. To prepare them for the offensive, Hanoi resupplied them with the latest Soviet-made weaponry, such as AK-47 assault rifles and this F1 fragmentation grenade.

BEFORE

In the early years of the war, the majority of Americans backed US participation in the war.

AMERICAN OPINION
The **Tonkin Gulf Incident** ≪ 80–81 in 1964 led to a massive escalation of the US military presence in Indochina. Yet most Americans had been too preoccupied with the Civil Rights Movement and the 1960s' counterculture to question America's role in Vietnam. More than **half of all Americans** approved of the war effort in polls conducted by Gallup in 1965 and 1966.

BADGE OF PRIDE

Mastermind at work
General Vo Nguyen Giap (in blue), veteran of the First Indochina War against the French, directed the execution of the Tet Offensive of 1968. He expected ARVN resistance to crumble.

By 1967, the Vietnam War had ground to a bloody stalemate, with neither side capable of achieving a final or even partial victory. The American military and its allies had proved adept at winning conventional battles, while the NVA and the Viet Cong excelled at gaining the upper hand in smaller skirmishes and at controlling large parts of the South Vietnamese countryside through guerrilla warfare.

Constant pounding
The number of American troops stationed in South Vietnam had grown by more than 100,000 by the end of 1966, reaching an all-time high of nearly half a million GIs spread between the Mekong Delta and the DMZ. Viet Cong positions in South Vietnam were pounded with B-52 Arc Light raids on a daily basis, as well as by naval guns and ground artillery.

Some 20,000 US troops had already been killed in action, yet Lyndon B. Johnson was pouring ever more men and machines into the anticommunist cause and there was no reason to believe the escalation would abate.

The communist leadership determined that the only way to break the stalemate—and snatch victory from the jaws of deadlock—was to undertake a massive military offensive against multiple targets in South Vietnam. At best, the assault might topple the South Vietnamese regime outright and drive the Americans into the South China Sea. At worst, it would demonstrate the communists' ability to strike anywhere, at anytime—and inflict massive damage—thereby forcing the Americans to the negotiating table.

Choosing their moment
In the fall of 1967, growing antiwar sentiment in the United States, as well as the continued unpopularity of President Nguyen Van Thieu and his corrupt, dictatorial regime in Saigon, encouraged North Vietnam's leadership to believe the time was ripe to launch a full-scale attack. There was also a growing fear that North Vietnam—its economy in shambles due to the ongoing American bombing—might soon lack the necessary resources to achieve a military solution to the conflict.

The initial plan of attack was drawn up by the Central Office for South Vietnam (COSVN), the high command responsible for coordinating communist military activities south of the DMZ. In the summer of 1967, the politburo in Hanoi approved the general offensive and authorized General Giap, commander of the NVA, to put the plan into action.

Giap determined that the only way to strike at so many places along such a broad front was a coordinated action by NVA regulars and Viet Cong guerrillas. He also decided that the best time to launch the assault was over Tet,

the Vietnamese New Year (at the end of January), when a ceasefire would be in place across South Vietnam and many ARVN troops would be on leave for the holiday.

In preparation for the offensive, the NVA bolstered its own arsenal and began resupplying the Viet Cong with arms. Through the fall of 1967, men and materials began moving down the Ho Chi Minh Trail in ever-greater volume.

Diversionary tactics
The final piece in Giap's strategy was to lure American troops away from their strongholds in urban areas and along the coast by attacking American and ARVN outposts along the DMZ and in the Central Highlands. In addition to diverting US troops, Giap hoped to conjure up fears of the siege he had mounted on French forces at the isolated base of Dien Bien Phu in 1954, a siege so terrible it had ended the First Indochina War.

In November 1967, US troops uncovered a communist document proposing a "general offensive." Astonishingly, it was dismissed by US intelligence agents as North Vietnamese propaganda.

Falling into line
An NVA column marches along the Ho Chi Minh Trail. In the months leading up to the Tet Offensive, an estimated 200,000 NVA troops and more than 80,000 tons of military supplies were moved into South Vietnam via the trail.

"Above all, **we wanted** to **show the Americans** that we were **not exhausted**."

GENERAL VO NGUYEN GIAP ON THE TET OFFENSIVE, INTERVIEWED BY STANLEY KARNOW IN THE *NEW YORK TIMES*, JUNE 24, 1990

AFTER »

In January 1968, General Giap put his plan into action, taking ARVN and US forces by surprise in towns and cities throughout the South.

POISED FOR ACTION
By the Vietnamese New Year, more than 320,000 communist troops (fairly equally split between North Vietnamese regulars and Viet Cong guerrillas) were in position for the **Tet Offensive 176–77** ». Among the peripheral attacks, **Khe Sanh 200–203** » threatened to be the new Dien Bien Phu.

US PUBLIC OPINION WANES
In February 1968, after **wide criticism of Tet in the US media 216–17** », Gallup released a new poll showing that only 32 percent of Americans approved of President Johnson's handling of the war. Secretary of Defense **Robert McNamara resigned** at the end of February. By spring, **Johnson** had decided **not to run for re-election**.

NORTH VIETNAMESE GENERAL Born 1911 Died 2013

General Giap

"I was **in command,** and I demanded **absolute obedience.**"

GENERAL GIAP, INTERVIEWED BY STANLEY KARNOW IN THE *NEW YORK TIMES*, 1990

A master of guerrilla warfare and one of the great military minds of the 20th century, General Vo Nguyen Giap piloted the Vietnamese resistance to the Japanese invasion during World War II, spearheaded the military insurrection against the French colonists in the 1950s, and led NVA and Viet Cong efforts against the US and its allies during the Vietnam War. He was also active in politics, serving as defense minister, deputy prime minister, and a member of the Communist Party Politburo.

Giap grew up in a staunchly anticolonial household. His father took part in early uprisings against the French and later died in prison after his arrest for subversive activities. One of Giap's sisters also died as a political prisoner and his first wife would perish in a French colonial prison. These events had a profound effect on Giap's world view and political leanings.

Young subversive
Following in his father's footsteps, Giap was active in politics from an early age. He joined underground revolutionary groups and spent the late 1920s and early 1930s agitating against French rule in Indochina. When the Communist Party was outlawed by the French at the start of World War II, Giap took refuge across the border in China, where he linked up with Ho Chi Minh and other Vietnamese nationalists. Giap secretly returned to Vietnam to organize the Viet Minh spy network, establish a paramilitary force, and start a propaganda campaign against the Japanese-supported government.

With the end of World War II, which halted the negotiations with France for independence, Giap and

Decorated commander
As commanding general, Vo Nguyen Giap led communist forces to victory in the First Indochina War and the Vietnam War. He received many medals and honors, including Vietnam's highest decoration: the Gold Star Order.

His greatest victory
Giap's 1954 victory at Dien Bien Phu is depicted in this propaganda painting on the walls of the old fort, where the French held out for 57 days before surrendering to the Viet Minh.

> "Any forces that … **impose** their will on other nations will … **face defeat.**"

GENERAL GIAP, IN AN INTERVIEW WITH BBC NEWS, 2004

TIMELINE

- **1911** Born on August 25 in An Xa, a village on the north bank of the Kien Giang River in Quang Binh province.

- **1924** Begins studies at the prestigious Quoc Hoc (National Academy) in Hue.

- **1930** Arrested for his participation in student protests against the French colonial regime.

- **1933–37** Studies law and political economics at Hanoi's National University.

- **1937** Joins the Communist Party.

- **1940** Ordered by the party to flee to southern China; meets Ho Chi Minh.

- **1941–45** Organizes guerrilla resistance against the forces of Nazi-occupied France and of Japan.

- **1944** Forms the Vietnam Armed Propaganda and Liberation Brigade.

- **1946** Issues a national call to arms; builds his army and fights against the French in the following years.

- **1951** Becomes a member of the Politburo, the executive committee of the Communist Party of Vietnam.

- **1954** Plans and leads the Viet Minh victory at Dien Bien Phu, forcing the French to relinquish control of Indochina.

- **1955** Becomes Deputy Prime Minister of the Democratic Republic of Vietnam.

- **1968** Develops the overall strategy used in the Tet Offensive, an assault on more than 100 targets in South Vietnam.

- **1972** Plans the Easter Offensive.

- **1975** Oversees North Vietnam's final offensive and the fall of Saigon.

- **1977** Helps mastermind the Vietnamese invasion of Cambodia that topples Pol Pot's genocidal regime.

- **1979** Leads a counterattack against a Chinese invasion in the north.

- **2013** Dies on October 4 at 102, and is buried near his birthplace in Quang Binh.

the Viet Minh launched a decade-long struggle to oust their colonial adversaries. Showing a natural flare for guerrilla tactics, Giap took the fight to the French.

Tactical brilliance

As a military strategist, Giap was adept at compelling the opposing army to divide its forces into smaller units spread across a huge area, which could then be isolated and attacked with force. Giap's

coup de grâce was the 1954 battle against the French at Dien Bien Phu, where he achieved a decisive victory with his unconventional battlefield tactics.

With this experience under his belt, Giap was key in planning the 1968 Tet Offensive, during which his forces struck more than 100 enemy targets on the same day. Giap and his troops may have lost on the field of battle, but they were the clear victors in the propaganda

struggle that followed. As the commander in chief of the North Vietnamese Army (NVA), Giap also masterminded the 1972 Easter Offensive and then the 1975 Spring Offensive that would retake Saigon and reunify Vietnam.

After the war

In 1975, although the US had been expelled from Indochina, the threat to Vietnamese sovereignty was not over. Hanoi found itself facing threats from former Communist allies—invasions by the Cambodian Khmer Rouge and Chinese—that Giap quickly quashed.

Although Giap retired from his military duties in the early 1980s, Giap persevered in politics for another decade, during which he wrote extensively and gave many interviews about military strategy and his own experiences. In 2013, with his health failing, the general died—aged 102—after four years in an army hospital.

People's hero
Taking time off from battlefield duties, Giap (center) lauds "Heroes of Socialist Labor" during Hanoi's May Day celebrations in 1968.

FUNERAL OF GENERAL GIAP

When intensive US bombing of North Vietnam failed to end the war, US Defense Secretary Robert McNamara looked for other solutions.

HIGH-TECH DEFENSE
McNamara decided that the war could only be won by stopping **NVA soldiers and supplies from infiltrating South Vietnam**. He proposed the contstruction of a high-tech barrier across the **DMZ** to cut off the **Ho Chi Minh Trail «< 56–57**.

Scientists in the Pentagon proposed all kinds of **devices to help secure the line**. In addition to the more usual barbed wire and minefields, they included "button" bombs the size of a beetle, bomb-dropping carrier pigeons, electronic sensors affixed to live insects, and acoustic devices to "listen" for the enemy (the only ones that were actually used).

Prelude to the Tet Offensive

Through the summer and fall of 1967, the NVA and Viet Cong attacked American bases along the DMZ. Their aim was to to draw US and ARVN forces into these areas and clear the way for a major communist assault on South Vietnam's cities and towns.

On September 7, 1967, Secretary of Defense Robert McNamara held a news conference to announce the construction of an infiltration barrier across the DMZ. The McNamara Line, as it became known, was intended to link a chain of new or reinforced firebases from the border with Laos to the South China Sea. However, when construction of the line began, North Vietnamese artillery harassed the construction crews to such an extent that General Westmoreland was forced to limit the project to firebases at Con Thien, Dak To, and Khe Sanh. Meanwhile, General Giap and the NVA high command, planning their "general offensive," saw how

they could use the American firebases to their advantage. If they could lure US and ARVN units away from their urban strongholds to firebases around South Vietnam, their offensives in Saigon and other major cities would have a greater chance of success.

Attack on Con Thien
Located in Quang Tri province just 14 miles (23 km) inland from the coast and 2 miles (3 km) south of the DMZ, Con Thien ("Hill of Angels") firebase came under attack on May 8, 1967, as US Marines repulsed an intense NVA ground assault with bloody hand-to-hand combat. Fighting continued around the firebase throughout the summer as the

Mobile ack-ack
One of the few ways the North Vietnamese could counter total American domination of the skies above South Vietnam was the use of mobile antiaircraft guns mounted on armored cars.

" **War painted the living** and the **dead** the same gray pallor on Hill 875."

WAR CORRESPONDENT PETER ARNETT, NOVEMBER 1967

stormed the summit. The firefight took more than two days to play out and included one of the war's worst friendly-fire incidents—42 soldiers killed and as many wounded when a US Air Force fighter dropped a bomb on a US position by mistake.

The siege was finally lifted during a fierce battle through the first three weeks of November, with heavy casualties on both sides. More than 400 American and ARVN troops and at least 1,000 NVA lost their lives in the battle. Three members of the 173rd Airborne Brigade were posthumously awarded the Congressional Medal of Honor for their actions.

Retaking Hill 875
US troops from the 2nd Brigade of the 503rd Airborne Infantry Regiment destroy enemy bunkers after retaking Hill 875 during the closing stages of the Battle of Dak To in November 1967.

Marines and their ARVN allies launched counterattacks to find and destroy NVA bunkers and artillery emplacements.

By the end of the summer, the NVA was bombarding Con Thien daily with long-range howitzers based across the DMZ. The Marines drove back an NVA ground assault before it could breach the inner defensive wire, but in the Siege of Con Thien, from September 19 to September 27, thousands of artillery and mortar rounds rained down on the beleaguered Marines. The US forces responded with their

Vulnerable to attack
The NVA targeted American outposts that were vulnerable to siege. Khe Sanh, near the Ho Chi Minh Trail, was massively reinforced and its landing strip upgraded through 1967. This aerial view was taken in November of that year.

own massive bombardment from land, sea, and air—a barrage that eventually broke the siege.

The siege of Dak To
A similar situation played out in June 1967 at Dak To firebase in Kontum province, near the Laotian border, not far from the Ho Chi Minh Trail. The siege began with a heavy mortar attack against US Special Forces stationed there. Fighting was so intense that US

airborne, infantry, and cavalry units, as well as ARVN forces, were deployed to hold the firebase and surrounding hilltops.

American forces eventually prevailed with a combination of close aerial support and a series of bold sweeps during which they dislodged the NVA from their elevated positions, which were connected by trenches and tunnels. Fighting was especially fierce on Hill 875 as US airborne troops

AFTER »

The McNamara Line did very little to halt North Vietnamese infiltration or the resupply of Viet Cong forces in the South.

POWER VACUUM
Following the **Siege of Khe Sanh 200–203** » in January 1968, the Americans dismantled the entire western portion of the McNamara Line and removed firebase troops from the region. By October of that year, the whole scheme to create a physical barrier along the DMZ had been abandoned.

The lack of US military power in the area around the DMZ made it even **easier for communist forces** to move men and materials along the **Ho Chi Minh Trail**. However, there was never another attempt to construct a defensive barricade between North and South Vietnam.

The Saigon Circle

In January 1968, the high command in Hanoi was ready to launch the Tet Offensive, simultaneous attacks on South Vietnam's cities. Their prime target was the "Saigon Circle," which included the US Embassy and the ARVN headquarters at nearby Bien Hoa.

BEFORE «

Before the Tet Offensive, Saigon and its surroundings had been relatively tranquil.

PARIS OF THE ORIENT
Before the war, South Vietnam's capital felt like a largely **French city**, with its tree-lined avenues, colonial villas, and Catholic churches. French and Vietnamese were the main languages. Until 1968, the South Vietnamese capital had been **comparatively free of violence**.

PRELIMINARY ATTACKS
Isolated **US Combat bases along the DMZ** « 176–77 had experienced bouts of fierce fighting through the summer and fall of 1967.

By January 1968, some 84,000 NVA and Viet Cong troops had taken up attack positions between the Mekong Delta and the DMZ. Ordered out of their jungle bases by the communist leadership in Hanoi, the Viet Cong secretly entered cities and towns across South Vietnam in readiness for a major offensive scheduled for Tet, the Vietnamese New Year, on January 31.

It was anticipated that many ARVN soldiers would be on leave over the holiday and urban areas filled with out-of-town visitors, providing a perfect cover for the civilian-clad Viet Cong to blend in with the general population. Meanwhile, NVA troops, who had been infiltrating South Vietnam since the previous summer, were set to take part in coordinated attacks on combat bases along the DMZ.

The infiltration coincided with the announcement of a ceasefire over the Tet holiday by both the Saigon government and the National Liberation Front (NLF), the

The initial thrust
Viet Cong troops charge from hiding places in the jungle during the initial phase of the Tet Offensive. Communist forces attacked more than 100 targets in South Vietnam.

Retaking Saigon block by block

ARVN infantry supported by US troops in tanks and armored personnel carriers counterattack Viet Cong units in northern Saigon during the Tet Offensive. Fighting in the capital lasted the better part of a week.

political wing of the communists in the South. With South Vietnam lulled into a false sense of security, the stage was set for the massive and unprecedented assault.

Night raids

Due to communication problems, the attack actually began on January 30, a day earlier than scheduled, with raids on US and ARVN bases in towns in the Central Highlands and along the north coast. This led General Westmoreland to place US forces

on high alert and South Vietnam's President Thieu to cancel ARVN leave. These measures were enough to quell the initial wave of attacks but not what was to come.

The main offensive erupted across South Vietnam in the early hours of January 31. The offensive, which included nearly every provincial capital and major city, was especially fierce in Saigon where around 5,000 Viet Cong attacked strategic targets around the capital, supported by North Vietnamese regulars in the countryside. Communist leaders were confident their forces would gain momentum as civilians rose up against the Americans and the Saigon regime.

Key targets

Dozens of South Vietnamese and American government buildings and bases were attacked between 2 and 3 a.m. Among the hardest hit were Tan Son Nhut airbase and the adjacent MACV compound, the headquarters of the US high command, nicknamed Pentagon East on account of its size and importance. Other targets included the presidential palace, the US Embassy, the ARVN headquarters, the national radio station, and the national police barracks. The embassies of the Philippines and South Korea, America's allies in the war, were also attacked.

Using sappers (engineers) to blast their way through fortified walls and front gates, the Viet Cong

managed to breach most of these compounds quickly. Their task was made easier by the leisurely pace at which ARVN troops returned from their leave and the fact that few US

combat troops were based in Saigon. The vast majority of American combat units were stationed up north where much of the fighting had taken place over the previous six months. Although an intervention by General Weyand had boosted the number of troops in the wider Saigon area, the city center was held by the undermanned ARVN Fifth Rangers and a small detachment of Marines guarding the US Embassy. Most of the US personnel remaining in Saigon were administrative staff rather than battle-hardened combat troops.

ARVN soldier

The US had put the ARVN in charge of the defense of Saigon just a few weeks before the Tet Offensive in recognition of its growing confidence in South Vietnam's army. The Fifth Ranger group led the defense of Saigon.

35 The number of communist battalions, totaling 35,000 men, in the Saigon Circle at Tet.

27 The number of US and ARVN battalions around Saigon, boosted from the initial 14 after the intervention of US General Weyand.

Using weapons smuggled into the city inside coffins and delivery trucks in the months leading up to Tet, the Viet Cong assembled in local hotels where they were staying under the guise of ordinary holiday visitors. Some were clad in civilian clothes, others dressed in stolen ARVN uniforms. Exiting their assembly points, the Viet Cong waylaid private cars and taxis to reach their targets. Along the way they gunned down South Vietnamese police or American MPs unfortunate enough to stray into their path. »

"An earth-shattering, mind-shattering event that **changed the course of the war.**"

NAVAL WAR COLLEGE HISTORIAN JAMES J. WIRTZ, 2004

Defending the South
South Vietnamese troops and policemen return fire from behind a wall as part of a counterattack against Viet Cong forces in Saigon. With the bulk of US forces deployed elsewhere, ARVN troops were key in repelling the communist attack.

Marines and military police guarding the diplomatic enclave. US troops managed to prevent the attackers from storming the building, but could not immediately drive them from the compound outside. Reinforcements were on their way to the embassy but had no idea of the obstacles they might face along the way.

The situation was far less desperate at Tan Son Nhut airbase on the outskirts of Saigon, where the Seventh Air Force Command had raised its security alert to the highest level just before Tet. Although Viet Cong sappers breached the perimeter and hundreds of attackers flooded into the airbase, USAF reaction forces were able to respond quickly and beat back the attack with relatively little loss of life or damage to Air Force aircraft and structures.

By daybreak, Saigon was shrouded in smoke from fires sparked by the overnight fighting, and the smell of cordite and the sound of gunfire drifted across the capital. Entire sections of Saigon were under Viet Cong control, including the Cholon district, where many of the city's ethnic Chinese resided. The streets were strewn with the bodies of combatants from both sides and hundreds of civilians caught in the crossfire. Civilians who survived the carnage huddled in their shops or houses, tending to wounded family and friends.

Counterattacks
Reinforcements started to arrive through the morning. By midday on January 31, most of the strategic targets around Saigon had been secured and the attackers had been driven back with heavy casualties. Counterattacks were launched to clear the capital of Viet Cong. There was house-to-house

fighting and civilian areas were bombed. It took nearly a month to clear Cholon of Viet Cong forces, but within a week American and South Vietnamese forces had recaptured the rest of Saigon and repelled NVA and Viet Cong attacks on most of the communist targets in the South.

The offensive caused immense destruction and heavy loss of civilian life, but no popular

Collateral damage
Civilians sort through the ruins of their shops and homes in the Chinese quarter of Cholon. The hub of economic activity in the city, Cholon saw some of the fiercest street fighting during the Tet Offensive.

》 Nearly overrun by the surprise attack, US and ARVN personnel grabbed any weapons they could find and hastily created defensive positions in offices, barracks, and supply rooms. Westmoreland and his staff were forced to take refuge in his command bunkers in the MACV compound. As the fighting around the US headquarters intensified, the general's staff drew

Spoils of war
Captured Viet Cong guerrillas are displayed alongside Soviet arms seized during fighting to retake Saigon's Cholon district. Among the weapons are automatic rifles, rockets, Sten guns, and ammunition clips.

their arms and joined the last-ditch defense. In a move indicative of the dire situation, Westmoreland mandated that many of the duties of the central command should be immediately transferred to the US Army headquarters in Long Binh.

Embassy and airport
A similar situation was unfolding at the US Embassy in downtown Saigon. Armed with mortars, grenades, automatic weapons, and explosive charges, the Viet Cong blasted their way through the front gate and into the landscaped area surrounding the six-story structure. As American diplomats sought safety inside, a firefight ensued between the Viet Cong and the

"We have reached an important point when the **end begins to come into view.**"

GENERAL WESTMORELAND ON THE TET OFFENSIVE, NOVEMBER 1967

insurrection against the South Vietnamese government took place. In total, an estimated 45,000 NVA and Viet Cong troops were killed, captured, or wounded.

The real winner

Although the Tet Offensive was a massive military defeat for the NVA and the Viet Cong, it also proved a major strategic victory for North Vietnam because of its psychological impact on the American public, media, and politicians. The overall attack, especially the communists' penetration of the US Embassy compound in Saigon, caused a media firestorm and a profound political backlash in America.

The Tet Offensive continued elsewhere through the spring, and erupted again in Saigon in May.

BATTLE GOES ON
Fierce fighting continued until late February In **Hue 190–93 »** and until April in **Khe Sanh 200–03 »**. In May, the **"Mini Tet" 210–11 »** broke out in Saigon.
  Overwhelmingly defeated during the Tet Offensive, the **Viet Cong took two years to rebuild**, during which the war was primarily against the NVA. In the wake of the atrocities committed against civilians, especially in Hue, their political influence also diminished in South Vietnam.

VIET CONG ROSETTE

NEW LOOK
After Tet, and as the war went on, the city took on an increasingly **American landscape**, with GI bars and military bases. At the same time, English overtook French as the second language after Vietnamese and vehicles came to supersede *cyclos* and handcarts on the streets of Saigon.

Tet Offensive

183

As the Tet Offensive exploded across South Vietnam, Saigon came under intense attack from Viet Cong units. Among their foremost targets was the compound of the US Embassy, held by a small contingent of military police and Marines with the help of a handful of embassy staff.

Diplomat Allan Wendt recalls how he reacted when he was woken at around 2.30 in the morning by an enormous explosion and the sound of masonry falling. Rockets were crashing into the building and the embassy was under a full-scale assault. Estimates put the number of Viet Cong guerillas at 20; they had blown open the wall and were pouring into the compound, firing rockets and AK-47 assault rifles into the building.

At this point, Wendt began making numerous phone calls to the military assistance command, to Washington, D.C., to speak to the Situation Room in the Whitehouse, to the Operations Center in the State Department, and to the military command headquarters at Tan Son Nhut airport, with whom he pleaded for relief.

❝ The American Embassy is 'the citadel' of the American presence in Vietnam. And for it to be in the hands of a Viet Cong guerrilla squad did not look good.**❞**

US EMBASSY WORKER ALLAN WENDT, VIDEO TRANSCRIPT FROM THE ASSOCIATION FOR DIPLOMATIC STUDIES & TRAINING, 1968

Attacking the seat of US power
As their dead comrades lie nearby, three US military police protect the American Consulate adjacent to the US Embassy in Saigon. Images like this one, showing the embassy compound in danger, caused consternation in the United States.

1 TROPICAL WR
CLASS II JACKET

2 MI HELMET

3 BOONIE
HAT

4 1941 BACKPACK

5 TROPICAL WR
CLASS II PANTS

6 M1956 PLASTIC CANTEEN

7 M1910 ALUMINUM CANTEEN

8 TROPICAL COMBAT BOOTS

US Gear and Weaponry

American uniforms changed significantly during the course of the conflict, with the introduction of lightweight, quick-drying materials suitable for combat in tropical zones. US forces were equipped with a range of standardized small arms.

9 CLAYMORE MINE BAG

10 M61 GRENADE 11 M67 GRENADE

[1] **Tropical WR class II jacket** Issued to the Marines and US Army, this design with ERDL pattern camouflage was worn from 1967 until the end of the war. [2] **M1 helmet** Made of steel, the M1 was a modified version of the helmet worn by GIs in World War II. This one is fitted with a radio receiver. [3] **Boonie hat** The US Army adopted this hat for jungle combat. [4] **1941 backpack** This example includes an M1951 entrenching tool and a rolled-up camouflage tent. [5] **Tropical WR II class pants** Made of lightweight fabric, these were designed to offer comfort in tropical combat zones. [6] **M1956 plastic canteen** Designs of this type were introduced in 1962. US infantrymen in Vietnam generally carried at least two canteens. [7] **M1910 aluminum canteen** Old-style canteens remained in use throughout the 1960s. [8] **Tropical combat boots** Combat boots made from nylon and canvas were introduced after leather boots proved unsuitable. [9] **Claymore mine**

bag Once the mine had been detonated, the bag could be used independently. [10] **M61 grenade** This fragmentation grenade was filled with 5.5 ounces (156 g) of explosive. [11] **M67 grenade** The M67 had replaced the M61 by the end of the war. [12] **M7 bayonet and M8 scabbard** A bayonet was attached to the M16 rifle. [13] **M16A automatic rifle** This became the US Army's standard rifle in 1969. This example is fitted with a later magazine. [14] **M1911 pistol** The magazine of the US Army's standard sidearm from 1911 to 1986 holds seven rounds. [15] **M14 self-loading rifle** This was the primary US infantry weapon in Vietnam until the arrival of the M16. [16] **M79 grenade launcher** Nicknamed the Blooper by US troops, the M79 could fire a variety of rounds, including explosives and smoke. [17] **M60 machine gun** The M60 was used to provide fire support. Extra ammunition was distributed across infantry squads to spread the weight.

12 M7 BAYONET AND M8 SCABBARD

13 M16A AUTOMATIC RIFLE

14 M1911 PISTOL

15 M14 SELF-LOADING RIFLE

16 M79 GRENADE LAUNCHER

17 M60 MACHINE GUN

The **Media** and the **War**

The first war shown extensively on television, Vietnam was the focus of increasingly critical coverage by the US media. As a result, many Americans lost confidence both in the Pentagon's version of events and the ability of US forces to triumph.

« BEFORE

The phenomenon of reporting from the battlefield was not new to the Vietnam War—nor was the use of photography to capture the horrors of combat.

HISTORIC PARTNERSHIP
The US media's **cozy relationship** with the military stretched back to the Civil War, when reporters began to dispatch **eyewitness stories from the battlefield**. Most of the coverage was slanted toward the "home side"—the Union or Confederacy. During World War I, General Pershing allowed reporters to be embedded with his troops on the Western Front, while World War II produced reporters such as Ernie Pyle. **War photography had an equally long history**—one of the first war photographers, Roger Fenton, took pictures during the Crimean War in 1854.

In 1960, there were more than 52 million American households with TV sets; the overwhelming majority were black-and-white units, and satellite broadcasts were still a thing of the future. Three big nationwide networks (CBS, NBC, and ABC) dominated the airwaves. News and entertainment programming was conservative and largely conformed to middle class, white American values. Nearly everyone tuned into the network news shows. Prior to US involvement in Vietnam, American TV technology and culture were relatively primitive.

Pentagon approval
During the early years of the US involvement in Vietnam, the media painted an optimistic picture of eventual and inevitable US victory in Vietnam. Due to this positive coverage, the Pentagon allowed journalists unprecedented access to US troops, bases, and battlefield operations. At the beginning of the war, the Pentagon had no reason to believe that its special relationship with the press would sour. However, media coverage of the civil rights struggle and antiwar movement back home was often slanted against the establishment. The rise of a popular counterculture press pushed the mainstream media into being more critical of US policies than it otherwise might have been.

Early controversies
Negative press coverage of the Vietnam War started before Tet. Deployed in 1962, *New York Times* reporter David Halberstam penned unsettling stories about what he witnessed in Vietnam. His

Embedded reporters
Photographers Terry Fincher of the *Daily Express* (left) and Larry Burrows from *Life* magazine take a break during an operation in 1968. Burrows often followed the same men for extended time periods—such as Captain Vernon Gillespie—to give a more complete glimpse into their lives.

reports seemed to counter General Harkins's famous quip that the war would be "over by Christmas." President Kennedy tried to pressure the *Times* into recalling the young reporter and Vice President Johnson inferred he was a traitor. But Halberstam held his ground and two years later won a Pulitzer Prize for his war coverage. An ever-growing number of correspondents refused to tow the Pentagon line during the 1960s, among them Neil Sheehan and Peter Arnett.

One the most controversial TV reports was broadcast in 1965, when CBS correspondent Morley Safer accompanied US Marines on a search-and-destroy mission. Rather than rooting out Viet Cong guerrillas, the Marines evacuated and burned an entire peasant

Rewind mechanism
Shutter speed dial
Aperture ring
Self-timer
Interchangeable lens

Battle-ready equipment
Long before digital cameras were invented, photographers used a variety of sturdy film cameras—like this vintage Nikon Model F single lens reflex camera. One of these cameras saved the life of photographer Don McCullin, taking a Viet Cong bullet as it hung from his neck.

village: images that did not play well with the American public. Larry Burrows's evocative photos for *Life* magazine depicted the plight of ordinary GIs in the face of horrible battlefield conditions.

Coverage after Tet

The Pentagon's policy of giving reporters extraordinary access would backfire in the wake of the Tet Offensive in 1968. Despite claims by American leadership that Tet was a US and ARVN victory, TV images, photos, and stories about the offensive seemed to prove otherwise. Witnessing carnage in the streets of every major South Vietnamese city, the media now painted a picture of looming defeat.

The Tet Offensive radically altered the perception of the war by media stars back home, many of whom had a great influence over American public opinion. CBS anchorman Walter Cronkite, venturing to Vietnam in the aftermath of the Tet Offensive, aired a scathing report on the state of the war effort. "We have been too often disappointed by the optimism of the American leaders, both in Vietnam and Washington, to have faith any longer in the silver linings they find in the darkest clouds," Cronkite declared.

President Johnson, upon viewing the report, reportedly quipped that "If I've lost Cronkite, I've lost Middle America." The conversion of Cronkite and other media gatekeepers from ambivalent onlookers to antiwar advocates was a major blow to the American effort in Vietnam.

"Vietnam was **the first war** ever **fought without any censorship.**"

GENERAL WILLIAM WESTMORELAND IN *TIME* MAGAZINE, APRIL 5, 1982

AFTER

American television evolved by leaps and bounds during the course of the war.

REVOLUTION ON THE AIRWAVES

By 1975, more than 71 million households had television. The launch of the Telstar satellite in 1962 enabled broadcasts from Vietnam, while progressive TV shows such as *M*A*S*H* (set in the Korean War) and *All in the Family* **brought pressing cultural issues and antiwar sentiments** into American living rooms. Later on, veteran war correspondents were instrumental in launching **news shows** such as *60 Minutes* and a **cable news network**, CNN, which debuted in 1980.

The turning point
CBS anchorman Walter Cronkite interviews Professor Mai from Hue University in February 1968, during one of his broadcasts. After the Tet Offensive, Cronkite remarked, "It seems now more certain than ever, that the bloody experience of Vietnam is to end in a stalemate."

Saigon Execution

One of the most famous images of the Vietnam War captures the moment ARVN General Nguyen Ngoc Loan executes a Viet Cong officer on a street in Saigon. The photographer, Eddie Adams, recalls both the moment he took the shocking image and the impact it had on the general's life.

On that day in February, Adams was taking occasional pictures as three men walked toward him. When they were about five feet away, the soldiers stopped and backed away. A man walked into his camera viewfinder, took a pistol out of his holster, and raised it to the head of the Viet Cong officer. Expecting this man to interrogate the officer, Adams got ready to take a picture. But the man shot the Viet Cong officer in the temple at the same time as Adams took the photo.

This photograph had a negative impact on the life of General Nguyen Ngoc Loan. Adams claimed he killed the general with his camera that day, and that he felt bad for him and his family for a long time after. Photographs capture a moment but they do not ask the viewer what they would have done if they were there at that time and place.

"Photographs are the most powerful weapons in the world. People believe them; but photographs do lie.**"**

EDDIE ADAMS, OBITUARY FOR NGUYEN NGOC LOAN, *TIME* MAGAZINE, JULY 27, 1998

The **Battle** for **Hue**

Communist forces overran the city of Hue at the start of the Tet Offensive and held fast in Vietnam's ancient capital for nearly a month. US and ARVN forces fought street by street—and often hand-to-hand—to oust them.

Storming the Citadel
Viet Cong troops storm the Citadel's Ngo Mon Gate at the start of the Tet Offensive. The Citadel contained the Tay Loc airfield and the headquarters of the ARVN Rangers, who were also known as the Black Panthers.

As the headquarters of the US military and the South Vietnamese government, Saigon was the primary objective of the Tet Offensive, but the ancient city of Hue was next in line. The city's imperial history made it highly symbolic, and in the eyes of the NVA and Viet Cong, capturing Hue would show the nation and the world that their struggle was against all forms of imperialism.

By the eve of Tet in 1968, some 10,000 Viet Cong guerrillas and NVA regulars had worked their way into clandestine positions all around the city. Synchronizing their attack with many others around South Vietnam, they launched their assault on Hue shortly after 2 a.m. on January 31. Disguised in ARVN uniforms, a small group of NVA soldiers tricked the guards and

◀◀ BEFORE

Hue became Vietnam's imperial capital in the early 19th century when Emperor Gia Long moved his royal court from Hanoi to the river city.

ROYAL ENCLAVE
Started in 1804, the **Citadel** was a fortress-palace complex surrounded by high walls and filled with palaces, temples, and gardens. It contained the Imperial City, where the **emperor and royal family** lived inside the Forbidden Purple Palace. Hue remained the royal capital until 1945, when **Emperor Bao Dai ◀◀ 16–17** abdicated and went to live in exile in Paris.

> "Hue is a **pleasant little town** with something of the leisurely air of a **cathedral city.**"
>
> W. SOMERSET MAUGHAM, *THE GENTLEMAN IN THE PARLOUR*, 1930

gained access through the western gate of the Citadel on the north side of the Perfume River. Communist troops poured into the sprawling royal compound on the hunt for South Vietnamese troops. Other battalions swarmed through the modern town on the south bank with the objective of disabling or destroying Hue's civilian government and any US military presence.

The city was even more lightly defended than Saigon. The attackers quickly captured most of their strategic objectives, including prisons where more than 2,000 political prisoners and 400 communist prisoners of war were being held. By daybreak, a Viet Cong flag was flying over the Citadel. Hanoi was able to claim that it had liberated a major South Vietnamese city for the first time.

Pockets of resistance

However, Hue was not completely in communist hands. A small detachment of US military advisers had barricaded themselves inside the compound of the MACV, in the commercial part of the city, and officers and clerks of the First ARVN Division had managed to repel the initial communist assault

on their headquarters inside the Citadel. The third group that survived the night was a company of ARVN Black Panther reconnaissance troops defending Tay Loc airfield inside the Citadel. As fighting continued through the day, General Truong commanding the First Division ordered the Black Panthers to organize a strategic retreat from the airfield and join the defense of the ARVN headquarters. However, there seemed little hope that the ARVN would be able to hold out for long.

Meanwhile, the popular uprising the communists had hoped to spark elsewhere in South Vietnam actually materialized in Hue as students, teachers, and Buddhist monks welcomed the attackers.

House-to-house in Hue
US Marines take refuge in a devastated building during the battle to retake Hue. The Marine in the foreground wields an M60 machine gun; his companion by the window has an M79 grenade launcher.

Reinforcements delayed

US Marines stationed at Phu Bai airbase and other spots within 10 miles (16 km) of Hue were ordered to reinforce the city, but they also came under fire, a combination of ground attacks and rocket-mortar bombardments that kept them either pinned down in the airbase or engaged in local firefights. Using a combination of armor and infantry, Marines from the First Battalion under the command of Lieutenant Colonel Marcus Gravel finally entered the city from the south. By mid-afternoon, battling sniper fire, Gravel's forces had reinforced the MACV compound.

Continuing their push, the Marines reached the south bank of the Perfume River. Crossing the main bridge, they came under heavy enemy fire and retreated to the MACV compound. As night fell on January 31, the compound was surrounded by NVA forces. There had been no reinforcements for the ARVN troops inside the Citadel.

Gas attacks
The Marines, wearing gas masks to protect themselves, flush out snipers with tear gas during the battle to retake Hue. Both sides used tear gas.

»

Moment of glory
A Marine sergeant celebrates the US victory in the throne room of the Thai Hoa Palace, which miraculously survived the battle. All but 10 of the 160 structures that stood inside the Citadel prior to the Tet Offensive were destroyed.

On the north side of the river, several battalions of ARVN airborne and infantry engaged communist troops in heavy fighting and eventually broke through into the Citadel and recaptured the airfield. Later that day, they were reinforced by more South Vietnamese troops, flown in under low clouds by Marine helicopters amid heavy mortar fire. Despite the arrival of the US Army First Cavalry troops on the western side of the Citadel,

progress in retaking the city remained painfully slow over the first few days of February. Communist resistance was much tougher than expected, and casualties mounted at an alarming rate as American GIs confronted a warren of snipers, machine-gun nests, spider holes, bunkers, and booby traps. US commanders eventually reversed their earlier decision not to bombard the city, but even then they and their ARVN allies had to fight hard. The Viet Cong base in the commercial

Civilians flee the fighting
A US Marine guards Vietnamese civilians caught up in heavy fighting on a residential street in Hue. It was difficult for the Americans to tell whether civilians were friends or foes.

>> By dawn on February 1, the US Marines and their ARVN allies had gathered enough troops around Hue to launch a counterattack on the communists. Their biggest challenge was the lack of intelligence regarding the size, power, and placement of Viet Cong and North Vietnamese units inside the city. American commanders had little choice but to order their units to advance. They could not have foreseen that it would take the better part of a month to clear Hue of communist troops or that along the way they would lose one man to every yard they gained inside the Citadel.

Intense fighting

Come morning, Gravel and his men tried to break out of the MACV compound and retake other strategic points in the commercial quarter, but they were thwarted by communist forces that had dug in overnight. Marine reinforcements began to arrive on the southern outskirts of Hue, but their progress was slowed by intense street fighting against veteran NVA units.

The counterattack was also hamstrung by foul weather, which thwarted air support, and an initial reluctance to use close-quarter bombing and artillery in advance of an attack for fear of causing high civilian casualties and damage to historic buildings.

" Gradually, the battling turned the **once beautiful city** into a **nightmare.** "

TIME MAGAZINE, FEBRUARY 16, 1968

quarter was finally taken on February 6, and the remainder of the south bank of the river over the next three days.

By then, the communists had destroyed the last bridge, forcing the Marines to cross the river in assault craft supported by helicopter gunships. More bloody fighting ensued as the Marines, Army, and ARVN attempted to dislodge the Viet Cong and NVA troops from their well-fortified positions.

The tide turned on February 21, when a break in the monsoon cloud enabled close air support from US airbases and carriers in the South China Sea. That same day,

600 The number of ARVN and US deaths at Hue.
5,000 The number of NVA and Viet Cong killed in the battle.

the communists were finally flushed from the Imperial palace and forced into a last stand in the Citadel's southwest corner. The handful of Viet Cong and NVA troops still inside the walls were ordered to retreat under cover of darkness. Clean-up operations continued in the new town and Citadel until February 25, when the Battle of Hue was finally over.

Aftermath
Half the commercial quarter of the city lay in ruins, as did nearly all of the historic

monuments in the Citadel. Casualties were immense on both sides: hundreds of American and ARVN troops and thousands of Viet Cong and NVA soldiers.

The toll on Hue's civilian population was also considerable. In addition to 800 civilians who died as a result of the battle, on February 26, the day after the battle ended, US and ARVN forces found the mass graves of around 3,000 civilians who had been massacred during the month-long occupation.

Communist atrocities
The discovery of mass graves containing government workers, policemen, and anyone suspected of collaborating with the Saigon regime turned much of Hue's civilian population against the NVA and Viet Cong.

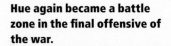

AFTER

Hue again became a battle zone in the final offensive of the war.

NEW ATTACK
In March 1975, the NVA attacked Hue as part of its **Final Offensive 316–17 »**. Mindful of the atrocities committed during the Tet Offensive, the population fled the city, impeding the ARVN defense.

RESTORING THE CITADEL
Postwar projects restored some of Hue's historic buildings. In 1993, UNESCO enshrined the Citadel and nearby royal monuments as a **World Heritage Site**, citing the walled city as a remarkable example of the **planning and construction of late feudal urban planning in East Asia**.

THE CITADEL'S RESTORED ENTRANCE

The **US Marines**

Among the first American units to arrive in Vietnam, the Marines came to the fore during the Tet Offensive, when their reputation for being the US's toughest infantry force was put to the test at Con Thien, Khe Sanh, and in the bloody battle to retake Hue.

« **BEFORE**

The Marines have served in nearly every US overseas conflict since the corps was founded during the Revolutionary War.

WORLD WAR I RECRUITMENT POSTER

BORN TO BE BOLD
On November 10, 1775, the **Continental Congress** instructed Samuel Nicholas to raise two battalions of **seaborne soldiers**. Their first mission was a raid on the Bahamas in 1776. Their nickname **leathernecks** derives from the stiff neckpieces of their early uniforms.

In World War I, the Germans called the Marines devil dogs for their ferocious performance at the **Battle of Belleau Wood** in 1918. In World War II, the Marines rose to world renown for their bravery in **battles against the Japanese** in the Pacific.

The United States Marine Corps (USMC) was an important component of US operations in the war. Between 1965 and 1975, around 450,000 Marines served in the conflict; some 13,000 were killed in combat, and more than 88,000 were wounded. Fifty-seven Marines were awarded the Medal of Honor for bravery under fire.

Recruitment and training

The Marine Corps is a self-contained combined-arms force with its own artillery and airpower, but it is best known for its infantry—rapid response ground forces that engage in close-range combat. The corps is part of the US Department of the Navy, reflecting its original role of supporting naval campaigns.

In Vietnam, the vast majority of Marine recruits were volunteers, typically between the ages of 18 and 20. (Only 10 percent of draftees became Marines.) They signed up for a minimum of three years, although this was reduced to two during the buildup of US troops in 1965 and again in 1967.

To ensure would-be recruits had the necessary physical and mental stamina, they were put through rigorous training at the Parris Island Recruit Depot, South Carolina, or its sister establishment in San Diego, California. The four-month program included an 80-day boot camp—cut to 60 days during parts of the war—beginning with an obligatory hair cut and drill. Further training in combat skills included long-range shooting, a specialty of Marines. This included learning the Rifleman's Creed, a guiding doctrine avowing the pact between man and gun. After this, they were deployed for their first 13-month tour of duty.

First troops

The first Marines to arrive in Vietnam stormed Red Beach Two in Da Nang on March 8, 1965, an entrance reminiscent of their amphibious landings in the Pacific during World War II. Rather than facing enemy troops, however, the "devil dogs" of the Ninth Marine Expeditionary Brigade were met by TV crews and welcome banners held by grateful South Vietnamese. It was not long before they were engaged in counterinsurgency activities and open combat against Viet Cong guerrillas and NVA regulars. Their first major offensive,

Flying ace

This Marine Corps patch shows Charles Schultz's cartoon character Snoopy flying an Mk4 pod gun, a weapon mounted on the exterior of various models of US Navy and Marine attack aircraft.

involving some 5,500 Marines, was Operation Starlite in August 1965, a mission to interdict and destroy Viet Cong forces massed around Chu Lai air base south of Da Nang.

By the end of 1965, the initial force of Marines had been augmented by units under the aegis of the III Marine Amphibious

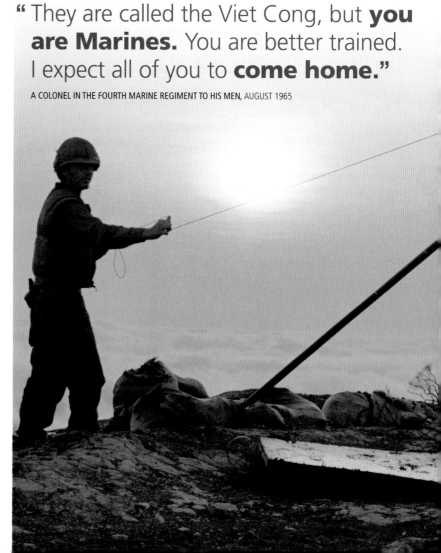

" They are called the Viet Cong, but **you are Marines.** You are better trained. I expect all of you to **come home.**"

A COLONEL IN THE FOURTH MARINE REGIMENT TO HIS MEN, AUGUST 1965

Force. Partnering with ARVN troops, the units protected rural hamlets along the DMZ. Later in the war, General Westmoreland sent these combined action platoons on search-and-destroy missions in the countryside. Typically, they were equipped with M-16 rifles, M60 machine guns, Ka-Bar combat knives, grenades, and machetes for hacking through the jungle.

GRUNT Slang for a member of the Marine Corps fighting in Vietnam. Later in the war, it was applied to all US soldiers on the frontline.

Center stage

The Marines faced their biggest challenge in 1967 and 1968, when communist forces attacked Marine bases along the DMZ prior to the Tet Offensive. They repelled a fierce attack on Con Thien, endured a brutal 77-day siege at Khe Sanh, and ousted NVA and Viet Cong troops from Hue in bloody house-to-house fighting.

By the summer of 1969, Marine units began to withdraw from the war zone, though they formed part of the invasion of Cambodia in 1970. Most of the last ground units left Vietnam on June 25, 1971, leaving a small detachment to guard the US Embassy. Twenty-six Marines were among the POWs handed over by North Vietnam after the 1973 peace treaty was signed. The Marines distinguished themselves again during the evacuations of the US embassies in Saigon and Phnom Penh (Cambodia), in April 1975, and in the rescue of the USS *Mayaguez* from the Khmer Rouge.

AVIATOR (1932–2015)

FRANK E. PETERSEN

When Frank Petersen graduated from the Naval Aviation Cadet Program in 1952, he became the Marine Corps' first African American aviator. Petersen served in the Korean War and the Vietnam War, making some 350 sorties over the course of the two conflicts. In Vietnam, where he flew a McDonnell Douglas F-4 Phantom, he was forced to bail out when his aircraft was shot down on a 1968 mission. He survived, and that same year became the first African American to command the Black Knights squadron. In 1979, he was made the first black general in the Marine Corps.

AFTER

The US Marines continue to be a vital part of American military action overseas.

INTO THE 1980s
By the end of the war, US strategic interest had begun to shift to the Middle East. Thirteen Marines were among 65 Americans taken captive when Iranian revolutionaries stormed the **US Embassy in Tehran** in 1979.

In 1983, 220 Marines were killed by a car bomb during an intervention in **Lebanon**. Later that year, Marines took part in the US invasion of **Grenada** in the Caribbean.

IRAQ AND AFGHANISTAN
Marine aerial and ground units led the invasion of Iraq during the **First Gulf War** (1991) and were called upon again during the **Iraq War** (2003–11) that toppled Saddam Hussein. Marines are still active in Iraq as well as in the ongoing conflict in **Afghanistan**.

Reveille at Khe Sanh
Marines raise the Stars and Stripes while a bugler renders honors to the nation atop Hill 881, near Khe Sanh, in January 1968. The dawn call signaled a new day in the 77-day Siege of Khe Sanh.

Reclaiming Hue's Citadel
US Marines battle their way along the devastated outer walls of Hue's Citadel, as they retake the imperial city. When ARVN troops eventually entered the imperial palace, they found the communists had already slipped away.

« BEFORE

WORLD WAR II WAC POSTER

World War II saw the first American WAC detachment activated in a war zone.

GOING IN GREEN

Vietnam was only the second US war to utilize a WAC detachment. While willing to serve in Vietnam, many women were **ill prepared** for the realities of a combat zone. Basic training consisted of classes on ironing, deportment, make-up application, manners, hair styles, and speech. For the vast majority of women, weapons training was not provided.

US Women at War

Ignored by many histories of the war, approximately 1,000 US military women who were not nurses served in-country in Vietnam from 1962 to 1973. Women were not allowed to serve in combat positions, but nonetheless fulfilled a variety of key support roles.

Women's service in Vietnam was both rewarding and challenging. Like the men, women experienced the stresses of life in a combat zone—walking by body bags, seeing the wounded, and hearing the incoming choppers. However, they also battled challenges unique to their gender, including sexism, harassment, and sexual violence. Women in the military were still rare: one female warrant officer (WO) described how General Westmoreland addressed her as "mister," because the Officers' Guide stated that this was how a WO should be addressed.

Varied roles

The first US woman to serve in Vietnam was US Army Major Anne Doering—a Combat Intelligence Officer fluent in French and Vietnamese. She was one female soldier among more than 10,000 US military personnel in Vietnam in 1962. In 1965, two US Army women, Major Kathleen Wilkes and Sergeant First Class Betty Adams, stepped off the plane to serve as advisers to the newly formed Vietnam Women's Armed Forces Corps. General Westmoreland soon decided to bring over more women as stenographers.

200 The number of women who served with the USAF in Vietnam.

35 The number of US women who served with the US Marine Corps.

They arrived in 1966 and 1967, followed by many others in the ensuing years. The majority of the women who served in Vietnam were members of the Women's Army Corps (WAC). The WAC Detachment was established at Tan Son Nhut airbase and moved to Long Binh for greater safety after the Viet Cong breached the Tan Son Nhut compound in 1967. Captain Peggy Ready was the first Detachment commander in Vietnam, and Marion Crawford was her First Sergeant.

Officers who agreed to have female staff members discovered that these women were not only highly competent, but would work long hours without complaint. The women took on a variety of roles, serving as intelligence analysts, translators, clerk-typists, flight controllers, couriers, physical therapists, or photographers.

Soon, many of the male holdouts wanted women assigned to their staff, even though senior military leaders did not believe women, other than nurses, should serve in a combat zone. Their success brought more women from the Air Force, Marine Corps, and Navy.

These first women arrived in country wearing dress uniforms. Most were untrained in weapons use, but all were willing to serve. Within a year, they were wearing jungle fatigues, boots, and helmets, and knew the fastest route to their bunkers during rocket attacks.

Firsts and figures

The majority of Army Women were assigned to Long Binh and Saigon, although some were stationed in distant places, such as Qui Nhon, Cam Ranh Bay, and Da Nang. In addition to Army women, the Air Force sent women to Vietnam, Thailand, and Hawaii. The Navy sent eight female officers, as well as four who served on the USS *Repose* and USS *Sanctuary*.

There were many firsts for US military women. In 1967, Marine Corps Master Sergeant Barbara

WAF pioneers

Lt. Col. Frances Chaffin (left) greets the first five enlisted Air Force (WAF) women and fourth WAF officer to arrive in Vietnam: June Hilton, Carol Hornick, Rita Pitcock, Barbara Snavely, Shirley J. Brown, and Eva Nordstrom.

All smiles

As they await training on their only visit to the shooting range, First Sergeant Crawford (pointing) jokes with Captain Ready to aim at the target, not the men, who "spread to the four winds" upon seeing women with weapons.

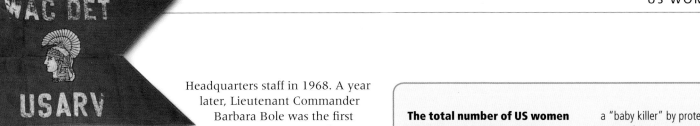

Pallas Athene
This Vietnam-era guidon was lost for years before it was returned, no questions asked, to the US Army Women's Museum. It bears the WAC insignia: the head of a goddess of battle, who led through victory to peace and prosperity.

Dulinsky was the first woman Marine to serve in a combat theater. Major Norma A. Archer was the first Air Force woman to give daily briefings of key air strikes to the Seventh Air Force

Headquarters staff in 1968. A year later, Lieutenant Commander Barbara Bole was the first Navy woman to get the Bronze Star with Combat "V" (for combat heroism), and in 1970, Army Colonel Clotilde Dent Bowen, MD, arrived in Vietnam to be chief psychiatrist—the only African American physician in the Army. That same year, Air Force Major Barbara Thompson became the first female engineer to be assigned to the Rapid Engineer Deployable, Heavy Operations Repair Squadron. The service of these women paved the way for US military women thereafter.

The total number of US women who served in Vietnam is unknown. US Army records are lost, while the Air Force records exist only in paper archives.

LOST TO HISTORY
Many remain unaware that there were US women, other than **nurses 242–43 »**, in Vietnam. They were called frauds or liars simply for wearing the combat patch they had earned, and were subjected to harsh criticism—Specialist Sherri Tipton recalled being called a "baby killer" by protesters. Women faced many of the same struggles as men upon **returning home 344–45 »**.

PROGRESS FOR WOMEN
Military women in Vietnam opened doors for later wars. Congress **disestablished** the WAC as a separate corps in 1978, and women now constitute about 15 percent of the US military. They can qualify for **combat assignments** and serve at all ranks.

> "Kids teased, '**Your momma** wears combat boots.' **I did!**"

CLERK-TYPIST CAROL A. WILLIAMS, IN *WOMEN VIETNAM VETERANS: OUR UNTOLD STORIES*, 2015

Hitting the ground
US Marines at Khe Sanh scramble to take shelter from incoming fire. The Marines endured up to 1,300 rounds of mortar and artillery each day, mainly from Soviet-made 122 mm rockets and 120 mm mortars.

« **BEFORE**

Siege of **Khe Sanh**

Khe Sanh was a US combat base in the northwest corner of South Vietnam.

FRENCH PRECEDENT
The Viet Minh's siege of the similarly isolated French army base of **Dien Bien Phu « 30–31** in 1954 had ended the **First Indochina War « 26–27**.

STRATEGIC VALUE
Early in the war, the **Green Berets « 64–65** established a reconnaissance post at Khe Sanh, 6 miles (10 km) from the **Ho Chi Minh Trail « 56–57**. In 1966, Khe San was reinforced with large numbers of Marines; the Green Berets moved to Lang Vei, a few miles west.

In early January 1968, the remote US combat base of Khe Sanh came under intense attack as part of General Giap's plan to divert US and allied troops from the targets of the Tet Offensive. The siege that ensued was one of the fiercest battles of the war.

Like other combat bases along the DMZ, Khe Sanh and the nearby Special Forces camp of Lang Vei had come under attack by communist forces through the summer and fall of 1967. US forces had successfully counterattacked, supported by aerial bombing.

There was no reason for the US to believe that the action around Khe Sanh in January 1968 would be any different from these earlier battles. However, General Giap had something special in mind for Khe Sanh: a reprise of his legendary victory over the French at Dien Bien Phu in 1954. The geography of Khe Sanh and Dien Bien Phu was remarkably similar—isolated hilltop forts near the Laotian frontier, surrounded by old coffee plantations and jungle that favored

guerrilla warfare. Giap also resolved that the 304th Division of the NVA—heroes of Dien Bien Phu—should be one of two NVA divisions (totaling around 18,000 troops) that would launch the strike. Two more divisions, with similar troop strength, were positioned to block Route 9, the only overland route to Khe Sanh from US bases on the coast.

Initial attack

Contingents of NVA troops attacked Khe Sanh on January 21—nine days before the Tet Offensive—with probes against Khe Sanh, Lang Vei, and small Marine units on the surrounding hilltops. No significant ground was gained, but the NVA destroyed the Marines' ammunition dump and other vital supplies. Khe Sanh commander Colonel David Lownds reacted to this initial assault by evacuating civilians from the area and calling in more Marines and elite ARVN Rangers, boosting allied numbers to around 6,000 men.

Over the week that followed, the communists tightened the noose around Khe Sanh and Lang Vei, creeping closer to the base's perimeter until their trenches were only 1,000 yards (900 m) from their opponents. As a prelude to a

Mapping the battle

These maps accompanied reports of the battle circulated by the United Press International news agency. A large number of journalists risked their lives to report on the siege, which received more media coverage than any other combat zone during the Tet Offensive.

ground assault, they unleashed a massive mortar, artillery, and rocket barrage on the American positions.

Low cloud and fog impeded close US air support, allowing the NVA to capture the road between the two bases, thus isolating Lang Vei. But the US airlift continued whenever weather permitted, the airplanes and helicopters dodging incoming fire.

> " I reached for my **helmet** and there was the **tail fin of a mortar** stuck in it."

SIEGE SURVIVOR JOHN "DOC" CICALA, INTERVIEW FOR *STARS AND STRIPES*, 2014

Second onslaught

As the Tet Offensive exploded across the rest of South Vietnam on January 30 and 31, the area around Khe Sanh remained eerily calm. It was not until February 5 that communist forces began to test US defenses again, in a fierce assault against Marines on Hill 861 and 861A that was repelled via bloody hand-to-hand combat. Two days later, thousands of ground troops from the NVA's

861 The hill, named after its height in meters, where US forces came under attack on January 21 and February 5. The opposing armies fought fiercely for control of the heights around Khe Sanh.

304th Division attacked Lang Vei, supported by light tanks. By this time the defense of the Special Forces camp included 24 Green Berets, a handful of Royal Laotian troops, and some 900 Montagnard militia.

By late afternoon, the NVA had broken through the perimeter and was overrunning the camp. With the NVA in control of the road and nightfall closing in, relief by ground or air from Khe Sanh was impossible. Faced with certain defeat and probably slaughter, the Green Beret commander called for a blistering artillery barrage to be directed on his own base and ordered his troops to retreat into the jungle. Out of around 1,000 defenders, fewer than 100 reached safety in Khe Sanh or elsewhere. »

Blood, sweat, and smiles
Under cover of darkness, female Viet Cong guerrillas transport supplies and ammunition down a section of the Ho Chi Minh Trail in 1968 as communist forces prepare for their attack on Khe Sanh.

Hide and seek
US soldiers set fire to Vietnamese huts between Khe Sanh and the coast during Operation Pegasus. After the bombing, Marines combed the area around Khe Sanh, flushing out any NVA troops hiding in the villages.

and napalm. The bombardment also destroyed large amounts of their weaponry and supplies of ammunition.

Last-ditch attempt
On February 29, Giap's forces made a final effort to storm Khe Sanh. The vaunted 304th Division—heroes of Dien Bien Phu and Lang Vei—launched a substantial ground attack along the eastern edge of the base. After heavy fighting, they were beaten back by the ARVN Rangers stationed there.

The siege and its incessant shelling continued through early April, when the US Army's First Cavalry Division kicked off Operation Pegasus to recapture Route 9 between the coast and Khe Sanh. To support the operation, Army and Marine engineers built a forward base with a landing strip just north of Ca Lu off Route 9, a feat achieved in just 11 days. Meeting relatively light resistance, First Cavalry Division were able to link up with Marines from the firebase on April 8, ending the 77-day siege.

» At sunrise on February 8, the situation looked bleak for the US soldiers at Khe Sanh. The nearby Special Forces camp at Lang Vei had been utterly destroyed with great loss, the main firebase was surrounded by tens of thousands of communist troops, and Route 9 to the coast was blocked. Although the Tet Offensive had been blunted nearly everywhere else in the South by early February, there was no sign of a communist retreat from the warren of bunkers and zigzag trenches around Khe Sanh. Under cover of darkness, foul weather, and artillery attacks, Giap's forces continued to inch closer to the American lines.

" The earth [was] churned into a moonscape by … US bombs."

LIFE MAGAZINE ARTICLE ON OPERATION PEGASUS, APRIL 19, 1968

sorties by B-52 bombers flying from bases in Guam and Thailand and by fighter-bombers based in South Vietnam. Together they dropped more than 110,000 tons of ordnance onto NVA positions

around Khe Sanh, often perilously close to the perimeter of the base itself. The vast majority of Giap's troops who lost their lives during the siege were killed by this downpour of conventional bombs

Operation Niagara
The Marines dug in for the siege, hunkering down in muddy bunkers strewn with garbage that attracted legions of rats. The lack of proper sanitation led to infections and disease while the constant stench and noise of explosives pushed defenders to the brink of mental breakdown.

The US responded to the initial attack and siege with the only logical means—a massive air strike. Codenamed Operation Niagara, the aerial assault entailed thousands of

KEY CONCEPT

CLOSE AIR SUPPORT

Khe Sanh provided many classic examples of Close Air Support (CAS), the battlefield doctrine of calling in air strikes against enemy positions located near your own lines. Carried out with helicopter gunships, fighter jets, and B-52 bombers, CAS was essential to American survival at Khe Sanh and Hue. Key to the concept is the use of Forward Air Controllers (FACs), small teams that assess the situation on the ground and advise the air units on where to strike. At the siege of Khe Sanh, B-52 crews relied on ground-force radar to direct them to their targets.

AFTER

Air agility
The First Cavalry Division led the relief of Khe Sanh. This shoulder patch recalls the division's descent from horse-mounted cavalry, used for the last time in World War I and also valued for agility and rapid response.

US and ARVN forces together lost around 500 men during the siege; NVA figures were never known, although estimates range from 5,500 to 15,000.

Despite the siege being lifted, fighting continued around Khe Sanh as Marines and Army units tried to expand their zone of control and eliminate communist units remaining in the region. Going into the jungle in small patrols, the US forces incurred far higher casualities than during the siege itself.

As communist shelling of the base resumed, the US high command decided to abandon and destroy the combat base rather than risk another costly siege. The final troops were evacuated on July 5 and a few days later the North Vietnamese flag was raised over the ruined combat base.

Khe Sanh and the wider Tet Offensive marked a watershed in the war.

POLICY CHANGE
Following Khe San, General Westmoreland ordered US troops to **abandon combat bases** along the McNamara Line. Shortly afterward, in June 1968, Westmoreland was replaced as commander of the MACV by **General Creighton Abrams**, who introduced a policy of **Vietnamization 228–29 ≫** —equipping and training ARVN troops to take on more of the combat.

ROUTE 9
In February 1971, Khe Sanh and Route 9 were reopened in preparation for **the invasion of Laos by ARVN troops 264–65 ≫**.

ECOLOGICAL IMPACT
In addition to the cost in human lives, bombing and napalm **destroyed much of the rainforest surrounding Khe Sanh**. Over the decades, the jungle reclaimed many of the bomb craters while much of the military ordnance left on the battlefield was collected and sold or repurposed by the hilltribes of the area.

Aerial workhorse
Soldiers jump out of a Bell UH-1 "Huey." Helicopters were vital in the resupply of Khe Sanh, the pilots braving both enemy fire and dangerous weather as they brought in troops and supplies and evacuated the wounded.

Siege of Khe Sanh

As part of the Tet Offensive, the North Vietnamese Army subjected the isolated Marine base of Khe Sanh to daily shelling for six weeks. Sometimes there was little that the besieged Marines could do but hunker down in their sandbag bunkers and hope that the US bombing campaign to repel the NVA would eventually prevail.

Outside the bunkers, Marines filling sandbags were caught by the first shell burst, and exploding rockets sent showers of hot fragments everywhere. Meanwhile, inside the bunkers the marines tried to make themselves as small as possible by hugging their legs and bowing their heads. As the tempo of the shelling increased, in their minds the small opening to the bunker seemed to grow and the 6,000 sandbags over the bunker seemed dangerously thin.

When the shells stopped, a few men climbed out of the bunker and checked if more dead or wounded men were outside. Medics rushed through the area. Inside the bunker, the marines resumed what they were doing: one continued to play the guitar, two men picked up their card game where they had left it, and another went back to his paperback book.

" The shelling wasn't worth discussing. "
ASSOCIATED PRESS CORRESPONDENT JOHN T. WHEELER, DISPATCH FILED FROM KHE SANH, FEBRUARY 12, 1968

Running for shelter
Three US Marines arriving to reinforce the besieged stronghold at Khe Sanh drop their duffel bags to run for shelter as a rocket explodes nearby. The only way to get in or out of Khe Sanh was by air.

1 HOMEMADE MORTAR (VIET CONG)

2 TYPE 31 60MM MORTAR (VIET CONG)

3 82-PM-41 MORTAR (NORTH VIETNAM)

4 BM-21 GRAD ROCKET LAUNCHER (NORTH VIETNAM)

5 152MM GUN HOWITZER M1955 (NORTH VIETNAM)

6 122MM HOWITZER M1938 (NORTH VIETNAM)

Artillery

All parties in the conflict employed artillery, including the Viet Cong. The Americans built artillery bases (FSBs) as defensive strong points and to allow infantry patrols to order strikes against enemy targets.

1 **Homemade mortar (Viet Cong)** Portable and light, such mortars provided valuable fire support. 2 **Type 31 60mm mortar (Viet Cong)** Produced by the Chinese, this mortar was captured from the Viet Cong by Australian troops in 1968. 3 **82-PM-41 mortar (North Vietnam)** This Soviet-produced mortar, and the Chinese Type 67 copy, saw extensive service in Vietnam. 4 **BM-21 Grad rocket launcher (North Vietnam)** Supplied by the USSR, this multiple rocket launcher is still in service in Vietnam. 5 **152mm gun howitzer M1955 (North Vietnam)** This Soviet artillery piece was known for its reliability. 6 **122mm howitzer M1938 (North**

Vietnam) The NVA also used this Soviet howitzer. 7 **M116 howitzer (North Vietnam)** Supplied to Chinese forces in World War II, this American howitzer was used by the Viet Minh against French forces. 8 **M114 155mm howitzer (US)** Developed during World War II, the M114 remained in widespread service with US forces. 9 **M2A2 105mm howitzer (Australia)** American-made, the M2A2 was the standard gun for most field units of the Royal Australian Artillery. 10 **Mortar smoke shell (US)** White phosphorus was used to create smoke screens. 11 **Howitzer shells (US)** Artillery pieces like the M114 fired 155mm shells.

7 M116 HOWITZER
(NORTH VIETNAM)

8 M114 155 MM
HOWITZER (US)

9 M2A2 105 MM
HOWITZER (AUSTRALIA)

10 MORTAR
SMOKE SHELL (US)

11 HOWITZER
SHELLS (US)

The negative press of the Tet Offensive gave Johnson a reason to once again seek conciliation.

RELUCTANT WARMONGER
Johnson began escalation of the war in Vietnam in 1964 following the **Tonkin Gulf Resolution « 80–81**, but would rather have focused on domestic policy. After the 1968 **Tet Offensive « 178–81**, the president was haunted by the seemingly futile war effort and sinking public approval.

PRESIDENT JOHNSON MEETS A US SOLDIER

Opening Negotiations

Following the Tet Offensive, President Johnson decided to seek peace talks with North Vietnam. Beginning negotiations, however, proved no easy feat, with each side stubbornly refusing to compromise on key starting points.

On the evening of March 31, 1968, President Johnson delivered a televised address to the American nation from the White House, during which he surprisingly announced a partial halt to the US bombing of North Vietnam— an olive branch that he hoped would lead to peace negotiations with Hanoi and a rapid de-escalation of the conflict. While Johnson had attempted in 1965 and again in 1967 to halt the bombings and appeal for peace talks, these earlier overtures had failed to lead to a resolution. Now, the president tried once more.

"Our purpose in this action," said Johnson, "is to bring about a reduction in the level of violence that now exists. It is to save the lives of brave men—and to save the lives of innocent women and children. It is to permit the contending forces to move closer to a political settlement."

The address was a remarkable (if perhaps unintentional) admission on Johnson's part, acknowledging that the NVA's Tet Offensive— despite failing to achieve its military objectives and largely neutralizing the Viet Cong as a fighting force—had achieved its major political aim. In the eight weeks since the offensive, the US media had turned against the war. By extension, so had US public opinion. Rather than extend a war that seemed unwinnable, Johnson pushed for peace.

Common ground
Several locations were suggested as potential settings for the peace negotiations, including Warsaw and Phnom Penh. However, after

79	**PERCENT** Johnson's Gallup approval rating in 1964.
35	**PERCENT** Johnson's Gallup approval rating in 1968.

Historic setting

Delegates from both sides gather in May 1968, under the crystal chandeliers in the ballroom of the Hotel Majestic in Paris. Once a palace owned by Isabella II of Spain, the hotel belonged to the French government from 1936 to 2008.

Peace was not reached in 1968. The war would continue for five years—and see a new US president—before peace accords took the US out of Vietnam.

NIXON'S INFLUENCE

White House audio tapes, declassified and released in 2013, reveal a new take on why negotiations failed in 1968: Johnson discovered that Richard Nixon had been secretly (and illegally) **pressuring President Thieu** into backpedaling his support for the talks, by promising him a much better deal than Johnson, if and when **Nixon became president**—as he did later that year **224–25 ≫**.

delegation, the primary hurdles to reaching an agreement were the US delegates balking at a proposal to include the National Liberation Front in a coalition government in the South and the Saigon government's refusal to recognize the legitimacy of the Viet Cong. South Vietnamese President Thieu was a surprising impediment; US Ambassador Ellsworth Bunker made note to Johnson of "Thieu's sudden intransigence."

Death and disorder

The peace talks were held against a backdrop of chaos in the streets of Paris that nearly toppled Charles de Gaulle's government. Student demonstrations coupled with widespread general strikes brought the entire country to a standstill for the better part of two weeks in the middle of May.

Talks stalled for four months, until November, when Johnson agreed to suspend all bombing and end Operation Rolling Thunder. In December 1968, US Secretary of Defense Clark M. Clifford remarked that delegates should "stop

squabbling." Despite claiming that the US was not at all at fault for the slow progress, he made a good point: "each day and each week that they delay, more men are dying on the battlefield of South Vietnam."

Voice of the Viet Cong

Nguyen Thi Binh (center) crashed the peace talks on behalf of the National Liberation Front (the political arm of the Viet Cong) and eventually got a place at the table. A skilled diplomat, she has served two terms as the vice president of Vietnam in the postwar era.

more than a month of discussion between Washington and Hanoi, it was decided the two parties would meet in Paris in the second week of May 1968. Officially called the International Conference on Vietnam, the talks unfolded at the Majestic Hotel near the Arc de Triomphe. Since French President Charles de Gaulle was hosting the meetings, it was determined that French would be the official language of the conference.

Discussions stalled

William Averell Harriman, former US ambassador to the Soviet Union and Great Britain, headed up an American delegation that also included future secretary of state

Cyrus Vance. On the other side of the table, the North Vietnamese team was led by former foreign minister Xuan Thuy, whom the US would soon come to view as a major obstacle to their goals during the peace process.

Diplomats on both sides hoped the talks would bring a quick end to the war in Indochina. However, weeks of negotiating yielded nothing, with both sides refusing to budge from their original positions.

The major sticking point for the US was the refusal of Xuan Thuy and his team to immediately withdraw all North Vietnamese troops from below the DMZ and recognize the legitimacy of the Saigon government. For the Hanoi

> "I call upon … **Ho Chi Minh** to respond positively … to this new **step toward peace.**"

PRESIDENT LYNDON B. JOHNSON, ADDRESSING THE NATION, MARCH 31, 1968.

The "Mini Tet"

As their leaders negotiated in Paris, war continued to rage in South Vietnam. Following close on the heels of their main offensive, the North Vietnamese launched another major assault on South Vietnam in May of 1968—the "Mini Tet Offensive."

The Mini Tet was the second NVA offensive in 1968. Striking against more than a hundred targets, it was also called Little Tet, the May Offensive, or Phase Two of the Tet Offensive. Fighting was especially fierce in and around Saigon—where a combined Viet Cong and NVA force captured part of Tan Son Nhut airbase—as well as Kham Duc in the Central Highlands.

The NVA's attack on Saigon unfolded in the hours before dawn on May 6, as communist troops infiltrated the city via several routes, including Phu Tho racetrack and the French cemetery on the western edge of Tan Son Nhut. Using rockets, mortars, sniper fire, and ground troops, Viet Cong units attacked the western and southern perimeters of the base and engaged US and ARVN troops in heavy fighting. Although parts of the airfield were damaged by rocket fire, the defenders responded quickly and by late afternoon had stemmed the attack.

Fall of Kham Duc

After the first phase of the Tet Offensive, Kham Duc in the Central Highlands west of Da Nang was the only remaining US Special Forces base along the Ho Chi Minh Trail. On May 10, the Viet Cong attacked and overran Ngok Tavak, an outlying post manned by a small Australian unit. Fearing that a major assault was imminent, airborne US reinforcements were rushed to protect Kham Duc.

By the morning of May 11, the base was completely surrounded by Viet Cong and NVA forces, who unleashed a blistering rocket and mortar attack on the base. Coinciding with the barrage, they began to capture isolated hilltop outposts around Kham Duc.

Determining that it was not as easily defendable as Khe Sanh, General Westmoreland and the US high command decided to evacuate the base. Surrounded, outmanned, and outgunned, the US executed a chaotic air evacuation of more than 1,500 personnel as B-52 strikes, close air support, and helicopter gunships kept the communists at bay. Nine US aircraft were lost to enemy fire during the evacuation. Major Bernard L. Butcher's C-130 transport plane was shot down, killing around 150 Vietnamese women and children as well as the American aircrew. Despite such setbacks, the US evacuation was punctuated by a conspicuous act of gallantry when Lieutenant Colonel Joe M. Jackson landed his C-123 under heavy fire on the airfield to retrieve three members of a combat control team who had been left behind. He was awarded the Medal of Honor for this heroic action.

Phase two

Communist forces attacked Saigon again on May 25. Rather than trying to capture or disrupt Tan Son Nhut airbase or other US facilities, the Viet Cong concentrated their efforts on Cholon, the city's main ethnic Chinese district. Assuming that religious shrines would be safe from attack, the Viet Cong took refuge inside Buddhist temples. The assumption proved wrong, however, and ARVN and US troops gradually drove them from the city.

The May offensive had proved ineffective. Better intelligence gathering in the wake of the first Tet Offensive enabled US and ARVN forces to intercept many NVA units before they could reach their targets.

Final push

The last phase of the Tet Offensive began in August and also yielded little success for the NVA. They attacked 27 cities, 100 districts and military posts, and 47 airfields. However, just as in the May offensive, many of these attempts were short-lived. At the end of 1968, both sides had gained little from the offensives, and at the expense of great loss of life.

BEFORE

The US had bases across South Vietnam, but Tan Son Nhut airbase, on the outskirts of Saigon, was the most important.

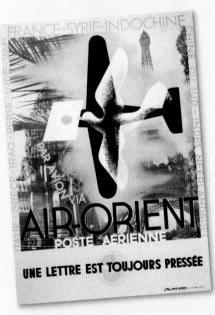

AVIATION POSTER

GATEWAY TO SAIGON
By the 1930s, Tan Son Nhut was the primary air gateway into southern Vietnam, served by carriers such as Air-Orient. It became an **American base** in 1961, and in 1967 became the headquarters of United States' Military Assistance Command Vietnam (MACV).

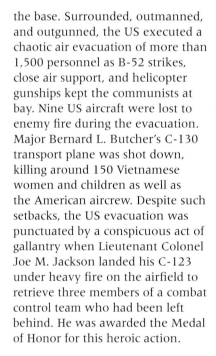

Holding their ground
ARVN artillerymen reload a 105 mm gun on May 6, 1968, inside the strategically important Phu Tho racetrack. Once a horse racing venue enjoyed by French officials, the track in western Saigon was later used to land helicopters.

AFTER ≫

The year 1968 resulted in heavy losses for both sides and gave neither any permanent gains. War continued to be waged for South Vietnam—and for Saigon.

EVACUATION HUB
Tan Son Nhut would once again be at the center of the action in 1975. Before it was retaken by the NVA, it was used in the **evacuation 322–23 ≫** of American and South Vietnamese people, fleeing Saigon to escape the invading forces of the **final offensive 316–17 ≫**.

LOST SOLDIERS
Thirty-one US soldiers were listed as **missing in action** (MIA) **344–45 ≫** after Kham Duc. When it was reoccupied by US infantrymen in July 1970—during Operation Elk Canyon I and II—patrols were sent out to look for the missing men. The bodies of crewmen from the Butcher crash were found in the 1990s, and were finally buried in the US in 2008.

"Undoubtedly the **most heroic action** in US Air Force history—**bar none.**"

US AIR FORCE VETERAN SAM MCGOWAN, ON THE EVACUATION OF KHAM DUC, OCTOBER 2015

Running for his life
Bleeding from a facial wound, an ARVN Ranger—identifiable by the Black Panther insignia on his arm and helmet—runs for cover in a lumber yard while his unit comes under heavy fire from Viet Cong infiltrators.

CORDS and Pacification

As part of the overall war effort, the US created a number of programs to assist, pacify, and make allies of South Vietnam's civilian population, in particular rural villagers more inclined to favor, shelter, and even join the communist forces.

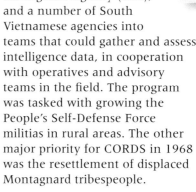

Pacification programs were designed to win over local people and lessen their desire to revolt. They encouraged people to live peaceably and cooperate with US and ARVN forces in spite of a turbulent situation. Early programs had not been especially effective, leading the US to devise new ways to win the "hearts and minds" of South Vietnam's rural population. Foremost among these was the Civil Operations and Revolutionary Development Support (CORDS) program created by US Ambassador Henry Cabot Lodge in 1967. Although it was technically a military program, White House Special Assistant Robert Komer was brought to Vietnam to head the program.

Setting priorities

Under Komer's leadership, CORDS integrated personnel from the military intelligence, Central Intelligence Agency (CIA), and a number of South Vietnamese agencies into teams that could gather and assess intelligence data, in cooperation with operatives and advisory teams in the field. The program was tasked with growing the People's Self-Defense Force militias in rural areas. The other major priority for CORDS in 1968 was the resettlement of displaced Montagnard tribespeople.

Appeal for aid
The American Red Cross established 50 camps to aid South Vietnamese civilians impacted by the conflict: facilities that provided food, shelter, clothing, and medical care, and helped villagers rebuild their war-ravaged homes and farms.

At the same time, the US Agency for International Development (USAID) made a push to bring modern health care into villages across South Vietnam. Their work ranged from efforts to eradicate malarial mosquitoes to staffing and equipping rural aid stations and provincial hospitals.

Flawed system
One of the offspring of CORDS was the Hamlet Evaluation System (HES)—through which the US collected and analyzed data on more than 9,000 hamlets and villages across South Vietnam. Compiled by US advisers stationed

« BEFORE

The "hearts and minds" campaign developed out of earlier civilian pacification programs launched by US forces.

EARLY EFFORTS
The US first experimented with proactive pacification techniques during the Philippine–American War (1899–1902), trying to win over the populace by building schools and public works.

AFTER THE ACCORDS
In Vietnam, pacification kicked off shortly after Vietnam became independent and was split into **separate nations** in 1954 **« 38–39**. From the very start, the programs concentrated on a rural, peasant population long abused under French colonial rule and most likely to have political, social, and economic gripes about the South Vietnamese regime. Early programs ranged from amnesties for Viet Cong rebels to the construction of fortified **strategic hamlets « 70–71** protected by government troops.

Militia patrol
Female volunteers of the People's Self-Defense Force (Popular Forces) patrol the perimeter of the hamlet of Kien Dien to discourage Viet Cong infiltration. By 1972, the PSDF's combat arm numbered around one million people, with another 2.5 million in support roles.

> "The **struggle** was in the **rice paddies** ... in and **among the people.**"
>
> GENERAL LEWIS WALT, COMMANDER OF THE US MARINE FORCES IN VIETNAM, 1970

in the countryside, the data rated the security situation in every hamlet, leading to a monthly report that supposedly reflected the increasing (or decreasing) loyalty of rural residents to the South Vietnamese regime and American war effort. Given the pressure on advisers to increase security in their zone, it was inevitable that data was frequently inflated. Worse was

Playtime

Sometimes hearts and minds were won with small, spur-of-the-moment actions, like this American GI interacting with a Vietnamese child as she uses the antibomb sandbags in front of her home as a playground.

the fact that hamlets under total communist control were not included in the system.

Limited success

The Tet Offensive of early 1968 proved a major setback for CORDS. The evacuation of rural areas, a massive flow of refugees to coastal and urban areas, and the diversion of personnel and funding to the counterattacks impacted the CORDS program. Once the NVA offensive was thwarted, the program regained its momentum.

By 1969, CORDS had established military-civilian advisory teams in more than 250 districts and had some 7,000 personnel involved in pacification. It also utilized two

types of local militia—Regional Forces (RF) and Popular Forces (PF), known collectively as Ruff-Puffs to their American advisers—who grew into an effective fighting force. Through them, CORDS could provide some security for villages vulnerable to Viet Cong attacks.

However, CORDS mostly failed when it came to convincing Viet Cong troops and other communist sympathizers to come to the side of the US and South Vietnamese. Appointed as the US Ambassador to Turkey in 1968, Komer turned over control of CORDS to his deputy: intelligence expert William Colby, who had once served as CIA Chief of Station in Saigon and later became director of the CIA.

Although the concept had mixed results in Vietnam, the US would use "hearts and minds" as a nonviolent companion to military might in later conflicts.

MIDDLE EAST PACIFICATION

First established in 2002, Provincial Reconstruction Teams (PRTs) became a **cornerstone of US policy** in both Afghanistan and Iraq. Composed of members of the US military, diplomats, civilian advisers, and representatives of USAID and other government agencies, PRTs build schools and hospitals, distribute aid, and assist farmers.

The **Phoenix Program**

Surprised by the ferocity and breadth of the Tet Offensive, the US examined the role of intelligence in the war. The result was the Phoenix Program, a systematic drive to destroy the political structure of the Viet Cong and root out communist sympathizers.

Set up by the CIA under President Johnson, the Phoenix Program (Phung Hoang in Vietnamese) was an attempt to boost intelligence efforts in South Vietnam. Active from July 1968 as part of the CORDS pacification program, Phoenix targeted the Viet Cong's political and administrative structures, known as the VCI (Viet Cong Infrastructure). The Phoenix Program's mandate went much further than previous intelligence initiatives. As well as authorizing the detention of communist agents and sympathizers, it sanctioned their torture and assassination.

Hunted down

The first task of Phoenix personnel in any operation was to identify the communist leadership in each province, district, and village. Thousands of committees were set up to gather information on

Pinning their hopes
This 1965 Viet Cong badge made of brass and enamel carries the phrase "National Liberation" (Dan Toc Giai Phong) and the red, blue, and gold Viet Cong flag. Such open allegiance became much less common once the Phoenix Program had been established.

individuals and compile lists of names. In theory, accusations had to be confirmed by at least three independent sources before suspects could be interrogated.

Arrests—usually made at night when the accused were sleeping—were made by Provincial Reconnaissance Units (PRUs): paramilitary teams comprising South Vietnamese security officers, the CIA, and the US military, including Special Forces and Navy Seals. The PRU then took the accused to a provincial interrogation center, where he or she could be detained for up to two years without trial. At their height, there were some 4,000 PRUs. Their members in South Vietnam were assigned to districts in which they already had contacts.

Their job was not easy. Much of the countryside, especially around the Mekong Delta, was effectively controlled by the Viet Cong. At the outset of the program, it was estimated that around

70,000 individuals were actively working for the communists in South Vietnam, and thousands of sympathizers performed small duties or favors for the cause.

Clandestine methods

PRUs used enhanced interrogation techniques—many of which were considered torture under the Geneva Convention governing the treatment of civilians in war—to extract information from captives. These torture methods included waterboarding, electric shocks, starvation, sodomy, and gang rape.

The PRUs used information obtained through such methods to identify other communist leaders and collaborators. In cases where suspects could not be detained, persuaded to surrender, or seek amnesty, PRUs were authorized to eliminate them by any means they deemed necessary. With little oversight of their activities and the

tacit approval of those higher up in the Phoenix Program, the PRUs became de facto hit squads charged with instilling terror in the VCI.

Wrongly targeted

Many of those who were detained, tortured, or assassinated under Phoenix were noncommunist opponents of the South Vietnamese regime. Villagers sometimes falsely accused neighbors out of revenge or for other personal reasons, often incriminating whole families.

> **81,000** The estimated number of communist cadres "neutralized"—killed, captured, or forced to defect—by the Phoenix Program. It is estimated that up to half this number were killed.

Informants were also paid for their information—leading to more false accusations—while others were persuaded to make accusations in order to avoid their own torture or death. Phoenix personnel also had quotas to achieve. At one point, they were required to identify several thousand suspects every month.

Without a doubt, Phoenix helped to cripple Viet Cong Infrastructure in South Vietnam. However, it was not until after the war that the organizers of the program began to realize how effective it had been. Colby claimed that communists had found the years the program ran to be the most difficult of the entire war.

BEFORE «

The Central Intelligence Agency (CIA) was involved in Indochina long before the first US military advisers or troops arrived.

OPS AND ASSASSINATIONS
The CIA opened its first covert station in Saigon in 1954. A year later, the agency laid the initial groundwork for a "secret war" in Laos against communist forces that would last for nearly 20 years.

Under **Project Tiger**, the agency inserted South Vietnamese spies into North Vietnam from the late 1950s. CIA agents also helped plan the coup that **toppled the government of President Diem** « 76–77 in November 1963.

PHUNG HOANG

ADVISOR HANDBOOK

Reining them in
The Phoenix Program handbook was produced in 1970. It aimed to combat negative publicity about the program in the US by laying out a legal framework for the program and establishing limitations on the PRUs.

Special services assist
A US Navy Seal team escorts a Viet Cong sympathizer along the Bassac River in the Mekong Delta during Operation Crimson Tide in September 1967.

"**Central** to **Phoenix** is the fact that it **targeted civilians,** not **soldiers.**"

HISTORIAN DOUGLAS VALENTINE, *THE PHOENIX PROGRAM*, 2000

AFTER

Enhanced interrogation tactics, including torture, were used in US intelligence operations after the Phoenix Program.

UNDER PRESSURE
In 1971, program architect William Colby attended a **Congressional hearing** on the Phoenix Program. He admitted that the program included illegal killings but said that this was a necessary element of war. Similar interrogation techniques were employed after Vietnam. Battalion 316, a CIA-trained military intelligence unit, used torture to gather information in **Central America** in the 1980s, and CIA interrogation techniques were also used during the **War on Terror**.

COLBY SPEAKS OUT

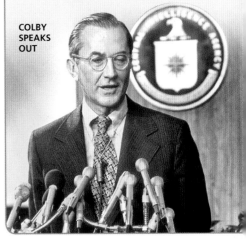

215

Protest and Elections

The Tet Offensive inflamed passions in the US, leading to widespread antiwar protests in the streets and on college campuses. These disturbances would spill over into the presidential election of 1968.

Pleading for peace
This silkscreen poster was one of eight designed and printed in 1968 by students at the Rhode Island School of Design, in Providence. The posters were sold for a few dollars each, mainly to the rising antiwar student population.

« BEFORE

The antiwar movement largely grew out of college campuses, where the radical Students for a Democratic Society (SDS) campaigned in the mid-1960s.

GROWING DISSENT
Before 1968, Americans **protested against the war** through campus teach-ins, draft resistance, and a large-scale march on Washington in 1967. Contemporary to the antiwar movement was the **Civil Rights Movement**, which also rocked the nation. Amid this growing turmoil, **Lyndon B. Johnson became president « 78–79** in 1963, in the wake of the assassination of John F. Kennedy. Johnson would be elected president in his own right in 1964, in a **landslide victory**.

Women speak out
Members of the "Women's Strike for Peace" activist group—one of the first groups to oppose the war—push their way to the doors of the Pentagon building to demand a meeting. A 30-minute lockdown ensued instead.

The year 1968 will go down as one of the most turbulent in US history: an emotional and sometimes violent confluence of war, politics, civil rights, and social revolution that rocked the country from coast to coast. In one protest, a full-page ad ran in the *New York Post*, *New York Review of Books*, and *Ramparts* magazine, explaining that nearly 530 writers and editors had pledged not to pay the 10 percent Vietnam War tax surcharge because they believed American participation in the war was "morally wrong." The list included Allen Ginsberg, Noam Chomsky, James Baldwin, and many other famous and influential writers who opposed the war.

Challengers step up

It was shaping up to be a hotly contested election year. Senator Eugene McCarthy, an antiwar senator from Minnesota, had already announced his intention to challenge Johnson for the Democratic nomination when the Tet Offensive in January 1968 threw the entire campaign into

Ready for victory
Richard Nixon flashes his signature "V for Victory" sign as he is carried by supporters at a rally in Miami Beach, Florida. Two days later he would accept the Republican nomination for the 1968 presidential election.

The blowback from Tet and mounting opposition within his own party contributed mightily to President Johnson announcing on March 31 that he would not seek reelection. Less than a week later, Dr. Martin Luther King Jr. was

California primary—threw the election and the nation into bedlam again. The protests spilled over into the August conventions. As Nixon was officially named as the Republican candidate, protesters rioted in the streets of Miami. Meanwhile, Hubert H. Humphrey emerged as the Democratic candidate in the midst of violence around the convention hall in Chicago.

The Chicago riots tipped the election in favor of the Republican candidate. Although the margin

AFTER

Sensing the antiwar sentiment that was growing in the country, President Nixon called for a de-escalation of American involvement in Vietnam.

SEEKING APPROVAL
After 1968, it was not only a small number of students and civilians who expressed their feelings against the war. Troops in Vietnam became **radicalized and demoralized** as the war dragged on 234–35 ≫.

Weary of the antiwar movement, in 1969, Nixon made a speech appealing to the "silent majority" of Americans to support **Vietnamization 228–29 ≫**, which increased the combat role of the ARVN and decreased US involvement.

was close (around half a million votes out of 73 million cast), Nixon eventually defeated Humphrey in the November general election, ending one of the most convulsive and violent periods in American political history.

> " These are **not ordinary times** and this is **not an ordinary election.**"
>
> ROBERT F. KENNEDY ANNOUNCING HIS CANDIDACY, MARCH 16, 1968

chaos. When McCarthy nearly bested Johnson in the New Hampshire primary in early March, others jumped into the fray. Robert Kennedy, brother of John F. Kennedy, declared his candidacy on March 16. Alabama's segregationist governor George Wallace was also in the race, running as a third party candidate with Vietnam veteran General Curtis LeMay as his running mate. Wallace would have one of the strongest third party campaigns in US history, carrying the southern states of Arkansas, Alabama, Mississippi, Louisiana, and Georgia.

On the other side of the race, former vice president Richard Nixon faced stiff competition from three high-profile Republican governors: Ronald Reagan, Nelson Rockefeller, and George Romney.

assassinated in Memphis, plunging the nation into one of its deepest crises since World War II.

Wave of chaos
Violence erupted in 60 cities across the US in the wake of King's assassination, with a wave of protests and riots that coincided with rising antiwar sentiment, especially on college campuses. New York's Columbia University was paralyzed by a student sit-in that mixed antiwar and civil rights sentiments. It ended with the arrest of more than 700 students.

By early summer, Kennedy had emerged as the favorite to capture the Democratic nomination and face presumptive Republican nominee Nixon. Robert Kennedy's assassination on June 6—on the heels of his victory in the

---

DECISIVE MOMENTS

BATTLE OF MICHIGAN AVENUE

The 1968 Democratic Convention in Chicago saw eight days of violent confrontation between thousands of demonstrators and the Chicago Police Department, accompanied by US Army troops and the Illinois National Guard. Leading the antiwar charge was the Youth International Party ("Yippies"), led by Jerry Rubin and Abbie Hoffman. Post-convention reports identified the Chicago police as the instigators of the violence, but seven antiwar leaders—including Hoffman and Rubin—were arrested and put on trial for inciting riots. Although convicted, not one of the so-called Chicago Seven was fined or imprisoned.

5

NIXON'S WAR

January 1969–December 197

The massive cost in both money and lives
begins to overturn public support for the v
As antiwar sentiment leads to mass protes
at home, the Nixon administration faces a
dilemma: how to de-escalate the war and
extricate American forces from Vietnam.

« Protest for peace

NIXON'S WAR
JANUARY 1969–DECEMBER 1971

President Richard Nixon took office in 1969 with the promise to "bring the boys home" without losing South Vietnam to communism. Under the policy of "Vietnamization," the US trained and equipped South Vietnamese (ARVN) troops to take on a bigger role in the war, and American troop presence was steadily de-escalated. With the burden of fighting handed over to them, the ARVN saw mixed results in battle against the North Vietnamese (NVA) due to poor leadership and morale. Peace talks in Paris soon stalled. Nixon responded by widening the war's scope: bombing Cambodia and launching cross-border incursions into both Cambodia and Laos. Cambodia, already destabilized by American action, also came under threat from communist Khmer Rouge guerrillas. Meanwhile, in the United States, antiwar protests would increase in scale.

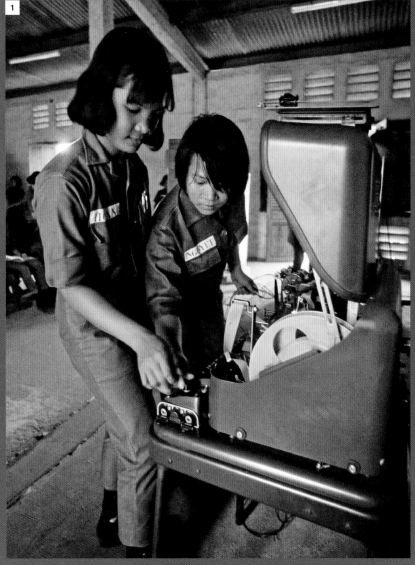

[1] Teletype operators were trained at an ARVN Signal School in Vung Tau. Vietnamization required extra provisions for training the ARVN. [2] Cambodian government troops were trained by the ARVN at Nha Trang. [3] The first American troops to be redeployed under Vietnamization departed from Da Nang.

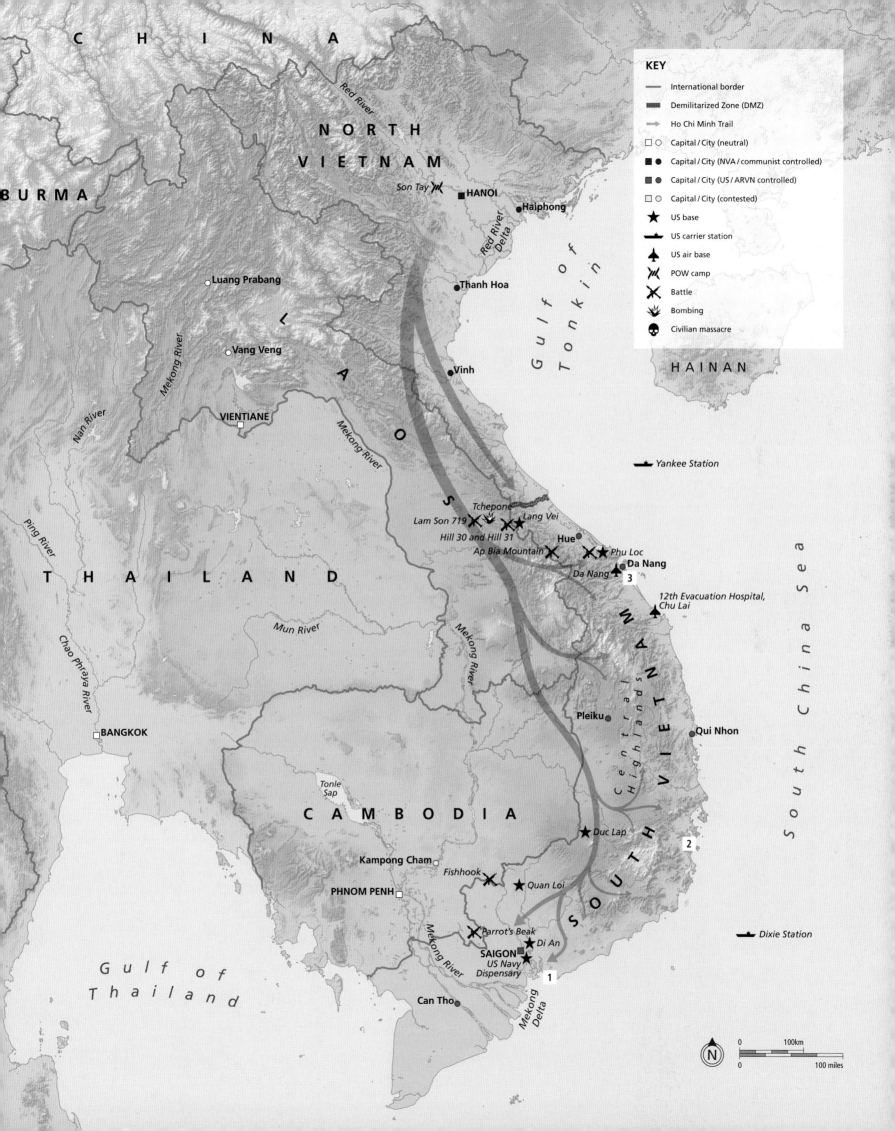

CHINA

NORTH
VIETNAM

Red River

Son Tay ⚔ ■ HANOI ● Haiphong

Red River Delta

● Thanh Hoa

○ Luang Prabang

L

○ Vang Veng

Mekong River

● Vinh

□ VIENTIANE

Gulf of
Tonkin

HAINAN

A
O
S

Mekong River

Tchepone
Lam Son 719 ✕ 💥 ✕ ★ Lang Vei
Hill 30 and Hill 31
Ap Bia Mountain ✕ ● Hue
✕✕ ● Phu Loc
Da Nang ★ ● Da Nang
3

Yankee Station

12th Evacuation Hospital,
Chu Lai ✈

THAILAND

Mun River

Mekong River

C
e
n
t
r
a
l

H
i
g
h
l
a
n
d
s

S
O
U
T
H

V
I
E
T
N
A
M

South China Sea

● Pleiku

● Qui Nhon

Ping River

Chao Phraya River

Tonle
Sap

CAMBODIA

★ Duc Lap

2

□ BANGKOK

○ Kampong Cham

Fishhook ✕
★ Quan Loi

PHNOM PENH □

Mekong River

Parrot's Beak ✕
★ Di An
SAIGON ■
US Navy
Dixie Station
Dispensary
1

Gulf of
Thailand

● Can Tho

Mekong Delta

N
0   100km
0   100 miles

BURMA

Nan River

KEY

—— International border
▨ Demilitarized Zone (DMZ)
→ Ho Chi Minh Trail
□ ○ Capital / City (neutral)
■ ● Capital / City (NVA / communist controlled)
● Capital / City (US / ARVN controlled)
□ ○ Capital / City (contested)
★ US base
⊥ US carrier station
✈ US air base
⚔ POW camp
✕ Battle
💥 Bombing
☠ Civilian massacre

TIMELINE JAN 1969–DEC 71

Richard Nixon becomes president ▪ **Secret bombing of Cambodia** ▪ Hamburger Hill
▪ **Secret peace talks** ▪ US-backed coup in Cambodia ▪ **Shootings at Kent State**
University ▪ Raid on Son Tay prison ▪ **Operation Lam Son** ▪ Rise of Khmer Rouge

1969

1970

MARCH
An investigation begins into the March 1968 massacre at My Lai, triggered by letters from Vietnam veteran Ronald Ridenhour.

JANUARY 20
Richard Nixon is inaugurated as US president, promising to bring peace with honor in Vietnam.

MARCH 17
President Nixon authorizes the secret bombing of enemy supply lines and bases in Cambodia.

⌄ Richard Nixon

APRIL 30 1969
American troop levels in Vietnam reach their peak at 543,400.

JUNE 8
President Nixon announces the withdrawal of 25,000 troops from Vietnam.

AUGUST 14
Cambodian leader Norodom Sihanouk appoints pro-American General Lon Nol as his prime minister.

OCTOBER 15
National Moratorium peace demonstrations take place across the United States.

NOVEMBER 3
President Nixon delivers a televised speech appealing for "the great silent majority of … Americans" to support his policy on Vietnam.

FEBRUARY 21
Henry Kissinger begins secret peace talks with Hanoi politburo member Le Duc Tho in Paris.

MARCH 18
In Cambodia, a US-backed coup led by General Lon Nol overthrows President Norodom Sihanouk.

⌃ Hard hat riot, May 1970

APRIL 30–JUNE 30
American and South Vietnamese forces carry out major operations across the Cambodian border, attacking communist base areas.

JANUARY 22
US Marines launch their last major offensive campaign of the Vietnam War, Operation Dewey Canyon.

MAY 10–20
Costly fighting at Hamburger Hill in the A Shau Valley causes a political outcry in the United States, leading to a ban on further major offensive action by US ground troops.

SEPTEMBER 2
Ho Chi Minh dies in Hanoi at the age of 79.

SEPTEMBER 6
Lieutenant William Calley is charged with the murder of Vietnamese civilians at My Lai.

NOVEMBER 15
About 250,000 antiwar protesters gather in Washington, D.C. for the "Mobilization" peace demonstration.

MAY 4
National Guardsmen shoot dead four students at Kent State University, Ohio, during antiwar protests provoked by the US invasion of Cambodia.

FEBRUARY 22
In a renewed offensive, the Viet Cong and NVA launch attacks against US bases and cities across South Vietnam.

« Listening to Nixon's Silent Majority speech

DECEMBER 31
By the year's end, there are 475,000 US troops in Vietnam. The American death toll for the year is 11,780.

« Headlines, May 1970

MAY 14
Two students protesting the war at Jackson State College, Mississippi, are shot by police.

"Let us be **united for peace.** Let us also be **united against defeat** ... Let us understand: **North Vietnam cannot defeat** or **humiliate** the **United States.** Only Americans can."

PRESIDENT NIXON, ADDRESS TO THE NATION, NOVEMBER 3, 1969

1971

»

JUNE 24
The Tonkin Gulf Resolution is repealed as the US Congress tries to reassert control over the president's power to take the country to war.

JUNE 30
US ground troops withdraw from Cambodia.

JAN 30–MAR 25
In Operation Lam Son 719, some 20,000 ARVN troops invade Laos with American support, aiming to cut the Ho Chi Minh Trail. They eventually withdraw having suffered heavy casualties.

JUNE 13
The publication of leaked Defense Department documents about the war begins. They are known as the Pentagon Papers.

» ARVN "tigerstripe" tunic

» Protest badge, September 1970

MARCH 29
A military court finds William Calley guilty of murdering 22 Vietnamese civilians in the My Lai Massacre.

SEPT 5–OCT 8
Operation Jefferson Glenn, inland from Hue and Da Nang, is the last major combat operation in which US ground troops take part.

LET THE PEOPLE VOTE ON WAR

VIETNAM REFERENDUM 70

OCTOBER
In Cambodia, the Khmer Rouge controls all territory east of the Mekong by the month's end and continues to make further gains.

MAY 1–5
A series of nonviolent acts of civil disobedience by antiwar militants in Washington, D.C. results in 12,000 arrests.

OCTOBER 2
Thieu is re-elected unopposed as South Vietnamese president.

OCTOBER 3
Cambodian government troops launch an offensive against Vietnamese communist and Khmer Rouge forces.

OCTOBER 9
An instance of combat refusal by troops of the Air Cavalry Division draws public attention to the poor morale of American troops in Vietnam.

» Returning sniper fire while on patrol, January 1971

Cắc

NOVEMBER 21
US Special Forces carry out a raid on Son Tay prisoner of war camp in North Vietnam, in an attempt to liberate Americans supposedly held there. The raid is codenamed Operation Ivory Coast.

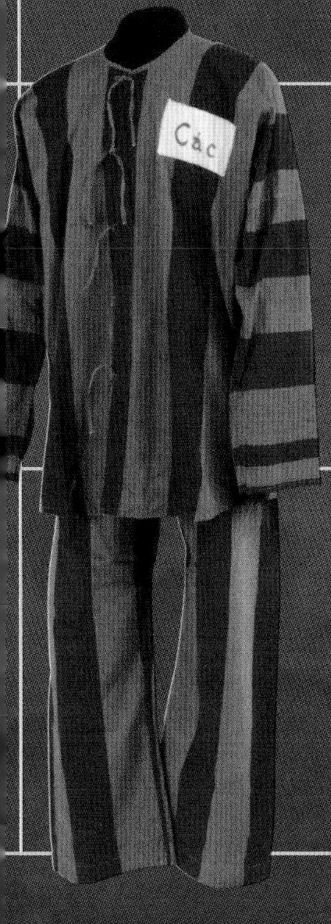

DECEMBER 26–30
President Nixon orders intensive bombing of southern North Vietnam in retaliation for breaches of the understanding that forms a basis for the peace talks.

« Prisoner of war uniform

DECEMBER 31
By the year's end, the number of US troops in Vietnam has fallen to 335,000. The American death toll for the year is 6,173.

DECEMBER 31
By the year's end, the number of US troops in Vietnam has fallen to 156,800. The American death toll for the year is 2,414.

The **Nixon** Administration

Richard Nixon assumed the presidency in January 1969, believing he could force Hanoi to negotiate, while also reducing US troop levels in Southeast Asia. Within a year, he was as frustrated with the war in Vietnam as his predecessors had been.

Inauguration day
In his Inaugural Address on January 20, 1969, Richard Nixon pledged to help lead the world out of the "valley of turmoil." Within hours, his presidential cavalcade was being pelted with rocks and beer cans from antiwar protesters.

« **BEFORE**

Americans hoped that the election of Richard Nixon would end the Vietnam War.

THE OLD NIXON
As vice president in the 1950s, Nixon had a reputation for being a **tough anticommunist**. He had urged President Eisenhower to use US troops and airpower in Indochina. Even after losing the 1960 presidential election to Kennedy, Nixon supported the new administration's decision to **increase American aid to South Vietnam**.

PROMISES OF PEACE
While campaigning for the presidency in 1968, Nixon suggested he had a **secret plan to end the war**. He promised "peace with honor" and created the expectation that he could end the stalemate and make Hanoi capitulate.

N ixon's initial efforts to end the war were as much improvisation as grand strategy. The president and his national security adviser, Henry Kissinger, guided the nation's foreign policy. Nixon was a veteran politician and Kissinger was an Ivy League international relations scholar. They shared a penchant for secrecy and crafted US policy in Vietnam without significant input from others. They had no blueprint for success in Indochina but they were confident that one existed and they would find it.

The Madman Theory

Both Nixon and Kissinger were convinced that diplomacy and the use of force had to be better coordinated. On January 25, 1969, they expanded the peace talks that Johnson had begun in Paris to include representatives of North Vietnam, South Vietnam, and the Viet Cong. Shortly afterward, on March 18, the US secretly began to bomb North Vietnamese military sanctuaries in neutral Cambodia. Nixon called this dual strategy the Madman Theory. He told Chief of Staff H. R. Haldeman that he wanted the North Vietnamese to believe that he was unpredictable and dangerous, a rampant anticommunist with his hand on the nuclear button. Secretly, the Nixon administration called the plan Operation Duck Hook. They deliberately leaked to the press that Nixon planned a "go for broke" air and naval assault to inflict punishing blows on North Vietnam.

The Silent Majority

On March 19, the administration announced the introduction of Vietnamization, a plan to increase the combat role of the South Vietnamese while reducing the number of Americans fighting the ground war. Such a prospect was widely welcomed by the American public, which was growing restless about the high cost of fighting the war, in terms of both human lives and resources. However, those who opposed continued US intervention in Vietnam were not willing to wait for de-escalation.

In October, large and peaceful antiwar protests occurred throughout the country.

To counter this public pressure and to shore up his image of determination, on November 3, Nixon made one of his most memorable public addresses—his Silent Majority speech, claiming that the antiwar protesters represented a minority that was prepared to surrender to tyranny.

Talking while fighting

Nixon's threats of massive bombing did not move the politburo in Hanoi, in part because it could see that the US public had turned against the war. Also, leadership in North Vietnam was in the hands of Le Duan following the death of Ho Chi Minh in September 1969.

While Ho Chi Minh had never ruled out negotiation, Duan was ruthlessly determined to win the heroic victory he thought was in sight.

Nixon and Kissinger, the global strategists, turned to Hanoi's chief patrons, Beijing and Moscow. Kissinger also undertook secret negotiations with North Vietnamese representatives in Paris, and Nixon made high-profile trips to the People's Republic of China and the Soviet Union in 1972. Despite a historic handshake with Mao Zedong in China and a nuclear arms treaty with the USSR, Nixon gained little leverage against North Vietnam from these trips.

> " I'm **going** to **stop the war. Fast.**"
>
> RICHARD NIXON TO CHIEF OF STAFF H. R. HALDEMAN, 1969

Meeting the troops
Nixon greets members of the First Infantry Division at their base camp in Di An, south of Saigon, in July 1969, during his first visit to Vietnam as president of the United States.

AFTER

Frustrated by the failure of his military and diplomatic moves, Nixon looked for alternative ways to deliver "peace with honor."

A NEW STRATEGY

Nixon knew that he had to try to end US intervention in Vietnam while preserving the credibility of his leadership at home and that of America abroad. As they turned to **Vietnamization 228–29 »** and diplomacy, Kissinger and Nixon spoke privately, not of victory in Vietnam, but of making South Vietnam strong enough to survive for a decent interval after US withdrawal. They wanted to avoid the appearance of abandoning an ally.

Photo opportunity
After Nixon's Silent Majority speech on November 3, White House staff invited the press to photograph Cabinet members reading telegrams from the so-called Silent Majority. In fact, the telegrams were part of a letter-writing campaign organized by the administration.

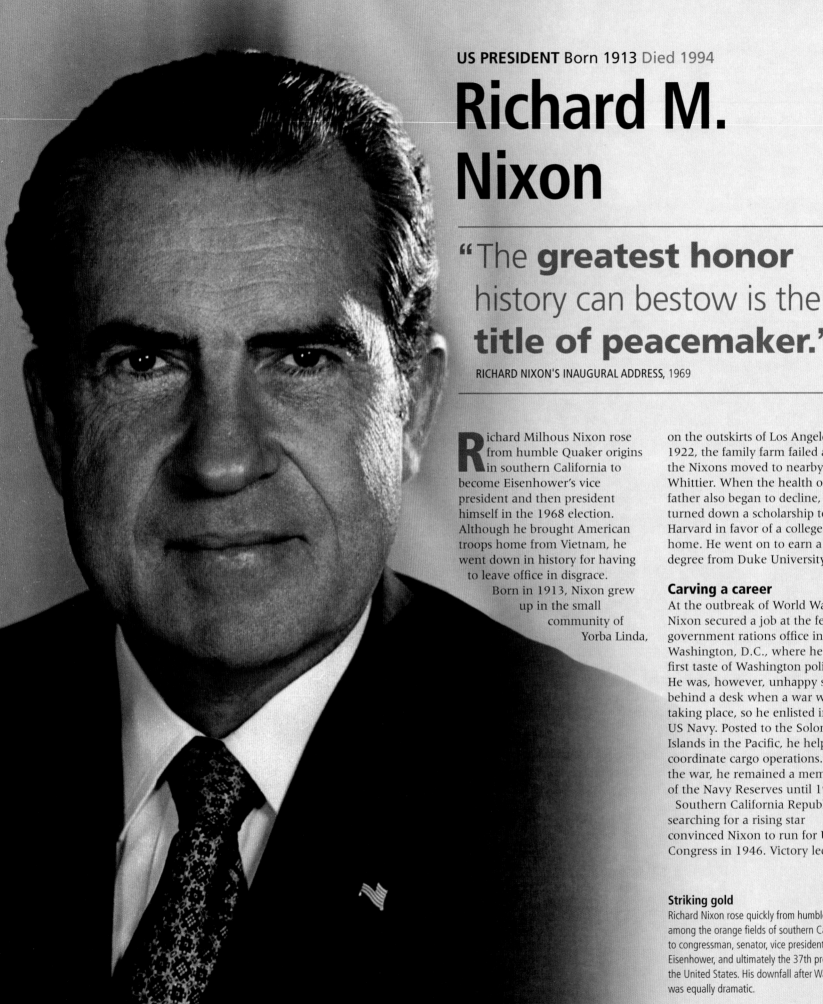

US PRESIDENT Born 1913 Died 1994

Richard M. Nixon

"The **greatest honor** history can bestow is the **title of peacemaker.**"

RICHARD NIXON'S INAUGURAL ADDRESS, 1969

Richard Milhous Nixon rose from humble Quaker origins in southern California to become Eisenhower's vice president and then president himself in the 1968 election. Although he brought American troops home from Vietnam, he went down in history for having to leave office in disgrace.

Born in 1913, Nixon grew up in the small community of Yorba Linda, on the outskirts of Los Angeles. In 1922, the family farm failed and the Nixons moved to nearby Whittier. When the health of his father also began to decline, Nixon turned down a scholarship to Harvard in favor of a college near home. He went on to earn a law degree from Duke University.

Carving a career

At the outbreak of World War II, Nixon secured a job at the federal government rations office in Washington, D.C., where he got his first taste of Washington politics. He was, however, unhappy sitting behind a desk when a war was taking place, so he enlisted in the US Navy. Posted to the Solomon Islands in the Pacific, he helped coordinate cargo operations. After the war, he remained a member of the Navy Reserves until 1966.

Southern California Republicans searching for a rising star convinced Nixon to run for US Congress in 1946. Victory led him

Striking gold

Richard Nixon rose quickly from humble origins among the orange fields of southern California to congressman, senator, vice president under Eisenhower, and ultimately the 37th president of the United States. His downfall after Watergate was equally dramatic.

Paving the way for Ford
President Nixon (center), Secretary of State Henry Kissinger (left), and White House Chief of Staff Alexander Haig (far right) meet with Congressman Gerald Ford in October 1973 to discuss Ford succeeding Spiro Agnew as vice president. Agnew had been charged with fraud.

"No event in **American history** is more **misunderstood** than the **Vietnam War.**"

RICHARD NIXON, *NO MORE VIETNAMS*, 1985

TELEVISED PRESIDENTIAL DEBATE, 1960

back to Washington and a meteoric political career that took him to the Senate in 1950 and then the White House in 1953, when be became Dwight Eisenhower's vice president. Nixon was known as a zealous anticommunist and a politician willing to cut ethical corners in order to win office—a reputation that earned him the nickname Tricky Dick.

TV politician

Nixon was one of the first politicians to exploit the power of television—he earned fame for his 1952 "Checkers" speech rebutting allegations of financial irregularities while campaigning as Eisenhower's running mate. However, his tired appearance in a televised presidential debate with John F. Kennedy in 1960 (Nixon was recovering from flu) probably cost him the White House. He was defeated again in 1962, running for governor of California, but won the presidential election in 1968 with his promise to bring the troops home from Vietnam.

Nixon did bring the troops home. His Vietnamization program, ping-pong diplomacy, and détente with China, including his landmark visit to Beijing in 1972, culminated in the Paris Peace Accords of 1973. Despite his conservative leanings, Nixon's environmental policies were often progressive. He created the Environmental Protection Agency (EPA) and supported the Clean Air Act of 1970. The Nixon White House also launched the controversial War on Drugs, which some thought was a way to attack two of the constituencies that most opposed him—African Americans and young, liberal whites.

Watergate and after

Despite running well ahead of Democrat George McGovern in the 1972 presidential election, Nixon could not divorce himself from the dirty tricks that had always marked his campaigns. On June 17, 1972, five men were arrested for breaking into the Democratic party

Mounting pressure
Campaigners outside the US Capitol state their demands on October 21, 1973, the day after Nixon fired Watergate Special Prosecutor Archibald Cox and Attorney General Elliot Richardson resigned in protest.

headquarters at the Watergate complex. *Washington Post* reporters Bob Woodward and Carl Bernstein linked the burglars to the White House. The scandal forced Nixon to resign in August 1974.

President Gerald Ford, Nixon's successor, granted him a full pardon in September 1974. Nixon began the process of rehabilitating his image by writing books and making high-profile foreign trips. He spent his last 15 years living in and around New York City, finally passing away at his home in New Jersey in April 1994.

« BEFORE

The escalation of the number of US ground forces in Vietnam peaked in the spring of 1969.

REEVALUATING COMMITMENT
US military personnel in Vietnam totaled 543,000 in April 1969, marking the highpoint of American ground combat forces and support personnel. ARVN strength was at 897,000. Since the first **build-up of US forces « 90–91** in 1965, US infantry and airmobile divisions had conducted large-scale offensive operations, while ARVN troops had provided **population security « 140–41** and conducted smaller operations. However, the 1968 **Tet Offensive « 178–93** had prompted the Johnson administration to reexamine its strategy in Vietnam. By 1969, public opinion and that in Washington had shifted against the war.

Vietnamization

Wary of the rising human costs and the unpopularity of the war in Vietnam, the Nixon administration was eager to withdraw American troops. As the US increased economic aid to South Vietnam, it also made moves to transfer the burden of fighting to the ARVN.

By 1969, the war had gone on longer and cost more than anyone had foreseen. General Creighton Abrams had replaced Westmoreland as the head of Military Assistance Command Vietnam (MACV)

Defending their homes
At the village level, Vietnamization entailed training a civil self-defense force to provide security against Viet Cong and NVA attack. These lightly armed local militias in each province received about 13 weeks of training.

in 1968, and after Nixon became president, Abrams began a process called Vietnamization.

The Nixon Doctrine
Reportedly coined by Nixon's Secretary of Defense Melvin Laird, Vietnamization was the operational term for what journalists called the Nixon Doctrine. It was the policy of transferring responsibility for combat in Vietnam from American forces to the ARVN, leading to the withdrawal of US troops from Vietnamese soil.

Citing improved ARVN capability, the White House announced the withdrawal of 25,000 US forces on June 8, 1969. Shortly after, Nixon met with South Vietnamese president Nguyen Van Thieu at Midway Island. He praised Thieu's leadership and reaffirmed US support for the Saigon government. Then, in a press conference on the Pacific island of Guam, in July 1969, the US president made a statement—quickly labeled the Nixon Doctrine—that while the US would continue to provide military

Operation Keystone Eagle
The First Battalion, Ninth Marine Regiment board the troop ship USS *Paul Revere* at Da Nang, headed for Okinawa. Their departure on July 14, 1969, followed a lavish ceremony for the Ninth Marines, who were some of the first troops redeployed as a result of Vietnamization.

and economic aid to its allies, those nations would henceforth be expected to use their own soldiers to bear the burden of any fighting.

Although Vietnamization was portrayed as evidence of progress in Saigon, it was actually central to Nixon's effort to end the drain of the war on the United States and reduce political pressure at home. Vietnamization was a policy, not a

73 PERCENT of the generals in the US Army believed that Vietnamization was so effective that it should have been implemented earlier, according to a 1974 survey.

plan, and its timing and evolution were determined almost entirely by US domestic politics. Fewer American service personnel in Vietnam meant fewer American casualties—and, the administration hoped, less public outcry against the war. While the program decreased the role of American troops, it also increased supplies to the ARVN, which reassured the war's supporters that commitment

to South Vietnam remained strong.

To be successful, Vietnamization had to be about more than simply substituting ARVN troops for US units—or South Vietnamese blood for American blood. Efforts to strengthen Saigon's military forces were straightforward. As US troop levels dropped sharply in 1969 and 1970, MACV returned to the advisory model for US units that had existed before 1965. MACV set up special schools and training activities in a "modernization and improvement program" for the expanded ARVN.

The three selfs
Nation building in South Vietnam also required many nonmilitary improvements. The country needed rural pacification, public services, economic viability, and security for its citizens. However, policing, land reforms, controlling inflation, holding local elections, rooting out Viet Cong, and increasing the rice harvest were not improvements that US military assistance alone could provide. The South Vietnamese summarized their needs as self-

The word from Washington
US Special Forces and Montagnard Civilian Irregular Defense Group members at Duc Lap listen to the radio broadcast of Nixon's November 3, 1969, speech, which affirms that South Vietnamese troops will assume full responsibility for the defense of South Vietnam.

defense, self-government, and self-development—known as the three selfs.

Vietnamization assessed
The success of the policy was difficult to measure. South Vietnam provided well for refugees, and succeeded at land redistribution. Roads that had been unsafe were made usable. The rice harvest in 1969 was the best in five years, and tractors replaced water buffalo for plowing. Accomplishments were modest, but genuine.

Success in terms of the war effort was harder to pinpoint. Viet Cong and North Vietnamese activity decreased in many areas of South Vietnam but likely not because of increased ARVN size. The politburo in Hanoi held back, biding its time for further US withdrawals. Meanwhile, low morale and weak leadership continued to plague Saigon's troops. Those tasked with training the ARVN struggled to keep up with the timetable created by Nixon's administration. There was simply not enough time.

VIETNAM SERVICE SLEEVE INSIGNIA

After just over two years in office, the Nixon administration had halved the number of US forces in South Vietnam. The burden of ground combat rested on the shoulders of the ARVN.

FIGHTING THEIR OWN FIGHT
The number of US military personnel in Vietnam fell to 239,000 in June 1971 and **continued to decline**. ARVN strength, on the other hand, was at 1,048,000, and these troops began to take on more responsibility for fighting the Viet Cong and NVA. When most **US troops left Vietnam « 234–35 »**, however, the ARVN struggled without US backup.

"Our **whole strategy** depended on whether this program **succeeded**."
PRESIDENT RICHARD NIXON, *NO MORE VIETNAMS*, 1985

US COMMANDER Born 1914   Died 1974

Creighton W. Abrams

"The way to **eat** an **elephant** is **one bite at a time.**"

CREIGHTON ABRAMS, LETTER TO FRIENDS, 1964

On July 2, 1968, General Creighton W. Abrams replaced General William Westmoreland as commander of the Military Assistance Command Vietnam (MACV). This change had been anticipated for many weeks. Westmoreland's war of attrition, designed to force Hanoi to abandon the South, had failed and a new approach was needed. Abrams believed that the security of the South Vietnamese, right down to village level, was the key to success.

Modest start
Born in 1914 in Springfield, Massachusetts, Abrams grew up in modest circumstances in the nearby town of Agawam. At the age of 17, he entered the US Military Academy at West Point, graduating in 1936 alongside William Westmoreland. He began his career in horse cavalry but soon switched to the armored branch.

Abrams first saw combat in World War II, commanding the tank battalion that spearheaded General George Patton's Third Army advance through Europe. An aggressive and talented leader, he led the relief of the besieged 101st Airborne Division at Bastogne during the Battle of the Bulge. Patton called Abrams "the best tank commander in the Army."

During the Korean War, Abrams served as chief of staff of three different army corps. In 1963, and by then a lieutenant general, he commanded V Corps in West Germany, on the frontline of

Dedicated public servant
Secretary of Defense James Schlesinger described the direct and plain-speaking Abrams as "an authentic national hero" for his personal bravery, tenacity, and unwavering dedication to service.

the Cold War. As US involvement in Vietnam deepened, President Johnson promoted Abrams to the rank of general (over the heads of several three-star generals), alongside Harold K. Johnson and William Westmoreland. From this group, the president made Johnson US Army chief of staff, Abrams vice chief of staff, and Westmoreland commander of MACV.

Upgrading the ARVN

From 1964 to 1967, Abrams and Johnson worked as a team to create an army that was fit for Vietnam, even though it contained a large number of draftees and inexperienced officers. Johnson and Abrams commissioned a report called "A Program for Pacification and Long-Term Development of Vietnam," or PROVN. From it, Abrams took the idea of "one war"—the integration of military operations and pacification.

In May 1967, Abrams reported to Vietnam as Westmoreland's deputy commander with the responsibility of upgrading the performance of the ARVN. Over the next six months he traveled to every ARVN command in the country. When

World War II hero

Abrams twice received the Distinguished Service Cross for extraordinary bravery. On both occasions, his tank advanced ahead of his battalion, against superior forces, inspiring his men and turning the course of battle.

the Tet Offensive erupted in January 1968, the ARVN's improved response was credited to him. Abrams himself directed the US–ARVN counterattack that retook Hue during the Tet Offensive.

Abrams's war

Upon replacing Westmoreland in July 1968, Abrams began implementing his "one war"

interrupt enemy supplies and provide more local security. While the shorthand for Westmoreland's method had been search-and-destroy, for Abrams it was reconnaissance in force—now referred to as clear-and-hold. Success was measured by the number of towns and villages under the control of Saigon. For Abrams, it was a complex effort that required more time to implement than he had at his disposal. The political will to continue US intervention was already gone by then.

Abrams commanded an American force that numbered only 47,000 when he turned MACV over to

"It's **the people ...** both sides are **struggling for.**"

GENERAL CREIGHTON ABRAMS BRIEFING JOINT CHIEF OF STAFF CHAIRMAN GENERAL EARLE WHEELER, OCTOBER 4, 1969

concept. He cut back on the heavy use of artillery against villages and on the large-unit rural sweeps that often hurt civilians. Instead, he employed small-unit patrols to

Cigar moment

General Abrams (left) and Secretary of Defense Melvin Laird (right) light each other's cigars as they listen to a briefing on pacification at the village of An Noi, 27 miles (43 km) northwest of Saigon, in 1970.

General Frederick Weyand in June 1972. In his new appointment as US Army chief of staff, Abrams worked to restore morale and purpose to the institution that had been his life, and whose pride and reputation had been battered by an unpopular war. He was still serving in this position when he died of cancer on September 4, 1974.

It is unknowable whether Abrams's "one war" approach, if started earlier, would have produced a better outcome for Washington and Saigon than what occurred, but within the US Army Abrams holds an honored place.

September 15, 1914 Born in Springfield, Massachusetts, the son of a repairman for Boston & Albany Railroad.

1936 Graduates from West Point and marries Julia Harvey.

1936–40 Serves as lieutenant and captain in First Cavalry Division.

1938 Birth of Noel, the first of six children. The three sons become army officers, and the three daughters marry army officers.

1940 Serves as tank company commander in First Armored Division.

1941–43 Becomes a lieutenant colonel and commands the 37th Tank Battalion, Fourth Armored Division, Third Army, under General George S. Patton.

September 1944 Leads Combat Command B in the Battle of the Bulge.

1945 Receives field promotion to colonel.

1949–52 Commands 63rd Tank Battalion and Second Armored Cavalry Regiment.

ABRAMS IN THE TURRET OF A TANK, 1945

1953–54 Serves as chief of staff for three corps commands in Korea.

1956 Promoted to brigadier general and serves as deputy chief of staff for reserve components.

1959 Promoted to rank of major general and becomes commander of the Third Armored Division.

1962 Transferred to the Pentagon as deputy chief of staff for operations.

1963 Appointed lieutenant general and commands V Corps in Europe.

1964 Promoted to general and named vice chief of staff.

May 1967 Named deputy commander of Military Assistance Command Vietnam (MACV). Becomes commander the following year.

June 1972 Appointed chief of staff of the US Army.

September 4, 1974 Dies of lung cancer in Washington, D.C.

The **ARVN**

Frequently maligned as the puppet army of foreign powers, and often the victim of its own leaders and patrons, the Army of the Republic of Vietnam (ARVN) became a scapegoat for South Vietnam's defeat by the North Vietnamese.

The ARVN was formally established by the government of President Diem in 1955, following the French withdrawal. The US then took over supplying and training the force. In spite of US support, morale remained low.

Organization
The ARVN grew from a modest strength of 150,000 in the 1950s to a seemingly robust total of one million by 1975. In addition to the army, there were separately organized and smaller air, naval, marine, and commando services. The ARVN was organized on three levels: regular forces, regional forces (RF), and popular forces (PF). American soldiers often referred to the last two of these as "Ruff Puffs." Equipment and training varied widely at the three

levels. The best was the regular army, consisting of 13 infantry divisions, seven ranger groups, and various elite and support elements. The regional forces supplied the troops for the ARVN's four regional commands, and the popular forces under the control of local councils provided security for cities, towns, and major installations.

Leadership
One of the major weaknesses of the ARVN was that senior officer positions were largely determined by patronage and there was little possibility of promotion of able soldiers into the officer class. The majority of commanders were Catholic, as was Diem, but most of the troops were Buddhist.

Corruption was endemic as the less-qualified officers pocketed funds intended for their units or kicked back funds to superiors to retain their positions. Reforms occurred under Vietnamization, but a toxic culture remained entrenched. Many of the top commanders adhered to vestiges of passive French defensive tactics, while their younger, American-trained juniors often favored aggressive operations—creating tension and confusion in the officer corps. A frequent charge was that the generals commanded from safe rear areas, rather than facing the enemy.

Life in the ranks
The enlisted men often lacked loyalty to their own government, felt pushed aside by the American commanders, and were ill-equipped

In recognition of valor
The highest military decoration of South Vietnam, the Military Merit medal was awarded mostly to enlisted men for valor in combat. Established in 1950, the medal was modeled after the French Médaille Militaire. It was last awarded in 1975.

> **"**I always returned to the fighting, but **close to home ...** that is how Vietnamese had fought for centuries.**"**
>
> INTERVIEW WITH PHAN THUY, ARVN ARTILLERY OFFICER, 1999

and poorly trained. Yet, in the end they were called upon to fight to save their country. American officers sometimes declared that the ARVN spent too much time complaining, but the conditions under which many served were deplorable. The official number of ARVN desertions was unusually high, although statistics were misleading because a soldier absent for even one day was listed as being a deserter, rather than absent without leave (AWOL). Many soldiers only missed reporting for duty on one or two days or joined another unit closer to their home while still listed as a deserter on another roster.

ARVN conscription methods were severe, and the Saigon government was largely unresponsive to the personal needs of its troops. ARVN soldiers received no mail, their pay was meager, and barracks and dependent housing were in short supply and corruptly allocated. Food rations were inadequate and frequently pilfered. American canned goods and soy sauce were poor substitutes for the fish, rice, vegetables, and nuoc mam cham (fish sauce) that were the staples of the South Vietnamese diet.

Camouflaged in combat
The "Tiger Stripe" camouflage pattern on this ARVN Marines shirt is believed to have been first used by the Vietnamese Marine Corps from 1959. The style was derived from the French "Lizard Pattern" of the early 1950s.

Manning a gun emplacement
Soldiers of the ARVN man a gun emplacement in June 1970. These largely conscripted troops were often very young and poorly trained. The arms and equipment were overwhelmingly supplied by the US.

Motivation to fight

Many US military observers were puzzled when they noticed how the North Vietnamese soldiers and the Viet Cong guerrillas seemed to fight with more determination than the ARVN. As the war progressed, the South Vietnamese forces became increasingly dependent upon American support. The continuous supply of replacement parts and new equipment, and the availability of massive air support when needed paradoxically seemed to inhibit the resourcefulness and self-reliance of the Southerners.

Nevertheless, many ARVN officers and troops fought effectively during the multipronged Tet Offensive of 1968 and then in the Easter Offensive of 1972. They also offered strong resistance during the final chapter of the war in April 1975.

It has often been observed that, in combat, soldiers in all armies fight for one another above all else. It is clear that the ARVN fought to protect their homes and families more than for the government. Some 200,000 ARVN soldiers died during the conflict.

Packing parachutes

Following the establishment of a training school for female soldiers in 1966, soldiers of the Women's Armed Forces Corps of the ARVN took on a variety of support roles. Here, a group of recruits are instructed on parachute packing at the 90th Aerial Equipment Depot.

AFTER »

When South Vietnam lost the war in 1975, the soldiers in the ARVN lost the country for which they had been drafted to fight.

THE FATE OF THE ARVN
When the victorious North assumed control of South Vietnam in April 1975, some conscripted soldiers of the ARVN **returned to their villages**. Decades after the end of the war, the families of those who supported the government of the South were subject to restrictions.

RE-EDUCATION
Anyone who held any degree of command responsibility was sent to a **re-education camp 332–33 »**, where many died in the harsh and dangerous conditions.

Withdrawal and Demoralization

As the war became more controversial, the feelings of Cold War anticommunism and patriotism that had previously inspired soldiers weakened. Personal survival increasingly became more important than the mission to many US soldiers and ARVN allies.

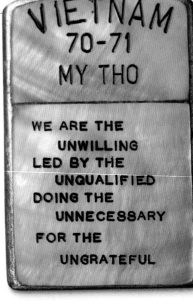

BEFORE

Throughout the war, American soldiers listened to rock and roll music and its protest lyrics as an outlet for their frustration.

WAR ANTHEMS
One of the most popular songs among the troops, the 1965 hit "We Gotta Get Out of This Place" by the Animals, was banned from Armed Forces Radio by the South Vietnamese government. With their portable cassette tape players, however, GIs had ready access to songs that voiced **resistance to authority,** including Jimi Hendrix's "Purple Haze," Los Bravos's "Black is Black," the Beatles' "Hey Jude," and John Fogerty's "Fortunate Son."

Desperate and fatigued
A US infantryman lies exhausted on the ground as he drinks from a canteen in the Fishhook region. The US suffered heavy losses during grueling combat there in 1970, relying on a steady influx of troops to replace the fallen.

American troop withdrawals did not happen all at once, but by the end of 1969, the number of troops in Vietnam had decreased by 115,000, and by December 1970, there would be only 280,000 left. In the year in between, a common feeling grew among US servicemen: nobody wanted to be the last to die in Vietnam. The strain of fighting

> ## "Hey man, tell them back in the world we're coming home, and we're never coming back."
> A US ARMY MEDIC SPEAKS TO DOCUMENTARY FILMMAKER JOHN PILGER FOR *THE QUIET MUTINY,* 1970

a war with poorly articulated objectives manifested itself in attacks on both officers and noncommissioned officers (NCOs), racial disharmony, and increasingly widespread drug use. Echoing debates at home, many soldiers began to question America's role

in Vietnam, their letters home damning the immoral, unlawful, and inglorious war they found themselves still fighting in.

Incremental exit
US troops were withdrawn from Vietnam in a series of incremental "redeployments" under the codename Keystone. The first troops withdrawn, the Ninth

Infantry Division, departed Vietnam in June 1969 in Operation Keystone Eagle. More followed: Keystone Cardinal, in late 1969, withdrew 45,000 US troops, and Keystone Bluejay, in spring 1970, saw another 50,000 return home. The troops sent home came from various branches of the military, so that proportional representation of each service was maintained. This was counter to General Abrams's original plan, which would have seen the bulk of initial redeployment focus on the Marine Corps; arguments about the makeup of each increment would continue into 1972.

Racial tensions
For those left behind in Vietnam, morale was in freefall. The US military during the late 1960s reflected the same issues prevalent at home. Before 1969, troops in

Unhappy service
This Zippo by artist Bradford Edwards—engraved with a quote from Czech historian Konstantin Josef Jireček—is a copy of a lighter used by a GI in Vietnam. Soldiers often had their lighters engraved with words showing dark humor, disillusionment, and references to death.

Vietnam were not immune to the racial tensions in American society, but combat had a way of bonding warriors. After 1969, however, the self-segregation of soldiers off duty or in rear areas away from active combat became ever more apparent. This practice likely mirrored attitudes brought over from the United States.

Threats to discipline
In an era when the youth culture was openly challenging authority in America on many fronts, strong leadership of young men in combat

also became a special challenge. The expansion of the Army had left a deficit in experienced small unit leadership—junior officers and sergeants. While most men placed in these roles performed well, there were some who exposed units to ambushes, firefights, or petty harassment. Six-month rotations of officers and one-year tours of duty in-country also made unit cohesion difficult and threatened the ability of leaders to command the respect of their men. Particularly disturbing

60 PERCENT of GIs used drugs to escape anxiety or boredom, according to a 1970 report by the Pentagon.

was the increasing incidence of fragging: the intentional use of a fragmentation grenade against unit leaders. Fragging was both murder and an attack on authority. Drugs and alcohol played a part in most of these disputes, threatening to undermine discipline. Marijuana and amphetamines, commonly used by young Americans in the late 1960s, were cheap and easy to obtain throughout Vietnam.

Escaping the war
GIs exchange heroin vials in a decorated bunk in Vietnam. Opium and heroin were cheap, and of a high quality, but used primarily in secure areas because their narcotic effect could get the user killed.

Counting the days
A tank crew member nicknamed Big Buddha stares morosely at his combat base in 1971. A hand-painted sign on the tank's protective shield expressed his desire to leave Vietnam, as ever more US units left the country.

AFTER

Studies of Vietnam veterans indicated that drug use primarily stemmed from combat exposure and that 90 percent of veterans stopped using drugs upon their return to the United States.

NEGATIVE IMAGES
Although the Nixon administration tried to downplay the military's concerns about drug use, **popular stereotypes** began to emerge back home of service members as "potheads" and drug addicts. These images were inaccurate overall, but sadly heroin addiction did afflict many **returning service men and women 344–45 ≫**, who often struggled to get the help they needed.

Longing for peace
US artillerymen take a break at the Laotian border in 1971. The proliferation of peace signs among US troops—who painted them on tanks and pinned them to helmets—showed their diminishing support for the war.

<< BEFORE

Hamburger Hill

The US top command in Vietnam had changed, but skepticism of American strategy remained.

THE END OF ATTRITION
Strategy under General Westmoreland had followed the **attrition model**, which relied on large unit operations intended to produce body count and to exhaust the enemy. By 1969, questions were being raised about what actual territory South Vietnam controlled, how the use of massive firepower conflicted with **pacification programs** << 212–13, and what moral price the US was paying for relying on attrition.

The American push for Ap Bia Mountain, later known as Hamburger Hill, was the product of General Abrams's positional strategy. A grim and grueling battle, it produced a high body count on both sides and further inflamed public debate on US conduct of the war.

Westmoreland's attrition strategy underestimated the value of holding territory. Just like his predecessor, General Abrams was prepared to use US combat power, but his new idea was to use it not just to take out the North Vietnamese Army (NVA), but to deny its forces access to major population centers. To accomplish that objective, he sought to target key locations and not just enemy personnel.

Abrams makes plans
In 1969, General Abrams designed a large-scale assault that utilized US and South Vietnamese (ARVN) units to prevent the NVA from launching attacks on cities in the I Corps Tactical Zone: the provinces of Quang Tri, Thua Thien, Quang Nam, Quang Tin, and Quang Ngai, all in the north of South Vietnam.

On May 10, 1969, Abrams launched Operation Apache Snow, which was intended to protect the

Mountain of the Crouching Beast. The US would later come to know it as Hamburger Hill—so called because the terrible carnage there made it akin to a human meat grinder.

Carnage on the hill

Units of the Third Brigade of the 101st Airborne Division, the Ninth Marine Regiment, and ARVN First Division's Third Regiment were flown in by transport helicopters, to approach up the hill and attack the NVA on the top. Rather than retreat, the NVA on the hill decided to stand and fight on the high ground, and combat raged there for 10 days.

After one US regiment attacked with little success, two regiments of the 101st Airborne, and the ARVN regiment, reinforced the attacking force. The tenacity of the US and ARVN ground forces—and the heavy bombardment by air support with B-52s—dislodged the defenders, but the fog of war prolonged the engagement. A torrential downpour on May 18 turned the mountain slopes into mudslides, and on two occasions US helicopter gunships mistakenly struck elements of the 101st Airborne approaching the ridge However, with all four US and ARVN regiments involved in the eleventh assault on the mountain, the NVA finally withdrew into Laos on May 20.

About 600 NVA died in the fighting, and around 70 US troops were killed, with a further 370 wounded. These numbers were not

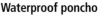

Waterproof poncho
US Army-issued multipurpose ponchos such as this one were worn during the downpour at Hamburger Hill, but could also be unbuttoned for use as tents, shelters, blankets, and ground sheets.

as high as those from single engagements in 1968 during and after the Tet Offensive, but the NVA had taken heavy losses and been forced out of the pivotal A Shau Valley. Operation Apache Snow's objectives had been achieved, and US forces and those of the ARVN withdrew from Hill 937. Although the NVA moved back onto the hill, they would not use the supply route through the valley for three years.

Unpopular strategy

In spite of this objective success, the battle sparked outcry in the US. The media painted a bleak picture of the battle. Senator Edward Kennedy labeled the engagement

Temporary fixes
Medics attend to wounded soldiers during the heavy rainstorm on Ap Bia Mountain. The wounded were hooked up to saline drips (pictured) and treated with field bandages before they were carried on litters to waiting Medevac choppers.

cities of Hue and Da Nang by targeting the NVA's logistical network and staging areas between the Laotian border and the coast.

Unpopular strategy

The heaviest fighting of Apache Snow occurred in Ap Bia Mountain in the A Shau Valley. Marked on US military maps as Hill 937— meaning it was 3,074 feet (937 m) high—it was known to locals as the

Keeping record
This 1967 Philips portable tape recorder was used in the field in Vietnam. Battlefield reports heavily influenced US public opinion on Hamburger Hill, with one such report by Jay Sharbutt for the Associated Press bringing the name "Hamburger Hill" into American discourse.

Hamburger Hill, and the outrage it provoked, was the catalyst for a re-evaluation of US strategy.

TERRIBLE TOLL
Under pressure from the public and the Pentagon, General Abrams switched to a strategy of **protective reaction**, which would minimize US casualties. However, the damage was already done. *Life* magazine printed "The Faces of the American Dead in Vietnam: One Week's Toll," with portraits of **242 men killed** in a week. Many did not die at Hamburger Hill, but the public associated them with the battle nonetheless.

at Hamburger Hill "senseless and irresponsible." War critics argued against continuing to endanger US troops in battles over territory that would not be held—and would likely return to enemy control soon after. It was difficult for those who were already against the war to appreciate the distinction Abrams made between denying the enemy a place and occupying that area.

" I'll take a **court martial** before I go up … again. It's **suicide.**"

A 19-YEAR-OLD GI, INTERVIEWED BY UPI STAFFER BERT W. OKULY, MAY 1969

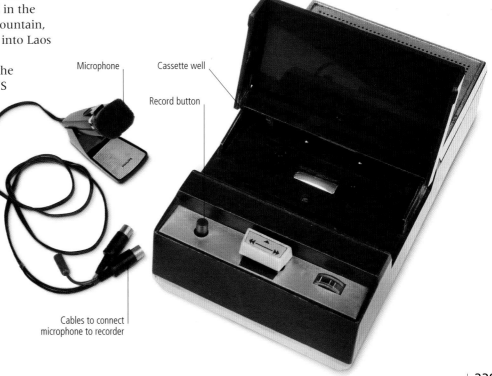

Microphone   Cassette well

Record button

Cables to connect microphone to recorder

Medevac and Treatment

The efficiency of evacuating wounded men by helicopter and the effectiveness of medical treatment in Vietnam sharply lowered the death toll compared to previous American wars, but also led to a larger percentage of survivors with serious permanent injuries.

BEFORE

Helicopters were first used by the US to evacuate wounded troops during the Korean War.

IMPROVED RESPONSE

In Korea, Medevac helicopters took soldiers from the front lines to makeshift **Mobile Army Surgical Hospitals**, pioneered by surgeon Michael DeBakey. While this allowed wounded men to be treated much more quickly than before, the war still saw **26 percent of casualties** die from their wounds.

TESTING SUPER GLUE

Dr. Harry Coover invented cyanoacrylate—labeled Eastman 910 Adhesive and now known as Super Glue—in the 1940s. In 1966, he got permission to test it as a sutureless wound closure on the battlefield and in field hospitals in Vietnam. The glue worked, successfully reducing bleeding and infection, but the version in use at the time was too concentrated and also caused irritation to the skin.

Medical support for US forces increased with the escalation of ground forces. In April 1965, the US Army had one field hospital at Nha Trang with 100 beds, and the US Navy had a dispensary at Saigon. By the end of 1968, there were more than 5,000 beds at Army hospitals,

All-purpose kit
Combat medics were expected to treat a wide range of problems. This medic's survival pack contained morphine sulfate lozenges for severe pain and tablets to treat seasickness, malaria, fever, diarrhoea, and sweating.

while the USS *Repose* and USS *Sanctuary*—Navy hospital ships— each had capacity for 800 patients.

In South Vietnam, the US created evacuation hospitals, surgical hospitals, field hospitals, and a convalescent hospital. These essentially permanent facilities had air-conditioning, sanitary environments, and high-tech equipment. US Army surgeons were also able to perform blood transfusions—even in the field— and other lifesaving procedures.

The hospitals were staffed with a wide range of surgical and other specialists. Each division of the army had its own medical specialists, including physical therapists, dieticians, and

pharmacists. Such roles were not limited to men, and some women served in these capacities.

Evacuating the wounded

The availability of medevac, commonly called "dust off," helicopters, and the proximity to the battlefield of well-equipped and staffed evacuation hospitals saved countless lives. The air ambulances were reconfigured UH-1 troop transports, known as "Hueys" or "slicks," that could accommodate up to nine litters. They could be in the air within three minutes of receiving a call and could have their patients in a hospital within 15 minutes of lift-off from the landing zone (LZ).

Despite large red crosses on the aircraft, they faced intense enemy fire when extracting the wounded. Armed escort gunships provided suppressing fire, but many times medevac pilots ignored standard procedures and flew into hot LZs without cover. Sometimes they had to hover and hoist the litters. They flew day and night and in all types of weather and terrain, performing seemingly impossible rescues. The peak year for the number of patients evacuated by dust off was 1969, when 206,000 US, ARVN, other allies, and

civilians were transported. The dust off pilots and crews and the medical corpsmen in each unit performed heroic service, and in the two-year period, 39 medevac crew members were killed in action in Vietnam.

Surviving the worst

Sixty-five percent of all wounds were to upper and lower extremities, leaving survivors with amputations or paralysis that would require

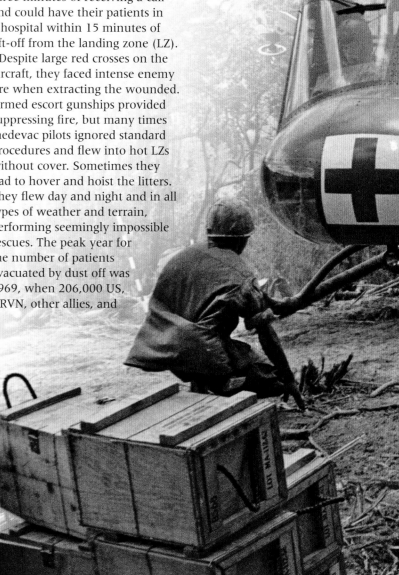

long-term recuperation and rehabilitation. Of those who made it through the first 24 hours after injury, only one percent died. Overall, 19 percent of US casualties died from their wounds in Vietnam. One reason for these survival rates, which were better than in previous wars, was the less destructive nature of North Vietnamese and Viet Cong weapons. More than half of US deaths were from small arms, mines, and booby traps.

Treated abroad

After treatment in-country, the wounded who required additional surgery or extended recuperation, or who were eligible for medical discharge, were flown in C-141 Starlifter medical transports, first to Japan and then directly to hospitals in the US. The transportation system, coordinated by Military Assistance Command Vietnam (MACV), sought to utilize Pacific and mainland US resources, while also maximizing the availability of beds and resources in Vietnam.

Many soldiers returned home with severe psychological and physical trauma, necessitating further care on US soil that was sometimes hard to come by.

CONTINUED CARE

Many combat veterans experienced **post-traumatic stress disorder** (PTSD), which was poorly understood and diagnosed. **Agent Orange** exposure led to serious conditions in veterans and birth defects in their children. The many **amputee** veterans would also require long-term or lifelong care.

AMPUTEE VETERANS

" You were just such a **target ...** [flying] the **medevac choppers.** "

MICHAEL BRADBURY, THIRD BATTALION OF THE 26TH MARINE REGIMENT, THIRD MARINE DIVISION, IN AN INTERVIEW, 2003

Rushed from the field

A wounded soldier of the 101st Airborne Division is carried to a waiting UH-1H after battle at Hamburger Hill. While medevac helicopters were required to be marked with a red cross, medics had stopped wearing this symbol.

US Nurses

The enduring image of American women serving in Vietnam is that of the nurse. These women provided a broad spectrum of care for soldiers and civilians alike, and many emerged from the war traumatized by what they had seen.

Most nurses in Vietnam served in US Army hospitals, but the war also saw the service of US Air Force flight nurses and US Navy nurses on hospital ships. All treated a steady stream of patients with horrific injuries and serious tropical diseases, and many experienced difficult social and professional readjustment after their service.

The maximum number of military nurses in Vietnam at one time was about 900 in 1969 at the peak of the overall US troop deployment. As many as 6,000 US nurses were posted to Vietnam over the course of the war. Most of them were young, in their early twenties, and had clinical training but limited experience with the injuries and illness they encountered in the war zone. All were volunteers, and most were patriotically motivated, but in many cases also attracted by recruiting incentives that subsidized nursing training. By 1969, about 20 percent of nurses were men.

83 PERCENT of US women who served were nurses.

60 PERCENT had less than two years of training.

Varied roles
Nurses performed a wide range of medical duties. Much of their work was in disease and infection control, pain management, and the provision of psychological comfort to the wounded. Malaria and dengue fever were prevalent in Vietnam, and both were life-threatening, as were encephalitis, typhus, hepatitis, and other infectious diseases. Nurses managed such cases and sometimes became infected themselves. They would also play a role in caring for those undergoing treatment for drug addiction.

In addition to taking care of American personnel, US nurses participated in humanitarian operations, such as the Medical Civic Action Program (MEDCAP), which provided vital outpatient medical services to South Vietnamese civilians in rural areas.

Earning recognition
US Navy nurses Lieutenant Barbara Wooster, Lieutenant Ruth Mason, and Lieutenant Ann Reynolds become the first women awarded purple heart medals in Vietnam, for surviving the Christmas 1964 Viet Cong bombing in Saigon.

Job stress
Nurses in a war zone suffered many kinds of emotional strains and stresses. The incidence of both post-traumatic stress disorder and emotional problems was high among nurses, who were faced with treating a relentless stream of horrific and painful wounds. The evacuation of severe cases to other hospitals or out of the country meant that nurses and doctors did not have the satisfaction of seeing all patients through to recovery. In addition, nurses experienced social isolation owing to the low number of women in the area and the tensions of living and working in the violent, male-dominated environment of war. These stresses left emotional scars. Nurse Judy Marron, writing about her time in Vietnam, described the horror of seeing cockroaches crawl out of amputees' stumps. One Navy nurse described the wounds as being so bad the operations that were carried out had no name: they were simply "horridzomas" or "horriblectomies." Female nurses also dealt with stresses that were unique to their gender. According to one study, 63 percent of them experienced sexual harassment, ranging from "small pranks" to rape.

Nurse casualties
Lieutenant Sharon Lane was the only nurse killed as a direct result of enemy action. The blast from an artillery round struck her while she was working at the 312th Evacuation Hospital in Chu Lai on June 8, 1969. In addition, several nurses died in helicopter crashes, including Second Lieutenant Carol Drazba and Second Lieutenant Elizabeth Ann Jones, both assigned to the Third Field Hospital in

« **BEFORE**

The US Army Nurse Corps was established in 1901, but American women had been providing care for troops in wartime since the Revolutionary War (1775–83).

HISTORY OF SERVICE
In the 19th century, **Clara Barton** was called the American Nightingale for her nursing of soldiers during the American Civil War, and about 10,000 US nurses **served overseas** during World War I.

At the beginning of World War II, women had to be white, unmarried volunteers, and graduates of a civilian nursing school to join the Nurse Corps. It had become **more diverse** by the end of the war, with African American nurses in all-black units. This diversity further increased in 1955 when the first man, Edward T. Lyon, joined the Corps.

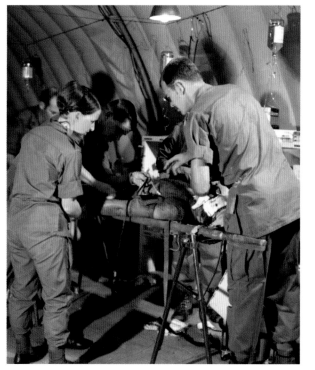

Teamwork in action
Captain Bernice Scott and several male officers of the US Army Nurse Corps take the blood pressure and cut the field bandages off a man who has just arrived at the 2nd Surgical Hospital in Lai Khe, in September 1969.

Saigon, and Captain Mary Therese Klinker, a flight nurse who died assisting the evacuation of orphans during Operation Babylift in 1975.

Expert care
As a result of their experiences, nurses in Vietnam became more specialized than they would have been in civilian practice. Especially in the areas of trauma, critical care, and anesthesia, military nurses often developed expertise that gave them increasing autonomy. In mass casualty situations, nurses also took on triage of the wounded—the responsibility for determining who received care first and who was beyond medical help. The important role of nurses was recognized. In 1970, Colonel Anna Mae Hays, the chief of the Army Nurse Corps who had built the nursing staff in Vietnam, became the first woman in the US military ever to be promoted to the rank of brigadier general.

In 1993, a new statue honoring the contribution of military women was dedicated at the Vietnam Veterans Memorial.

THEY WERE VETERANS TOO
Paid for through public donations, Glenna Goodacre's **Vietnam Women's Memorial** statue shows three nurses aiding a wounded soldier. While not exclusively for nurses, this memorial highlights their contributions.

Like soldiers, many of these nurses experienced **difficulty readjusting 344–45 »** to life at home. Judy Marron was an extreme example of this difficulty: alienated and plagued by alcohol abuse, she later committed suicide.

VIETNAM WOMEN'S MEMORIAL

Ready to serve
Twenty-three-year-old Army Second Lieutenant Roberta Steele alights from a medical supply truck in Qui Nhon in 1966. Steele, from Tillamook, Oregon, was eager to serve in Vietnam and had traded places with a recently married nurse in 1965.

"**Nothing** could **prepare you** for the sight of the **mangled bodies.**"

MARGUERITE GIROUX, NURSE, THIRD SURGICAL HOSPITAL, BIEN HOA, 1965–66

Nursing the Seriously Wounded

Nurses, like combat soldiers, went to Vietnam with a resigned sense of service to their country. However, the reality of war was often shocking and permanently transforming. On returning to the US, Nancy Randolph, a nurse from the South who served in Vietnam for a year, found a medical culture and society from which she felt alienated.

"I must say that I believe there were more reasons than one for my decision to go to Vietnam … When you are twenty-two, glory presents itself in various ways. To be a combat nurse brought all sorts of visions to mind …

The saddest thing I'd ever encountered after I'd been there a while was to see the human body and what war does to it … Once the doctor triaged them, if they were in the expectant category [expected to die] … they were medicated and bathed if they were dirty … They were cared for, but still, it was so sad just to put them behind a screen and check them every so often so you could get the time of death right …

Back in the United States as a professional nurse has had its complications. The Vietnam nurses were good. You had to be good … I came back to rural counties, and I … have to ask permission to give an aspirin? Come on, give me a break … Or I'd have to listen to some doc … chew me out for whatever, after what I'd seen and done … I just didn't need it … [Vietnam] made me a better person. It showed me, up front, at the ripe old age of twenty-two, what I could do without and still survive—what was important and what wasn't."

US ARMY NURSE NANCY RANDOLPH, INTERVIEWED IN *THE HUMAN TRADITION IN THE VIETNAM ERA* (SCHOLARLY RESOURCES, AN IMPRINT OF ROWMAN & LITTLEFIELD), 1998

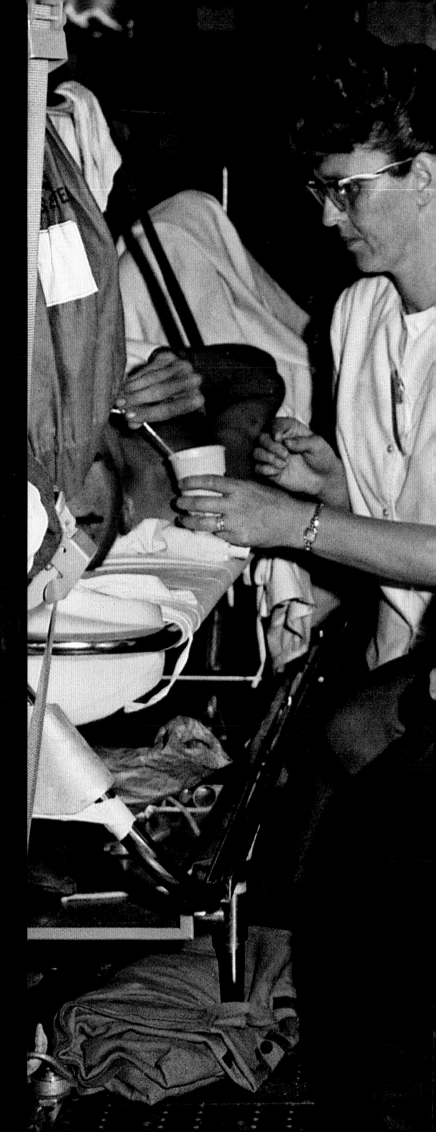

Air ambulance
Nurses attend to wounded American soldiers as their plane prepares to evacuate them from Vietnam. Seriously wounded soldiers were transported to army hospitals in the Philippines and Japan for treatment.

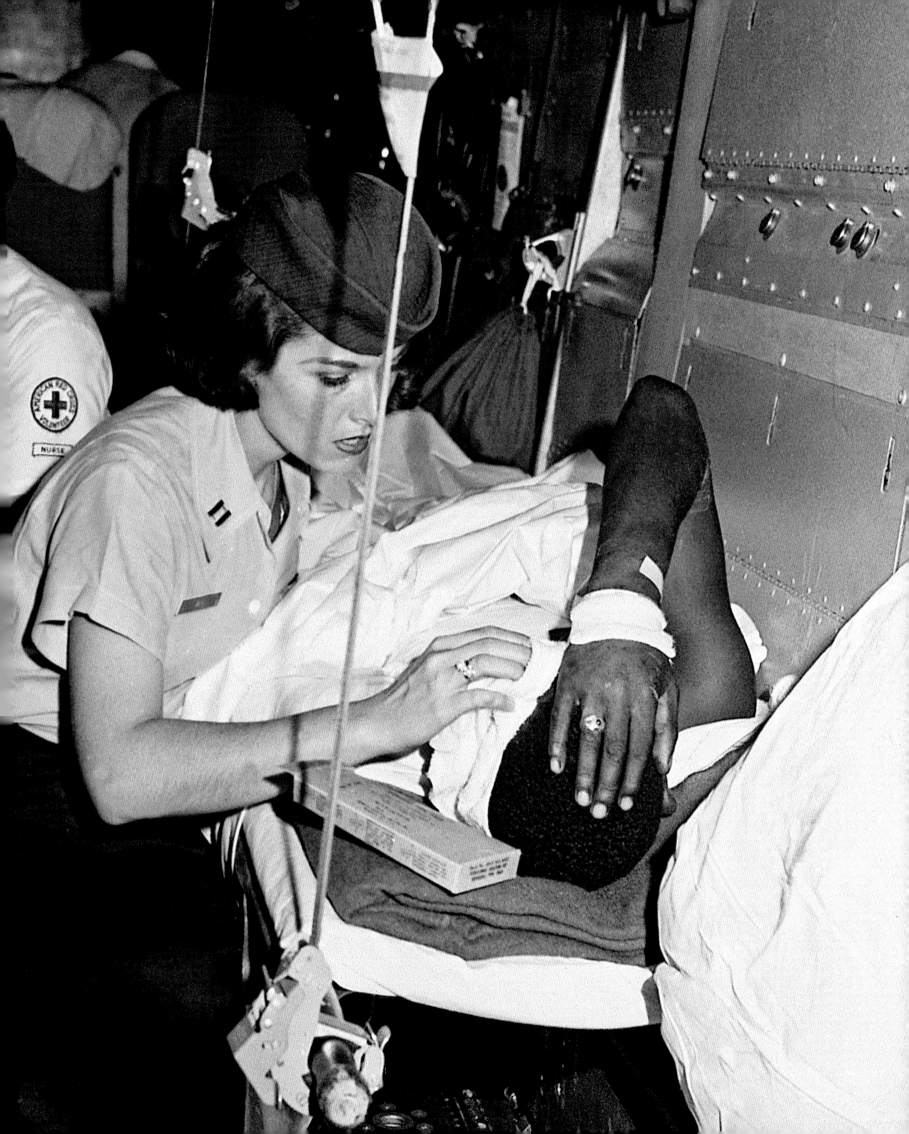

Evidence of atrocity
Two children lie on the ground at My Lai. This picture—and others of women and children at My Lai—were taken by army photographer Ronald Haeberle on his personal camera. Fearing they would be destroyed, he did not turn in the photos.

« BEFORE

Atrocities such as targeting innocent civilians and torturing prisoners were not new to American history or limited to one side of the confict.

A VIOLENT HISTORY
In the 19th century, US soldiers killed innocent Native American women and children in massacres such as the one at **Wounded Knee**.

MASSACRE IN HUE
In the **1968 struggle ‹‹ 190–93** for control of Hue, NVA forces murdered hundreds of civilian residents, who were buried in mass graves .

The **My Lai Case**

The My Lai massacre was the largest single American atrocity in the ground war in Vietnam. In 1969, the exposure of what had happened and the search for explanations prompted troubling questions about the moral risks the war posed for the United States.

I n 1971, controversial court martial proceedings captured the attention of the nation. The trials revolved around an incident some years before, in 1968, when an infantry company had killed 504 unresisting Vietnamese civilians in a hamlet known as My Lai, in the village of Son My. The event had been covered up by the participants and their immediate commanders for a year and a half, until Ron Ridenhour—a soldier who had learned what happened from men in the company—began writing letters to the Army, members of Congress, and even the president. Soon, *Life* magazine and CBS News were reporting the story. Ridenhour's persistence prompted an official inquiry in 1969. Led by Lieutenant General William Peers, their report in March 1970 recommended that no fewer than 28 officers be charged.

Details emerge
The court martial that began in November 1970 charged only 14 officers, who were called upon to

Evidence and guilt

The courts martial at Fort Benning, Georgia, would last four months, as the testimonies of 91 witnesses were heard, and documents, depositions, and photographs were scrutinized by the prosecutors. Thirteen of the officers charged were acquitted owing to lack of evidence. One officer was tried on charges of a cover-up and acquitted for the same reason.

The blame for My Lai was laid on the shoulders of the man who ordered the shootings: Lieutenant William Calley. He was tried for the murder of 109 civilians, but that number later dropped to 102. Calley said he had only been following orders, and claimed that his only crime was to value the lives of his troops above those

The media coverage and trials brought public attention to the massacre and raised serious issues about the conduct of the war. Were the men of this company defective, or was the entire war defective? The military prosecutors, Aubrey

Ready to be tried

Lieutenant Calley leaves a preliminary hearing on August 24, 1970, with a civilian attorney and a military escort. Calley's court martial was a general court martial—the most serious court of military trial—for which a preliminary Article 32 hearing is mandatory.

> " It was **terrible.** They were **slaughtering the villagers** like so many **sheep.**"

SERGEANT LARRY LA CROIX, QUOTED BY RON RIDENHOUER, MARCH 29, 1969

of the enemy. Witnesses told a different story. Rifleman Paul Meadlo testified that Calley had ordered him to help kill the civilians. They pushed them into a ravine and shot them where they fell. Witness Dennis Conti described Calley firing on villagers as they cowered in a ditch.

Lack of justice

At the end of the trial, only Calley was convicted—for personally killing 22 villagers. Despite an initial life sentence for premeditated murder, the lieutenant served only three months in military prison and three and a half years under house arrest. Nixon reduced the sentence under public pressure from those who saw Calley as a scapegoat for the failures of the Army.

Daniel and William Eckhardt, claimed that politics interfered with the army's ability to bring the perpetrators to justice.

The Pentagon Papers

My Lai tarnished the reputation of the Army and shocked the American public. "No My Lais" became a key mantra for infantry officers in the US Army.

Other questions were also being raised about US conduct of the war. On June 23, 1971, the *New York Times* began publishing excerpts from a secret record of the Department of Defense. These "Pentagon Papers" revealed shallow motivations behind important military decisions. Although Nixon tried to quash public access to the report, the damage was already done.

FREE LT. CALLEY NOW

Protest button

The "Free Calley" movement believed that the lieutenant had been unfairly blamed for the orders of those higher up in the chain of command. They made a hero of him, holding rallies and writing songs in his honor.

explain their actions. The story that emerged was bleak. As part of the post-Tet operations in 1968, a task force, including three infantry companies, was sent to Son My. Charlie Company, under Captain Ernest Medina, landed outside My Lai on March 16. Expecting to find a Viet Cong unit, two platoons entered with guns firing and began to round up the inhabitants.

By noon, all of the men, women, and children in the hamlet were dead. The only US casualty was self-inflicted. The commanding general reported a victory with 128 killed, but there were no hostile forces present. Within the division, it was a secret that My Lai was cold-blooded brutality, which included rape as well as murder.

AFTER ≫

The My Lai case helped turn US public opinion even further against the war in Vietnam.

ANTIWAR SYMBOL

After admitting to murdering men, women, and children at My Lai, Paul Meadlo was asked, "and babies?" by the prosecutors. A popular **antiwar** poster emerged from his response, with his reply, "and babies," superimposed onto a photograph of the massacre.

My Lai was a **symbolic moment** in the American view of the war. Today, many veterans make pilgrimages to the site, hoping to make peace with these memories.

MEMORIAL AT SON MY

BEFORE ««

From May 1965 to July 1969, there were no formal diplomatic relations between Cambodia and the United States.

TROUBLED RELATIONS
Against the backdrop of **historic border disputes** and ethnic tensions between the Cambodians and their Vietnamese neighbors **«« 42–43**, the rapidly **intensifying war** in Vietnam made it increasingly difficult for Cambodia to maintain its neutrality.

US INCURSIONS
Repeated **cross-border raids** against Viet Cong hideouts by ARVN forces, backed up by US advisers and air support, **brought tensions to a head**. Following an incident that left 17 Cambodian villagers dead, Norodom Sihanouk ordered US diplomats out of Phnom Penh.

Cambodia is Drawn into the War

The Johnson administration had attempted to manage Cambodia's precarious neutrality, but the Nixon government launched several major operations within this small country that dragged it further into the wider war.

President Johnson had placed some restrictions on US military and intelligence actions along the Cambodian border and had rejected a request from General Westmoreland for B-52 strikes along the frontier. Nevertheless, US reconnaissance and land-mining patrols, codenamed Salem House and later Daniel Boone, repeatedly entered Cambodia, and Cambodian villagers continued to suffer from ARVN raids planned with the US command.

Relations restored

Norodom Sihanouk did not like the Vietnamese communists' use of his country for their operations, but he wanted the United States to recognize Cambodia's borders, stop the incursions, and sever the ties that he perceived the Americans to have with his domestic rivals.

As a presidential candidate, Nixon had criticized Sihanouk as not truly neutral and agreed with military strategists who wanted more US operations in Cambodia. Once in office, however, he surprised almost everyone, including the

Prince in Paris
Shortly before his overthrow, Norodom Sihanouk addresses the media outside the Elysée Palace, Paris, after a meeting with French President Pompidou. Sihanouk argued for a halt to US involvement in Cambodia. A few days later, he visited Moscow and Beijing.

leaders of South Vietnam, by recognizing Sihanouk's demands for respect for his country's rights and territory, and in July 1969 diplomatic relations were restored between the two countries. Nixon and Kissinger created a public image of cooperation with Sihanouk but the reopening of the US Embassy in Phnom Penh was also useful for intelligence gathering, a factor that was of growing importance as these diplomatic moves occurred in the wake of significant military developments.

Ready to fire
Troops of the Cambodian army take up firing positions behind a bank near Kampong Cham in the Mekong Delta region in May 1970. Cambodian forces were fighting in operations linked to the US and South Vietnamese incursions that followed the fall of Sihanouk.

vote of no confidence removed him as head of state. The war had caused the urban middle class and many in the military to lose faith in Sihanouk's ability to defend the country. Cheng Heng, Chairman of the National Assembly, was appointed interim head of state.

Operation Menu
The Nixon administration was intent upon one thing, defeating North Vietnam and the Viet Cong, and had little regard for Cambodia. In journalist William Shawcross's phrase, Cambodia was only a "side show." On March 18, 1969, the US Air Force had begun Operation Menu, a covert bombing campaign of eastern Cambodia, known to be a support area for the infiltration of North Vietnamese forces into South Vietnam. American commanders also thought it was the location of the headquarters of the Central Office for South

Vietnam (COSVN), the base of operations for communist forces in the South. The nature of so-called sanctuaries and of COSVN itself had been in dispute—one reason Johnson had refused to bomb Cambodia—but Nixon and many

of his military advisers were committed to this strategy. General Abrams promised that a single B-52 sortie would destroy COSVN. In the event, almost 4,000 sorties were flown, but COSVN, a main target, was not destroyed.

New blood
General Lon Nol had not plotted the coup, but in the preceding weeks he had been urging Sihanouk to be tougher with North Vietnam. Public demonstrations in Phnom Penh after the overthrow of Sihanouk provided the pressure for parliamentary leaders to invite Lon Nol to take charge.

> " A ... **change of policy** toward Cambodia ... should be one of the [priorities] when we get in."
>
> RICHARD NIXON, NOTE TO HENRY KISSINGER, JANUARY 8, 1969

AFTER »

General Lon Nol failed to halt the activities of communist forces—both from Cambodia and Vietnam—in spite of military support from the United States.

INCURSION AND RETREAT
In April 1970, US forces launched a **massive incursion 252–53** » of ground forces into Cambodian territory with the aim of disrupting communist networks in the country. This produced such a **storm of domestic protests 254–55** » in the United States that the administration had to retreat.

SUPPORT WITHDRAWN
This experience left the United States reluctant to commit to further action on the ground, leaving the weak government of Lon Nol **unable to resist** the ever-increasing strength of the Khmer Rouge **326–27** ».

ARMY OFFICER AND POLITICIAN 1913–85

GENERAL LON NOL

Lon Nol served in the French colonial service from 1937 and entered the police force in 1951. He joined the army in 1952, taking part in the fight against Vietnamese communist insurgents. In 1960, he became commander in chief of the Cambodian army. Subsequently, he held the posts of defense minister and prime minister, alternately or simultaneously. Following the overthrow of Sihanouk in March 1970, and despite a debilitating stroke in 1971, he led the government in Phnom Penh until March 1975, when he left Cambodia.

Effects of the bombing
Many Cambodian villagers died in these raids, however. The Vietnamese communist forces moved westward from the border and further into Cambodia, increasing their political influence on the Cambodian population. The United States had never asked Sihanouk for approval of these bombing operations.

In addition to the devastating impact of the American bombing and continued ground operations on the Cambodian population as a whole, US strategy also had a catastrophic effect on Sihanouk's hold on power.

In March 1970, while Sihanouk was absent in Europe supposedly for medical care, a parliamentary

The **Khmer Rouge**

During the first two years of the Nixon administration, a combination of US actions and political intrigue in Phnom Penh helped to mold Cambodia's radical communist faction into a dangerous threat to both Cambodia and to American interests.

In 1963, the general secretary of the Communist Party of Kampuchea (CPK) was a shadowy figure named Saloth Sar. A leading figure in the resistance to French rule in Cambodia, he later became committed to the overthrow of the government of Prince Norodom Sihanouk, who steered a neutral line in foreign policy.

Under Sar's leadership, the CPK was transformed into the extreme and violent movement that became the Khmer Rouge. Sar—known as Brother Number One—assumed the name Pol Pot.

Although the communists of North Vietnam initially supported the Khmer Rouge, by the mid-1960s, this alliance had broken down. The pact between Sihanouk

deep inside the countryside, the Khmer Rouge leadership created a strike force of teenage soldiers, described by one witness as "grim, robotlike, brutal."

Unintended consequences

Operation Menu, which was launched by the United States in March 1969, upset the political balance in Cambodia. The Khmer

Strange bedfellows

The overthrow of Sihanouk by conservative factions of the ruling class, led by Lon Nol, created a moment of opportunity for the Khmer Rouge. They now found it expedient to form an

<< BEFORE

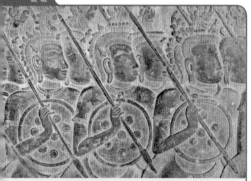

BAS RELIEF OF KHMER SOLDIERS FROM ANGKOR WAT

Historical antagonism between Cambodians and Vietnamese inhibited fraternal relations between the communist movements in each country.

HANOI AND SIHANOUK
Vietnamese leaders had dominated the Indochinese Communist Party created by Ho Chi Minh in the 1930s. When a small group of **communist-led rebels** formed in Cambodia in the 1950s to oppose Sihanouk, they received little help from the Vietnamese communists. The Politburo in Hanoi saw a neutral Cambodia as an advantage. It made an **arrangement with Sihanouk << 248–49** to allow it to resupply and rest its troops in Cambodia in return for not aiding Sihanouk's enemies.

> "The **Khmer Rouge** [should] realize that their existence **depends** on ours … Cambodia is **our staging area**."
>
> A VIET CONG DOCUMENT, CAPTURED IN APRIL 1970

and the Vietnamese communists led the Khmer Rouge to hate both in equal measure.

Although versed in the ideologies of the French revolution, Marxism, and Stalinism, Pol Pot believed that Cambodia had nothing to learn from external influences and envisioned the restoration of the old glory of the Khmer Kingdom. He and his followers viewed all Vietnamese people—from the North or South—as enemies.

The Forest Army

For years, Sihanouk considered what he called the Khmers Rouges little more than a nuisance. They remained a small, isolated group of extreme zealots, nurturing their own vision of "pure" revolution and extolling suffering and sacrifice. It was a rural-based agrarian communism roughly modeled on Mao Zedong's peasant movement.

The extreme secrecy of the Khmer Rouge made it a mystery to most Cambodians, who referred to it as the "forest army." In its camps

Rouge took advantage of the weakness in Phnom Penh under Sihanouk and subsequently Lon Nol, and the spread of the Vietnam War to Cambodia to expand their membership among disaffected rural Cambodians. Although Nixon had bluntly declared that "no Cambodians had lived in [the area bombed] for many years" and that "it was totally occupied by the North Vietnamese Communists," American intelligence knew otherwise. Terrified villagers fled the B-52 attacks, and some of the survivors ended up in the ranks of the rebels. Those who did not join the militants became sympathetic to the enemies of the United States. Very young, displaced villagers were radicalized and trained as guerrillas.

Khmer Rouge guerrillas

Few photographs exist of Khmer Rouge soldiers in their camps in the 1960s and 1970s. Pictured at their base in western Cambodia in February 1981, these Khmer Rouge guerillas are as young and committed as those of earlier decades.

alignment with the ousted prince whom they had long opposed and with the Vietnamese communists, whom they distrusted.

At the time of the coup, France briefly floated a proposal for an international conference that might secure Cambodian sovereignty and neutrality, but failed to get support from enough nations to make this a reality. Understandably angry and feeling betrayed, Sihanouk took refuge in Beijing. He made the surprising announcement that he was forming a coalition with the communists to "liberate our motherland." In later years, he

Peasant support
The Cambodian peasantry was overwhelmingly apolitical, but had royalist sympathies. After Sihanouk voiced his support for the Khmer Rouge, their numbers swelled from 6,000 to 50,000.

would defend this impetuous move as an effort to avenge himself against Lon Nol.

Responding to anarchy

Cambodia descended into a violent anarchy of rival gangs, Khmer Rouge guerrillas, and Vietnamese troops of various kinds grasping for

advantage. Prompted by US officials in Phnom Penh, Lon Nol appealed for outside help, and the Nixon administration was more than ready to respond. But the Khmer Rouge was also ready to make a "recruiting sergeant" of the misery caused by continued US and Vietnamese incursions.

AFTER »

Under Prime Minister Lon Nol, Cambodia began the creation of a Cambodian national army with the advice and training of US Army Special Forces operators.

FANK FAILS
Lon Nol's military organization was known as FANK (Forces Armées Nationale Khmer). In spite of the training provided by the US and its Australasian allies, this army was unable to resist the **Khmer Rouge advance 326–37 »** in 1975.

MAKAROV PISTOL USED BY THE KHMER ROUGE

Cambodian Incursion

In spring 1970, Nixon decided to risk public criticism and attack Viet Cong and NVA bases in Cambodia, an officially neutral country. He also wanted to shore up Lon Nol, Cambodia's newly installed pro-American premier, and send an intimidating message to the North.

The heat of battle
Armed with M16 rifles, an M60 machine gun, and a sniper rifle—but without shirts, flak jackets, or helmets, because of the oppressive heat—members of the Ninth Infantry Division fight enemy forces in Cambodia's forest terrain.

Following the coup in Phnom Penh in March 1970, the new prime minister General Lon Nol quickly offered military cooperation with the United States as a way of controlling communist activity. Although Nixon had publicly declared that the United States had no advance warning of the coup, it was clear that the change of leadership was welcomed by the United States.

Entering the Parrot's Beak
On April 30, 1970, at the request of General Abrams, Nixon ordered incursions into Cambodia. The plan and execution of the incursion was a joint operation with South Vietnamese forces and a combat test of Vietnamization.

or in brief raids. Some stayed to occupy an area to provide support for the army of Lon Nol's Cambodian government (FANK), and others quickly went back to South Vietnam. The FANK forces largely retreated toward Phnom Penh. All of these actions had US

air and artillery support. Also, strict rules of engagement were observed that limited US forces to proceed no more than 18 miles (30 km) into Cambodia and required ARVN to stay within 31 miles (50 km) of

> " **Electrify** people with a **bold decision.** [They will] **make history.** "
> RICHARD NIXON, MAY 1, 1970

BEFORE

By 1970, President Nixon and Henry Kissinger were conducting peace negotiations in private.

FIGHTING AND TALKING
On February 21, 1970, Henry Kissinger had begun secret **talks with North Vietnam's Le Duc Tho** in Paris. Private meetings were evidence of Nixon's and Kissinger's **secretive conduct** of the war and of their concern to use political pressure as well as military means to force a settlement. Le Duc Tho demanded US withdrawal from Vietnam and a role for the **People's Revolutionary Government**, the political arm of the Viet Cong.

The operation opened with an 8,000-man ARVN force accompanied by about 100 US advisers attacking the portion of the border known as the Parrot's Beak, only 24 miles (40 km) west of Saigon. The goal was to encircle and destroy a large concentration of North Vietnamese (NVA) forces there. Two days later, a primarily American force attacked the "Fishhook," some 48 miles (80 km) north of Saigon and believed to be the site of the Central Office for South Vietnam (COSVN), the nerve center of the Viet Cong, which US intelligence believed was operating out of Cambodia.

Over the following weeks, the attacking ARVN and US forces often operated independently in multibattalion cross-border attacks the border. Within a week, a joint force of 31,000 US troops and 19,000 ARVN were ranged along a 100-mile (160 km) stretch of the South Vietnam-Cambodian border.

Costs versus benefits

The attack lasted throughout May and June. It was the largest military sweep since Operation Junction City in 1967. The incursion was intended to force communist units away from Vietnam's border, thus buying time for Vietnamization and reducing pressure on Lon Nol's pro-American but precarious

regime. US commanders claimed the operation killed around 11,000 enemy troops, destroyed 8,000 bunkers, found thousands of weapons and tens of thousands of rounds of ammunition, and seized tons of rice and medical supplies. The costs to the US and ARVN were also considerable, including 388 Americans and 638 South Vietnamese killed and more than 1,500 Americans and 4,000 ARVN soldiers wounded.

This costly effort did not have a significant impact on the strength of communist forces in Vietnam or move Le Duc Tho from his hardline

position in the Paris peace talks. Moreover, the incursion failed to locate the COSVN. Instead of the jungle headquarters that the Pentagon had envisioned, there was what one journalist described as "a scattering of a few empty huts." The COSVN was not a place but a leadership group that moved frequently between various meeting sites in order to avoid attack or capture.

At a time when Washington was attempting to reduce the scale of its engagement in Indochina, the theater of war had expanded with the accompanying costs and risks.

US forces pull out

On June 30, 1970, US forces left Cambodia. Without US or ARVN troops to defend Phnom Penh, the Cambodian Army now faced the emerging Khmer Rouge alone. US airstrikes had killed tens of thousands of Cambodians. Within four months of the US withdrawal, the Khmer Rouge controlled the country east of the Mekong, and much beyond. While Lon Nol's government held on to the capital, it was unable to regain any territory. Cambodia's economy quickly deteriorated and poverty and hunger took hold.

Captured enemy weapons
Members of the First Cavalry Division and 11th Armored Cavalry Regiment at their base at Quan Loi near An Loc survey some of the thousands of enemy weapons captured in the Fishhook area during the incursion of May and June 1970.

AFTER

The incursion into Cambodia inflamed antiwar protests and provided added impetus to the scaling down of US operations. It did nothing to hold back communism in Indochina.

INDIRECT ENCOURAGEMENT
The Khmer Rouge only continued to grow in strength after 1970, and finally **took Phnom Penh 326–27 ≫** in 1975. The US Air Force's **secret bombing** of Cambodia by B-52s also continued to turn many people there against the US. The bombing campaign was **not called off** until 1973, after it became public knowledge in the United States.

**US AIR FORCE
FLYING
HELMET**

Victory rally

Demonstrators fill the streets around the Capitol in Washington on October 3, 1970. The fundamentalist preacher who organized the event, the Reverend Carl McIntire, called it not a pro-war rally, but one advocating for "peace by victory."

Political Storm

In the wake of the Cambodian incursion, political challenges to Nixon's determination to keep fighting the war snowballed—from the halls of Congress to the ranks of service members returning home.

In President Nixon's televised address on April 30, 1970, he declared that he had rejected all political considerations when deciding to move against the enemy sanctuaries in Cambodia. He said that his primary concern had been to save American lives. He also said that he sought to bridge the country's deep differences over the war.

Instead, Nixon ignited a political firestorm that would engulf his presidency. A siege mentality began to develop inside the White House as it assessed domestic politics. Many members of Congress who were already opposed to the war exploded in anger over Nixon's Cambodian incursion. Some charged that the administration had lied outright to Congress, as only days before the incursion Secretary of State William Rogers had testified to the Senate Foreign Relations Committee that there were no plans for operations in Cambodia. Nixon and Kissinger had not informed Rogers of the imminent attack.

Congressional doves

On May 1, two bills challenged the president's authority. Republican John Sherman Cooper of Kentucky and Democrat Frank Church of Idaho sponsored a measure to cut off all funds for military operations in Cambodia after June 30. Republican Senator Mark Hatfield of Oregon joined Democrat George McGovern of South Dakota to propose a stronger requirement: that all US forces be withdrawn by the end of 1971. Neither bill became law, but in June the Senate voted for a resolution to terminate the 1964 Tonkin Gulf

Young martyrs

Four students were killed and nine more were wounded during 13 seconds of gunfire at Kent State. Only two of the four students killed, Jeffrey Miller and Allison Krause, had actually taken part in protests.

since the Moratorium protests of late 1969. On hundreds of college campuses, antiwar voices called the incursion an invasion. Nixon intensified the outcry by calling students "bums." One tragic outcome of this turmoil was at Kent State University, Ohio, where National Guardsmen opened fire on protesters on May 4. Ten days later, two students were killed in a similar incident at Jackson State in Mississippi.

Both sides rally

Protests over the incursion showed a national divide. On the antiwar side, the Vietnam Veterans against the War (VVAW) expressed their discontent. In February 1971, they conducted the "Winter Soldier Investigation," a public forum in which speakers detailed the

had been used to commit terrible acts of violence in the name of freedom, against a people who posed no threat to the US.

On the other side were the so-called hard-hat demonstrators. On May 8, 1971, 200 construction workers assaulted antiwar protesters in New York City. Chanting "America, love it or leave it," these counter-protesters beat some peace marchers with work tools. On May 20, at least 100,000 paraded in New York City in support of Nixon's administration.

« **BEFORE**

The selective service system had long been a point of controversy. In December 1969, the US draft lottery began.

DRAFTEES TO VOLUNTEERS

Congress—concerned about requiring young Americans to participate in an increasingly unpopular war, and the fairness of the selection system—decided to draw birth dates by lottery to set the order of induction. However, the **continued unpopularity** of the draft led Congress to end the lottery in 1972 and institute an all-volunteer service.

> " How do you **ask a man** to be the **last man to die** in Vietnam? … [To] **die for a mistake?**"
>
> LIEUTENANT JOHN KERRY TO THE SENATE FOREIGN RELATIONS COMMITTEE, APRIL 22, 1971

Resolution upon which Johnson and Nixon had claimed authority to deploy US forces to Vietnam.

Campus chaos

Congress was not alone in its anger. The Cambodian incursion inflamed domestic opposition to the war that had been mounting

misconduct they had witnessed. "Operation Dewey Canyon III" followed in April—during which veterans in green fatigue shirts tossed medals earned in Vietnam across police barricades and onto the steps of the Capitol. Lieutenant John Kerry, a Navy veteran, argued that loyal young Americans

AFTER »

Stung by the intense public criticism, Nixon responded to the protests by taking action.

THE HUSTON PLAN

Convinced that radical groups in the US were linked to foreign governments, Nixon authorized the **Huston Plan** to wiretap and burglarize the homes of ordinary Americans. This brazen attack on privacy would later come to light in the **Watergate scandal 310–11 »**.

NO CONSEQUENCES

Nixon created the President's Commission on Campus Unrest in response to the events at Kent State. However, the guardsmen were **not punished**, and were acquitted by a Grand Jury in 1974.

THE NATIONAL DRAFT LOTTERY

Horror at Kent State

In demonstrations that started on May 1, 1970, students marched, damaged businesses, and burned the old ROTC building at Kent State University, Ohio, in protest over the perceived expansion of the war into Cambodia. By Monday, May 4, armed National Guardsmen occupied the campus. Tom Grace, a sophomore on the way to a history exam, was caught up in the tragedy that followed.

The students felt that it was their campus and they were doing nothing wrong, and that the armed National Guardsmen had no right to order them to disperse. Many students screamed at them to get off their campus. At the same time, some students were wandering through the area with textbooks, unaware of what was taking place around them.

All of a sudden, the National Guardsmen got to the top of the hill where they began to fire rifles. Tom Grace describes turning and running as fast as he could, before being knocked off his feet by a bullet through his left heel. There was no cover and farther down the hill in the parking lot, he could see people were dropping. He didn't know if they were being hit by bullets or if they were just hugging the ground.

"It ... kept going and going and going. And I remember thinking, 'When is this going to stop?'**"**

TOM GRACE, ORAL HISTORY IN *FROM CAMELOT TO KENT STATE: THE SIXTIES EXPERIENCE IN THE WORDS OF THOSE WHO LIVED IT*, 1987

Picture of despair
Fourteen-year-old Mary Ann Vecchio screams over the body of 20-year-old Jeffrey Miller in this Pulitzer Prize-winning image by photojournalism student John Filo. Instead of firing blanks, National Guardsmen shot 67 live rounds in 13 seconds, killing four and wounding nine.

« BEFORE

Some Americans became prisoners of war in Vietnam in the early 1960s well before the major deployment of US forces later in the decade and remained in captivity for many years.

THE FIRST PRISONER

Lieutenant Everett Alvarez was shot down over North Vietnam on August 5, 1964, in Operation Pierce Arrow, the initial bombing raid in the immediate aftermath of the **Tonkin Gulf Incident «** **80–81**. He became the first pilot to be **held prisoner** in North Vietnam and remained in captivity for eight and a half years.

LONGEST CAPTIVITY

The longest-held American prisoner was US Army Special Forces Captain Floyd James Thompson who was **captured** in South Vietnam on March 26, 1964, after only three months in the country. He was not released for almost nine years.

Prisoners of War

The number of Americans held prisoner or categorized as missing was relatively small, but the fate of American prisoners of war in North Vietnam became a burning political issue during the war, throughout the peace negotiations, and after the conflict was over.

" What [our North Vietnamese captors] wanted was to **subdue** us and then **win us over** to the point where we would routinely **do their bidding.** They **failed.**"

JEREMIAH A. DENTON JR., *WHEN HELL WAS IN SESSION*, 1976

Taken prisoner

First Lieutenant Gerald Santo Venanzi. is taken prisoner by a young Vietnamese woman. Venanzi was copilot of a plane that was brought down in North Vietnam on September 17, 1967. He spent over six years in captivity.

In February and March 1973, 691 Americans (mostly military but also a few civilians) were released from prisons in North Vietnam. Four American prisoners held in China also were freed. Many of these surviving prisoners had suffered extreme hardships in captivity. Estimates are that 55 to 75 POWs died. About 2,300 other Americans were deemed to be missing in action (MIA). Most of them died in fiery crashes or at the hands of guerrillas in remote areas, and few remains were ever found. Most of these men were later reclassified as KIA/BNR (Killed in Action/Body Not Recovered).

Hanoi Hilton

American captives were held in 11 different prisons, but the majority of the approximately 700 POWs were crowded into the cell blocks of Hoa Lo Prison in Hanoi. Known to Americans as the Hanoi Hilton, it was once a French jail holding Viet Minh suspects. A large fortress covering a city block, it had 20-foot (6 m) high walls that were topped with electrified barbed wire. Sanitation, food, and health care were poor.

Many prisoners were isolated and tortured in special interrogation rooms in attempts to secure confessions for propaganda use. Mistreatment included beatings, shackling, being held in darkness for extended periods, and being denied washing facilities. Despite often inhumane treatment,

prisoners devised ingenious methods of surreptitious communication and found ways to keep up morale. The Hanoi Hilton held some prisoners who were destined for later prominence, including Medal of Honor winner and later admiral James B. Stockdale and future senator and presidential candidate John McCain.

Conditions in the prison began to improve after 1969. The reasons are unclear but may have related

> **The longest-held American civilian prisoner was Ernest Brace, a contract pilot taken in Laos in May 1965 and held for nearly seven years.**

to North Vietnam's perceptions of US military de-escalation and the possibilities for negotiation raised by the POW issue.

The POW issue

As a counter to the peace movement and to acquire political support for the administration, Nixon and his aides began to prioritize the demand for the release of American prisoners of war. The tactic produced mixed results. Many Americans had been willing to fight communism, but they had become opposed to the continuation of a costly war to maintain the unpopular Saigon regime. By making POW release an issue, Nixon gained backing from POW families and from pro-war individuals, notably millionaire H. Ross Perot, who headed the United We Stand organization, which lobbied to

Captive guerrillas
Suspected Viet Cong fighters await interrogation by the US Marines in July 1967. They had been rounded up near the DMZ. US forces did not hold prisoners long term, but took advantage of their capture to question them for information about enemy plans.

Zoo inspection
American POWs stand for an inspection by international observers in the yard at Hanoi's Nga Tu So prison, nicknamed the Zoo, on March 29, 1973, just before their release. They left the prison shortly after, still dressed in their prison uniforms.

continue the war primarily for the purpose of POW release. Backed by the administration, some members of Congress, and the media, the National League of Families of American Prisoners and Missing in Southeast Asia was formed in May 1970.

While successful in gaining support at home, diplomatically the focus on POWs backfired. The North Vietnamese reasoned that their negotiators could use offers to release POWs as leverage to gain the concessions it wanted from the United States to reduce its support for the Thieu government.

Vietnamese POWs in the South
The US military did not hold Vietnamese POWs—these were held by the South Vietnamese— and North Vietnam did not make its own prisoners or missing an issue in the peace negotiations, even though their numbers were far greater.

Name of serviceman

Date of capture

» The North Vietnamese representatives in Paris sometimes casually mentioned they had many more missing than did the United States, but the government in Hanoi simply labeled their missing as "martyrs of the revolution" and demonstrated no formal interest in their fate.

After interrogation by American intelligence, all North Vietnamese and Viet Cong prisoners were placed under the jurisdiction of the ARVN military police. The South Vietnamese Ministry of the Interior operated four prisoner of war camps, one in each military region. Conditions in these camps were harsh and degrading.

Communist political operatives who were not soldiers were placed in a number of local jails or in the infamous Tiger Cages on Con Son

Enduring reminder
A student organization called Voices in Vital America first issued these bracelets in May 1970 as part of their campaign to ensure that POWs would not be forgotten. Those who wore the bracelets vowed to leave them on until the soldier, or their remains, were returned.

Island. Originally forming part of a French colonial prison, the Tiger Cages were only 5 feet (1.5 m) square and 9 feet (2.7 m) high with an open roof of metal bars. No North Vietnamese soldiers—except

for some POWs convicted of murder in prison camps—were held at Con Son. Conditions at the prison were so terrible that in July 1970 the Red Cross declared it in violation of the Geneva Convention prohibiting inhumane treatment of prisoners. Reports on the prison helped to convince the US Congress to begin to curtail aid to South Vietnam—a significant turning point in the war.

Raid on Son Tay

In tandem with diplomatic efforts to obtain the release of US prisoners, the Nixon administration wanted a military success in Vietnam to demonstrate to the North and the American public that the US political will to fight the war remained strong. In June, military intelligence had reported

"The prisoners of war have **not been forgotten."**

RICHARD NIXON, REMARKS AFTER SON TAY RAID, NOVEMBER 25, 1970

Operational success
USAF General Leroy Manor, who planned the Special Forces raid on the Son Tay prison camp in North Vietnam, points to a model of the camp as he declares to a news conference on December 2, 1970, that the raid was an "operational success."

50 American POWs at a camp at Son Tay about 23 miles (37 km) north of Hanoi. This seemed to provide the opportunity to liberate American prisoners from the heart of North Vietnam, which would be a valuable propaganda coup.

On the night of November 20, 1970, US Air Force helicopters ferried 56 US Army Rangers into Son Tay. What the intelligence had failed to discover was that, due to flooding from heavy July rains, the North Vietnamese authorities had moved the prisoners about 15 miles (24 km) away. There were no prisoners to be rescued at Son

Going home
Newly freed prisoners of war show their joy as their military aircraft lifts off from Hanoi on February 12, 1973. Between February and April 1970, the mission dubbed Operation Homecoming returned 591 American POWs to their home country.

Tay. No American lives were lost in the raid, which was considered a tactical success and could well have rescued prisoners had they still been there. Press reaction was mixed. Some commentators saw it as a courageous attempt worth the risk, though others labeled it a foolhardy and provocative act. While Nixon did not get the kind of accolades he wanted, the action did impress the North Vietnamese. The United States had inserted and extracted troops very near to their capital and had inflicted a significant number of casualties on the camp's defenders. Following

this incident, the North Vietnamese closed the scattered prison camps and consolidated all POWs in Hanoi. Living conditions became very crowded in the Hanoi Hilton, with some men sleeping shoulder to shoulder, but the increased contact had the benefit of enhancing prisoner morale.

Homecoming heroes

Operation Homecoming was the name given to the repatriation of American POWs in 1973 following the signing of the Paris Accords in January 1973. The North released the prisoners as the last remaining US forces withdrew from South Vietnam, except for a small contingent at the American embassy in Saigon. With great fanfare, the returnees were welcomed home as heroes, a reception few other service members received when they came back from the controversial war.

Although Nixon proudly proclaimed that all POWs had returned in 1973, many Americans remained skeptical that the North had cooperated fully.

HOPE SURVIVES

Reports of live sightings and other "evidence" of POWs allegedly still held in Southeast Asia fueled speculation and **kept hope alive** for many families. However, separate congressional and Department of Defense investigations in the 1970s concluded that no US prisoners remained anywhere in Southeast Asia. Nevertheless, for a further two decades the US demanded that the Vietnamese government provide a **full account of all missing US servicemen** before diplomatic relations could be established.

REPATRIATION OF MIA REMAINS FROM HANOI IN 1984

1 TOOTHPASTE AND PACKET

2 TOOTHBRUSH

3 CIGARETTES

4 MATCHBOX

5 SOAP

6 CLOTHES PEGS

7 METAL SPOON

8 CUP

9 METAL CUP

10 WHITE CUP

11 ROSARY

Prisoners of War Objects

From 1964 to 1973, hundreds of US servicemen were made prisoners of war (POWs) by the Viet Cong and the North Vietnamese. Conditions were often atrocious and the POWs had only the most basic necessities for daily life.

1 **Toothpaste and packet** The lead tubes were sometimes made into pencils by POWs. **2** **Toothbrush** Items for personal hygiene such as toothbrushes were provided. **3** **Cigarettes** Locally produced cigarettes were given to prisoners. **4** **Matchbox** POWs were only allowed matches toward the end of the war. **5** **Soap** Highly valued by prisoners, small pieces of soap were pressed together to form larger bars. **6** **Clothes pegs** These bamboo pegs were produced by POWs. **7** **Metal spoon** This NVA issue spoon was used by Commander David Rollins, who was held from 1967 to 1973. **8** **Cup** POWs used wire around the handles of cups like this one

to make needles. **9** **Metal cup** This was issued to Colonel Carlyle Harris, who was a POW for nearly eight years. **10** **White cup** This lidded cup was made of enamel. **11** **Rosary** Commander Paul Schulz, who owned this rosary, spent six months in solitary confinement. **12** **Paper towel** POWs were given one towel each day. **13** **Pen and pencil** Writing materials were in short supply. **14** **Letters** From 1969, POWs could send one short letter a month. **15** **Pajamas** These were worn by POWs at Hoa Lo Prison, the "Hanoi Hilton." **16** **Belt** This belt was improvised by a POW to hold up his pants. **17** **Sandals** Simple sandals were issued to POWs.

12 PAPER TOWEL

13 PEN AND PENCIL

14 LETTERS

NGÀY VIẾT (Dated) 2 Oct 1971

Dear Joan. Peachy in college? Cathy and Bill's plans? How are your folks? The Jivotts? My best to them. Describe the house. Car? Please send coffee, pipe tobacco, pictures and tee shirts. Big love to you and all. Dad.

GHI CHÚ (N.B.):

1. Phải viết rõ và chỉ được viết trên những dòng kẻ sẵn (Write legibly, and only on the lines).

2. Gia đình gửi đến cũng phải theo đúng mẫu, khuôn khổ và quy định này (Notes from families should also conform to this proforma).

GỬI MÁY BAY
PAR AVION

To: Mrs L.T. Profilet
and children
441 Nevada Avenue
Palo Alto, California 94301
United States of America

15 PAJAMAS

Các

16 BELT

17 SANDALS

263

Lam Son 719

On February 8, 1971, the ARVN sent a task force of 15,000 troops into Laos with heavy US air and artillery support. Their goal was to disrupt and block off the Ho Chi Minh Trail. Codenamed Lam Son 719, the operation was a major test of Vietnamization.

Transporting intel

This map case was used by Viet Cong and NVA troops to carry important documents along the Ho Chi Minh Trail. Cases like this one often held information about enemy supply routes and intelligence from Hanoi regarding enemy positions or strategy.

« **BEFORE**

By 1971, the Ho Chi Minh Trail had been operational for 16 years, bringing soldiers and supplies from North Vietnam through Laos and Cambodia into South Vietnam.

SUPPLY ROUTE

Despite steady **air bombardment « 94–95** during the 1960s, and the **Cambodian incursion « 252–53** in 1970, men and materiel continued to flow south. During 1970, an estimated 8,000 men and 10,000 tons of supplies moved along the trail each month.

FORBIDDEN ZONE

After the Cambodian incursion, Congress repeatedly attempted to limit the US president's war powers and block any expansion of the war beyond Vietnam. The **Cooper-Church amendment** to a military appropriation bill finally passed Congress in December 1970. It clearly **prohibited** the use of US ground forces in Laos.

I n early 1971, General Creighton Abrams planned an operation to interdict the flow of North Vietnamese (NVA) and supplies into South Vietnam along the Ho Chi Minh Trail. The initiative was welcomed by both the US and South Vietnamese administrations. Both President Nixon and President Thieu were eager to see the South Vietnamese Army (ARVN) succeed as US troop strength declined, to show that the ARVN was capable of holding its own in battle.

Because of the Cooper-Church Amendment, US ground forces could not enter Laos, through which much of the Ho Chi Minh Trail passed. Therefore, it was decided that the operation would be an ARVN ground attack with

function. Truck convoys of 40 to 60 vehicles moved through the area each night on a maze of roads.

Marching into Laos

The ARVN advance along Route 9 toward Tchepone went easily for a few days. As trained by the US, South Vietnamese troops built fire support bases as they went. After an advance of about 12 miles (19 km) in two weeks, the ARVN column came under heavy attack. Contrary to earlier intelligence assessments indicating that the NVA in the area mainly consisted of logistics personnel with some security forces, the North Vietnamese quickly moved five divisions with field

and antiaircraft artillery against the ARVN. Counting on US air support, the southern forces hunkered down in the firebases, but low clouds, antiaircraft fire, and the proximity of enemy to friendly forces negated the use of B-52s or low-level fighter bombers.

Despite heavy opposition, Thieu ordered the ARVN commander, General Hoang Xuan Lam, to launch an air assault on Tchepone itself. American UH-1 Hueys—with Cobra

> " I hope **Thieu understands ...** that this may be his **last crack** at **massive US support.** "
>
> HENRY KISSINGER, IN A CABLE TO AMBASSADOR ELLSWORTH BUNKER, MARCH 1971

American air, long-range artillery, transportation, and intelligence support. There were no American advisers or forward air controllers with the ARVN units.

Target Tchepone

The once vibrant Laotian market town of Tchepone, about 27 miles (43 km) from the Vietnamese border, was a key transfer point along the trail and had attracted more bombing tonnage than any industrial city in Germany during World War II. All of the houses had been destroyed and the local people were living in caves, but the roads, communication network, antiaircraft artillery, and a rebuilt Buddhist temple continued to

gunship protection—lifted two South Vietnamese battalions into the town. However, by March 1, Tchepone had been abandoned by the North Vietnamese, and the assault therefore had no military consequences. With the town successfully taken, President Thieu considered his objectives realized, and ordered Lam's forces to retreat.

Disorderly Retreat

The real battle, however, was yet to come. Nearly 40,000 NVA troops attacked the ARVN as they left the town, and the withdrawal quickly became a rout. Many ARVN troops lacked battlefield experience. In this test of Vietnamization, many fought well, but the army faced some overwhelming challenges. An orderly retreat under fire would have been a difficult maneuver even for veteran troops, and the ARVN forces lacked both the

Taking control

North Vietnamese troops attack a fire support base at Hill 31, Laos, 15 miles (24 km) northwest of an American border base at Lang Vei. Some 250 ARVN troops were killed, and Hill 31 fell to the NVA on the third day of heavy pressure. They soon set their sights on the nearby Hill 30.

training and leadership needed to accomplish the task. The ARVN sustained heavy losses. It was only the bravery of US helicopter crews, going in despite poor weather and devastating antiaircraft fire, that enabled the rescue of thousands of ARVN troops.

Lam's forces lost at least 5,000 men, killed or wounded, plus 2,500 missing in action. Some 700 US helicopters were destroyed or damaged beyond repair, and 253 US personnel lost their lives. Radio Hanoi termed the operation "the heaviest defeat ever for Nixon and Company." Traffic along that part of the Ho Chi Minh trail was only briefly stopped, and plans to expand the trail farther into Laos were underway.

This bleak reality, however, did not stop Nixon and Thieu from proclaiming a great victory for Vietnamization and for the ARVN. In April 1971, Nixon announced the withdrawal of another 100,000 US troops from Vietnam.

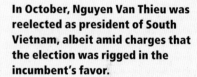

AFTER »

In October, Nguyen Van Thieu was reelected as president of South Vietnam, albeit amid charges that the election was rigged in the incumbent's favor.

THE ONE-MAN ELECTION

In 1971, Thieu forced a list of criteria for presidential candidates through the National Assembly that not even Vice President Nguyen Cao Ky could satisfy. One popular general met the criteria, but chose not to run despite **CIA efforts** to pay him to stay in. Thieu went to the polls **unopposed** in October and received almost 80 percent of the vote, with a 90 percent turnout. Thieu's own ambassador to the US wrote that this election only reinforced the image of the regime inside and outside of Vietnam as a corrupt and repressive **dictatorship**.

Help on its way

Four South Vietnamese rangers wounded during Lam Son 719 await medical evacuation to Phu Loc, a firebase near Khe Sanh and not far from the Laotian border. The NVA had attacked Phu Loc during the ARVN's advance in February, but it remained under South Vietnamese control.

6
EASTER OFFENSIVE TO US EXIT

January 1972–January 1973

In 1972, North Vietnam launches another big offensive, which the South Vietnamese struggle to repel. In an attempt to bring all parties back to the negotiating table, the US rains bombs on strategic targets in the North.

≪ Helicopters in action
A Sikorsky HH-53B Super Jolly Green Giant of the 40th Aerospace Rescue and Recovery Squadron flies alongside as a gunner of the US Air Force 21st Special Operations Squadron surveys the landscape during a search-and-rescue operation in October 1972.

EASTER OFFENSIVE TO US EXIT
JANUARY 1972–JANUARY 1973

At Easter 1972, North Vietnam launched a major offensive against the South, using tanks and heavy artillery. The North Vietnamese Army struck southward across the DMZ to capture Quang Tri and across South Vietnam's western borders toward Kontum and An Loc. The United States responded with extensive bombing of the North and provided air support for South Vietnamese ground troops. After initial reverses, the South Vietnamese army halted the offensive on all fronts. In the fall, the Paris peace talks broke down after coming tantalizingly close to agreement, prompting President Richard Nixon to order air raids by B-52 bombers against key targets in Hanoi and Haiphong. A resumption of negotiations in January 1973 brought swift agreement on terms for a ceasefire and the final withdrawal of American forces from Vietnam.

1 Blocking Route 13, the road to Saigon, became a key objective for South Vietnamese soldiers during North Vietnam's Easter Offensive at An Loc. 2 In May 1972, the US unleashed Linebacker 1, an air campaign against strategic targets in North Vietnam. 3 The devasation wreaked by the Easter Offensive caused thousands of civilians to flee their homes.

CHINA

NORTH
VIETNAM

Red River

Luang Prabang

Mekong River

Nan River

L
A
O
S

VIENTIANE

Vang Veng

Noi Bai
Long Bien Bridge
Hai Duong Bridge
HANOI
Hoa Lac
Linebacker I,II
Bach Mai
Kien An
Linebacker I, II
Haiphong
Cat Ba
Haiphong Harbor

Thanh Hoa Bridge
Thanh Hoa

Red River Delta

Gulf of Tonkin

HAINAN

Vinh

Udorn

Nakhon Phanom

T H A I L A N D

Ping River

Chao Phraya River

Takhli

Korat

Mun River

Ubon

Mekong River

Yankee Station
2

Camp Carroll
Tchepone
Khe Sanh
Dong Ha
Quang Tri
Hue
3

Da Nang

Mekong River

Tan Canh
Firebase Delta
Kontum
Pleiku

Dak To

Central Highlands

Qui Nhon

S
O
U
T
H
V
I
E
T
N
A
M

South China Sea

BANGKOK

Tonle Sap

C A M B O D I A

PHNOM PENH

Mekong River

Loc Ninh
An Loc
1

Trang Bang
SAIGON

Can Tho

Mekong Delta

Dixie Station

Gulf of Thailand

U R M A

KEY

——	International border
▦▦▦	Demilitarized Zone (DMZ)
➡	Ho Chi Minh Trail
□ ○	Capital / City (neutral)
■ ●	Capital / City (NVA / communist controlled)
■ ●	Capital / City (US / ARVN controlled)
□ ○	Capital / City (contested)
★	US base
⊥	US carrier station
✈	US air base
✕	Battle
✲	Bombing

N

0 ——— 100km

0 ——— 100 miles

TIMELINE JAN 1972–JAN 1973

US de-escalation ▪ **Major NVA offensive** ▪ Linebacker raids ▪ **Siege of An Loc** ▪ Operation Enhance ▪ **Battle over Quang Tri** ▪ Haiphong Harbor attacked ▪ **Christmas Bombing** ▪ North Vietnam returns to the negotiating table ▪ **Paris Peace Accords** ▪ Ceasefire agreed between North and South Vietnam ▪ **Operation Homecoming**

JANUARY–APRIL

FEBRUARY 21–28
President Nixon visits communist China and meets with Chairman Mao Zedong, leading to a rapprochement between the US and China.

MARCH 30
The NVA launches the Easter Offensive, a large-scale invasion of South Vietnam, using armored vehicles and artillery to strike across the DMZ toward the city of Quang Tri.

APRIL 4
In response to the Easter Offensive, President Nixon authorizes the bombing of North Vietnam up to the 18th parallel.

APRIL 10
B-52 bombers begin large-scale raids on targets deep inside North Vietnam as America escalates the air war.

MARCH 10
The US 101st Airborne Division leaves South Vietnam, the last US ground combat division to be withdrawn. Vietnamization is complete.

APRIL 7
After a three-day battle, North Vietnamese and Viet Cong forces capture the town of Loc Ninh, near the Cambodian border north of Saigon.

APRIL 12
Communist forces advance from base areas in Laos and Cambodia toward Kontum.

APRIL 13
The city of An Loc, north of Saigon, comes under attack and its defenders are placed under siege by communist forces.

❯ NVA volunteer corps soldier with an antiaircraft gun, 1972

APRIL 27
F-4 Phantoms armed with laser-guided bombs strike the Thanh Hoa bridge, a vital communications link in North Vietnam.

MAY–AUGUST

MAY 11–28
An Loc and Kontum resist major assaults by communist forces. B-52 bombers are used in devastating strikes against the attackers.

≪ Kontum, June 1972

JUNE 28
ARVN troops in northern South Vietnam launch a counteroffensive with the aim of retaking Quang Tri province.

MAY 1
The city of Quang Tri is occupied by the NVA as South Vietnamese troops retreat southward in disorder.

MAY 5
South Vietnamese forces stabilize a defensive line, halting the North Vietnamese advance toward Hue.

MAY 17
President Nixon approves Operation Enhance, the provision of large quantities of American military equipment to the South Vietnamese armed forces.

JULY 20
The Siege of An Loc ends in an NVA defeat after 95 days of fighting.

❯ ARVN soldiers at La Vang (Quang Tri), July 1972

MAY 8
President Nixon orders the mining of Haiphong Harbor and other North Vietnamese ports to block the import of war materiel.

MAY 10
US air forces begin Operation Linebacker, a sustained bombing campaign against North Vietnam, which attacks military installations, supply routes, and storage facilities.

JUNE 9
Communist forces are cleared from Kontum City, ending the threat of South Vietnam being cut in two.

AUGUST 11
The last combat patrol carried out by American troops in Vietnam is completed near Da Nang.

AUGUST 27
US Navy vessels carry out a night raid against the defenses of the port of Haiphong.

"We tend to think only in terms of **what this war has cost us,** but by **comparison** to what it has cost so many Vietnamese, **our price pales.**"

LETTER FROM COLONEL WILLIAM NOLDE, LAST US COMBAT CASUALTY IN VIETNAM, KILLED JANUARY 27, 1973

SEPTEMBER–DECEMBER

JANUARY–MARCH 1973

OCTOBER 22
The communist Easter Offensive ends. The American Linebacker bombing campaign against North Vietnam is halted.

NOVEMBER 14
Nixon assures President Thieu that if Hanoi does not abide by the terms of the proposed peace deal, the US will retaliate swiftly and severely.

DECEMBER 20
Six B-52 bombers are shot down by North Vietnamese SAMs, forcing a revision of American bombing tactics.

JANUARY 9
Peace talks resume in Paris; a breakthrough is announced.

FEBRUARY 12
Operation Homecoming— the transfer of US prisoners of war from North Vietnam to the United States—begins.

≫ Christmas Bombing, December 1972

SEPTEMBER 16
South Vietnamese forces retake Quang Tri City, lost to the communists at the start of May.

≫ ARVN recapture Quang Tri, September 1972

DECEMBER 14
As peace negotiations in Paris stall, Nixon and his advisers decide to resume the bombing of North Vietnam.

DECEMBER 18
Operation Linebacker II, known as the Christmas Bombing, begins. American B-52 bombers attack targets in Hanoi and Haiphong.

FEBRUARY 21
A peace agreement is signed between the Royal Laotian government and the Pathet Lao. The US bombing of Laos is halted.

OCTOBER 8
Meeting in Paris, North Vietnamese negotiator Le Duc Tho and US National Security Adviser Henry Kissinger agree a draft peace agreement.

OCTOBER 26
Henry Kissinger declares that "peace is at hand" in Vietnam, despite the rejection of the peace deal by South Vietnam's President Thieu.

≫ Henry Kissinger

DECEMBER 26
North Vietnamese cities are attacked by 120 B-52s. North Vietnam proposes a resumption of peace negotiations in January.

JANUARY 21
President Thieu reluctantly accepts the proposed peace terms. The "land grab" begins as communist and South Vietnamese forces fight for control of villages across South Vietnam.

≫ Commemorative badge

PEACE AT LAST
JAN. 27 1973
VIETNAM CEASEFIRE

OCTOBER 20
The US begins Operation Enhance Plus, the supply of military equipment and transfer of bases to South Vietnam ahead of an expected peace agreement.

NOVEMBER 7
Richard Nixon is re-elected as president in a landslide victory, winning over 60 percent of the popular vote.

DECEMBER 29
Linebacker II is halted. The US Air Force has lost 16 B-52s shot down in the raids. The bombing has caused 1,624 civilian deaths.

JANUARY 27
The Paris Peace Accords are signed. The provisions include a ceasefire and the withdrawal of all American forces from Vietnam within 60 days.

MARCH 29
The last American combat troops leave Vietnam. More than 58,000 Americans have died in the conflict.

Decision to Attack

The combination of US withdrawal, the relative inexperience of ARVN troops in combat, and antiwar opinions in the US created a window of opportunity for North Vietnam. In the spring of 1972, it decided to act.

I n the latter half of 1971, the North Vietnamese Politburo began to make plans for a major new offensive into South Vietnam for spring 1972. It was to be a campaign unlike anything they had tried before, with troops waging conventional warfare, employing massed tanks and heavy artillery. The North Vietnamese planned to coordinate closely among main force, regional, and local troops and to fight in urban and rural areas alike; unlike the Tet Offensive, which had unfolded in waves, the attack would be relentless. Diplomacy would proceed in parallel.

Supplies and training
Hanoi's allies, China and the Soviet Union, had scheduled talks with American leaders in 1972. Anxious to cushion the shock these diplomatic openings might cause Hanoi, they supplied North Vietnam with additional increments of military aid. China tripled shipments of artillery guns, sending nearly 7,900 pieces to Hanoi in 1971 alone, and delivered 300 tanks between 1971 and 1972. Moscow also sent tanks, along with modern cannons and more sophisticated missiles, such as the shoulder-fired SA-7 "Strella" antiaircraft weapon and the AT-3 "Sagger" antitank missile.

Hanoi prepared for the much greater supply needs that were anticipated. It built a pipeline to pump oil to the South, and supplemented the existing

2,000 **The number of trucks sent to Hanoi by China between 1971 and 1972, increasing capacity along the Ho Chi Minh Trail by 50 percent.**

Keeping up the fight
This Viet Cong propaganda poster, published in 1972, was designed to keep up morale among the guerrilla force during the lull in combat leading up to the Spring Offensive.

road net with a new Secret Road that connected Tchepone in Laos with the Cambodia-Laos-Vietnam "triborder" region. Able to carry trucks and built entirely under jungle canopy, it could be used 24 hours a day, and accelerated the movement of troops (who had previously marched), reducing deaths and sickness. A mock-up of

The T-54 Tank
Communist allies augmented the NVA's supply of light PT-76 tanks with medium T-54 or T-55 vehicles, which were a better match for the US M48. Crewed by four, the T-54 had a top speed of 34 mph (55 km/h).

Infrared gun sight

Fume extractor

100 mm gun

Driver's hatch

Machine gun slit

Track idler

BEFORE

At the end of 1971, Hanoi was in a strong position, especially after the ARVN failure in Lam Son.

RECOVERING FROM TET
North Vietnam's failed **Tet Offensive** ‹‹ 178–93 decimated Viet Cong forces, but they were replenished through continued infiltration along the Ho Chi Minh Trail. The failure of South Vietnam's **Operation Lam Son 719** ‹‹ 264–65 in Laos in early 1971 revealed the weakness of ARVN forces.

VIET CONG IN ACTION IN 1968

a US or ARVN-style base camp of regimental size was also built at Bach Mai, outside Hanoi, so that the NVA could practice assaults.

North Vietnam's military planners also refined the offensive concept. Corps-level commands were set up to lead multidivision forces of combat troops throughout South Vietnam—a capability that Hanoi's forces had previously managed only in the vicinity of the DMZ. The combat divisions themselves—tasked with mastering the new mass tactics in a very short time—each specialized in certain types of attack, such as urban or mountain fighting, or ambushes.

NORTH VIETNAMESE LEADER (1907–86)

LE DUAN

Preparations for the 1972 invasion of the South were masterminded by Le Duan. A veteran strategist, who had led the Viet Minh against the French in the Mekong in the 1950s, Le Duan became the effective ruler of North Vietnam after Ho Chi Minh's death in 1969, eclipsing rival Pham Van Dong. Evidence suggests that Le Duan took part in a 1967 purge of pro-Soviet leaders that had marginalized Dong.

Placing the troops

The ambitious plans called for forces of several divisions to attack across the DMZ, in the Central Highlands, and north of Saigon. Priority was initially given to the Saigon area but this shifted to the northern provinces of Quang Tri and Thua Thien shortly before the attack began. Hanoi expected to overrun those provinces, as well as Kontum and Pleiku in the Central Highlands. In the Saigon region, the 301 Group was to take the capital. The final pieces in the plan were for the Viet Cong to attack in the Mekong Delta and for more NVA troops to enter northern Laos.

The NVA committed almost all its forces, keeping only one division in reserve. Evoking a heroic figure in Vietnamese history, Hanoi called the campaign the Nguyen Hue Offensive, after the warrior (also known as Quang Trung) who defeated a Chinese invasion in 1789 and went on to become a modernizing emperor of Vietnam.

AFTER »

North Vietnam's preparations for war did not go unnoticed by US intelligence.

NIXON VISITS CHINA
While North Vietnam prepared for its **Easter Offensive 276–87 »**, President Nixon visited China in February 1972, with a view to building relations with Vietnam's ally and isolating Vietnam politically. Peace talks between the North Vietnamese and Henry Kissinger continued in Paris. Hanoi worried that a Chinese-American rapprochement had begun at its expense.

TIME TO STRIKE
By its military offensive, Hanoi sought both to demonstrate its resolve and **break the deadlock** in the peace talks. It believed the US was **stalling for time in the peace talks** while Washington rebuilt the military capablities of the South Vietnamese.

Commander's hatch

Domed turret shaped to deflect shells

Engine, placed at the back, away from attack

Drive sprocket, which moves the track forward or backward

> "[We] **must annihilate** as much … of the **US and** [its] **puppet's potential** as possible."
>
> TRUONG CHINH, SPEECH TO THE VIETNAM FATHERLAND FRONT, PUBLISHED FEBRUARY 3, 1972

American Strategy in 1972

When US intelligence reported a surge in North Vietnamese military activity, American leaders and commanders pondered the prospect of an attack—when would it come, where would it fall, and would the South Vietnamese be able to cope?

« BEFORE

RALLYING THE ARVN

President Nixon had been elected on his promise to end the war in Vietnam.

KEY POLICIES
Nixon's policy of **Vietnamization** **« 228–29** gradually led to ARVN forces replacing US troops in all combat operations in Vietnam. Meanwhile, Nixon had instructed Henry Kissinger to conduct **secret talks « 224–25** with the North Vietnamese in the hope of reaching a peace deal.

It was apparent to US strategists that Hanoi was planning something major for 1972, but they had no clear idea of what it might be. In September 1971, the Director of the CIA, Richard Helms, had briefed the National Security Council that something was afoot and expressed most concern about the DMZ and the Central Highlands. However, Washington's attitude remained upbeat and confident. In a presidential conversation with Henry Kissinger in November 1971, Nixon had expressed his desire for the US to take a hard "pop" against Hanoi after the 1972 presidential election, regardless of who became president. Nixon instructed Kissinger to reinforce the US fleet off Vietnamese shores.

" The day after the election … we will **bomb the bejeezus** out of them."

RICHARD NIXON, NOVEMBER 20, 1971

Cause for alarm

At that point, the intelligence turned dark. North Vietnamese infiltration, which had been at a very low rate in summer and fall of 1971, increased exponentially over the winter, with 20,000 soldiers setting out along the Ho Chi Minh Trail in one week and 63,000 more following over a four-month span. Watchers at MACV noted the increase. Meanwhile, aerial reconnaissance detected a tank concentration bigger than anything they had seen previously, North Vietnamese jets at airfields in the southern panhandle of North Vietnam, and two dozen NVA surface-to-air missile battalions taking position in the DMZ-Trail area. Defense Intelligence Agency staff had also noticed a more aggressive tone in NVA and Viet Cong pronouncements.

Indications of a major offensive mounted. General Creighton Abrams and Joint Chiefs of Staff Chairman Admiral Thomas Moorer

Fighting the propaganda war
Actress and activist Jane Fonda delivers an antiwar message on Hanoi Radio in North Vietnam in July 1972. Exploiting the propaganda value of Fonda's visit to the full, Hanoi got her to sit on an antiaircraft gun while she made the broadcast.

believed the attack would fall in the Central Highlands, but Washington focused on both the Highlands and the DMZ. On January 17, 1972, senior officials meeting in Washington tentatively predicted an attack in the DMZ in March and discussed how it could

be met—ARVN capabilities and the scale of US support in terms of tanks, planes, and artillery. On January 20, General Abrams asked Washington to authorize more airstrikes and extend US air support for the ARVN, including into Laos.

Warning the public

On January 25, the president went on national television to prepare the public for what might unfold. His speech revealed the secret peace negotiations that had been taking place with the North Vietnamese, including a peace proposal presented to them in the previous October. He stated that if this proposal was rejected, he would take action to defend the remaining personnel in Vietnam.

By the end of January, the president had confirmed General Abrams's requests, and airstrikes were stepped up against the Ho Chi Minh Trail in Laos. Planners studied the intersections, choke points, and river crossings of the Trail, designating "blocking belts"—strategic points that when destroyed made escape difficult—and laying electronic sensors to provide target intelligence. The US also added to the Seventh Fleet in the South China Sea, and began preparations to operate B-52 bombers from the island of Guam and from Thailand.

Reaching out

Strategy in Washington in 1972, however, was not solely focused on Vietnam. As the war there dragged on, Nixon surprised the US public by visiting the People's Republic of China in February to normalize relations. Later that year, he visited the Soviet Union to pursue a détente. Both nations had previously supplied aid to Hanoi. Nixon's visits marked a shift in Cold War diplomacy.

AFTER

The US were proved right in their expectation of a major offensive. In March, the NVA and Viet Cong unleashed their most ambitious offensive of the war.

THREE-PRONGED ATTACK
The **Easter Offensive 276–87 ≫** began on March 30. It turned out to be a three-pronged attack, across the DMZ, from the west into the Central Highlands, and from Cambodia toward Saigon in the south, employing conventional tactics and weapons. The **ARVN**, supported by massive US airpower, faced its greatest test so far.

BOMBING THE NORTH
In May 1972, Nixon ordered **Operation Linebacker 292–93 ≫**, the bombing of **military sites, roads, and bridges** in North Vietnam. He also ordered the mining of **Haiphong Harbor 290–91 ≫**, a major entry point for armaments and supplies from North Vietnam's allies.

Final preparations
Nixon meets with bipartisan Congressional leaders in the White House Cabinet Room on February 17, 1972, to discuss his upcoming trip to China. That afternoon, he left for Hawaii, where he would stay for four days before flying west.

Standing by for action
US Marines train in 1972, using helicopters and amphibious vehicles. By this point in the war, the last US Marines in Vietnam were preparing to stand down, or training the ARVN, but the prospect of a new North Vietnamese offensive saw numbers increase, readying for combat.

Easter Offensive: Quang Tri

US and ARVN commanders had been anticipating a major North Vietnamese offensive in the early months of 1972, but when the action began, the South Vietnamese forces were in disarray and US support was limited because of ongoing Vietnamization.

B y March 1972, the American policy of Vietnamization had reduced the American presence to a fraction of its former might. Yet the ARVN still depended heavily on American support to operate effectively against the NVA and Viet Cong. US Army advisers were working with the ARVN Third Division, in charge of defending the Quang Tri region of Military Region 1, the northernmost zone bordering the DMZ, but the ARVN forces were thinly stretched.

Late in March, the ARVN Joint General Staff (JGS) learned the North Vietnamese attack would begin on March 29 and ordered an alert. However, ARVN forces were unprepared. General Giai, commanding the Third Division, was in the process of switching his Second Infantry with the 56th Infantry, which meant that neither regiment was in protective strongpoints when the attack commenced. Moreover, both Military Region 1 commander, General Hoang Xuan Lam, and General Giai expected the

Countering air attacks
The NVA used the Soviet-made 9K32 Strela-2 shoulder-fired surface-to-air missile launcher to counter US air attacks during the Quang Tri Offensive. They managed to shoot down 14 fixed-wing aircraft and 10 helicopters.

attack to come from the west, descending from the hills to the coastal plain, rather than across the DMZ, and the most effective regiment, the Second Infantry, was being removed from this sector.

Line of defense
South Vietnamese troops and tanks take counteroffensive action against North Vietnamese forces attacking Highway 1, southwest of Dong Ha, on April 20, 1972.

« **BEFORE**

Bordering the DMZ, Quang Tri province had been a key target for communist attacks since the start of the war.

HISTORY OF BATTLES
In 1967, US forces tried to secure the border area with a **chain of firebases** along the DMZ. These came under attack in the **run-up to the Tet Offensive** « **178–81**, as did Quang Tri City, the capital of the province. The **siege of the combat base at Khe Sanh** « **200–203** was one of the fiercest engagements in the war.

CHANGING THE GUARD
In October 1971, the ARVN's newly formed **Third Division**, under General Vu Van Giai, replaced the departing US 101st Airborne Division, which had previously defended Quang Tri province.

South Vietnamese Marines holding some of the firebases behind the DMZ line had experienced NVA probes and seen activity over the previous days. Some artillery and air strikes had countered these attacks, but Giai felt he had no strength for a ground operation beyond his defense line.

The North Vietnamese had more than 30,000 troops backed by many guns and a full armored regiment. Their prongs of attack across the DMZ, which included tanks, took the ARVN by surprise.

Cloud descends

The skeleton group of US advisers sprang into action. Lieutenant Colonel George Turley, the deputy chief Marine adviser in South Vietnam, who was visiting Quang Tri sector, found himself thrust into the role of senior US adviser in the DMZ. B-52 bombers hit NVA

Fleeing the battle
Thousands of civilians were forced to flee their homes and villages during April 1972 as North Vietnamese forces advanced through Quang Tri province. Many were killed by NVA bombardment of the routes along which they were fleeing.

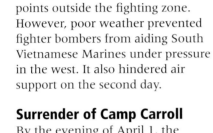

" [The] **disorder** and **panic** among these refugees … was **contagious.**"

GENERAL NGO QUANG TRUONG DESCRIBING CIVILIANS FLEEING QUANG TRI, 2010

staging areas at Khe Sanh and points outside the fighting zone. However, poor weather prevented fighter bombers from aiding South Vietnamese Marines under pressure in the west. It also hindered air support on the second day.

Surrender of Camp Carroll
By the evening of April 1, the western firebases had become untenable for the South

Vietnamese and General Giai was forced to move his headquarters east to Quang Tri City. On April 2, Easter Sunday, the situation for the ARVN defenders in the west deteriorated further. Camp Carroll, the most important of the DMZ firebases, and the best equipped militarily, was surrounded by enemy forces. The South Vietnamese surrendered the base with hardly a shot fired.

With the loss of Camp Carroll went all the Vietnamese Marines' artillery and the ARVN's heaviest guns. The US advisers stationed there only just escaped in time, while some 1,500 ARVN soldiers were captured. Pressure against the remaining South Vietnamese positions in Quang Tri province immediately increased and a full-scale ARVN retreat was soon underway.

»

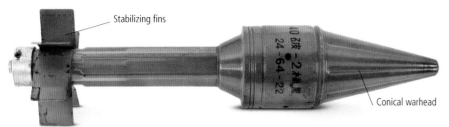

Stabilizing fins

Conical warhead

Communist firepower
Made in China for the NVA, the CHICOM Type-50 antitank grenade was a copy of the Soviet RPG-2. "CHICOM" was a US intelligence term for Chinese technology—US soldiers used it as pejorative slang for captured equipment.

» The bridge is blown
Following the loss of Camp Carroll, General Giai ordered his forces to withdraw behind the Cua Viet River, setting up a battle for the town of Dong Ha. This was a critical location because the bridge carrying the main north–south transportation route, Route 1, crossed the river there. A second bridge, built by the French, stood nearby, and a third bridge crossed the river near Camp Carroll. The three crossings formed the gateway to the heart of Quang Tri province and the cities of Hue and Da Nang.

By April 2, the Vietnamese Third Marine Battalion, ordered up from reserve, had entered the town, along with the 20th Armored Squadron on M-48 Pershings, the ARVN's heaviest tanks. To the north, across the river, the North Vietnamese tanks had taken up positions. Before they could sweep across the Route 1 bridge, Colonel Turley ordered Captain John Ripley, top adviser to the Third Marines, to blow up the bridge. Captain Ripley displayed extreme bravery and skill as he climbed through the steel structure of the bridge to set the explosives. The blast destroyed both the road bridge and the railway crossing.

Fresh attacks
By forcing the NVA tanks to make a lengthy detour westward to cross the river, the destruction of the bridge at Dong Ha effectively sapped the momentum of the NVA advance. Supplies to their forces also had to

be replenished. The interruption provided the ARVN with time to regroup its forces and attempt a counteroffensive, but without much effect. On April 23, the North Vietnamese renewed their attacks, this time slowly grinding away in an attempt to wear down ARVN morale.

The ARVN forces abandoned Dong Ha on April 28, and Quang Tri was lost on April 29. Cloud cover had prevented US air strikes in support of the ARVN.

The loss of Quang Tri and the NVA bombardment of villages and towns in the area led to a mass of refugees fleeing down Route 1 toward Hue. The NVA targeted the road, and the loss of civilian lives there comprised one of the worst atrocities of the war.

In the wake of this catastrophic defeat, President Thieu replaced Military Region 1 commander Lam with General Ngo Quang Truong,

10,000 The estimated number of NVA troops killed in the battle for Quang Tri City.

5,000 The estimated number of ARVN killed in the retaking of Quang Tri city.

South Vietnam's best field commander. General Giai was fired, tried by a military tribunal, and sentenced to jail, his place taken by Nguyen Duy Hinh.

New broom
General Truong reorganized the ARVN defenses. The First Division, which Truong had once led, was far more organized in its defense of Hue, the next assumed target. Difficulties of supply meant that the NVA lacked the weight of artillery and armor it had enjoyed along the DMZ. When ARVN defenses held to the west and north of Hue, Truong moved to stabilize the line along the My Chanh River, about halfway between Quang Tri and Hue.

By May 13, ARVN forces had regained enough confidence to make further attacks and they gradually expanded their efforts west and north of the city of Hue. On June 14, General Truong presented a plan for the recapture of Quang Tri and reached the town on July 4. Both the assault and the defense were fierce, with house-to-house fighting. The Vietnamese Marine Division replaced the Airborne on July 27. NVA soldiers began to call the town

Hamburger city for the way new men arrived at night but were dead before dawn. The South Vietnamese fought them every step of the way and took the last positions in Quang Tri's citadel on September 15. With both armies exhausted and the city in ruins, the offensive in Quang Tri province was over.

AFTER »

The Easter Offensive in Quang Tri showed that the ARVN was capable of fighting well, but only when circumstances were right.

MIXED RESULTS
The Quang Tri campaign proved that **US air support**, and the good weather required, was critical to the success of ARVN actions. The **vital part played by US advisers** was also clear. As Vietnamization progressed, the ARVN would **struggle** with **inadequate supplies, low morale, and poor leadership 310–11 »**.

MEASURING SUCCESS
Although the ARVN regained Quang Tri city, it fought to a standstill that left the communists with **permanent territorial gains**.

ARVN TROOPS

Victor of Quang Tri
ARVN General Ngo Quang Truong (right), here talking to a junior officer while commander of the Mekong Delta, was placed in charge of Military Region 1 after the fall of Quang Tri in late April 1972.

Faith among the ruins
An ARVN soldier prays in the ruins of the church at La Vang, south of Quang Tri City, destroyed by bombardment in 1972. The Quang Tri region had a high proportion of Catholics, many of whom feared communist rule.

Napalm Attack

The NVA occupied the village of Trang Bang during the Easter Offensive in 1972. As families fled, South Vietnamese pilots dropped napalm bombs, believing their targets to be enemy soldiers. Photographer Nick Ut captured nine-year-old Phan Thi Kim Phuc screaming "Too hot!" in agony, as she ran naked from her village. Phuc sought asylum in Canada in 1992, and now speaks publicly about what happened.

She describes running from Cao Dai temple in Trang Bang and seeing an airplane getting lower. It dropped four bombs and then there was fire all around. It spread over her body, especially her left arm, burning off her clothes. On Road No.1 from Saigon to Phnom Penh, her photo was taken and then a soldier gave her a drink and poured water over her body. She lost consciousness and woke up in hospital, where she spent 14 months and had 17 operations.

When she eventually went home, she found that their house was destroyed and they had lost everything. They survived from day to day. Despite the pain, itching, and headaches she suffered almost constantly, Phan Thi Kim Phuc dreamed of becoming a doctor. But her studies were cut short by local government who refused to allow her to go to school anymore.

"They wanted me as a symbol of the state.**"**

PHAN THI KIM PHUC, FROM *THE LONG ROAD TO FORGIVENESS*, NATIONAL PUBLIC RADIO, JUNE 30, 2008

Shocking the nation
The Associated Press initially rejected Nick Ut's image of the terrified Phan Thi Kim Phuc fleeing the napalm attack, on the grounds of nudity. Editors, however, believed the news value of the photo overrode any reservations.

Easter Offensive: Kontum

The security of the Central Highlands was a paramount concern for South Vietnamese and US strategists in early 1972. Loss of the Highlands and adjacent coastal plains would cut South Vietnam in two.

BEFORE

From the start of the war, the Central Highlands had been a key area of conflict.

REPEATED ASSAULTS
In 1965 and in 1967, there was **major fighting** in the Central Highlands. The North Vietnamese used operations in this area to distract US and ARVN forces while they prepared for the **Tet Offensive ❮❮ 178–81**. This strategy was repeated two weeks before the start of the Easter Offensive when NVA units increased their activities in the area.

An attack from the west through the Central Highlands—Military Region (MR) 2—was one of the three prongs of attack that comprised North Vietnam's plan for a spring offensive. For this advance, the

Montagnard defenders
Soldiers from the hilltribes, or Montagnards, played a key role in opposing the NVA advance during the campaign in the Central Highlands. Here, Montagnard troops rest in camp at Kontum while B-52s bomb the surrounding area.

North Vietnamese assembled three infantry divisions along with a tank unit, two artillery regiments, and three regiments of independent infantry—roughly 20,000 troops. The ARVN defenders included the 22nd and 23rd Infantry Divisions, widely regarded as the weakest in the ARVN. The South Vietnamese, aware of the threat, also posted a brigade of the ARVN Airborne Division to the region.

The ARVN benefited from a formidable US adviser, John Paul Vann, who was able to convince

The NVA in action
In a photograph released by the North on April 28, 1972, North Vietnamese soldiers are seen in action as they fire rockets at ARVN tanks. The location of the photograph was identified as "Dak Can," but the location is probably Tan Canh or Dak To.

General Abrams to prevail upon the ARVN to send a second airborne brigade to the Highlands.

Even so, not every key point could be garrisoned. Rocket Ridge, which overlooked Route 14, the

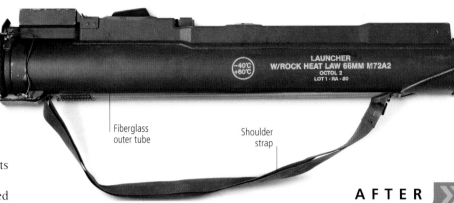

of additional ARVN forces from Pleiku to forward positions above Kontum.

The action unfolds

Serious fighting began at the end of March with clashes in Binh Dinh province, where the NVA attempted to cut Route 19, which connected the coastal ports with the upland cities. In the Highlands, the NVA troops carried out bombardments on March 30, but held off on ground assaults for several more days. A serious engagement came near Dak To, where on April 1, ARVN troops faced NVA sappers. On April 3, Firebase Delta on Rocket Ridge was assaulted. By April 11, fighting had become generalized from Rocket Ridge to Dak To and Tan Canh. One by one the firebases fell in spite of B-52 air strikes.

north-south backbone of the Highlands, had several firebases but it was still a tempting target for North Vietnamese forces looking to cut off Kontum from Dak To and Tan Canh, MR 2's northerly outposts. Further preparations for the expected offensive included the deployment

> "Even a tank we 'destroyed,' ... might be repaired to **fight again** another day."

LIEUTENANT COLONEL THOMAS P. McKENNA, *KONTUM: THE BATTLE TO SAVE SOUTH VIETNAM*, 2011

Meanwhile, the South Vietnamese chose to move the airborne brigades out of the Highlands in exchange for the Sixth Ranger Group from Quang Tri. The Rangers were exhausted from nearly a month of fighting, and moving up troops of the 23rd Division at Pleiku simply weakened the defenses. Rocket Ridge positions collapsed, after which the NVA swiftly attacked the major base at Tan Canh, using tanks. Some tanks were destroyed from the air, but the ARVN at Tan Canh and Dak To collapsed on April 24.

Holding Kontum

Kontum lay only 25 miles (40 km) away, but this was a major challenge for the North Vietnamese forces. Their advance forces were in need of supplies, and weeks passed until the NVA was able to mount its assault on the town. By then, the ARVN leadership had sent back one of the airborne brigades and President Thieu had appointed a new corps commander and a fresh leader for the 22nd Division. This officer, Ly Tong Ba,

Opposing tank attacks

The M72 LAW (light antitank weapon) was the primary ground-operated US antitank weapon during the Vietnam War. Operable by one person and highly portable, it provided mobile defense against tank assaults by the NVA such as those during the Kontum campaign.

became one of the heroes of the Easter Offensive, holding out against numerous challenges.

General Abrams designated Kontum for a day of B-52 strikes on May 12, just as the North Vietnamese were resuming their attacks. The most serious actions took place on May 14 and May 20. For a time, Kontum had to rely upon aerial supply.

By late May, ARVN forces were able to launch a counterattack. By May 30, the area was sufficiently secure for President Thieu to make a visit. A tragic footnote to the story occurred on June 9, when Vann's helicopter was shot down in the area where he had declared the last NVA positions to be eliminated.

Lucky mascot

US troops, members of a tank-killing unit, are carried by helicopter into Kontum in the Central Highlands on June 3, 1972. One of the soldiers holds on to his lucky teddy bear.

Armored Vehicles

The terrain and the unconventional nature of warfare in Vietnam restricted both sides' use of armored vehicles. While tank battles were rare, armored vehicles provided greater mobility and were key to the NVA's offensives.

1 **M41 Walker Bulldog (US/South Vietnam)** This American light tank was also used extensively by the ARVN. 2 **M24 Chaffee (South Vietnam)** This World War II-era American light tank saw service with both French and South Vietnamese forces in the 1950s. 3 **M48 Patton (US/South Vietnam)** A versatile battle tank, particularly good for mine-sweeping, the M48 was used by the US Army and Marines. The US also used the M60, an improved version of the M48. 4 **M551 Sheridan (US)** Arriving in Vietnam in 1969, the Sheridan was designed to accompany airborne assaults, as it was light enough to be be landed via parachute. 5 **Centurion MK 5 (Australia)** This battle tank was deployed by the Royal Australia Armored Corps in Vietnam. 6 **M42 Duster (US/South Vietnam)** Designed as a self-propelled antiaircraft gun, the Duster's guns also proved effective in breaking up infantry assaults. 7 **M55 (US)** A self-propelled howitzer, the lightly armored M55 required a crew

of just six men. It could be deployed in terrain unsuited to trucks. 8 **M706 Commando (US/South Vietnam)** This amphibious armored car was used mainly as a reconnaissance and patrol vehicle. 9 **LVTP-5 (US)** The LVTP (Landing Vehicle, Tracked Personnel), the most common amphibious vehicle used by US Marines, had variants for mine sweeping, command, recovery, and fire support. 10 **M113 (US/South Vietnam)** This armored personnel carrier (APC) was usually armed with an M2 Browning machine gun. 11 **BTR-40 (North Vietnam)** Around 100 of this APC and reconnaissance vehicle were given to North Vietnam by the Soviet Union. 12 **PT-76 (North Vietnam)** An amphibious tank exported to allies of the Soviet Union, the PT-76 first saw service in Vietnam during the Tet Offensive. 13 **T-34 (North Vietnam)** North Vietnam used the Soviet T-34 after World War II. By 1965, the NVA had begun to use a Chinese copy of the Soviet T-54—the Type 59.

1 M41 WALKER BULLDOG (US/SOUTH VIETNAM)

2 M24 CHAFFEE (SOUTH VIETNAM)

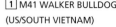

3 M48 PATTON (US/SOUTH VIETNAM)

U S AR
ORDNA

US ARMY
9A 5213

4 M551 SHERIDAN (US)

5 CENTURION MK 5 (AUSTRALIA)

6 M42 DUSTER (US/SOUTH VIETNAM)

7 M55 (US)

8 M706 COMMANDO (US/SOUTH VIETNAM)

9 LVTP-5 (US)

10 M113 (US/SOUTH VIETNAM)

11 BTR-40 (NORTH VIETNAM)

12 PT-76 (NORTH VIETNAM)

13 T-34 (NORTH VIETNAM)

Easter Offensive: An Loc

The area between Saigon and the Cambodian border, known as Military Region 3, was crucial for South Vietnam: it formed a safety belt for Saigon and contained most of the country's industry. The North Vietnamese made it the focus of their Easter Offensive.

It is thought that Hanoi's objective in Military Region 3 (MR 3) was to strike down Route 13 from the Cambodian border and storm Saigon. Initial proposals to make it the main focus of the offensive, however, were changed because of supply problems.

Cardboard tanks

The assault opened on April 2, 1972, with a diversion—an NVA regiment advancing toward the province of Tay Ninh. The North Vietnamese had even placed cardboard T-54 tanks opposite the city of Tay Ninh to convince South Vietnamese leaders that the attack would come there. In fact, the real attack began three days later, when North Vietnamese General Tran Van Tra led his main force of three divisions from Cambodia into Binh Long province. The NVA Seventh Division aimed to block Route 13 and isolate the battlefield, while other forces conquered the province and prepared for the pursuit south into Saigon.

Colonel William H. Miller, senior US adviser to the ARVN Fifth

Division, responsible for this part of MR 3, was not fooled by Tran Van Tra's diversions but he was not able to convince his South Vietnamese counterpart, Brigadier General Le Van Hung, to concentrate his forces on Binh Long.

On April 5, General Tra sent two regiments supported by two dozen tanks plus heavy artillery, to Binh Long's town of Loc Ninh, just north of the province capital of An Loc. US Army gunship helicopters, Navy carrier aircraft, Air Force close support planes, and Vietnamese planes all responded, but on April 6, Tra's Seventh Division blocked a section of Route 13, and surrounded Binh Long province. Loc Ninh fell to the Viet Cong's Ninth Division on April 7, making An Loc, the NVA's next target.

The ARVN had scattered groups of its Fifth Division across the province, which General Tra's forces took some time to drive back. President Thieu summoned a full division, the 21st, from MR 4 (south of Saigon), to block the road to Saigon, while bringing up the ARVN First Airborne Brigade to back the An Loc defenders. Colonel Tran Van

> **4,499** TONS **The amount of supplies airdropped by US and South Vietnamese planes during the 55-day siege of An Loc.**

Nhut, the province chief, who had been at a conference when the attacks started, hastened to An Loc to reorganize the available Regional Forces troops. General Hung also received the Third Ranger Group as a reinforcement. An Loc's garrison and the town of 15,000 had to be supplied by air.

Artillery bombardment

What became the siege of An Loc began on April 12 with an NVA attack, accompanied by a 7,000-shell barrage. ARVN soldiers initially ran away from the T-54 tanks, but soon discovered the effectiveness of both their shoulder-fired light antitank weapons (LAWs) and the support of US gunship helicopters. In spite of their efforts, however, the ARVN lost the northern half of the town.

General Tra made a second wave attack on April 19. By then, the ARVN's First Airborne Brigade had reached nearby positions and joined the defense, taking charge of recovering the airdropped supplies. On April 29, Tra's troops employed the SA-7 antiaircraft missile, forcing the air drops to a high altitude that demanded special parachute techniques.

Tra then assembled his troops for another pitched attack on May 11. As the NVA crowded into An Loc, with second echelon forces concentrated behind them, General Abrams ordered a full day of B-52 strikes on the town. The destruction blunted the North Vietnamese attack. From that moment, South Vietnamese efforts shifted to the restoration of ground links between Saigon and An Loc. The Siege of An Loc ended on June 1.

War companions
US adviser Lieutenant Colonel Burr M. Willey, accompanied by his dog Moose, fires his rifle as he moves up Route 13 toward An Loc with a South Vietnamese army unit. Willey and his dog later died in the relief effort.

USAF BOMBER

The Easter Offensive was over, but the North Vietnamese had gained territory.

BEYOND AN LOC
Although the ARVN had regained An Loc, it did not attempt to recapture the Loc Ninh district of the province. Washington's next step was to **widen its bombing campaign 292–93 »**.

PRAYER OF THANKS
The ARVN paid a heavy price for its victory at An Loc, with some 5,400 casualties, half of whom were killed. **Pesident Thieu visited An Loc** on July 7. He knelt and prayed before a statue of Christ that had survived the shelling.

" If the **[NVA] pull back,** do the South Vietnamese have the capability to **chase them?**"

UNDER SECRETARY OF STATE JOHN N. IRWIN, WASHINGTON SPECIAL ACTION GROUP MEETING, APRIL 10, 1972

Tasting success
ARVN forces stand and cheer on a knocked-out NVA tank as airlifted reinforcements arrive on July 3, 1972. The soldiers ignited a flare on the battered vehicle to celebrate.

Besieged at An Loc

To those besieged at An Loc, the NVA's shelling felt endless, as the bombardment turned their city to rubble. Captain Harold Moffett Jr., who survived the barrage of more than 50,000 rounds of artillery, rockets, and mortars over one night, compared An Loc to Berlin after World War II. Lieutenant Colonel Ed Benedit also recorded the destructive transformation of the city.

Captain Harold Moffett Jr. describes how they counted the rounds as they came in to An Loc by the hour until they increased so much they could not keep up. It seemed almost impossible to put so many rounds into one small area in such a small period of time. The shelling annihilated well over 100 civilians, mostly women and children.

Lieutenant colonel Ed Benedit saw the intermittent shelling transform the once bustling, rural metropolitan area into a cemetery where nothing moved. All the people and livestock disappeared underground.

❝ Every living creature, person, or animal had his own crawl space and would remain there for what would seem like an eternity.**❞**

LIEUTENANT COLONEL ED BENEDIT, SENIOR ADVISER IN AN LOC, QUOTED BY PHIL CLARKE IN *THE READER'S DIGEST*, MARCH 1973

Reduced to rubble
Vietnamese civilians search through the remains of An Loc's main market for food and valuables on June 22, 1972. Once the siege was over, the inhabitants emerged from underground hiding places to find their homes and livelihoods destroyed by the bombardment.

Mining Haiphong Harbor

The port of Haiphong, on the Gulf of Tonkin, provided the entry point for the major share of North Vietnam's imports, in particular of supplies from its ally the Soviet Union. Disruption of this lifeline to the North became a priority for the United States.

In the spring of 1972, President Nixon, fresh from the diplomatic triumph of his visit to China in February, thought he had isolated the North Vietnamese regime. But the Easter Offensive forced back the South Vietnamese on front after front. On April 5, Joint Chiefs of Staff chairman Admiral Moorer asserted that the president wanted new options. The first proposal would have been a focused bombing campaign like that of 1967. The second, named Pocket Money, envisioned mining Haiphong and other North Vietnamese ports. Nixon accepted the latter. Secretary of Defense Melvin Laird protested that mining Haiphong would achieve little unless North Vietnam was also bombed. Nixon promptly approved plans for the first "Linebacker" operation of bombing the North.

Diplomatic moves

Under international law, mining was an act of war. However, no state of war existed between the United States and any country in Southeast Asia. A full menu of diplomatic notices and private meetings therefore accompanied Pocket Money. Nixon also surrounded this planned escalation with the trappings of a decision-making process, including meetings of the National Security Council, consultations with senior members of Congress, and a televised address to the nation. The major worry concerned the response of the

Attack on Haiphong

US jets bomb warehouses and shipping areas in Haiphong on May 17, 1972. The mining of Haiphong occurred alongside the Linebacker I bombing campaign.

« BEFORE

PRO-WAR BUTTON, 1965

Joint Chiefs of Staff contingency plans dating back to 1965 regularly envisioned sealing off North Vietnam's Haiphong harbor, by mining or blockade.

THUNDER ROLLS OVER HAIPHONG
The **Rolling Thunder « 94–95** bombing campaign in the summer of 1967 included **major attacks** on Haiphong in order to disrupt the import of supplies from North Vietnam's allies and therefore degrade its war effort. The strikes included dropping land mines along key transportation routes such as the **Ho Chi Minh Trail « 138–39** and also "seeding" mines in the inland waterways of North Vietnam.

Operational base
The USS *Coral Sea* waits on Yankee Station, an area used as a naval "base" in the Gulf of Tonkin. This aircraft carrier launched many of the aircraft that seeded mines at the entrance to Haiphong Harbor from May 1972.

Soviet Union, North Vietnam's ally. Nixon was shortly due in Moscow for a summit conference and signature of agreements on the nuclear arms race. The fear was that the Russians might cancel the summit and boost their aid to North Vietnam. It was also conceivable that they might respond to the mining of Haiphong with force.

Although the USSR responded by sending submarines and a flotilla of warships into the South China Sea, they kept the date for the summit.

It was fortunate for the Americans that Soviet agricultural production that year had fallen far short of its needs and the USSR needed to secure grain supplies from the United States.

Mines in place
Initial preparations for Pocket Money were advancing in high gear by April 20 and the tactical plans were complete by April 23. Only one shipping channel led into Haiphong. It could be plugged with just a few strings of mines (in total, 36 were used). Mineman Second Class Robert D. Gill Jr. was sent from his duty post in Charleston, South Carolina, to the USS *Coral Sea* in the Gulf of Tonkin to prepare the mines.

On May 8, the operation was launched. Six LTV A-7 Corsair aircraft and three Grumman A-6A Intruders dropped the mines at the entrance to the harbor. Although the North Vietnamese retaliated, no planes were lost. The mines were programmed to activate at 6 p.m. local time on May 11. A number of visiting merchant vessels given warning of this deadline left port. Others, still unloading, remained, to be penned in until the end of 1972.

The mines were programmed to deactivate after a certain period of time. Thus the channel had to be "re-seeded" periodically. By early 1973, US forces had deposited 11,603 mines in North Vietnamese ports and waterways at a total cost of $9.5 million.

" We want to **strike** in a fashion that **maximizes their difficulties.** "
HENRY KISSINGER TO US AMBASSADOR ELLSWORTH BUNKER, MAY 6, 1972

Advocate of mining
Admiral Elmo R Zumwalt Jr., commander of riverine warfare in South Vietnam (1968–70), was chief of naval operations from 1970 to 1974. He was a leading proponent of the strategy of mining Haiphong Harbor.

The success of the US mining operation is extremely difficult to judge. The CIA had repeatedly warned that the North Vietnamese army requirements for war in the South were so small that stopping entry into Haiphong would not affect their supplies. Although the NVA's move to conventional warfare in the Easter Offensive had greatly increased its logistics requirements, and that offensive died down after May 1972, it is not clear if the cessation was a result of the mining operation. The most intense phase of the offensive had halted before the mining of the harbor began.

AFTER

The Paris Accords committed the United States to clearing the mines from Haiphong Harbor.

ASSESSING THE IMPACT
The CIA estimated that North Vietnam's **imports** in June and July 1972 fell to about 3,000 tons a day, less than half the 6,100 ton daily level of the previous year, but still more than the estimated daily requirements of 2,700 tons.

OPERATION END SWEEP
The need to clear the mines became a **bargaining chip** during the **Paris peace negotiations 294–95 »**. Eventually, it was agreed that the US would take responsibility for removing the mines. This was undertaken by the US Navy's Mine Warfare Service in an operation codenamed **End Sweep** between February and July 1973.

《 BEFORE

CELEBRATING RESISTANCE AGAINST US BOMBING

The US had conducted bombing strikes on targets in the North from the mid-1960s onward.

LIMITED IMPACT

The US bombing of the North at first mainly targeted **military and naval** installations in the Hanoi and Haiphong areas **《 94–95**. This strategy had little impact on the North Vietnamese war effort and later bombing campaigns extended the targets from bridges, roads, and railroads to **whole areas** to demoralize the population. However, this also proved ineffective.

TECHNOLOGY

LASER-GUIDED BOMBS

The laser-guided bomb (LGB), or "smart" bomb, was a first generation "precision-guided munition." In Vietnam in 1972, these were available in two sizes: 2,000 lb (900 kg) and 3,000 lb (1360 kg). An aircraft equipped with an LGB could plant bombs within 20 feet (6 m) of the intended target, which was a massive improvement on the accuracy of fighter-bombers (500 feet/150 m) equipped with standard munitions.

2,000 LB PAVEWAY II LASER-GUIDED BOMB

Linebacker I

From the beginning of the war, the bombing of North Vietnam had been the United States' major means of hitting directly at the North. The Rolling Thunder campaign had ended in 1968, with only sporadic later bombing. In early 1972, a new air campaign was planned.

Early in 1972, the US had begun planning a renewed bombing campaign of North Vietnam, and the Spring Offensive of April reinforced a determination to disrupt supply lines from the North. Advances in aerial bombing technology made the precise targeting of military objectives without excessive collateral damage a real possibility.

aircraft attacked the notorious and highly defended Thanh Hoa Bridge, a key conduit for supplies down the panhandle of North Vietnam. During Rolling Thunder the bridge had been bombed many times but never destroyed. The strike, with two dozen laser-guided bombs, demolished the western span of the bridge. Repeat raids ensured the North Vietnamese were unable to

that remained problematic throughout the bombing campaign. As of August 12, some 22,400 sorties had been scheduled but 15 percent were abandoned due to bad weather. Henry Kissinger expressed rage at the shortfall. Although barely half the listed targets had been hit, the operation was unquestionably more successful than the raids that preceded it.

> " We **know very little about** the situation in **the north.**"
>
> PHILIP A. ODEEN (NATIONAL SECURITY COUNCIL STAFF) TO HENRY KISSINGER, AUGUST 12, 1972

Precision attack

The planning for the operation that would be named Linebacker I was well underway by March. The Air Force and Navy had assembled significant reinforcements of aircraft and ships from South Korea, Taiwan, Japan, and the United States.

The first day of the operation was May 10, 1972, when strike formations of Navy and Marine aircraft flew into North Vietnam from Yankee Station in the Tonkin Gulf, and Air Force planes from US bases in Thailand flew in along the Mekong River. Over the ensuing days and weeks, the Americans destroyed bridges, railroad facilities, roads, and tunnels. One of the big successes occurred on May 13, when US

repair the damage during the war—but they were ingenious at finding alternatives.

The smart bombs were a highly effective addition to the US armory, but their use required good weather. This was a disadvantage

Losses minimized

In Linebacker I, the US Air Force flew 18,000 sorties and lost 44 aircraft (five to flak, 12 to SAMs, and 27 to North Vietnamese interceptors). The US Navy flew more than 23,600 sorties and lost 45 planes (27 to flak, 17 to SAMs, and one to fighters). While the Air Force provided very elaborate electronic countermeasures and flak suppression for its missions, special training in aerial maneuver

Preparing to strike

Crewmen on the aircraft carrier USS *Constellation*, positioned off the coast of North Vietnam during Linebacker I, fit bombs to an F-4 Phantom jet on May 23, 1972.

Both US losses and damage to North Vietnam mounted as the bombing continued.

NEW EDGE
Special training for US naval air crews and **new weapons** for air forces improved American survivability and destructiveness and immediately put Washington in a stronger position for air warfare.

TALKS RESTART—AND STOP
The **peace talks in Paris 294–95** » resumed in early November. However, although a draft agreement was reached, both North and South Vietnamese negotiators found cause to resist signing.

Successful strike
US Navy bombers destroy the Hai Duong railroad bridge over the Song Thai Binh River southeast of Hanoi on May 10, 1972, during Linebacker I. One of the spans of this strategic bridge was destroyed in the action.

tactics enabled Navy crews to achieve a 13 to 1 kill-to-loss ratio against Hanoi's planes. Flying at a low altitude also reduced Navy losses to SAMs.

Losses of both Navy and Air Force aircraft were minimized by warnings of North Vietnamese fighter activity provided by US warship radars and Air Force intelligence units.

The worst day for the Americans was on June 27, when four Air Force Phantoms were shot down, three by MiGs, with no North Vietnamese losses.

Assessing the impact
In all, North Vietnam lost 62 of its own fighter interceptors to the Americans. The United States had demonstrated to North Vietnam that

Washington would respond forcefully to its actions in the South and would exact a cost for supplying the insurgents. However, as US National Security Council staffer Philip Odeen argued at the time,

155,000 TONS The quantity of bombs dropped on North Vietnam during Linebacker I.

US intelligence depended heavily on photography, which provided scant data about the state of North Vietnam's economy, logistical problems, or morale. Hence Washington knew almost nothing about the composition of imports, stock levels, or other key indices, and this made definitive judgments about the effectiveness of the bombing impossible.

Tentative negotiations to end the war had consistently failed as a result of the conflicting positions of both sides.

SOUTH VIETNAMESE CONCERNS
The Thieu **government's objectives** were the removal of North Vietnamese forces from the South, the disarming of the Viet Cong, and securing the continued leadership of Thieu.

OPPOSING MOTIVES
The major concern of the North was to secure a **total withdrawal of the US** from South Vietnam, ensuring the Viet Cong was brought into the Saigon government, and, if possible, ousting President Thieu.

ANTIWAR BADGE

At the negotiating table
US and North Vietnamese negotiators, including Henry Kissinger (fourth from right) and Le Duc Tho (fourth from left), meet in Paris on January 13, 1973, to continue discussions on terms for a ceasefire agreement.

Progress of the Peace Talks

Open, or "plenary" talks, with permanent delegations from all the participants had got underway in Paris by 1972. These proceeded alongside secret talks involving Henry Kissinger for the United States and Le Duc Tho for North Vietnam.

By 1972, it had become clear that any progress in Vietnam peace talks would have to come from the meetings between Henry Kissinger and Le Duc Tho, which left out the intensely wary South Vietnamese. Although the US played its hand very close to its chest, the South Vietnamese received periodic updates. After January, when President Nixon revealed the existence of the secret talks, public pressure to reach an agreement grew more intense.

The negotiators met in Paris on May 2. The North Vietnamese refused to call off their offensive and the US negotiators rejected a proposal to unseat President Thieu. With the peace talks in a state of deadlock, the next scheduled discussion was cancelled.

Breaking the deadlock
During a summit with the Russians in Moscow, Nixon sent the North Vietnamese another message via Soviet hands—that a commission that would be created to carry out a new presidential election in the South could function as an interim coalition government. That proposal interested the North Vietnamese, and meetings on July 19 and August 1 began to break the deadlock. The US agreed to include both political and military elements in an agreement and the North Vietnamese, assuming Thieu would resign before any election, relented on their demand that he give up power immediately. They then presented an outline framework for an agreement.

North by making them just one player. Meanwhile, Kissinger's deputy, Alexander Haig, arrived in Saigon at the end of September. Unbeknown to the South Vietnamese, Haig carried a new plan for bombing North Vietnam, which he discussed with American air commanders.

Thieu pushes back

After a final round of Paris talks, Kissinger returned to Saigon with a final draft ceasefire agreement. He had intended to go on to Hanoi, where the paper would be initialed ahead of a formal signing. Thieu, however, rebelled, making the very same objections that he had tabled earlier. Instead of traveling to Hanoi, Henry Kissinger returned to Washington. At that point the North Vietnamese went public and revealed the text of the draft peace

AFTER »

On December 13, 1972, Kissinger recommended that Nixon approve massive bombing of North Vietnam.

DEMONSTRATING COMMITMENT
With the South unhappy with the terms of the draft agreement, Nixon was keen to demonstrate his commitment to the South. This reassurance took the form of **Operation Linebacker II ‹‹ 298–99 ››**, an 11-day intensive bombing campaign against targets in Hanoi and Haiphong.

BACK TO THE TABLE
The Vietnamese returned to the negotiating table. A **ceasefire agreement ‹‹ 300–01 ››** was signed on January 27, 1973.

"There is no doubt **we must ... move** ... to **readjust ... our** overall **relationship with Thieu.**"

DEPUTY NATIONAL SECURITY ADVISER ALEXANDER M. HAIG, CABLE TO HENRY KISSINGER, OCTOBER 4, 1972

agreement, and the US was forced to seek revisions in accordance with Thieu's demands.

A new round of talks started in November 1972, but they were again inconclusive. Thieu sent Nguyen Phu Duc to Washington. Both the president and Kissinger told him that from January 1973, following the opening of the next session of the US Congress, it would not be possible for them to continue the war, but Duc refused to budge. Further secret talks between Kissinger and Le Duc Tho took place without result, and Kissinger yet again broke off the negotiations.

Rapprochement with China
President Nixon and Chinese Premier Chou-En-Lai toast each other during a reception in China in February,1972. Nixon's contacts with China played a key part in preparing the ground for peace talks with North Vietnam.

POLITICIAN 1911–90

LE DUC THO

Born Phan Dinh Khai, Le Duc Tho was one of the founders of the Indochinese Communist Party. He fought against the French during the 1930s and 1940s. The key negotiator for North Vietnam in the peace talks that led to the 1973 Peace Accords, he refused the Nobel Peace Prize he was offered jointly with Henry Kissinger.

First draft emerges

By August 10, there was a draft ceasefire agreement. Kissinger and Le Duc Tho met on August 14 to hammer out details. Kissinger visited Saigon on August 17. Thieu rejected the idea of a "commission" that could become a coalition government, and any ceasefire that did not force the North Vietnamese to withdraw from the South. Kissinger nevertheless asked Thieu to help to extend the negotiations until Nixon, with a renewed presidential mandate in November, could unleash a new show of force against the North.

Thieu reiterated his objections and made a bid for a grand negotiation at an all-Southeast Asia conference where he might hope to minimize the influence of the

US SECRETARY OF STATE Born 1923

Henry Kissinger

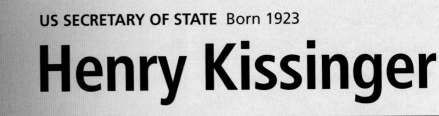

" [The] problem of **politics** is … the **limitation of righteousness.**"

HENRY KISSINGER, *A WORLD RESTORED*, 1954

Henry Alfred Kissinger is a controversial public figure who divides opinion: to some, he is a visionary strategist executing a grand design; to others, a priggish humbug obsessed by details. Such mixed reactions are partly the result of his route to power. Unlike the diplomats and generals who have populated his career, Kissinger did not work his way up through the ranks, but went straight to the top, due to his skills as a policy analyst—and by the judicious cultivation of patrons. As the adviser of presidents and politicians, he was widely viewed as an operator: a man who identified a goal and then sought to achieve it through a series of discrete maneuvers.

From Germany to Harvard

Born in 1923—the first of two sons—to orthodox Jewish parents in Fürth, Germany, Kissinger began life as Heinz Alfred. The family moved to England in 1938 to escape Nazi persecution, and then to the United States, where Heinz became Henry. The young Kissinger attended City College of New York before being drafted in 1943. His native German led to assignments in Army intelligence, and toward the end of World War II to a role in military government, overseeing a district of occupied Germany.

Kissinger always reached for the top. After the war, he won admission to Harvard, graduated with high honors, and went on to gain a doctorate in history, crafting a prize-winning dissertation on the Congress of Vienna and the end of the Napoleonic Wars. He used this to gain admission to analytical ranks at the Council on Foreign Relations and to the Rockefeller Brothers Fund, a policy research

Man of peace?

Ending the Vietnam War was a highlight of Kissinger's career, and one for which he was jointly awarded the Nobel Peace Prize with Le Duc Tho, North Vietnam's chief negotiator. Duc declined the prize on the grounds that real peace had not been achieved.

and advisory institute. He also served as rapporteur for study groups on key national security issues of the day, then turned his notes into books.

As Kissinger's stature increased, Harvard invited him back as a lecturer. He directed a prestigious Defense Studies Program, attended by future world leaders, and became a professor in 1962.

Right-hand man

By this time, Kissinger was already advising the US president. He counseled President Kennedy on the 1961 Berlin Crisis—a Cold War confrontation over the status of Berlin—and advised both Kennedy and President Johnson on Vietnam.

Kissinger remained close to Republican Party circles even as he assisted President Johnson on certain Vietnam peace feelers. During the presidential election of 1968 there are reports, never refuted, that Kissinger supplied inside information to Republican candidate Richard Nixon. After the election, Nixon made Kissinger his national security adviser.

Kissinger's penchant for tactics quickly became clear—he set the bureaucracy to work on extensive

Mr. Fix It
Kissinger talks with Mao Zedong in 1973. Kissinger's first visit to China in July 1971 recognized the legitimacy of the People's Republic and prepared the ground for President Nixon's visit in 1972.

> " He did what had to be done to acquire **power**—and to exercise it in **secret.**"
JOURNALIST ANTHONY LEWIS WRITING ABOUT KISSINGER FOR THE *NEW YORK TIMES*, 1982

policy reviews on every imaginable subject, diverting its staff while he created National Security Council (NSC) mechanisms for key policy areas, including Vietnam. Kissinger then used these NSC sub-committees to take control of policies in selected areas.

It is a measure of Henry Kissinger's power that US policies advanced in areas where he exercised control. In other areas, progress remained fitful. Both the Vietnam negotiations and those on nuclear arms control—as well as Nixon's opening to China—involved dominant Kissinger roles.

In Nixon's second term, Kissinger became secretary of state as well as NSC adviser. President

Gerald Ford kept him as secretary of state but appointed a new national security adviser at the end of 1975.

Post-government
Kissinger left government in 1977 and opened an international consulting business. President Ronald Reagan appointed Kissinger to a policy review commission for Central America, and Kissinger advised George W. Bush on the Iraq war. Hillary Clinton also courted Kissinger when she was secretary of state in the Obama adminisitration. Meanwhile, some critics continue to accuse Kissinger of war crimes for his role in various conflicts, including Vietnam.

KISSINGER WITH HIS WIFE NANCY MAGINNES

Elder statesman
Kissinger, a regular fixture on international lecture circuits, greets the audience at a ceremony at China's Hopkins-Nanjing Center, in 2007. Kissinger saw the rise of China, and the potential of economic cooperation, from an early point in his career.

On target
A US Air Force Boeing B-52 Stratofortress drops its bombs over North Vietnam during the Linebacker II offensive. Some B-52s were brought down by surface-to-air missiles.

« **BEFORE**

By late 1972, domestic pressure to end US involvement in the war and bring prisoners of war home from Hanoi was becoming intense.

NEGOTIATING SUCCESS
In October 1972, the North Vietnamese negotiator at the Paris peace talks, Le Duc Tho, agreed that **President Thieu could remain in powe**r in the South after a ceasefire was signed. However,

Thieu was unhappy that the draft ceasefire agreement did not insist on the NVA leaving the South and **the talks came to a halt** « **294–95**.

B-52S IN PLACE
In preparation for a winter bombing campaign, a B-52 force was assembled in nearby countries by late 1972. Meanwhile, the North Vietnamese were **evacuating civilians** from Hanoi.

Christmas Bombing

In the closing weeks of 1972, the United States planned a high-intensity bombing campaign, codenamed Linebacker II, that had both military and diplomatic objectives. This onslaught took place over 11 days, starting on December 19, 1972.

When the peace talks in Paris broke down on December 13, US forces were already gathering for Linebacker II, a successor to the Linebacker I bombing campaign that had ended in October. Ostensibly, the reason was to force North Vietnam back to the negotiating table, but as recordings of President Nixon's December 16 meetings with Vice President Spiro T. Agnew and Henry Kissinger reveal, the true aim of Linebacker II was to convince President Thieu that the US promise to execute massive retaliation against the North was not an empty one. That way, the Saigon leader might stop blocking the peace agreement.

Ready and waiting

Hanoi expected the attack. General Van Tien Dung had approved the final defense plan on November 24, and had ordered that everything be ready by December 3. Hanoi knew that a night attack would hamper their defense efforts: their fighter interceptors mostly lacked onboard radars and their antiaircraft gunners needed to see their targets.

On the morning of December 18, President Nixon telephoned Admiral Moorer, chairman of the Joint Chiefs of Staff, to emphasize that Linebacker II represented the military's last chance to hit hard at the DRV. That evening, B-52s in the lead wave took off from Thailand, flew up the Mekong River valley and approached Hanoi. Navy and Air Force attack planes entered from seaward hoping to distract the North Vietnamese. There were

20,000 TONS The amount of bombs dropped on North Vietnam during the bombing.

129 B-52s in the strike. The lead bomber, piloted by Captain Hal Wilson, reported wall-to-wall surface-to-air missiles (SAMs) ahead. About an hour into the raid NVA headquarters learned a SAM from the 261st Missile Regiment had downed a B-52. Two more would be lost that night, one of them Captain Wilson's.

Over the succeeding days the attacks continued, with a halt for Christmas itself. The bombers blasted air defenses, railroads, and industries; tactical aircraft added armed reconnaissance. The North Vietnamese tried mass firings of SAMs, missile launchings in unguided mode, fighter intercepts, even a deliberate midair crash. The Americans lost 15 B-52s and nine more were damaged, out of 795 B-52 sorties. Tactical aircraft flew 640 sorties and lost seven planes. Nearly 40 US airmen were taken prisoner.

Political firestorm

In America, where pundits dubbed the operation the Christmas Bombing, a firestorm of political protest ensued. Newspaper editorials uniformly rejected the bombing. Marches and protests took place in many cities despite the winter cold. There were rumors of Air Force pilots refusing orders—and actual instances of the radio spies of the Teaball (radio interception) unit halting work. Alexander Haig said later that

Briefed for action

Prior to flying out from Andersen Air Force Base on Guam, B-52 crews are briefed for their missions in Linebacker II. Thirty B-52s from this base were involved in the first wave of attacks on the night of December 18, 1972.

AFTER »

Linebacker II achieved its objective in forcing all sides back to the negotiating table. However, it did not impinge significantly on communist forces in the South.

BACK TO THE TABLE
The scale of the bombing had a swift effect on the peace process. The **Paris Peace Accords 300–01 »** were signed on January 27, 1973, bringing to an end direct US military involvement in the conflict.

FIGHT ANOTHER DAY
With the bombing leaving the **NVA forces in the South untouched by the bombing**, and the Ho Chi Minh Trail not targeted, the North Vietnamese could renew their operations at any time.

Witnesses to destruction
American singer Joan Baez and two other antiwar activists visit the ruins of Hanoi's airport on December 21, 1972. The airport had been bombed in a Linebacker II raid. Antiwar protests were reignited by the campaign.

Nixon gave up the Christmas Bombing because his cabinet deserted him and there were threats of impeachment. The bombing was not sustainable politically any more than it was militarily. Admiral Moorer told his colleagues on the Joint Chiefs of Staff that he had tried to get Nixon to continue the bombing until the North Vietnamese signed an agreement, not simply agreed to reopen talks, but that he had failed in that endeavor.

The Peace Accords

With all parties sitting down in Paris to discuss peace, hopes were high for a resolution of the conflict. However, many details had to be worked out, and some important issues were still outstanding when the final document was signed.

Peace at last

This button commemorates the Peace Accords of 1973 with a white dove of peace. Doves had previously been a popular feature on badges, buttons, and posters designed by protesters against the Vietnam War.

« BEFORE

Peace talks had been held in parallel with military action since 1968. From August 1969, additional peace talks were conducted in secret in Paris.

PRESSURED INTO PEACE
US bombing **« 292–93** of strategic targets in North Vietnam in the wake of North Vietnam's 1972 **Easter Offensive « 276–87** brought North Vietnam back to the negotiating table. Talks stalled in the fall of 1972 over South Vietnam's President Thieu's insistence that NVA troops should leave the South. **Bombing was resumed just before Christmas 1972 « 298–99**.

CONGRESSIONAL BLOCK
The American public was against the continuation of the Vietnam War, and so was Congress. In early January 1973, the Democratic majority in both houses of Congress voted to **deny military aid** when Nixon next requested it.

The deal is sealed

Henry Kissinger shakes hands with Le Duc Tho on January 23, 1973, to conclude their negotiations. This final, four-hour meeting was held in the Peninsula Hotel on Avenue Kleber in Paris; previous talks had taken place in private apartments and villas.

I n a succession of messages over the Christmas holidays, Hanoi and Washington agreed to reopen the peace talks in Paris. On December 30, 1972, the US called a halt to the bombing of the North. By January 5, both sides were discussing ways in which a peace agreement would be enforced, including locations for checkpoints to monitor people and equipment entering or leaving

additional lure for the South Vietnamese was the supply of extra equipment by the US in operations Enhance and Enhance Plus. To maximize South Vietnam's arsenal in advance of the Peace Accords, supplies included broken items that would be eligible for replacement under the one-for-one rule.

Kissinger reported the agreement as an achievement, but warned against too obvious a show of

> ❝ [All parties] **undertake** to … ensure a **lasting** and **stable peace.** ❞
>
> AGREEMENT ON ENDING THE WAR AND RESTORING PEACE IN VIETNAM, JANUARY 27, 1973

The ceasefire agreed between North and South Vietnam soon eroded. After a brief respite, the "War of the Flags" began.

VIETNAMS AT WAR
Despite the provisions for a ceasefire, the **war did not end**: the accord simply removed the US from the equation. No national reconciliation council was created, and in the 36 hours before the ceasefire was to begin, the NVA attacked more than 400 towns and villages. Fighting between the two Vietnams **continued 324–25 »**.

NIXON'S END
Back in the United States, Nixon was driven from office in 1974 as a result of the **Watergate Scandal 310–11 »**, in which he was shown to have abused his powers. Nixon resigned rather than be impeached. **Gerald Ford** became president in his stead.

ANTI-NIXON CARTOON

South Vietnam. The agreement also included a provision that military equipment could be replaced on a one-for-one basis, which then raised the question of monitoring. It was decided that an International Commission for Control and Supervision (ICCS)—with contingents from Indonesia, Canada, Poland, and Hungary—would handle all such issues.

Details resolved
The Paris agreement provided for a "standstill" ceasefire, which left all military forces in the positions they occupied at the instant fighting stopped. This meant no North Vietnamese forces would leave South Vietnam, but all of the remaining American forces would withdraw and US prisoners of war would be handed back. Two joint military commissions would be created among the Vietnamese: a two-party one of South Vietnam and the National Liberation Front (NLF) to discuss enforcement of the ceasefire; and a four-party one (North Vietnam, South Vietnam, the US, and the NLF) concerned with overall issues. The two South Vietnamese parties were supposed to agree to work toward elections through a National Council of Reconciliation and Concord.

Kissinger flew to France and met with Le Duc Tho on January 8. The next day, the sides agreed on all outstanding issues in the agreement's main text, leaving only details to be settled. An

celebration, which might induce Hanoi to rescind its approval. By January 11, Kissinger and Nixon were deliberating on a schedule that would involve signing the agreement in Paris and Kissinger subsequently visiting Hanoi.

Final drafts
The popular history of these last months of talks is that Kissinger and Le Duc Tho came to a draft accord, to which South Vietnam demanded numerous changes that Hanoi would reject. In this version

of events, North Vietnam meekly accepted Thieu's demands after the Christmas Bombing, and the Paris agreement was based on the revised formula. However, a comparison of the draft agreement of October 1972 and the one signed in January 1973 tells a different story. The most significant change was that the national council would not be an "administrative structure,"

> **Under Operation Enhance, the United States supplied South Vietnam with 63 working trucks— and 1,350 broken ones—along with weapons and other vehicles.**

which minimized the possibility of it emerging as a coalition government. Le Duc Tho agreed to that on December 8—before the Christmas Bombing. There was some new language on the DMZ, but the failure to convert it to a border was a success for North Vietnam. The removal of NVA forces from South Vietnam was delegated to the joint committees, which would frustrate Saigon's representatives.

Peace agreed
The signing took place on January 27, with William Rogers the US signatory and Nguyen Duy Trinh North Vietnam's. Protocols that included the two South Vietnamese parties were signed by Saigon's Tran Van Lam, and Nguyen Thi Binh of the NLF's Provisional Revolutionary Government (PRG). At 8 a.m. on January 28, 1973, the guns fell silent. The American war was over.

Homecoming welcome
Women at the Miramar Air Station, California, wait for their husbands to arrive back on US soil in February 1973. Their husbands, US Marines, were among the first POWs released following the Peace Accord.

Burst of joy
This iconic image, entitled "Burst of Joy," has come to define the end of the war. It was taken on March 17, 1973, and shows the family of Lieutenant Colonel Robert L. Stirm rushing to greet him at Travis Air Force Base, California.

7

ENDGAME AND AFTERMATH

After January 1973

Despite the Paris Peace Accords, the Vietnamese remain embroiled in conflict. While South Vietnam struggles without help from its American allies, North Vietnam only grows stronger. After a final push for Saigon in 1975, the fate of all of Indochina is sealed.

« Somber homecoming
US servicemen and women salute over aluminum coffins containing the remains of men reported missing in action (MIA) during a 1986 repatriation ceremony. In the 1980s, the US worked with the governments of Vietnam and Laos to bring MIA and prisoner of war remains home.

ENDGAME AND AFTERMATH
AFTER JANUARY 1973

The departure of American forces did not end the war in Vietnam. Despite an official ceasefire, fighting continued between the ARVN and communist troops. In America, the political will to support the Saigon government rapidly evaporated. Realizing the United States would not intervene, North Vietnam embarked upon a final offensive in spring 1975. The last American personnel were evacuated from Saigon as NVA tanks entered the city. Vietnam was then reunited under a hardline communist regime. Meanwhile, Cambodia fell to the communist Khmer Rouge, its population suffering immense hardship. Vietnam fought further wars against the Khmer Rouge and China before a kind of peace prevailed. In America, the process of coming to terms with the war and its consequences was painful and prolonged.

1 Crew of the USS *Mayaguez* were seized by the Khmer Rouge in May 1975, triggering the last action of the war. 2 Refugees from Xuan Loc tried to flee to Saigon during North Vietnam's Spring Offensive. 3 The last American POWs were released in February 1975.

C H I N A

N O R T H
V I E T N A M

Cao Bang

Red River

Phongsali

Xam Neua

HANOI
3
Hoa Lo
Haiphong

Ha
Long
Bay

Luang Prabang

Thanh Hoa

Gulf of Tonkin

Vang Veng

H A I N A N

Mekong River

Ang Nam Ngum

Nan River

VIENTIANE

L
A
O
S

Vinh

B U R M A

Ping River

Mekong River

T H A I L A N D

Mun River

Chao Phraya River

Mekong River

Attapeu

Khe
Sanh   Quang Tri
Hue   Lang Co

Da Nang

Central Highlands

Kontum

Pleiku

Qui Nhon

BANGKOK

Angkor

Battambang

Tonle
Sap

C A M B O D I A
(DEMOCRATIC KAMPUCHEA)

Tuol Sleng
PHNOM PENH
Choeung Ek

Mekong River

Gulf of
Thailand

Kompong Som

Operation Eagle Pull
Mayaguez Incident
1

Ba Chuc Massacre   Chi-Lang

Can Tho

Mekong
Delta

Battle of
Phuoc Long

Buon Ma Thuot
Buon-Dao

S
O
U
T
H

V
I
E
T
N
A
M

Phan Rang

Tuy Hoa

South China Sea

Bien Hoa
Tan Son Nhut   2   Battle of Xuan Loc
SAIGON   Long Thanh
(HO CHI MINH CITY)
Phuoc   Xuyen-Moc
An

USS Okinawa (Operation Frequent Wind)

Bac Lieu
Ca Mau   Ganh-Hao

KEY

International border

Demilitarized Zone (DMZ) (up to 1975)

Ho Chi Minh Trail

□ ○ Capital / City (neutral)

■ ● Capital / City (NVA / communist controlled)

▢ ◯ Capital / City (contested)

★ US base

US carrier station

✈ US air base

POW / Re-education camp

✗ Battle

Naval battle

Bombing

☠ Civilian massacre

N

0   100km
0   100 miles

TIMELINE AFTER JANUARY 1973

Ceasefire broken ▪ **The Case-Church Amendment** ▪ The Ho Chi Minh Campaign
▪ **Saigon falls** ▪ Communist victories in Cambodia and Laos ▪ **Vietnam reunified** ▪ Third
Indochina War ▪ **Economic and international growth** ▪ Vietnamese war tourism

1973–74

1975

JUNE 19, 1973
US Congress approves the Case–Church Amendment, which prohibits American military activity anywhere in Vietnam, Laos, or Cambodia.

DECEMBER 31, 1973
About 25,000 ARVN troops have been killed in combat by the end of 1973 despite a supposed ceasefire.

JANUARY 6
Phuoc Long falls to communist troops.

MARCH 13
President Thieu decides to withdraw his forces to a defensive perimeter around Saigon and the Mekong Delta.

APRIL 21
President Thieu resigns, denouncing the Americans for abandoning South Vietnam to its fate.

APRIL 28
General Tran Van Minh becomes South Vietnamese president and seeks a deal to end the fighting.

AUGUST 15, 1973
As the Case-Church Amendment comes into effect, the US Air Force carries out its last bombing mission over Cambodia.

MAY 9, 1974
US Congress begins impeachment proceedings against President Nixon in response to his role in the Watergate scandal.

AUGUST 6, 1974
Congress votes to cut aid for South Vietnam to $700 million in 1975.

APRIL 29–30
The United States carries out a hasty evacuation of Saigon by helicopter.

APRIL 30
Communist tanks drive into the center of Saigon and the government of South Vietnam surrenders. The war ends.

≪ Fall of Saigon, April 1975

AUGUST 9, 1974
Nixon resigns rather than face impeachment. The office of president passes to Nixon's vice president, Gerald Ford.

JANUARY 21
President Ford rules out renewed American military intervention in Vietnam.

MARCH 30
Da Nang quickly falls to communist forces as South Vietnamese military and civilian morale collapses.

⩒ Protester at a rally against Richard Nixon, October 1973

DECEMBER 13, 1974
The NVA and Viet Cong attack the provincial capital of Phuoc Long to test both the morale of the ARVN and the US response to an open breach of the Paris Peace Accords.

MARCH 10–11
The seizure of Ban Me Thuot in the Central Highlands opens the final communist offensive in South Vietnam.

APRIL 9–20
At Xuan Loc, outnumbered South Vietnamese troops put up valiant resistance but are eventually forced to fall back on Saigon.

MAY 15
In the *Mayaguez* Incident, US Marines recapture a merchant ship that had been seized by the Khmer Rouge.

NOVEMBER 7, 1973
Overriding a presidential veto, Congress passes the War Powers Resolution, which severely limits the president's authority to commit US forces to armed conflict.

APRIL 17
In Cambodia, Khmer Rouge guerrillas occupy the capital Phnom Penh and forcibly evacuate the population to the countryside.

DECEMBER 3
The Pathet Lao overthrows the Laotian monarchy and declares Laos a People's Democratic Republic.

≫ Khmer Rouge guerrilla in Phnom Penh, April 1975

> "The **ultimate irony** was that ... the soldiers' war, which the United States had **insisted on fighting ...** with massive military force, was **finally won** by the enemy."
>
> WILLIAM COLBY, DIRECTOR OF THE CIA, 1975

1976–PRESENT

« Stamp commemorating the first national assembly after Vietnam's reunification

DECEMBER 25, 1978
The Vietnamese Army launches a full-scale invasion of Kampuchea in association with Cambodian rebels.

JUNE 1979
The Boat People exodus peaks, with 54,000 refugees fleeing Vietnam in a month.

SEPTEMBER 26, 1989
Vietnam completes the withdrawal of its military forces from Cambodia after an 11-year occupation of the country.

JULY 11, 1995
President Bill Clinton announces the restoration of full diplomatic relations between the United States and Vietnam.

JANUARY 7, 1979
Vietnamese forces occupy Phnom Penh and overthrow the Pol Pot regime, installing a new government under Heng Samrin.

DECEMBER 1990
Vietnam adopts a Law on Private Enterprise that encourages private business, triggering a period of rapid economic growth.

FEBRUARY 17, 1979
China launches a punitive offensive into northern Vietnam, in response to the Vietnamese invasion of Cambodia.

NOVEMBER 13, 1982
The Vietnam Veterans Memorial wall is dedicated in Washington, D.C.

APRIL 15, 1992
Vietnam amends its constitution to open the country to foreign investment in the pursuit of economic growth.

⌃ Faux Ho Chi Minh propaganda poster, made for the war tourist market

⌄ Vietnam Veterans Memorial dedication, November 1982

⌃ Choeung Ek, a "Killing Field" in Phnom Penh, Cambodia

JANUARY 7, 1976
The Khmer Rouge renames Cambodia as Democratic Kampuchea. Pol Pot is the key figure in a regime that massacres about a quarter of the Cambodian population.

APRIL 30, 1977
Kampuchea launches a border attack against Vietnam. Sporadic border fighting between the two countries continues into 1978.

JANUARY 13, 1993
A US Senate Select Committee announces that there is "no compelling evidence" that there are US prisoners of war still held captive in Vietnam.

NOV 16–19, 2000
Bill Clinton becomes the first US President to visit Vietnam since the end of the Vietnam War.

JULY 2, 1976
North and South Vietnam are formally unified as the Socialist Republic of Vietnam under hardline communist rule.

SEPTEMBER 1978
Large numbers of people begin fleeing Vietnam by sea, and are dubbed the Boat People.

MARCH 16, 1979
Chinese troops complete a withdrawal from northern Vietnam, claiming their mission has been successfully completed. The Vietnamese claim to have repulsed the Chinese invasion.

DECEMBER 18, 1986
Nguyen Van Linh becomes General Secretary of the Vietnamese Communist Party. He liberalizes Vietnam's economy with the *doi moi* (renovation) program.

SEPTEMBER 24, 1993
Norodom Sihanouk is reinstated as king of Cambodia under a new monarchical constitution.

2015
Almost eight million tourists visit Vietnam in the year, 490,000 of them from the United States.

Breaking the Ceasefire

The Paris Peace Accords allowed the withdrawal of American forces from Vietnam, but did not end the war. Fighting continued between South Vietnamese and communist forces, while political developments in the US undermined support for its allies.

« BEFORE

An NVA offensive in Easter 1972 succeeded in occupying substantial areas of South Vietnam, but was halted by American airpower.

AMERICA PUSHES PEACE
Peace talks took on new momentum when the US agreed to accept a ceasefire without the withdrawal of NVA troops. After the **US bombing** of Hanoi and Haiphong, on January 27, 1973 a **peace agreement « 300–301**

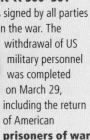

was signed by all parties in the war. The withdrawal of US military personnel was completed on March 29, including the return of American **prisoners of war**.

CELEBRATING THE HOMECOMING

Neither side in Vietnam had any intention of observing the provisions of the Paris Peace Accords. President Thieu would not accept the continued presence of North Vietnamese forces inside South Vietnamese borders as legitimate, while the North Vietnamese government still aimed to unite all of Vietnam under communist rule.

Land grabs

In the period immediately before and after the signing of the accords, both sides engaged in land grabs, attempting to extend the area under their control and seize strategic sites. Hundreds of South Vietnamese villages changed hands, some several times, in the attacks and counterattacks across the country. The international commission, which was meant to supervise the ceasefire, proved ineffectual. Armed conflict never stopped.

South Vietnamese forces lost some 25,000 men in combat in 1973, but generally performed better in the piecemeal fighting. The US had flooded Saigon with military equipment before its withdrawal, while North Vietnam took time to

Nixon and Thieu
President Thieu meets with President Nixon at San Clemente, California, in April 1973. Although Nixon renewed his promise to give military support to South Vietnam if the peace accords were violated, Congress would place severe limits on the president's ability to act.

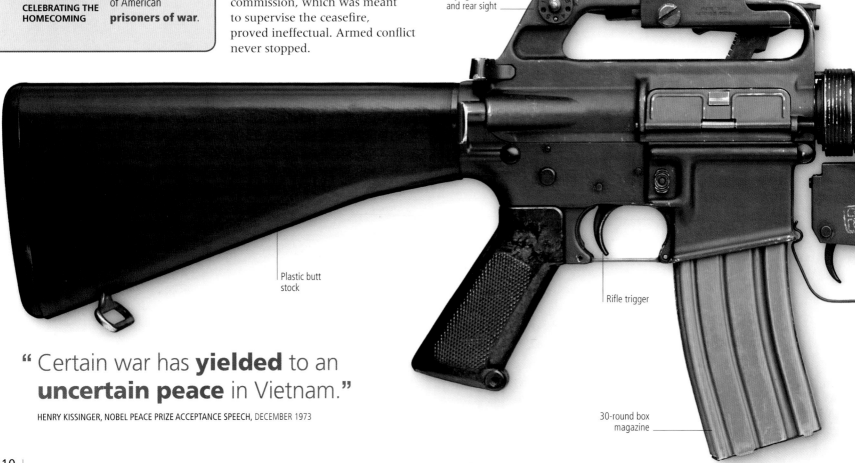

Carrying handle and rear sight

Plastic butt stock

Rifle trigger

30-round box magazine

" Certain war has **yielded** to an **uncertain peace** in Vietnam.**"**

HENRY KISSINGER, NOBEL PEACE PRIZE ACCEPTANCE SPEECH, DECEMBER 1973

DECISIVE MOMENT

WATERGATE SCANDAL

On June 17, 1972, five men were arrested for breaking into the Democratic National Committee headquarters at the Watergate building in Washington, D.C. Investigators linked this break-in to a committee working for the re-election of President Richard Nixon. As evidence mounted of attempts to block the investigation, and of other abuses of power, on August 9, 1974, Nixon resigned to avoid impeachment. His successor, Gerald Ford, would oversee the end of US military involvement in Vietnam, and pardon Nixon for all crimes against the US.

THE NEW YORK TIMES

NIXON RESIGNS
HE URGES A TIME OF 'HEALING';
FORD WILL TAKE OFFICE TODAY

THE END OF THE NIXON ERA

In spring 1975, South Vietnam underwent a rapid military collapse, its morale and fighting efficiency fatally undermined by the withdrawal of American aid.

THE DEMISE OF SOUTH VIETNAM
A victorious offensive at **Phuoc Long 314–15 »** confirmed to North Vietnamese leadership that South Vietnam was getting **weaker** and that the US would not intervene. This led to further successful **communist offensives 316–17 »**. In April 1975, North Vietnam had little trouble entering and occupying **Saigon 324–25 »**.

recover from losses incurred in the 1972 Easter Offensive and from the Christmas bombing of its ports. Hopes of resuming guerrilla warfare in South Vietnamese-controlled territory proved in vain.

North Vietnam bides its time
By October 1973, the North Vietnamese politburo was preparing a full-scale offensive on South Vietnam. They accepted, however, that this could not happen, as long as there was still a

The American public's frustration with the war was, by this point, reflected in Congress. In June 1973, it passed the Case-Church Amendment, which banned further military action in Asia. In November, this was followed by the War Powers Resolution, which severely restricted the president's ability to engage the United States

case, by the time the War Powers Resolution was passed, Nixon's authority was all but collapsing under the Watergate scandal.

Changing fortunes
South Vietnam had inherited from the US a costly way of waging war. The impact of financial cuts on the ARVN, combined with a global

again, with senior officers devoting themselves to black market deals rather than attending to their men.

Preparing for an attack
Meanwhile, North Vietnam built up its strength. With no American bombers to threaten its security, the Ho Chi Minh Trail became a paved highway with an oil

Grenade launcher foresight

Rifle with grenade launcher
The M16A1, here fitted with an M203 grenade launcher, became the US military's standard assault rifle during the Vietnam War. The Americans left the South Vietnamese army well equipped with such state-of-the-art weaponry.

Barrel

M203 grenade launcher

chance that the United States would re-enter the war. Since President Nixon had assured Thieu that America would intervene if North Vietnam breached the peace accords, the North's offensive had to wait for the right moment.

in war without Congressional approval. Support for South Vietnam in Washington had all but vanished. Congress cut military aid to Saigon from $1.6 billion to $1.1 billion for 1974, while aid for 1975 was just $700 billion. In any

oil crisis, was severe. Aircraft and helicopter use was strictly limited to save fuel. Soldiers' wages did not keep up with inflation, which undermined morale and increased the rate of desertions. South Vietnam's corruption and poor leadership came to the fore yet

pipeline. As men and munitions flowed into South Vietnam, the North made significant gains in 1974, especially around Da Nang, in coastal Quang Ngai province, and north of Saigon. In spite of these gains, the North Vietnamese politburo remained cautious—while they planned a major offensive for 1975, they did not expect victory until 1976.

PRESIDENT OF SOUTH VIETNAM Born 1924 Died 2001

Nguyen Van Thieu

> "**Thieu is right ...** our terms will **eventually destroy him.**"
>
> US SECRETARY OF STATE HENRY KISSINGER TO PRESIDENT NIXON, OCTOBER 6, 1972

An often-maligned figure, former ARVN general Nguyen Van Thieu served as the president of South Vietnam until 1975. He was the last South Vietnamese president to govern for a substantial period of time—his successor, Duong Van Minh, was president for just two days before Saigon fell to North Vietnamese forces. Thieu was criticized during his presidency for his authoritarian style, and for his perceived intransigence, which Nixon and Kissinger blamed for stalling the peace negotiations in 1972. Thieu, on the other hand, felt betrayed and abandoned by the United States, and publicly expressed great anger toward his American allies in the final years of his presidency.

Young commander

Nguyen Van Thieu was born in November 1924, but would later change his birthday to April 5, on the advice of an astrologer. The son of a fisherman, he grew up in the poor, coastal province of Ninh Thuan, and chose to join the Viet Minh in the struggle against the French. Despite rising in its ranks, after a year he renounced the brutal communist front and chose instead to ally with the French— even attending infantry school in Coëtquidan, France.

Thieu fought well against the Viet Minh. He drove them from his village in 1954, even attacking those hiding in his family home, and from there his military career picked up momentum. After the First Indochina War ended, Thieu joined the new South Vietnamese Army (ARVN) and underwent military training in the US in 1957 and 1960. In 1960, commanding the Seventh Division, Thieu sent troops to defend President Diem from a coup attempt, but later turned on him; he led an attack on the presidential palace during the coup that ousted Diem in 1963.

Thieu's political and military ascent continued. Appointed a general, he became a member of a group of young officers known as the young Turks. In 1964, they helped to oust the ruling military junta, and the group also played a role in a subsequent coup in 1965. That year, Thieu became chief of state under the new government of fellow young Turk Nguyen Cao Ky.

Struggling leader

South Vietnamese President Nguyen Van Thieu was a decorated soldier, whose ascent to power was supported by the ARVN. However, his capability as a general was questioned after the loss of the Central Highlands, and as a politician he was not particularly beloved by his people.

NGUYEN THI MAI ANH

Addressing his allies

President Thieu addresses 7,000 American troops and a crowd of journalists during a visit from US President Lyndon Johnson to Cam Ranh Bay in October 1966. A major US Navy base, Cam Ranh Bay also had a large Air Force base and a substantial US Army presence.

President and general

Thieu had taken a back seat to Ky in 1965, but this all changed in the 1967 election. With ARVN support, Thieu displaced Ky to run as the presidential candidate, making Ky his running mate. The ticket won with nearly 35 percent of the vote. Thieu promised to preside over a

warned that he would only support it if the US continued to supply funds and equipment to the ARVN.

As the war continued, concern from the West about Thieu's regime grew, especially after the 1971 election, which appeared to have been rigged in his favor. As the US became more determined to reach a peace agreement, Thieu became a major obstacle, angered by the secret talks between Hanoi and Washington.

Standing alone

Thieu eventually signed the 1973 Peace Accords, on the basis that the US would continue to supply

aid and air support. When US support diminished, Thieu publicly accused Henry Kissinger of tricking him into signing the agreement.

With the US out of the war, Thieu and the ARVN were left to fight the North Vietnamese Army (NVA) alone. During the final NVA offensive in 1975, Thieu and his army were proved inadequate by the communist forces, which soon closed in on Saigon. Time and again, Thieu expressed his bitterness over being left to fight alone by his former allies.

Thieu realized that he would not emerge victorious. On April 21, 1975, Thieu made an emotional final speech to South Vietnam, and resigned as president, leaving the task of surrendering Saigon to his successor. Five days later, he flew out of Vietnam, and eventually moved to the US. He lived a quiet life in Foxboro, Massachusetts, until his death in 2001.

> "We're having to **bargain for aid** from the United States like **haggling for fish** in the market."
>
> NGUYEN VAN THIEU, IN HIS TELEVISED FAREWELL SPEECH, APRIL 21, 1975

democratic government, enact social reforms, and crack down on corruption. However, he also increased mobilization, swiftly removed rivals, and engaged in censorship—his authoritarian style causing some to call him a dictator.

When peace talks began in 1968, Thieu did not attend, refusing to acknowledge the communist National Liberation Front (NLF) as a legitimate authority. He hesitantly accepted Nixon's Vietnamization policy in 1969, but

Greeting the general

President Nguyen Van Thieu is saluted by ARVN servicewomen during a visit to South Vietnam's Quang Tin province on February 5, 1969. During his presidency, the general often made inspection visits to ARVN units in the field.

Prelude in Phuoc Long

The fall of Phuoc Long in January 1975 opened the final phase of the war. It showed that neither the United States nor South Vietnam had the resolve to stop a communist victory.

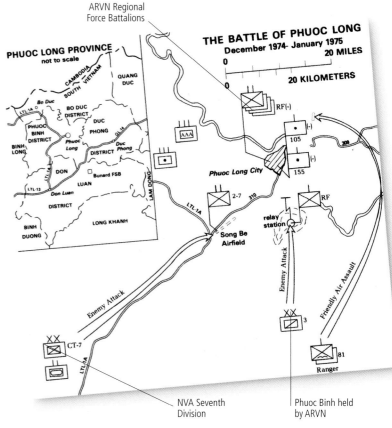

ARVN Regional Force Battalions

PHUOC LONG PROVINCE not to scale

THE BATTLE OF PHUOC LONG
December 1974- January 1975

NVA Seventh Division

Phuoc Binh held by ARVN

I n October 1974, the North Vietnamese leadership held a meeting to discuss how best to proceed toward their goal of final victory in Vietnam. On the one hand, Le Duan and his colleagues

« BEFORE

After the withdrawal of American forces from Vietnam, scattered but persistent fighting continued in spite of an agreed ceasefire.

TESTING THE WATERS
President Richard Nixon had promised renewed military intervention in defense of South Vietnam if required. However, Congress was determined to block any such action. Facing impeachment as a result of the **Watergate scandal « 310–11**, in August 1974 Nixon resigned the presidency. Meanwhile, the North Vietnamese prepared for a future major offensive, **building up their forces** and developing their supply routes to the South.

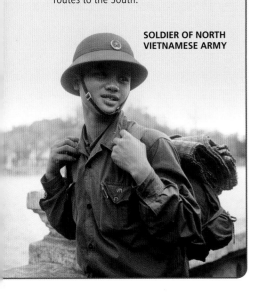

SOLDIER OF NORTH VIETNAMESE ARMY

believed that the resignation of Richard Nixon had sharply reduced the chances of any renewal of US military intervention. They also noted that the performance of South Vietnamese (ARVN) forces had deteriorated over the year.

On the other hand, their efforts to build up stores of heavy equipment and develop a supply system to their troops in the South were still far from complete. The members of the politburo also continued to be wary of the possible US response to a full-scale offensive, even under the presidency of Gerald Ford. The result of their deliberations was to authorize an all-out assault to capture Phuoc Long province, in the Central Highlands near the Cambodian border. If the United States failed to respond and the ARVN performed poorly, the communists would sense the way was open for them to escalate operations further in 1975.

Battle plan
This map of the battle of Phuoc Long from the US Center of Military History shows the initial attack by two divisions of the NVA 301st Corps and the airlift of ARVN reinforcements into Phuoc Binh (Phuoc Long City).

militia were hastily reinforced by an ARVN infantry battalion, helicoptered in from their base at Lai Khe, North Vietnam's superiority in numbers and

> " I appeal to the **entire population** to reserve three days to … **pray.** "
>
> PRESIDENT THIEU, APPEAL FOR MOURNING AFTER FALL OF PHUOC LONG, JANUARY 7, 1975

NVA superiority
The attack on Phuoc Long, set to be launched in December 1974, was masterminded by General Tran Van Tra, who amassed a force of two infantry divisions, a tank battalion, an artillery regiment, and an antiaircraft regiment, plus support units. In contrast, remote and thinly populated Phuoc Long was initially defended only by South Vietnamese Regional and Popular Forces. Even when these

firepower was overwhelming. The US reaction, meanwhile, was underwhelming. The Third Marine Division in Okinawa was put on alert and the USS *Enterprise* was sent closer to Vietnam, but no other action was taken.

The fighting in Phuoc Long began on 12 December. The provincial capital of Phuoc Binh—also known as Phuoc Long City—was quickly isolated, its defenders dependent on aerial resupply. Heavy

antiaircraft fire deterred ARVN pilots from flying low enough to achieve accurate airdrops or provide effective close air support to ground troops.

North Vietnamese (NVA) artillery were pouring 3,000 rounds a day into Phuoc Binh by early January. Two companies of elite Airborne Rangers were flown in as the situation worsened for the ARVN, but this was no more than a sacrificial gesture. On January 6, Phuoc Binh fell. It was the first provincial capital lost by the South Vietnamese government since Quang Tri at Easter 1972.

Decisive moment
Only 850 of the 5,000 or more South Vietnamese troops engaged in the fighting escaped either death or capture. President Thieu announced three days of national mourning after the defeat and vowed to retake Phuoc Binh. However, this promise was empty bravado. With the loss of Phuoc Binh and the evident withdrawal of American support, Thieu saw his prestige plummeting.

The communist victory at Phuoc Long was decisive for two reasons. Firstly, the lack of any active response from Washington showed that the US was no longer prepared to guarantee the existence of South Vietnam. The US made a formal protest, accusing Hanoi of seeking to impose a military solution on Vietnam, but at a press conference on January 21, 1975, President Ford stated that he could foresee no circumstances under which America would reenter the war in Vietnam. North Vietnam no longer had to fear American B-52s.

Secondly, the loss of Phuoc Long underlined the weakness of the South Vietnamese forces and leadership. The initial successes of the NVA were to be expected, given their ability to concentrate forces against a weakly defended point, but the failure of the ARVN to organize a substantial response revealed the fatal waning of both its morale and resources.

AFTER »

After its victory in Phuoc Long province, North Vietnam continued to plan its conquest of the South, envisaging a final offensive for 1976.

TAKING SAIGON

Hanoi decided to start with a local offensive in the Central Highlands. The initial blow was to fall on another poorly defended provincial capital, Buon Ma Thuot. Launched in March 1975, this attack unexpectedly precipitated a widespread **collapse of the ARVN**. The US launched a hurried **evacuation of the capital** as South Vietnam was defeated and **Saigon fell to the NVA 324–25 »** in April 1975.

DAUGHTER OF AN ARVN SOLDIER AWAITS EVACUATION

Celebrating conquest
After the unification of Vietnam under communist rule, the Victory Monument was erected in Phuoc Long City to celebrate the defeat of South Vietnamese government forces in Phuoc Long province.

PHƯỚC LONG CHIẾN THẮNG

6-1-1975

Final Offensive Begins

In March 1975, North Vietnamese forces commanded by General Van Tien Dung launched a major offensive at Buon Ma Thuot in the Central Highlands. This precipitated a collapse of South Vietnamese defenses that left the way open for a final drive to take Saigon.

Buon Ma Thuot was a provincial capital near the border with Cambodia. It had an army base and airfield, but in March 1975 was garrisoned only by a single ARVN infantry regiment and a Ranger Group, supplemented by Montagnard regional forces and militia. Holding the strategic initiative, the North Vietnamese forces were able to concentrate overwhelmingly superior forces against this poorly defended target, deploying three whole divisions in their attack.

Beginning on March 4, the NVA cut all the highways around Buon Ma Thuot, isolating the town. Then, with a swift infantry assault supported by heavy artillery, on March 10–11 they seized their objective. Ordered to retake Buon Ma Thuot, two ARVN regiments were airlifted to nearby Phuoc An, but instead of mounting a counterattack on the NVA, large numbers of demoralized South Vietnamese troops fled the scene, and joined a stream of civilian refugees attempting to escape the fighting.

Fateful decision

Faced with this crisis, on March 13 President Thieu made the fateful decision to abandon the defense of the Central Highlands and all of the northern provinces except the coastal enclaves. He envisaged a withdrawal to a line from Tay Ninh on the Cambodian border to the coast at Nha Trang. The area south of this line contained most of the

« BEFORE

The fall of Phuoc Long province to North Vietnamese forces in January 1975 emboldened the leadership in Hanoi to pursue a final military victory over South Vietnam's President Thieu.

WEAKENED BY CUTS

South Vietnamese armed forces had been weakened by severe **cuts in American financial aid** « 310–11, leading to shortages of fuel, munitions, and money for soldiers' pay. The United States had made it clear that no further military support could be expected. Meanwhile, North Vietnam's leaders, although remaining cautious, decided to mount a **spring offensive** in the Central Highlands.

SOUTH VIETNAMESE DEFENSES

Birthday celebrations

A North Vietnamese family celebrates Ho Chi Minh's birthday on May 19. This was the target date set by Hanoi in spring 1975 for the capture of Saigon at the end of what had been dubbed the Ho Chi Minh Campaign.

GIA ĐÌNH SỬA SOẠN MỪNG NGÀY 19-5

country's population and resources. It was theoretically a good strategy to concentrate South Vietnam's limited military strength on the defense of this region, but attempting such a withdrawal under the circumstances prevailing in spring 1975 invited disaster.

General Pham Van Phu, the commander in the Central Highlands, was ordered to move all his regular forces immediately from the major bases at Kontum and Pleiku to the coast at Tuy Hoa. The only road open to them was Provincial Route 7B, a jungle track requiring repair, bridge-laying, and mine-clearance to be passable. The withdrawal turned into a debacle. Discipline broke down as senior commanders abandoned their troops. Tens of thousands of fleeing civilians impeded the movement of military vehicles. The 320th NVA Division, pursuing the retreating South Vietnamese, threatened to cut the road entirely. NVA artillery bombarded the packed mass of troops and refugees as ARVN engineers worked valiantly to bridge rivers.

On 27 March, the disorganized remnants of the ARVN corps reached Tuy Hoa. About two-thirds of the original force of 60,000 men had been lost.

Vital bases fall

Thieu's decision to concentrate his forces in more defensible positions precipitated a string of disastrous events in the northern provinces.

> " Commanding officers ran; everywhere **commanding officers ran first.** "
>
> SOUTH VIETNAMESE VICE PRESIDENT NGUYEN CAO KY ON THE ARVN ROUT, TV INTERVIEW C.1980

Responding to the sudden collapse of South Vietnamese resistance, the North Vietnamese leadership set General Dung a new target—to capture Saigon before the onset of the monsoon season in May.

FROM XUAN LOC TO SAIGON
The advance of North Vietnamese forces was **temporarily stalled** by determined resistance by the ARVN at **Xuan Loc 320–21 »**. In a fierce two-week battle, South Vietnamese troops acquitted themselves with credit, but the town eventually fell.

President Thieu **accepted the inevitability of defeat 324–25 »** and resigned on April 21. The remaining units of the ARVN were in disarray, and North Vietnamese forces rapidly advanced toward the largely undefended Saigon **324–25 »**.

The area commander, General Ngo Quang Truong, was told to hold the base at Da Nang at all costs, but his crack Airborne Division was withdrawn to strengthen the defense of Saigon. To replace the airborne troops, South Vietnamese Marines were pulled out of Quang Tri province to reinforce Da Nang. The withdrawal of the Marines triggered an exodus of civilian refugees southward from Quang Tri and the city fell to the NVA on March 19 without a fight. Deserted by civilians and military units, Hue was occupied by the NVA six days later. A flood of refugees and soldiers reduced Da Nang to chaos.

On March 29, General Truong evacuated some 10,000 troops, who waded out to ships from the beaches where US Marines had disembarked 10 years before. The city fell the following day.

Chaotic retreat

The roads from the northern provinces were choked by a stream of military personnel and civilians fleeing south from Quang Tri and Hue ahead of the North Vietnamese advance.

NVA OFFICER (1917–2002)

GENERAL VAN TIEN DUNG

Dung joined the Indochinese Communist Party in the 1930s and was imprisoned by the French colonialists for subversion. From 1945, he served as a general in the Viet Minh guerrilla movement and then as chief of staff of the North Vietnamese Army.

In 1974, he replaced General Vo Nguyen Giap as commander of the NVA and led the final offensive in South Vietnam. He went on to command the NVA in wars with Cambodia and China in 1979 before retiring in 1986.

Desperate escape
Fleeing the advancing enemy, refugees from the northern provinces of South Vietnam are lowered into a navy boat at Da Nang in March 1975. Thousands flooded transportation routes in the so-called Column of Sorrow.

The **Battle** of **Xuan Loc**

Amid the general collapse of South Vietnamese forces in spring 1975, the determined resistance of troops at Xuan Loc was a beacon of hope for President Thieu. Although the ARVN salvaged some honor, the North Vietnamese advance could not be halted.

« BEFORE

Although the ARVN fought well against communist forces directly after the 1973 Paris Peace Accords, South Vietnam's military and political position worsened drastically in 1974.

THIEU'S REGIME DWINDLES
The US Congress **blocked** further US military intervention in Vietnam and **sharply reduced funding for Saigon « 310–11**. The resignation of Richard Nixon as US president in August 1974 was another blow to President Thieu. Victory for the NVA at **Phuoc Long « 314–15** in December revealed that the ARVN was suffering from demoralization and a lack of finances. In March 1975, a communist **offensive « 316–17** precipitated the break-up of the ARVN and a mass flight of civilians. Thieu's regime was left a small area around Saigon and the Mekong Delta.

The sudden collapse of South Vietnamese forces in March 1975 took the North Vietnamese leadership by surprise. Having not expected final victory before 1976, the North Vietnamese politburo altered its timetable. On March 25, NVA commander General Van Tien Dung was ordered to proceed to the capture of Saigon and the end of the war.

The ARVN took positions on the five main roads to Saigon in a defensive circle around the city. General Dung's forces were his enemy's superior in every way. He planned to avoid a battle inside the city by crushing each of the ARVN formations outside Saigon. Given the South Vietnamese troops' recent performance, it was reasonable to expect a swift victory.

Ultimate defense
At the eastern end of the ARVN defensive ring was the town of Xuan Loc. Standing on Route 1, almost 40 miles (65 km) from Saigon, it protected the vital air base at Bien Hoa as well as the road into the capital. Both sides recognized it as the keystone of the South Vietnamese defenses.

Xuan Loc was garrisoned by the previously undistinguished 18th ARVN Division, commanded by General Le Minh Dao. They faced the NVA IV Army Corps—three divisions with plentiful tanks and artillery. Despite the imbalance of forces, President Thieu ordered Xuan Loc held at all costs. General Dao told the world's media that however many divisions the communists sent against him, he would "smash them all."

Spectacular resilience
On April 9, the NVA pounded Xuan Loc with artillery fire, while infantry and armored vehicles surged forward to overrun the defensive perimeter. ARVN resistance was unexpectedly resolute and the NVA suffered heavy losses of men and tanks.

> " I don't care **how many** divisions **the other side** sends against me … I will **knock them down!**"
>
> GENERAL LE MINH DAO, ARVN COMMANDER AT XUAN LOC, TV INTERVIEW, APRIL 1975

Counterattacks by ARVN troops from outside Xuan Loc meant the NVA diverted their resources from the assault to defend their flanks.

Bien Hoa airbase
Some 16 miles (26 km) outside Saigon, Bien Hoa airbase served the US and South Vietnamese air forces during the Vietnam War. It came under artillery fire during the Battle of Xuan Loc and was occupied by advancing communist troops on April 25, 1975.

On April 10, the NVA was forced to withdraw from positions they had seized in the town.

The spectacle of ARVN troops fighting with skill and dedication roused understandable excitement among supporters of the South Vietnamese government. Impressed with this display, the Ford administration pushed for a new American aid package, which they argued would allow the South Vietnamese to continue resisting

The fall of Xuan Loc left Saigon indefensible, but how the North Vietnamese would choose to end the war remained uncertain.

NORTH VIETNAM TAKES CONTROL
Political leaders in Saigon hoped for a **negotiated end** to the conflict that would stop short of a total communist takeover, but the NVA **struck Saigon directly 324–25 »**. The United States belatedly organized a **final evacuation 322–23 »** of its staff and selected Vietnamese. Left behind, many of the heroes of Xuan Loc ended up in **communist re-education camps 332–33 »**.

---

the NVA. However, opinion in the US Congress was unmoved by stories of soldiers' courage or the sufferings of civilians.

Reinforcing both sides
Thieu had the ARVN First Airborne Brigade lifted into Xuan Loc to aid defense, but the NVA had far greater resources. On April 16, the NVA II Army Corps captured Phan Rang and was released to join the advance on Saigon. In desperation, President Thieu set the ARVN's remaining reserves against the NVA

Honor denied
The National Order of Vietnam was bestowed for outstanding courage. Instead of receiving this accolade, General Dao served 17 years in a re-education camp after the fall of Saigon.

forces surrounding Xuan Loc, but the NVA fought them off. The NVA bombardment of Bien Hoa airbase, curtailed the South Vietnamese air force's efforts to support ground

troops. With no hope of further reinforcements, the evacuation of Xuan Loc began.
The ARVN First Airborne Brigade experienced heavy losses and, when General Dao's 18th Division reached Saigon, it had lost around a third of its men. Taking responsibility for his country's military collapse, Thieu resigned his presidency on April 21, as

Air assistance
Chinook heavy-lift helicopters belonging to the Vietnam Air Force take part in the movement of people and supplies out of Xuan Loc during the evacuation of the city. The South Vietnamese were able to hold out for a fortnight against overwhelmingly superior forces.

communist troops moved in to occupy Xuan Loc. In effect, the outcome of the war had now been decided—conditions were primed for the communists to launch an assault on Saigon.

Tragic accident
Rescuers search the wreckage of a Lockheed Galaxy transport aircraft that crashed near Tan Son Nhut airport on April 4, 1975. Those on board included South Vietnamese children being evacuated under Operation Babylift.

‹‹ BEFORE

The Paris Peace Accords of January 1973 provided for the exit of US military personnel from South Vietnam, but thousands of US civilians remained in Saigon.

LAST STAND
The communist **Spring Offensive ‹‹ 316–17** in March 1975 led to the widespread collapse of South Vietnamese forces. President Thieu tried to organize a defense of Saigon and the Mekong Delta, throwing his last forces into the battle for **Xuan Loc ‹‹ 320–21**.

SURRENDER
After Xuan Loc fell, President Thieu resigned. His departure raised hopes for a negotiated end to the war, but NVA commander General Van Tien Dung **attacked and occupied Saigon**. South Vietnam could only surrender.

Waiting to escape
South Vietnamese civilians hoping to be included in helicopter evacuation wait anxiously outside the US Embassy in Saigon on April 29, 1975. Many who believed they had been promised a flight to safety were in fact left behind.

Evacuation

The final act of US involvement in Vietnam badly damaged the country's global image. America was left humiliated in defeat, as frantic helicopter evacuations left desperate Vietnamese civilians behind.

The sudden collapse of South Vietnamese forces in spring 1975 left the United States with a dilemma. The Ford administration was looking to Congress for aid to South Vietnam that might support the defense of Saigon and pave the way for a negotiated end to the war, avoiding a humiliating total defeat for America's ally. On the other hand, the rapid communist advance posed a clear threat to Americans and other foreigners in Saigon, and to Vietnamese military personnel and civilians who had worked for the Americans or been prominent in government or the ARVN.

Postponing the inevitable
Detailed plans were worked out for a mass evacuation, but implementation was obstructed by concerns that a rapid pullout might fatally undermine the chances of

" I **still grieve** over those we were **unable to rescue.**"

PRESIDENT GERALD FORD, WRITING ABOUT THE APRIL 1975 EVACUATION, JUNE 15, 2000

Any way out
Evacuees board a CIA Air America helicopter from an improvised helipad on an apartment building in Saigon. Taken by Dutch photojournalist Hubert van Es, this became the iconic image of the evacuation.

continued South Vietnamese resistance. Graham Martin, the US Ambassador in Saigon, was especially resistant to authorizing a general evacuation, producing elaborate arguments for postponing action. Nonetheless, by early April, US fixed-wing military transport aircraft were making regular flights out of Saigon's Tan Son Nhut airport to evacuate nonessential American personnel and certain categories of "at risk" Vietnamese.

Tragedy and chaos

The highly publicized Operation Babylift, which transported Vietnamese orphans to the United States, was interrupted by a tragic accident on April 4, when a Lockheed Galaxy transport aircraft crashed, killing many of the children on board. Meanwhile, many American personnel earmarked for evacuation refused to leave unless they could take Vietnamese dependents and friends with them. This led to a bureaucratic tussle that wasted more valuable time.

After the fall of Xuan Loc and the resignation of President Thieu on April 21, there was no longer any serious question of defending Saigon. Evacuation by fixed-wing aircraft continued at a more rapid pace, but without sufficient urgency, as some senior figures, including US Secretary of State Henry Kissinger and Ambassador Martin, did not believe that Saigon would be attacked.

Panic sets in

On April 28, two US Marine corporals at Tan Son Nhut, Charles MacMahon and Darwin Judge, were killed during a bombardment. They were the last Americans killed in the Vietnam War. The next day, Ambassador Martin at last accepted that fixed-wing flights were no longer possible and authorized implementation of a backup plan, codenamed Frequent

Wind, for final evacuation by helicopter. US Navy carriers were in position off the Vietnamese coast to carry out the plan. After gathering at assembly points in response to a signal—the playing of the song "White Christmas" on the radio—most evacuees were bussed to the Defense Attaché Office compound. A subsidiary evacuation was arranged from the US Embassy building. US Marines were used to provide security,

> **7,000** The approximate number of people evacuated from Saigon by helicopter on April 29–30, 1975.

which was very much needed as desperate Vietnamese flocked to the evacuation sites.

Flying back and forth between Saigon and the fleet, helicopter crews acted with outstanding skill and efficiency under trying

conditions. Flight decks were disrupted by the arrival of fleeing Vietnamese in their own helicopters or fixed-wing aircraft. Parked helicopters had to be ditched overboard to make space for new arrivals to land. At the same time as the airborne evacuation, more than 40,000 fleeing Vietnamese escaped by sea to join private or naval vessels.

By the early hours of April 30, the only remaining evacuation point was a helipad on the roof of the US Embassy. Ambassador Martin was among the last to be flown out as panic-stricken Vietnamese stormed the embassy building, desperate to escape the city. A few hours after the final helicopter left the embassy's roof, North Vietnamese tanks reached the presidential palace in the heart of Saigon.

Going overboard
A helicopter landed on the deck of USS *Okinawa* by a South Vietnamese pilot is manhandled over the side to make room for further arrivals. South Vietnamese fleeing on their own initiative complicated the evacuation.

BEFORE

Fall of Saigon

The Vietnam conflict had begun as a guerrilla war, but victory came to a military force plentifully equipped with armored vehicles and heavy artillery. Hopes of a negotiated end to the war vanished when the North Vietnamese Army entered Saigon as conquerors.

After the withdrawal of US troops from Vietnam in 1973, fighting continued between the South Vietnamese government and the joint forces of North Vietnam and the Viet Cong.

ISOLATED AND OVERPOWERED
Political developments at home **‹‹ 310–11** led to the US abandoning its promise to provide military support to South Vietnam. **Weakened and demoralized** by the drying up of American aid, South Vietnamese forces collapsed under heavy attack in **Spring 1975 ‹‹ 316–17**. The **evacuation of Saigon ‹‹ 322–23** began at the start of April 1975.

By resigning on April 21, 1975, President Nguyen Van Thieu signaled the opening of the Vietnam conflict's brief concluding phase. His departure was a public admission that South Vietnam had lost the war, as the last hope of US intervention had disappeared. Vice President Tran Van Huong, who had succeeded Thieu, called for a ceasefire and negotiations to end the war through adherence to the Paris Peace Accords. This proposal was rejected by the communist leadership.

Intent on offensives

Back in early April, the North Vietnamese politburo had given its senior commander, General Van Tien Dung, orders to pursue the military offensive until Saigon was taken. They had no reason to change their attitude once their forces were on the verge of victory.

General Dung launched the final drive against Saigon on April 26. The city was surrounded, with all major roads cut by Dung's forces. South Vietnamese troops had not given up—there was an especially fierce encounter between the rival armored forces at Long Thanh east

Victorious army
NVA soldiers flying the flag of the Provisional Revolutionary Government sit atop a T-54 tank outside the Independence Palace in Saigon on April 30, 1975. The mood of the victors was relaxed after South Vietnamese troops obeyed orders to lay down their arms.

Minh. The leader of the coup that overthrew the Diem regime in 1963, Minh had lost out in the subsequent power battles between South Vietnamese generals. He advocated a "Third Force" to keep contact with the communists and seek peace on the basis of shared nationalism. On April 28, Minh was chosen to replace Huong as president, in the belief that he was the man who could reach a deal with the communists.

No more negotiations
President Minh's inaugural speech proposed a ceasefire and a coalition government of reconciliation. Minutes after his speech, North Vietnamese pilots flying captured A-37 attack aircraft hit the city's Tan Son Nhut airport. The timing was not planned, but effectively showed the communists' disregard for talks. General Dung set April 29 as the day for the final assault on the city—rockets at 4 a.m. signaled the start of the action.

American casualties if possible. General Dung was ordered to allow a pause, offering the Americans time to complete their evacuation.

Seizing control
The occupation of the city began on the morning of April 30. Some South Vietnamese generals wanted to keep resisting, but at 10:24 a.m. Minh made a broadcast ordering his troops to stop fighting. As South Vietnamese soldiers abandoned their weapons and uniforms, NVA tanks and infantry in trucks rolled unopposed into the center of Saigon. A dozen tanks approached the seat of South

282,000 The estimated number of ARVN troops killed in the war.

882,000 The estimated number of NVA troops and Viet Cong killed.

Vietnamese government, Independence Palace. With unnecessary violence but a fine sense of theater, the lead tank crashed through the palace gates onto the lawn in front of the building. Minh's government, waiting inside ready for formal surrender, was informed by a North Vietnamese officer that all power had passed into the hands of the revolution and they could not hand over what they did not have.
  In the afternoon, taken into custody by the conquerors, Minh was ordered to make his second

AFTER ≫

The aftermath of the communist victory was a disappointment to people who had longed for peace and reconciliation—Vietnam still suffered hardship and warfare.

COMMUNISTS IN CONTROL
Saigon was renamed Ho Chi Minh City and Vietnam was formally reunited under the communist government in Hanoi. Soon hundreds of thousands of **"boat people" 334–35** ≫ were fleeing the communist rule, as misjudged economics brought **widespread poverty**. In 1979, **China invaded North Vietnam 340–41** ≫ to avenge Vietnam's overthrow of China's allies in Cambodia's Khmer Rouge government.

"UNCLE HO" WITH A CHILD

surrender broadcast of the day. Saigon's new rulers announced the liberation of the city and that the administration accepted unconditional surrender. The war had ended.

"Between Vietnamese there are no victors and no vanquished. Only the Americans have been beaten."
NVA COLONEL BUI TIN, ADDRESSING PRESIDENT MINH, SAIGON, APRIL 30, 1975

of Saigon—but the superiority of the communist side in numbers and weaponry was overwhelming. On April 27, the first NVA rockets were fired into Saigon's center.

Desperate hope
South Vietnamese and American politicians kept pursuing a fantasy of settlement without surrender. US Secretary of State Henry Kissinger declared that he expected a negotiated end to the war. In Saigon, hopes focused on General Duong Van Minh, known as Big

The only obstacle that remained to delay the North Vietnamese occupation of Saigon was the continuing American presence. Still cautious about a possible military reaction from Washington, the politburo preferred to avoid

Meeting the press
General Tran Van Tra, deputy leader of communist forces during the final campaign, addresses a press conference after the fall of Saigon. The city in effect came under military rule, with General Tra as area commander.

Khmer Rouge Victory in **Cambodia**

General Lon Nol proved an unstable ruler for Cambodia. Following sustained attacks against Nol's regime and the withdrawal of US aid, the Khmer Rouge achieved their goal of ultimate control. The extermination of all threats to the new order soon followed.

« BEFORE

With Cambodia dragged into the war, the Khmer Rouge steadily grew while the Cambodian government unraveled.

DOMESTIC UNREST

The **Khmer Rouge « 250–51** spent years gaining strength in the countryside. In 1970, a **coup** left general Lon Nol in charge of Cambodia. Phnom Penh had been the Cambodian capital since the fall of the Angkor kingdom. Although the city benefited from **American aid** during Lon Nol's goverment, Nixon's **secret bombing « 252–53** of the Cambodia/Vietnam border placed great strain on the city. Many **refugees** flocked to Phnom Penh or into the ranks of the Khmer Rouge.

Operation Eagle Pull
April 12, 1975 saw the final evacuation of US nationals and Cambodian allies to ships in the Gulf of Thailand. Several Cambodian officials refused to leave the city, even though the Khmer Rouge had marked them for execution.

After the Paris Accords in 1973, the Khmer Rouge separated themselves from the NVA and conducted an independent insurgency against Lon Nol's Cambodian Republic. US bombing shifted from North Vietnam and Laos to concentrate on the rebels in Cambodia. The Khmer Rouge intensely increased their efforts to secure the country. Their ultimate target was the capital of Phnom Penh. During 1973 and 1974, the Khmer Rouge encircled the capital and engaged the Cambodian Republic Army. US bombing protected Phnom Penh from the Khmer Rouge in 1974, but Lon Nol's army was systematically weakened.

Mysticism and corruption

In his years in power, Lon Nol had become increasingly authoritarian. His deteriorating health led him to depend on soothsayers and Buddhist mystics—during one Khmer Rouge assault on Phnom Penh, he sprinkled a line of holy sand around the city in order to defend it. Overrun by desperate refugees from the countryside who lived in squalor and were exploited by the government, Phnom Penh depended on US aid to survive. Lon Nol's regime was despised by both the city's refugees and native inhabitants.

Khmer Rouge attack

By 1975, the Khmer Rouge had conquered almost all of Cambodia, with the exception of Phnom Penh and the Preah Vihear Temple at the northern border with Thailand. They controlled the roads into the city and placed mines in the Mekong River to stop river traffic.

Their artillery and rocket bombardment of Phnom Penh got underway in

government. The fate of the Lon Nol regime was sealed. On April 1, Cambodian government and military leaders forced Lon Nol to resign and leave the country.

They hoped, fruitlessly, that the gesture would lead the Khmer Rouge to open negotiations

> " We are **entering the capital** by **force of arms.**"
>
> THE KHMER ROUGE INTERRUPT A GOVERNMENT BROADCAST, APRIL 17, 1975

January 1974. More than 100,000 homes were destroyed and thousands of people were killed. By March 1975, the city's airfield was destroyed and the US could no longer airlift ammunition and rice into Phnom Penh. Under pressure from the antiwar movement at home, and the failure of the campaign to deter the Khmer Rouge, the US terminated further assistance to the Cambodian

rather than assault the capital. On April 12, the US closed its embassy. After months spent on the outskirts of the city, the Khmer Rouge forces entered Phnom Penh on April 17, 1975. The soldiers were a mixture of fighters who had been at war in the countryside for years and young peasants with no concept of urban life, abducted and recruited by the Khmer Rouge. Glad that the Lon Nol regime was gone, many citizens came out in the streets to welcome the rebels—but their hopes for an end to strife were quickly dashed.

Tyranny begins

The Khmer Rouge leadership was already determined to eliminate all threats to their new order. Within

hours of entering the city, they ordered more than two million people to leave Phnom Penh for the countryside. Those who resisted or were unable to travel were murdered. The "new people," urbanized and of mixed ethnicities, unlike the pure Khmer peasants, were the main target of the mysterious Saloth Sar (now known as Pol Pot). The people were told that they must evacuate for safety from American bombing, assured that they would return within a few days when the city was secure. Restoring their old homes and old lives, however, was not Pol Pot's true plan.

Hundreds of thousands perished in enforced marches to the countryside and the labor camps that waited there.

BLANK SLATE

Pol Pot's conception of a peasant revolution against modern culture exceeded even the 1960s' Cultural Revolution in China. Cambodia's new life as "Democratic Kampuchea" started at **"Year Zero"** with no trace of the old regime. Hospitals, schools, and factories were targeted, as well as scores of

people. Cambodia now marks this horror with an annual **Day of Remembrance**, formerly called the National Day of Hate.

DAY OF HATE CEREMONY

Celebrations and eliminations
The "Mouvement National" takes to the streets of Phnom Penh to welcome the Khmer Rouge in 1975. Despite its popular support, the group was thought to be run by members of Lon Nol's regime and was soon eliminated.

The **Mayaguez Incident**

When Cambodian gunmen boarded a US cargo ship two weeks after the fall of Saigon, the American response was robust. The only known engagement between US ground forces and the Khmer Rouge, the incident was also the last military action of the Vietnam War.

Aerial evidence
This photograph taken by a USAF reconnaissance plane shows a patrol boat belonging to the Khmer Rouge alongside the USS *Mayaguez*, soon after the attack on the container ship.

« **BEFORE**

In 1975, after decades of internal strife in Cambodia, the Khmer Rouge, led by the dictator Pol Pot, came to power.

THE CIVIL WAR
A **long and bloody civil war** intensified after the overthrow of King Norodom Sihanouk by the prime minister, General Lon Nol, and the disastrous **US incursion** « **252–53** into the country in 1970. The conflict ended when the communist **Khmer Rouge entered the capital city** « **326–27** of Phnom Penh on April 17, 1975.

Retaking the *Mayaguez*
When the USS *Harold E. Holt* (left) approached the USS *Mayaguez* to recapture the ship, the crew found it already abandoned. Marines from *Holt* conducted the first hostile ship-to-ship boarding by the US Navy since 1826.

On May 12, 1975, a month after the Khmer Rouge takeover in Phnom Penh, Cambodian gunboats seized an American container ship, the USS *Mayaguez*, on its way to Thailand. The Khmer Rouge claimed that the ship had violated Cambodian waters by sailing inside the 12 mile (19 km) territorial limits of the tiny, uninhabited island of Poulo Wai, 59 miles (95 km) off Cambodia's coast—the US recognized only a 3 mile (5 km) limit. Exactly how close the ship had been was later disputed.

The US branded Cambodia's move "an act of piracy." Efforts at diplomatic resolution through the People's Republic of China failed when China refused to mediate. Reminded of the capture of an American spy ship, the *Pueblo*, by North Korea in 1968, when the crew had been held hostage for 11 months, President Ford ordered a significant military response to Cambodia's action.

Ford orders the attack
The Khmer Rouge took the ship to Koh Tang, an island about 32 miles (52 km) from the Cambodian coast, where they transferred the 39 crew members to fishing vessels. These boats took the *Mayaguez* crew to another small island nearby and then attempted to move them to the mainland at Kompong Som (the former Sihanoukville).

Realizing that the crew would be harder to track once they reached the mainland, Ford determined to rescue them first. However, American pilots lost track of the boat among the hundreds of fishing vessels in Kompong Som's harbor, and the Pentagon's lack of information about the area complicated its rescue plans.

President Ford authorized a naval, air, and landing operation to retake the *Mayaguez*, assault Koh Tang

> **"A violent** response is in order … we will **act** and we will act **quickly."**
>
> VICE PRESIDENT NELSON ROCKEFELLER DURING A NATIONAL SECURITY COUNCIL MEETING, MAY 12, 1975

island, and bomb Kompong Som. While the first and last objectives were achieved easily—the ship itself had already been abandoned—the attack on Koh Tang was more challenging. The Marine and Air Force landing party found the island far better defended than their intelligence briefings had indicated.

Developing debacle
Alarmed at the strength of the US response to the incident, the local Khmer Rouge conveyed the captors' readiness to end the affair to the captain of the *Mayaguez*. As a result, the Khmer Rouge released the *Mayaguez* crew not long after the US assault on Koh Tang started, and three

Landing on Koh Tang
Helicopters drop Marines on Koh Tang on May 14. Intelligence had incorrectly indicated that the assault, a combined action operation involving 230 Marines, supported by USAF planes, would meet minimal resistance.

hours later they were delivered to the USS *Henry B. Wilson* by a Thai fishing boat.

Upon hearing of the release of the American sailors, President Ford ordered the suspension of the invasion and a withdrawal of US forces. However, aborting the assault mid-battle was not possible.

The initial landing had been costly. Several troop-carrying helicopters were hit and destroyed, including one that was blown up in the air, killing 13 servicemen and injuring the pilot. The rescue of the US forces proved to be just as dangerous as the assault. In a 14-hour battle, 15 US servicemen died, while 23 perished in a helicopter crash in Thailand, where troops were preparing for action.

Left behind

Three Marines—in addition to the unrecovered bodies of dead servicemen—were left behind in the precarious extrication from the island, which was conducted at night under heavy fire. Not knowing the fate of the lost men, and certain that more would die in any rescue mission, the US command denied the Marines' request to return for their stranded comrades. The Khmer Rouge commander of Koh Tang later reported that one of the Marines had been captured and executed immediately afterward. The other two were also captured and subsequently killed, although accounts of the timing and circumstances differ.

AFTER »

In retrospect, the Mayaguez mission was seen as poorly planned and executed, in spite of the heroism involved.

ON REFLECTION
The US recognized the heroism displayed by Marines, Navy, and Air Force personnel in the combined response to the Mayaguez Incident by awarding one Navy Cross and 12 other major citations, in addition to bronze stars to the 23 men who died in the helicopter crash in Thailand.

Their service has not been forgotten. In 2008, more than 30 years after the incident, a law was drafted to award the Vietnam War Service Medal to veterans of the mission, who had previously been ineligible. In addition, collaborative efforts between Cambodia and the US to **find and repatriate bodies** from Koh Tang continue today.

VIETNAM WAR SERVICE MEDAL

Pathet Lao Takeover

The American withdrawal from Vietnam in 1973 and the subsequent communist victory gave a boost to the Pathet Lao, who had won control of large areas of their country.

Celebrating modern Laos
The victory of the communist Pathet Lao forces in 1975 led to the establishment of a one-party state, which celebrated its achievements through posters and other forms of propaganda.

BEFORE

The battle against North Vietnamese forces in Laos and along the Ho Chi Minh Trail made that country a crucial theater in the war in Indochina.

DIVIDED COUNTRY
Following the 1954 Geneva Conference, the Pathet Lao established control in two northern provinces. A coalition government between Royalists and communists collapsed in 1959 and a **long civil war** ensued.

In an attempt to disrupt the Ho Chi Minh Trail, the US bombed Laos extensively and organized and funded a **clandestine army of Hmong people ≪ 42–43** to operate against the North Vietnamese.

The US exit from Vietnam affected all of Indochina. In February 1973, the Pathet Lao and the Royal Laotian Government signed a ceasefire—the Vientiane Treaty—but the Pathet Lao did not disarm and the NVA remained in the country. With the communist takeovers in Phnom Penh and Saigon in April 1975, the Pathet Lao stepped up attacks on the Royalist forces.

The prime minister Souvanna Phouma knew that his forces could not prevail against this assault. He had little choice but to accept a promise of moderation from the leader of the Pathet Lao, his half-brother Prince Souphanouvong, and invite the communists to participate in a coalition government.

On August 23, 1975, 50 Pathet Lao troops entered Vientiane, the capital city, claiming to "liberate" it. Over the ensuing months the communists extended their control to the rest of the country.

500 The number of US fliers shot down over Laos.

14 The number of US POWs repatriated from Laos.

> " [The Pathet Lao] said 'We **need young soldiers**—we need every man around to be a soldier.'"
>
> CHUE VANG ON BEING ORDERED TO FIGHT FOR THE PATHET LAO AT AGE 8, *MISSOULA TIMES*, MAY 27, 2015

Coalition collapses

For a few months the Pathet Lao cooperated with the Royalists in the government. Souvanna Phouma ordered the Royalist . military forces not to oppose the Pathlet Lao. The US cut off economic aid, but maintained a diplomatic presence. However, on December 2, 1975, the Pathet Lao moved to take full power. They swept aside the noncommunist members of the coalition, forced King Savang Vatthana to abdicate, and abolished the monarchy. The king and the royal family were sent to a brutal re-education camp in November 1976 and all died within the next two years. The regime broke economic relations with China, while Soviet and other Eastern bloc countries provided economic aid. The newly proclaimed Lao People's Democratic Republic signed a treaty with the Socialist Republic of Vietnam that allowed Vietnam

From 1975 to 1996, the US resettled some 250,000 Lao refugees in the United States.

URBANIZED AND EDUCATED

Many refugees from Laos were ethnic Lao people: officials from the former government and those from the educated classes. Initially housed in refugee camps in Thailand, by 1995 more than 183,000 had been **resettled worldwide**.

HMONG DIASPORA

After some hesitation based on the belief that the Hmong people would not be able to adapt to life in America, the United States accepted some 140,000 Hmong from camps in Thailand. They settled mainly in California, Minnesota, Wisconsin, and North Carolina. Among them was General Vang Pao, whose death in California in 2010 was widely mourned by the Hmong.

HMONG WOMEN AT VANG PAO'S FUNERAL

Forced return

A Pathet Lao soldier orders a group of Meo hill people to return to their homes following an attempt by the Meos to march to the Laotian capital to protest against repression by the new communist-led government in May 1975.

to appoint advisers to help oversee the country and to station armed forces there. The US withdrew entirely and Laos fell almost totally under Vietnamese hegemony.

Genocidal retribution

Some resistance continued against the Pathet Lao regime, which announced that it would hunt down "American collaborators." The main targets of this campaign were the Hmong people. The new government set out to punish the Hmong who had fought with or supported General Vang Pao,

a Hmong leader who had collaborated with the United States in fighting the communists in Laos. This quest for revenge expanded into a genocidal campaign aimed at eradicating the Hmong people and their culture. As many as 200,000 Hmong fled into Thailand and a number of Hmong fighters took refuge in mountains. In later negotiations Laos agreed to repatriate 60,000 Lao refugees living in Thailand, including several thousand Hmong people. Fearing violence against them, the Hmong resisted return—their

concern was well founded. The communist government bombed their villages with poison gas and allowed atrocities against those who returned.

Re-education

The Hmong were not the only people to suffer under the new Laotian government. Thousands of both Lao and Hmong were

imprisoned for up to ten years in so-called "re-education" camps similar to those in Vietnam, located in remote areas. About 10 percent of the population, including most among the business, professional, and educated classes fled the country. Nevertheless, the US State Department's annual report on human rights violations did not mention Laos in 1976, 1977, or 1978. In 1979, the report noted some improvements in human rights in the preceding two years and rejected the charge of genocide, downplaying torture in the re-education camps. It reported evidence but not "absolute proof" of chemical warfare against the Hmong.

The **Fate** of South Vietnam

For those living in the former South Vietnam, life under the new communist regime could be difficult. Many people were persecuted due to their politics, religion, or even career choice, causing large numbers of South Vietnamese to flee their homeland for good.

United at last
This stamp commemorates the 1976 session of the Vietnamese National Assembly—the first for unified Vietnam. Of the 492 members of the Assembly, 243 were South Vietnamese.

In the frantic evacuation of the US Embassy, officials left behind many undestroyed files. Among these was a list of 30,000 Vietnamese who had worked in the Phoenix Program, helping to root out Viet Cong agents in rural areas. These individuals were quickly rounded up—later reports suggest that they were executed.

Although the feared bloodbath on a larger scale did not occur immediately, South Vietnamese citizens suffered deeply at the hands of the new regime. The North Vietnamese swept aside the People's Revolutionary Government (the political organ of the earlier Viet Cong) and in 1976 unified North and South as the Socialist Republic of Vietnam (SRV).

Sent away
As many as 2.5 million South Vietnamese—former military officers, civil servants, capitalists, priests, teachers, intellectuals, and others identified with the former regime—were dispatched to more than 300 "re-education" or "thought reform" camps in the countryside. Survivors, some of whom spent as many as 10 years incarcerated, described hard and

« BEFORE

The government in Saigon did not last long after the departure of US forces in 1973.

FALL OF SAIGON
In Spring 1975, a North Vietnamese **offensive « 316–17** swept through South Vietnam and the ARVN collapsed. President Thieu fled the country. After the ARVN were defeated at Xuan Loc, the NVA marched uncontested toward Saigon. A last-minute **evacuation « 322–23** of US personnel and some South Vietnamese from the rooftop of the US Embassy ensued as the communist forces **entered the city**.

SEIZED PRESIDENTIAL PALACE IN SAIGON

dangerous work (including mine sweeping), a glaring shortage of food and medical care, and harsh punishments for misbehavior. An estimated 165,000 people died in the camps—from starvation, disease, exhaustion, suicide, and by execution.

Bribery and extortion payments by family members inside and outside of Vietnam allowed some of the incarcerated to survive and even buy release. Commenting on their propaganda efforts to hide the horrors of the camps, an SRV

official joked that "We've been worse than Pol Pot, but the outside world knows nothing."

Singled out

Religious people, especially Christians, were persecuted, as were ethnic minorities, including the significant Chinese population. Among the major targets were approximately 30 tribes of Montagnards (today called Degars), who had cooperated with the French and later the US in the two Indochina wars. Fighting for their

Children's burden
Orphans eat at the Bamboo Shoot Orphanage in Ho Chi Minh City, in April 1980. Many of the orphaned children in Vietnam had American fathers, or birth defects as a result of chemical defoliants like Agent Orange.

cultures and autonomy, many Montagnards continued to resist for both ethnic and religious reasons. The new regime responded harshly, slaughtering thousands of tribespeople.

Economic adaptation

Persecution, however, was not the only item on the SRV government's list of punishments. Between 1975 and 1980, more than one million North Vietnamese citizens were sent to live in the south and central regions of the former South Vietnam, apparently to balance the population. Meanwhile, up to one million South Vietnamese people were relocated, and families were moved to previously uninhabited areas in the mountains called New Economic Zones. Estimates vary, but suggest that between 20,000 and 155,000 South Vietnamese people died performing hard labor in situations that were described by eyewitnesses both as "prefabricated hell" and "place[s] one comes to only if the alternative to it would be death."

Seeking asylum

Unsurprisingly, many former South Vietnamese people chose not to remain under the new regime. After the communist takeover, two

70 PERCENT of boat people died at sea, according to SRV sources. Other estimates are lower—around 50 percent.

million people fled Vietnam by boat. These refugees, who became known as the "boat people," risked their lives to escape. Even the most fortunate of them had horrendous experiences— hunger, thirst, pirate attacks, and rape—but the lucky ones made it to UN camps, before migrating to countries such as Canada, Australia, and the US.

AFTER

A sizable Vietnamese refugee community (Viet Kieu) resides in the US, especially in California.

A BETTER LIFE
Vietnamese people in America have achieved **notable distinctions**, for example, as scholars and professionals, high-ranking military officers, and, in one case, as an NFL professional football player. Many first- and second-generation Viet Kieu have acquired wealth and return to Vietnam for business ventures.

Economic renovation (*dao moi*) in 1986 created a market system to help Vietnam's integration into the world economy. Since 2000, its growth rate has been among the highest in the world.

Paying the price
Prisoners do manual labor in a re-education camp. The camps engaged in indoctrination but, despite the name, were more about punishment than converting people to communism.

Boat People

After the unification of Vietnam, many South Vietnamese people fled by boat to avoid persecution under the new regime. Vuong Thanh Loc's middle-class family owned a grocery store, and two of his brothers had worked for the South Vietnamese government. Vuong had tried to escape seven times and had been jailed twice, before he embarked on the difficult journey that would eventually take him to Australia.

The boat was very small, around 26 ft (8 m) long and 10 ft (3 m) wide, but fifty people were crammed into it like sardines in a can. It was unseaworthy; the engine was very old and it did not have a hooded cover, exposing it to the elements. The owner had promised a bigger ship would be waiting for them out at sea, but he had tricked them. In the hope a ship at sea could save them, they carried on with their journey. The weather was good and they prayed to keep their hopes up.

But the engine broke down after ten hours at sea, and with no sails or paddles, the boat was left adrift. Food was scarce and ran out two days later. On the third day, some ships appeared but did not stop to help. Finally, on the night of seventh day the boat came ashore but they did not know where they were until the police came. They had arrived in Malaysia.

❝We realized now how important escaping was, it was too late for us to return.**❞**

VUONG THANH LOC, FROM *VIETKA*, ARCHIVES OF VIETNAMESE BOAT PEOPLE, 2005

Seeking sanctuary
Vietnamese refugees arrive at the island of Tai A Chau, Hong Kong in 1989. Boat people were moved to this previously uninhabited island that summer, but rioted in September due to terrible conditions: crumbling huts, lack of electricity and toilets, and even an outbreak of cholera.

As a prelude to a mass execution, the victims are strung together with rope that was threaded through holes that had been cut into their hands, to prevent their escape

BEFORE

Although the movement had existed for a long time—and had ideological roots in 1950s' Paris—the Khmer Rouge was born officially in 1968.

COMMUNIST GROWTH

With assistance, albeit inconsistent, from North Vietnam, Khmer Rouge guerrillas **launched an insurgency ≪ 248–49** against the Cambodian government. It remained relatively weak until 1970, when Lon Nol overthrew Prince Norodom Sihanouk and invited the US to **invade Cambodia ≪ 252–53** to wipe out North Vietnamese and Viet Cong sanctuaries. A **civil war escalated ≪ 326–27** between the Lon Nol government and the Khmer Rouge, causing the insurgency to grow.

Cambodia Under Communism

Pol Pot and his regime sought to transform Cambodia, now called Democratic Kampuchea, in accordance with their radical ideology. Almost a quarter of Cambodia's population were brutally slaughtered in the name of progress and purification.

Totally renouncing the modern "capitalist, imperialist" world represented by cities, Khmer Rouge leader Pol Pot dreamed of a communal, agrarian, communist society, inspired by an idyllic image of pre-modern Cambodian peasants. He declared 1975 "Year Zero" of the new order and the country was given a new name: Democratic Kampuchea.

Road to agrarianism

Pol Pot believed that to cleanse society, all people must return to the land. Untold numbers of people perished on long marches from urban areas to rural work camps. The so-called "new" people, the products of urban culture—intellectuals, professionals, the educated, and those with worldly possessions—were ferreted out and often executed, as were many

Never forgotten

This bas relief at Wat Samrong Knong near Battambang, Cambodia, is one of a series of scenes detailing the atrocities committed by the Khmer Rouge. Here, victims are cruelly joined together en route to their mass execution.

these camps was Tuol Sleng prison—known as S-21— which was presided over by the notorious Comrade Duch, Kang Kek Iew. In such prison camps, interrogators employed heinous torture methods to gain confessions from supposed "traitors against the revolution," many of whom were casualties of the internecine power struggles among the Khmer Rouge factions, or were accused of being Vietnamese sympathizers.

Of the 17,000 people who passed through Tuol Sleng, only a few—one source says seven—survived. The others were executed at nearby Choeung Ek, a former orchard that became known as the most infamous of "The Killing

Born near Kompong Thom in May 1928, Saloth Sar emerged onto the political scene in 1953, and rose to become secretary general of Cambodia's secret Communist Party in 1963. The leader of the Khmer Rouge guerrillas, he became prime minister after Phnom Penh fell in 1975. He adopted his revolutionary name, Pol Pot, in 1976.

After Vietnam invaded Cambodia, Pol Pot went to Thailand. He relinquished his

army in 1985 and lived a shadowy life until his death in 1998. Many details about his life remain shrouded in secrecy.

three million were killed under the Khmer Rouge regime. Mass graves have been identified to account for nearly 1.4 million individuals. Like the Nazis during World War II, the Khmer Rouge torturers kept meticulous records and thousands of pictures of their victims.

China in the mid-1960s. However, like Mao, the Khmer Rouge soon realized that their regime would not survive without the restoration of the very institutions and skills they had sought to eradicate.

> " He who **protests** is an **enemy** [and] he who **opposes** is a **corpse.** "
>
> COMMON KHMER ROUGE SAYING, QUOTED IN *POL POT'S LITTLE RED BOOK* BY HENRI LOCARD, 2004

non-Khmer minorities. Starvation, disease, and work exhaustion killed hundreds of thousands more.

Systematic genocide

Numerous prison camps and execution centers were set up in the countryside to hold and punish those considered enemies of the regime. The most infamous of

Fields." Prisoners there were often hacked, beaten, or bludgeoned to death to save bullets.

Extensive research by the Yale University Cambodian Genocide Program and by the Cambodian Documentation Center estimates that total deaths in the country reached more than two million. Some claims suggest more than

Dismantling society

Pol Pot's assault on urbanity also included the repudiation of many institutions: hospitals and factories, but also foreign relations and financial structures. Money was abolished. Religion was outlawed, and communal living replaced single-family homes. The regime disrupted normal patterns of family life. Children were removed from their parents in order to be indoctrinated, while married couples were allowed to visit each other only on a limited basis. Those caught engaging in sexual activity could be executed on the spot.

The radicalism of Pol Pot was even more extreme than Mao Zedong's Cultural Revolution in

Denouncing modernity

A Cambodian cyclist passes broken cars on the roadside. One of many possessions associated with urbanization and the West, cars were destroyed under the Khmer Rouge regime.

AFTER

Although Vietnam had sponsored the Khmer Rouge originally, Hanoi's politburo never ceased wanting to annex Cambodia.

POWER CHANGES HANDS

After many mutual provocations, on December 25, 1978, Vietnam **invaded Cambodia 340–41 »**. By the beginning of January, they had ousted Pol Pot and replaced the Khmer Rouge with a Vietnamese **puppet regime**. However, the Khmer Rouge continued to fight the Vietnamese, and its guerrilla forces returned once more to bases in the jungles.

KHMER ROUGE GUERRILLAS

Victims of genocide
Pictures of some of the victims of the Khmer Rouge are displayed at the Tuol Sleng Genocide Museum in Phnom Penh. These photographs were included in the meticulous records kept by the regime.

Aftermath in Indochina

« BEFORE

Long-disputed boundaries and hostility toward migrants made it easy for conflicts to emerge.

DIFFERENCES ASIDE

The Indochinese powers had buried their difficulties during the **First Indochina War « 26–27** against the French, and both Cambodia and Laos had been attacked by North Vietnam's enemies during the Second Indochina War. North Vietnam had built their main supply route, the **Ho Chi Minh Trail « 138–39**, through Laos, and Cambodia was sucked into the war by Nixon's **Cambodian incursion « 252–53**. However, the three nations, along with their Chinese neighbor in the north, had an ancient history of **border and ethnic disputes** dating from long before French colonization.

The last United States citizens departed from Indochina in 1975, and Vietnam was reunified. The American war was over, but there was little respite: for the Indochinese, conflict merely moved into another stage, referred to as the Third Indochina War.

The Second Indochina War came to an end in 1975, with communist governments in power in all three Indochina countries, but the scars of the conflict were deep. Whatever levels of cooperation under the fraternal banner of communism might have existed during the war quickly fell apart, as historical animosities prevailed. The following decades were a dark and violent time in Vietnam, Cambodia, and Laos.

Centuries of antipathy between Cambodia and Vietnam, somewhat covered over during the Indochina Wars, resurfaced after the triumph of communist regimes in both countries in 1975.

Ancient grudge

Tensions soon erupted into armed conflict. Ethnic and border issues, as well as conflicting claims over islands, resulted in military skirmishes that escalated to major engagements. Following months of attacks on Vietnamese villages, in

September 1977 Democratic Kampuchea (the new Khmer Rouge regime in Cambodia) sent six divisions into Vietnam's Tay Ninh province. The new Socialist Republic of Vietnam (SRV) was

Angkor Wat temples

Khmer troops pass through Cambodia's Angkor Wat temples. Pol Pot saw Angkor Wat as proof of what the Khmer people could accomplish. Bullet holes from battles between the Vietnamese and the Khmer Rouge can still be seen around the temples today.

quick to respond; it amassed eight divisions, invaded Kampuchea, and by January 1978 its troops came within 24 miles (39 km) of Phnom Penh before withdrawing.

More border conflicts resulted in another Vietnamese incursion in June and a full-scale invasion was launched on December 25, 1978. Employing 13 divisions, 150,000 soldiers, and abundant artillery and airpower, Vietnam wiped out half of the Kampuchean Revolutionary Army in only two weeks. Khmer Rouge political leaders fled to the western regions of the country.

On January 7, 1979, Vietnam installed a puppet government, the People's Republic of Kampuchea, headed by Heng Samrin and other former Khmer Rouge defectors.

Sino-Vietnamese conflict

Despite China's support during the Vietnam War, Sino-Vietnamese relations also had a long history of

Battling with China

A Vietnamese soldier captures a Chinese tank driver in Vietnam's Cao Bang province. While the province's mountains had offered protection to Vietnamese communists for decades, Chinese troops invaded the city of Cao Bang in 1979.

hostility. Vietnam and the People's Republic of China had border disputes and mutual claims to the Paracel and Spratly Islands.

> "Beijing has said **time and again** that they will teach us a **second lesson.**"

PHAM VAN DONG, PRIME MINISTER OF VIETNAM, 1979

Vietnam's treatment of the 1.5 million ethnic Chinese who lived in Vietnam (known as the Hoa) also angered China. After 1975, more than 170,000 Hoa fled Vietnam and many became "boat people." The final straw for China was Vietnam's 1979 takeover of Kampuchea, an ally of China.

That February, China launched a punitive invasion with 200,000 forces penetrating about 25 miles (40 km) into Vietnam before they got bogged down and withdrew. It is estimated that China suffered at least 7,000–8,000 deaths in the three-week war. Vietnam never released military casualties but announced that 10,000 of its civilians died in the invasion. Border engagements continued through the 1980s until a settlement was reached in the late 1990s.

Cambodia and Laos

A peace agreement signed in 1991—yet again in Paris—brought an end to Vietnam's occupation of Cambodia and allowed the countries in the Association of Southeast Asian Nations (ASEAN) to increase their economic activity with Vietnam. In 1995, Vietnam became a member of the organization, and also restored its diplomatic relations with the United States.

Cambodia and Laos fared less well after 1991. The Khmer Rouge disaster, Vietnamese occupation, and continuing civil war in Cambodia prevented stability and development. In 1992, the United Nations Transitional Authority in Cambodia (UNTAC),

Vietnam made discernible political and economic progress as it moved into the 21st century.

PROGRESS AND STRUGGLE

Although it had to contend with land devastated by war, a brutal dictatorial government, a burgeoning population, and the costs of hegemony over its neighbors, Vietnam was still able to prosper as it moved **into the 21st century 342–43 »**, especially as it embraced a new economic system. Meanwhile, Cambodia and Laos, two of the poorest, most corrupt, and dysfunctional countries in the world, continued to suffer from the impact and legacy of the Indochina Wars.

negotiating Vietnamese withdrawal from Cambodia, accepted a mandate to administer the country, organize an election, and address the Khmer Rouge's crimes. Laos remained under Vietnamese control, but had a civil war of its own to fight, between the Lao People's Army—with Vietnamese allies—and a Hmong insurgency.

Warning sign

A sign in Cambodia warns travelers to beware of mines. Unexploded ordnance remained an unseen danger throughout Indochina, and represented just one of many ways in which the landscape was weaponized against the communist forces during the First Indochina War.

ប្រយ័ត្នគ្រាប់មីន!!

Danger!! Mines!!

Friendly association
US President Barack Obama with Vietnamese President Tran Dai Quang are greeted by a military guard in Hanoi during Obama's 2016 visit to Vietnam. The two leaders worked to open trade and reconcile relations during the trip.

◀◀ BEFORE

Indochina saw almost constant war for nearly 50 years, from World War II until the 1990s.

A TROUBLED PAST
The struggle to emerge from their **colonization ◀◀ 16–17** by the French led the freedom fighters of Indochina to adopt a communist ideology, which in turn brought the liberation movements into **conflict with the United States ◀◀ 28–29.**

LEGACY OF CONFLICT
The resulting warfare left a legacy of economic, political, and humanitarian **damage to Vietnam ◀◀ 340–41** and its neighbors, presenting a huge challenge for its people to overcome as they entered the new century.

Indochina into the 21st Century

Indochina entered the 21st century with outmoded political systems, causing social and economic stagnation, while their Asian neighbors embraced modernization. Vietnam has since started down this path, but Cambodia and Laos still lag far behind.

With a population of more than 90 million, Vietnam is the 14th most populous country in the world, and it is one of only five remaining single-party communist countries in existence. It now enjoys diplomatic relations with most of the world and is a member of 63 international organizations, including the United Nations (UN), Association of Southeast Asian Nations (ASEAN), and the Non-Aligned Movement, as well as 650 non-governmental organizations. The establishment of diplomatic relations with the US in 1995 opened doors, and the two have engaged in both military exchanges and joint exercises.

In spite of this apparent progress, however, Amnesty International continues to cite severe restrictions on freedom of speech and assembly in Vietnam, the persecution of

Commercializing history
This modern poster imitates Vietnam War era propaganda to satisfy a market for "war souvenirs." Other popular modern imitations include Zippo lighters, dog tags, and grenades turned into key chains. Dan Sinh market in Ho Chi Minh City is full of supposed "war surplus."

dissidents, state control over the media and judiciary, and harsh treatment of minorities.

Economic achievement

Since 2000, Vietnam's economic growth rate has been impressive; in 2008, PricewaterhouseCoopers projected that it could become the world's fastest-growing emerging economy by 2020. Vietnam has attracted significant foreign investment (including from Vietnamese people who now live overseas), seen a construction boom, and dramatically increased foreign trade. In 2007, Vietnam became a member of the World Trade Organization, which opened up new world markets.

International tourism, which brings in seven million visitors a year, is important: more than a third of Vietnam's gross domestic product is generated by services, including tourism, and the number of first class hotels and restaurants continues to grow. Hanoi is now often cited as one of the top 10 cities in the world to visit. The stunning Ha Long Bay is popular

and the tunnels of Cu Chi have been opened up as a tourist attraction. Increasingly, American Vietnam veterans have returned to visit, and even though this is an aging cohort, the Vietnamese consider war tourism to be an expanding market.

Cambodia struggles

It has been a less optimistic story in Cambodia. The Prime Minister Hun Sen, a former Khmer Rouge, has ruled with an iron fist since 1985, repressing several uprisings against him. He has stated that he will remain in power until 2026. King Norodom Sihanouk, who had served as the titular head of the Khmer Rouge and as Cambodia's nominal monarch since 1993, abdicated in 2004.

The actions of the United Nations Transitional Authority (UNTAC) in 1992 did little to improve the situation. Cambodia continues to have one of the worst records of corruption, human rights abuses, sexual exploitation of young girls, and HIV/AIDS in the world. Although very poor and largely agricultural, the country nevertheless experienced one of the world's highest growth rates from 2004 to 2011, when household consumption increased by 40 percent, and the poverty rate fell from 52 percent to 21 percent.

International genocide tribunals have proceeded slowly: due to both financial reasons and a lack of commitment by Hun Sen. Comrade Duch received a life sentence for crimes against humanity in 2012; Nuon Chea, Pol Pot's right-hand man, and

| 94 | **PERCENT The literacy rate in Vietnam in 2015.** |
| 77 | **PERCENT The literacy rate in Cambodia in 2015.** |

Khieu Samphan, Pol Pot's successor as leader of the Khmer Rouge, were both arrested in 2007 and given life sentences in 2014.

Poverty in Laos

In contrast to Vietnam, Laos remains one of the world's poorest countries. It has one of the lowest annual incomes in the world, with a third of its people living below the poverty line. In 2015, it ranked 29th among countries with the world's worst hunger problems.

During the US war, more than two million tons of bombs were dropped on Laos. An estimated 30 percent of these bombs did not explode— leaving an estimated 78 million pieces of unexploded ordnance in Laos. These bombs continue to kill about 300 people a year. The unearthing and sale of scrap metals from these bombs has, however, become a major industry on the Plain of Jars.

Legacies of war
Bomb craters scar the Laotian landscape. Today, scrap and unexploded bombs lie with megalithic burial urns in an area known as the Plain of Jars. New areas of the site are made safe for visitors as bombs are cleared.

AFTER

The future of the region is unclear. All three countries have young burgeoning populations and some natural resources.

UNCERTAIN FUTURE
All three Indochinese countries have the potential for further development and political liberalization. Vietnam will likely continue its **growth**, while Cambodia, appears set to **stagnate** under Sen's leadership for at least the near future. In Laos, some foreign investment, the rapid expanse of tourism, and rich **deposits of minerals** offer some hope to improve its bleak status.

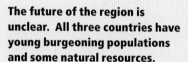

Facing the music
Former Khmer Rouge head of state Khieu Samphan stands trial in Phnom Penh. Samphan maintained his innocence throughout his trial, calling the charges against him a fairytale.

American Homecoming

Americans' antipathy to the war was shown not only toward the policymakers and generals, but also toward returning servicemen and women. For some veterans, especially those who saw combat, homecoming was a difficult adjustment.

Most Vietnam veterans returned to the US to live stable, productive, and distinguished lives. Studies demonstrate that 85 percent made successful transitions to civilian life after their time in Vietnam, and 91 percent of veterans indicated that they were proud of their service. Compared to their peers who did not serve in the war, Vietnam veterans enjoy a higher annual income, and a lower percentage of them have spent time in prison. There is no difference in statistics on drug addiction or homelessness. Their record of leadership in public life is noteworthy.

« BEFORE

The men and women who returned from Vietnam received a very different reception from that enjoyed by the veterans of World War II.

TARNISHED IMAGE
By the time the **US exited Vietnam « 300–01**, the war had become extremely unpopular, and this was reflected in the public's attitude to the returning troops. Moreover, **media coverage « 186–87**, including photographs such as Nick Ut's "Napalm Girl" and Ron Haeberle's shots of the My Lai massacre, had brought some of the atrocities of the war up close.

Call for help
A homeless veteran panhandles in Penn Plaza, New York City, in 1988. Many veterans still struggle to get compensation for disabilities caused by their service, and the Veterans Association reports that the number of Vietnam veterans making claims continues to grow.

Service honored
More Purple Heart medals (for miliary merit) were awarded in Vietnam than in any other American war but World War II. Three soldiers earned the medal a record eight times in Vietnam.

Life after warfare
Some veterans did suffer greatly after returning to the US. Adjustment problems immediately on return— particularly for the 10 percent of veterans who actually engaged in combat operations—included drug and alcohol addiction, post-traumatic stress disorder (PTSD), inadequate medical and mental health services, and negative perceptions of Vietnam veterans, ranging from simple indifference to outright hostility.

African Americans returned to the same discrimination that they had experienced before their departure, and a more radical Civil Rights Movement. Many African Americans from the South had been forever changed by their war experiences, but their rural communities expected them to return quietly to the traditional racial patterns of Southern life. Some urban black veterans found militant groups such as the Black Panthers appealing.

Unemployment was also a serious problem among African American veterans. In 1973, unemployment for white veterans aged 20–24 was just under 6 percent, but for comparable black veterans it was nearly 33 percent. US veterans organizations, dominated by those who served in World War II, did not welcome the new generation of veterans, and were especially resistant to African Americans.

Untold stories
The 6,400 female Vietnam veterans, who experienced an unusually high degree of trauma from the war, were often ignored and their experiences trivialized. Nurses' stories dominate the conversation about female Vietnam veterans, while those who served in other capacities have found their experiences largely ignored; the Women's Army Corps records were lost, and remain so despite veterans' calls to find them. Some female veterans have expressed their struggle to see themselves in the Vietnam Women's Memorial, which depicts an Army nurse tending to a wounded soldier.

The triumphant homecoming of prisoners of war (POWs) caught the nation's attention, but thousands of men missing in

In memoriam
A crowd gathers at the dedication of the Vietnam Veterans Memorial in November 1982. The two-acre wall is inscribed with the name of every member of the US Armed Forces who served in the war.

action (MIA) did not come home. Families grieved as the government appeared to give up on these men, treating them like inconvenient remnants standing in the way of new relations with former foes.

Hopeful future

At the end of the war, change came quickly to America's armed forces. The draft was ended, an all-volunteer military inaugurated, and more emphasis was placed on improving reserve forces. The number of women in the military increased, from less than 2 percent at the end of the Vietnam War to over 15 percent in 2015, with most combat positions open to them.

The dedication of the Vietnam Veterans Memorial in Washington, D.C., was a decisive event and other memorials soon followed. The GI Bill, inaugurated in 1984, expanded benefits for Vietnam veterans. The 1991 Gulf War elevated the honor of patriotic military service, a trend reinforced by 9/11. Vietnam veterans today stand alongside those who have served in the various theaters of the war on terrorism as worthy heroes—however shocking the new mantra of "Thank you for your service" may be to Vietnam veterans who experienced a totally different reception when they came home.

DESERT STORM VICTORY PARADE

For America, losing the Vietnam War provoked an intense re-examination of everything about the war.

LEARNING FROM THE PAST

From small unit tactical procedures to overall political and military strategy, all facets of war were debated and assessed in response to "the lessons of Vietnam." The leadership of America's military engagements in the **Balkans**, **Iraq**, and **Afghanistan** came from men such as Generals Colin Powell, Norman Schwarzkopf, Tommy Franks, and Alexander Haig, who each drew on their own lessons from their service in Vietnam.

" [When] soldiers **came home** from Vietnam, there were no parades, **no celebrations.**"

GENERAL WILLIAM WESTMORELAND ON THE BUILDING OF THE MEMORIAL IN WASHINGTON

FUSE-HOT ADVENTURE IN THE TIME BOMB OF THE WORLD!

a YANK in VIET-NAM

actually filmed under gun-fire!

MARSHALL THOMPSON

ENRIQUE MAGALONA *introducing* KIEU CHINH and JANE WARDELL and JACK LEWIS

Produced by WRAY DAVIS · MARSHALL THOMPSON · *an* ALLIED ARTISTS *release*

1 *A YANK IN VIET-NAM*, 1964

They had to be the toughest fighting force on earth— and the men who led them had to be just a little bit tougher..

THE GREEN BERETS

2 *THE GREEN BERETS*, 1968

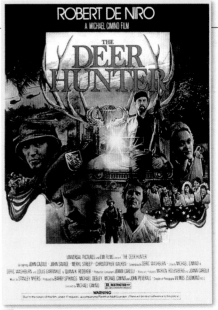

ROBERT DE NIRO

A MICHAEL CIMINO FILM

THE DEER HUNTER

3 *THE DEER HUNTER*, 1978

4 *APOCALYPSE NOW*, 1979

The **War** in **American** Popular Culture

The deep divisions that the war created in American society are found in the portrayal of the conflict in popular culture. Almost all the movies and novels about the war reflect subtle or overt pro- or antiwar bias.

1 *A Yank in Viet-Nam*, **1964** This was one of Hollywood's first portrayals of the war. 2 *The Green Berets*, **1968** Co-directed by and starring John Wayne, this took a clear pro-war stance. 3 *The Deer Hunter*, **1978** This focused on the psychological impact of the war on veterans. 4 *Apocalypse Now*, **1979** Francis Ford Coppola's acclaimed film offered a hallucinogenic rather than realistic view of the war. 5 *Rambo: First Blood Part II*, **1985** This Sylvester Stallone vehicle tackled the issue of MIA soldiers. 6 *Platoon*, **1986** Written and directed by veteran Oliver Stone, the movie was intended as a rebuke to 1968's *The Green Berets*. 7 *The Hanoi Hilton*, **1987** This movie tells the story of US soldiers who were prisoners of war in Hoa Lo Prison. 8 *Full Metal Jacket*, **1987** Stanley Kubrick's movie was based on veteran Gustav Hasford's semi-autobiographical novel

The Short-Timers. 9 *Good Morning, Vietnam*, **1987** Containing comedic elements, this also examined the politics of the conflict within Vietnam. 10 *Born on the Fourth of July*, **1989** Oliver Stone adapted paralyzed Marine Ron Kovic's autobiography into a film dealing with the conditions facing wounded veterans. 11 *The Ballad of the Green Berets*, **1966** This was a prominent pro-war song. 12 *Born in the USA*, **1985** Bruce Springsteen's seventh album addressed the loss of American lives in Vietnam and the hardship faced by veterans. 13 *Chickenhawk*, **1983** This memoir was written by veteran helicopter pilot Robert Mason. 14 *Battlefield Vietnam*, **2004** This first-person-shooter video game allows users to play as any of the war's major forces, using contemporary weapons in simulations of famous battle sites.

STALLONE

They sent him on a mission and set him up to fail. But they made one mistake.

They forgot they were dealing with Rambo.

RAMBO
FIRST BLOOD PART II

5 *RAMBO: FIRST BLOOD PART II*, 1985

6 *PLATOON*, 1986

7 *THE HANOI HILTON*, 1987

8 *FULL METAL JACKET*, 1987

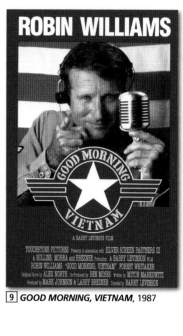

9 *GOOD MORNING, VIETNAM*, 1987

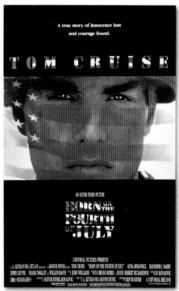

10 *BORN ON THE FOURTH OF JULY*, 1989

11 *THE BALLAD OF THE GREEN BERETS*, 1966

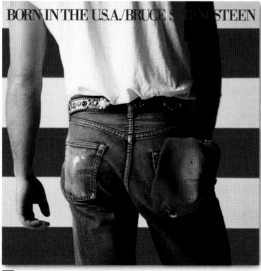

12 *BORN IN THE USA*, 1985

13 *CHICKENHAWK*, 1983

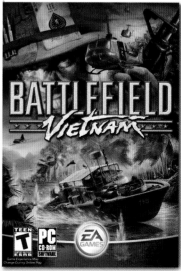

14 *BATTLEFIELD VIETNAM*, 2004

JOHN E HEFTY · MICHAEL L HEITGER · STEVEN W HEITMAN · JOHN E
...RGE H HEPPEN Jr · DEWEY W HEROY · SAMUEL E HEWITT · JOHN E H
...ERREL HINES · CARL R HINKLE · REGGIE W HINSON · DENNIS R HINTON · LEE C HIT
...LLMAN · RAYMOND R HOLLOPETER · THOMAS E HOLLOWAY · LONNIE M HOLMES ·
· WILLIAM H HOSEA · DONALD R HOSKINS · DARCY A HOUCHIN EARL F HOUCK ·
...HOWELL · GEORGE A HOWES · DENNIS L HUBBARD · RONALD C HUDSON · BURREL
· RONALD W HURT · CLARENCE R HUSK · DAVID G HUTCHINGS ...ALPH C HUTH · B
· WILLIAM L JARBOE · ROBERT W JARONIK · JOHN P JARO...CAK · ...AVID C JASPER · GA
...SON · JACK L JOHN...SON · JAMES R JOHNSON · JIMMIE L JOHNSON · RALPH E JOHNSON
...NES · GRAYLAND JONES · GUY T JONES · JACKIE D JONES · ...AMES E JONES · LARRY JON
...OBERT M KAIL · JAMES N KALIL · PAUL J KAPPMEYER · WILLIAM J KA...ES · KENNETH E KA
...G · GLENNIS R KELLAMS · RAYMOND E KELLEMS · JEROME ...EL E KELLY ·
...OMAS P KINDT · FREDRICK B KING · JOHN E KING · ARTHU...EPH K KIRK
...HARLES A KNOCHEL · THOMAS M KOCH · JOHN F KOEHLER ... · MICHA
...ER · JAMES H KURDELSKI · MICHAEL J KURELLA · ROBERT V ...F A LABUD
· JAMES P LANIER · JOHN T LANKASTER Jr · DAVID A LANNIN... · ...ARAWAY ·
...OMAS E LEAP Jr · ROGER R LEASER · RICHARD T LEAVELL · B... E LEE · JA
...KI · MICHAEL LEWIS · ROBERT D LEWIS · JOSE LEZAMA Jr · BO... ...ARLES W
...ALCOLM E LOMAX · LORIN E LONG · ROBERT L LONG · RO... ...RBERT J LO
...LUTTEL · ANTHONY R LUX · PHILLIP E LYNCH · RICHARD ... Y J LYNCH
...DY · JAMES A MANGER · ROBERT L MANN · THOMAS R MAN... ...R D MANNS ·
...MARTIN · DONALD E MARTIN · DONNIE J MARTIN · JE... · ROBERT A MART
...AS L MCBRIDE · FRANK E MCCLELLAN · CHESTER R M... ...EORGE F MCCOY
...Y C MCELFRIDGE · RICHARD W MCGEE · STEPHEN ... ...LD R MCINTOSH ·
...MCLHERN · DENNIS M MEAD · DAVID L MEADOWS ... ...EY Jr · VINCENT J ...
...AVID L MEYERS · GEORGE H MEYERS · WAYNE A MIC... ...ICHALSKI · JAMES
...ETT G MILLER · GEORGE D MILLER · GERALD L MILLE... ...R Jr · JACK W MILL
...RD T MILLS · ROGER D MILLS · JIMMIE L MINCKS · CI... ...BBY MINTON · WI...
...ERY · RONALD W MONTGOMERY · ALLAN J MOORE ... ...ORE · FRED MOOR
...LOREN L MORFORD · DENNIS E MORGAN · SAMUEL ... WILLIAM E MORMA...
...DELL · HAROLD E MUNDY · RAY MURPHY · STEVEN E MUR... ...AROLD E MUSSELMAN ·
...A NASH... · JOHN M NASH · RONALD W NEAL · WILLIAM E NEAL · DENNIS P NEELEY ·
...ICKEL... · WILLIAM D NICODEMUS · HARRY T NIGGLE · JAMES H NOBLE · FLOYD R N
...AN ... ...ICHAEL G O'CONNELL · DAVID C O'CONNOR · TIMOTHY J O'CON
... ...OSBORN · LYNN A OSBORN · WILLIAM C OSBORN · GEORGE ...
...A ...OHN W PARCEL · EUGENE A PARISH · IRVING G PARK · ROBERT L PARK ·
...NDALL PELL · DALE A PENNINGTON · MARVIN E PENRY · WILLIAM C PERDUE · OFALEE
...DREW PHILLIPS · KERRY W PHILLIPS · KENT D PIERCE · RICHARD A PIERCE · LARRY J

Remembering their service
Dog tags hang from the Vietnam
Veterans Memorial in Washington, D.C.
Tags are often left at the wall—as are
boots, photographs, and personal
objects—in honor of Vietnam veterans.

Visiting Vietnam

War tourism is a growing industry in Vietnam and attracts many veterans—especially American veterans. Today, visitors can tour museums, prison camps, and tunnels, or visit monuments and cemeteries, to learn more about the war or pay respects to the fallen.

BA RIA-VUNG TAU

Con Son Island
This island was first used as a penal colony during the French colonial period. The island's prisons remained in use until the fall of Saigon in 1975. In 1970, the prisons were visited by US Congressional representatives who notably reported seeing prisoners kept inside tiger cages. Today, Hang Duong Cemetery on Con Son is a site of pilgrimage, housing the remains of the 22,000 prisoners who died on the island.

BINH DUONG

Binh An Cemetery
This cemetery—previously known as the Bien Hoa Military Cemetery—was established in 1965 for soldiers of the South Vietnamese Army (ARVN), but does not appear to have been used until 1968. The cemetery's location on Highway 1 is marked with a sculpture, nicknamed "Thuong Tiec," of a tired ARVN soldier.

BINH PHUOC

Phuoc Long Victory Monument
The Battle of Phuoc Long, which began in December 1974, was a key defeat for the ARVN and an important precursor to the final North Vietnamese (NVA) offensive. The monument bears the date, January 6, 1975, when the NVA victory was sealed and the province was "liberated."

BINH THUAN

Ho Chi Minh Museum, Phan Thiet
Set on the banks of the Ca Ty River, this small museum contains artifacts from the life of leader Ho Chi Minh.

DA NANG

Zone 5 Military Museum
This museum in Da Nang's Hai Chau District has both indoor and outdoor displays of objects, weapons, aircraft, and vehicles that were used in Tactical Zone 5 during the Vietnam War. http://www.danang.gov.vn/portal/page/portal/danang/english/tourism/

Ho Chi Minh Museum
Next door to the Zone 5 Museum, this Ho Chi Minh museum contains three galleries of photographs and documents pertaining to the leader, as well as a reconstruction of his home in Hanoi. http://www.danang.gov.vn/portal/page/portal/danang/english/tourism/

DIEN BIEN

A1 Hill
One of the last French strongpoints to fall during the Battle of Dien Bien Phu, A1 Hill offers visitors a view of the entire battlefield and surrounding valleys.

Bunker of General de Castries
The capture of the French commander's bunker was a key moment in the 1954 Battle of Dien Bien Phu. The bunker has been preserved—and in places, reinforced with stronger materials—for visitors, but US visitors should be aware that information within is mainly presented in Vietnamese and French.

Dien Bien Phu Military Cemetery
This peaceful burial ground contains the remains of Vietnamese soldiers who fought against the French in 1954. While many graves are unmarked, memorial walls give the names of those who died in the battle, listed by province.

Dien Bien Phu Military Museum
Containing objects, weapons, and photographs from the Battle of Dien Bien Phu, this military museum also contains some oddities—such as a bathtub owned by French commander de Castries.

Dien Bien Phu Victory Monument
The sculpture, commemorating the Vietnamese victory at Dien Bien Phu, was installed at D1 Hill for the 50th anniversary of the battle. http://vietnam.vnanet.vn/english/dien-bien-phu-victory-monument/17837.html

DONG HA

Dong Ha Mine Action Center
Showcasing the ordnance dropped by American forces during the Vietnam War, the Mine Action Center in Dong Ha contains bomb fragments, unexploded devices, photographs, and warnings to children to beware of mines. http://landmines.org.vn/visitor-center/

DONG NAI

Bien Hoa Air Base
This was a major US base from 1961 to 1973, and was also used by the ARVN Air Force. While the public cannot enter the old base, day tours drive visitors around the complex to see the main gate and crumbling walls, as well as uphill to Buu Phong Pagoda, from which the base can be seen through binoculars. The "veterans return" tour also drives by the bars frequented by US pilots, and the major US base of Long Binh Post.

Dong Nai Province Museum
The museum on Nguyen Ai Quoc Street is home to the original Long Tan Cross, as well as other Vietnam War artifacts from Dong Nai.

Long Tan Cross and Battlefield
The Sixth Battalion, Royal Australian Regiment erected the Long Tan Cross in 1969 to commemorate the site of the August 1966 battle between the First Australian Task Force and the NVA and Viet Cong. The current cross at the site is a replica of the original, which is now in the Dong Nai Province Museum. Visitors may not visit the battlefield site without official authorization.

Ma Da Cemetery
Known as the "cemetery of no tombs," this burial ground is located in the old D military base in the province's Vinh Cuu district. The cemetery gets its name from the fact that thousands of remains buried there during the war have not yet been discovered.

Military Cemetery, Long Khanh
This cemetery, near the Xuan Loc Victory monument, contains the graves of both Viet Minh and NVA soldiers.

Xuan Loc victory monument
The Battle of Xuan Loc was a key victory for the NVA during their final offensive of 1975. The grand monument in Long Khanh, commemorating the battle, is dedicated to the soldiers of the North Vietnamese Army.

HANOI

B-52 Victory Museum
An American B-52 Stratofortress was downed in a surburban pond—known as Huu Tiep Lake—on the first night of Operation Linebacker II. The plane's remnants were later removed to this nearby museum, which commemorates aerial combat during the Vietnam War, and specifically NVA antiaircraft artillery.

Ho Chi Minh Mausoleum
Open from November until September, this marble building was built from materials gathered from across Vietnam to house the glass sarcophagus of communist leader Ho Chi Minh.

Ho Chi Minh Museum
Built in 1990 for the centennial anniversary of the leader's birth, this museum showcases photographs, personal possessions, and information on the Vietnamese communist movement. http://www.baotanghochiminh.vn/en/

Ho Chi Minh Stilt House
"Uncle Ho" lived in this modest wooden house between 1958 and 1969, refusing to live in the grander Presidential Palace. The building is now open to the public.

Hoa Lo Prison
Called the Hanoi Hilton by its American inmates, Hoa Lo Prison is one of the most infamous sites to house American prisoners of war during the conflict. The prison now contains exhibits on US pilots who were imprisoned there—notably Senator John McCain—as well as on the prison's use during the First Indochina War.

Vietnam Military History Museum
Built in 1956, this museum contains weapons, uniforms, and photographs from the Vietnam War. The museum also contains information about the famous tunnel systems, and shows archival film footage to tell the story of the war from the Vietnamese perspective.

Vietnam War Memorial
Opposite the Ho Chi Minh Mausoleum, this memorial was built in 1993 to commemorate those who fought alongside the NVA. It is a popular place for veterans and visiting foreign dignitaries to pay their respects.

Vietnamese People's Air Force Museum
This museum has a substantial collection of aircraft, helicopters, and weapons from the Vietnam War. The collection includes aircraft lost by US forces—for example, the wreckage of USAF Colonel Joseph Kittinger's F-4 Phantom, downed on May 11, 1972, and the gear he was wearing when taken prisoner.

HAIPHONG

Haiphong Museum

The museum's interior contains a gallery on the city from 1955 to present day, while the garden contains relics from the war—namely vehicles and aircraft.

HO CHI MINH

Cu Chi Tunnels

The most famous of the Viet Cong tunnel networks, the tunnels of Cu Chi, span a large amount of underground territory around Saigon, and were a major base for Viet Cong operations during the 1968 Tet Offensive. Today, the tunnels have been preserved and modified for tourists.

Day tours to Nui Dat, Long Tan, and Vung Tau

Of particular interest to Australian veterans are day trips from Saigon to Nui Dat, Long Tan, and Vung Tau. These private guided tours visit the former sites of Australia's Nui Dat Task Force Base, the location of Horseshoe fire support base, the Long Tan Cross Memorial, the Long Phuoc Tunnels, and the site of the Australian base at Vung Tau.

Ho Chi Minh Campaign Museum

Dedicated to the final NVA offensive of 1975, the museum has an outdoor exhibit with tanks and planes, such as a South Vietnamese Air Force Cessna A-37 and a US-built F-5E Tiger. The museum is home to one of the very tanks that entered the grounds of the Presidential Palace to capture Saigon in 1975.

Ho Chi Minh City Museum

This museum contains artifacts from the First Indochina War and Vietnam War, as well as "Souvenirs of War Resistance:" personal items belonging to those who fought alongside the NVA and Viet Cong. http://www.hcmc-museum.edu.vn/en-us/home-page.aspx

Museum of Vietnamese Women

Women served on both sides during the Vietnam War. Their service is memorialized on the second floor of this museum in Ho Chi Minh City.

Reunification Palace

The current building at this site was built in 1962, after President Ngo Dinh Diem's own Air Force bombed the previous presidential residence. The fall of Saigon saw tanks crash through the gates. South Vietnamese President General Minh surrendered on the palace steps.

St. Francis Xavier Catholic Church, Cholon

In an attempted flight from the coup that would oust him in 1963, South Vietnamese President Ngo Dinh Diem was arrested at this church as he took mass. En route to Tan Son Nhut, Diem and his brother were executed at close range in the back of an armored personnel carrier.

Tet Offensive memorials

Two memorials stand at the site of the US Embassy, which was demolished in 2002. One commemorates the efforts of the Viet Cong during the 1968 Tet Offensive; the other pays tribute to the fallen US Marines and embassy employees who lost their lives in that same struggle.

Vietnamese People's Air Force Museum, Ho Chi Minh City

Adjacent to the site of Tan Son Nhut Air Base—a major US airbase during the war—the Vietnamese People's Air Force museum contains a collection of aircraft and objects associated with North Vietnam's Vietnam People's Airforce (VPAF). It also includes an outdoor exhibit featuring US and ARVN planes.

War Remnants Museum

Pulling no punches, this attraction is one of the most popular stops for war tourists in Vietnam. The exhibits contain weapons, vehicles, and artifacts from both US and Vietnamese veterans, as well as harrowing photographs and accounts of the conflict. It also contains replicas of the notorious "tiger cages," in which communist prisoners were confined on Con Son Island.

Xa Loi Pagoda

A key site of resistance to President Ngo Dinh Diem, the pagoda today has a shrine honoring the martyrdom of Buddhist monk Thich Quang Duc, whose self-immolation nearby captured the eyes of the world in 1963.

KONTUM

Skull Slope

Kontum was the site of a major battle between the NVA and ARVN during the Easter Offensive of 1972. While few visual reminders of the battle remain, Kontum does have a monument to the war. Known as Skull Slope or Skull Hill, the monument occupies ground where 700 NVA soldiers' remains were unearthed after the war. An ARVN cemetery occupies the land opposite.

Dak To

A monument on a roundabout in the town of Dak To celebrates the liberation of the Dak To-Can Tanh base by North Vietnamese forces in the 1972 Easter Offensive. At the monument are two Russian-made tanks that took part in the offensive, and placards paying tribute to the North Vietnamese soldiers who died there.

NGHE AN

Kim Lien Museum

This free museum was the childhood home of Ho Chi Minh. who lived there between 1890 and 1895. He moved to nearby Lang Sen at the age of six—visitors to the town can see a replica of the home he lived in there, and visit a local shrine to the beloved leader.

QUANG NGAI

Son My Memorial Park

In March 1968, American soldiers massacred innocent civilians at a hamlet known as My Lai, leading to the court-martialling of its leaders. The tranquil site is now home to statues and memorial walls paying tribute to the dead, but the scars of the massacre remain visible in bullet holes and the foundations of burned down houses—each with a plaque commemorating the fallen.

QUANG TRI

DMZ (Demilitarized Zone)

Vietnam was divided into two territories along the 17th Parallel in 1954. The area around this division was technically a demilitarized zone (DMZ), although in practice it saw its fair share of military action. Today, visitors to the DMZ can see the Rock Pile, which was used as a US Marine Corps lookout and artillery base, and the remains of Camp Carroll—a base from 1966 to 1972. Day trips to the area go past the Rock Pile, McNamara Line, Khe Sanh, and Hamburger Hill.

Guides into DMZ territory mostly operate from the former US Marine post at Dong Ha; going into this territory without a guide is not recommended, due to the amount of unexploded ordnance that remains there, unmarked.

Hien Luong Bridge and Ben Hai River Museum

Destroyed in 1967, the original Hien Luong Bridge marked the division of Vietnam along the 17th Parallel, and was painted half red and half yellow to acknowledge this physical and ideological boundary. The bridge was reopened in 1975, now blue and yellow, as a symbol of Vietnam's reunification. Today, tourists can visit the Ben Hai River Museum, on the bridge's north side, for exhibitions on life in the DMZ territory during the war.

Khe Sanh Museum

This base near the DMZ was a major target of the NVA's Tet Offensive, with US troops besieged there under heavy artillery fire. The Khe Sanh Museum commemorates the battle with a reconstruction of an American bunker, as well as vehicles, weapons, and objects.

Truong Son Cemetery

This hillside cemetery was built for those who died on the Ho Chi Minh Trail—the major supply route from the North to the South—which was known to them as the Truong Son Trail. The cemetery is home to around 10,000 graves, which is only two-fifths of the total number of people who died on the trail.

Vinh Moc Tunnels

An entire coastal village was driven to seek refuge inside these tunnels, sometimes for days or weeks at a time, as shelter from American bombs. They built their three-level network nearly 100 feet (30 m) below ground to avoid US bombs that were capable of burrowing down around 30 feet (10 m). More spacious than the Cu Chi tunnels, Vinh Moc's underground network has been partially reopened for visitors.

THUA THIEN-HUE

Ho Chi Minh Museum, Hue

Hue's museum focuses on the schooling of the revolutionary leader, who studied there from 1895–1901 and 1906–09.

Hue Citadel

A major target of the 1968 Tet Offensive, the imperial city of Hue bears the scars of battle. While some of the buildings have been destroyed, the northern sector in particular is riddled with bullet holes and crumbling walls.

HO CHI MINH TRAIL

Biking the trail

The Ho Chi Minh Trail was a key supply route into South Vietnam, making it a target for US bombings during Operation Rolling Thunder. Many visitors wanting to learn more about the trail visit the Ho Chi Minh Trail Museum in Hanoi. Others choose to traverse the trail themselves, by motorbike. Motorcyclists can drive through scenic mountain passes, following the same route used during the war, which largely remains unchanged. Even with a guide, the full tour—from the north, through Laos, and back into the south—takes around two weeks to complete.

VETERANS' TOURS

Returning to Vietnam

Many of the war's major battlesites, crash sites, landing zones, and the remains of former bases are now gone—or, if they were particular to US troops, have not been well preserved. However, many local guides specialize in "veteran return" tours, and will, for a fee, locate and take veterans to the places where they served.

Index

Acknowledgments

The publisher would like to thank the following for their kind permission to reproduce their photographs:

(Key: a-above; b-below/bottom; c-center; f-far; l-left; r-right; t-top)

1 The Vietnam Center and Archive, Texas Tech University: 1332museum1151, Darryl (Bud) Skuce Collection. **2-3 Getty Images:** Bettmann. **4 akg-images:** Paul Almasy (cra). **Getty Images:** Bettmann (cr); SeM / UIG (br). **5 Alamy Stock Photo:** World History Archive (bl). **Getty Images:** Paul Schutzer / The LIFE Picture Collection (ca); Larry Burrows / Time Magazine / The LIFE Picture Collection (br). **6 Getty Images:** Bettmann (cl, cra); Jonathan Blair / Corbis (bl). **Press Association Images:** AP (br). **7 Bridgeman Images:** Pictures From History (tl). **Getty Images:** Bettmann (br); Robert Nickelsberg / The LIFE Images Collection (c). **Press Association Images:** Nick Ut / AP (bl). **8-9 Getty Images:** Bettmann. **10-11 akg-images:** Paul Almasy. **Press Association Images:** DANG VAN PHUOC / AP (Background). **12 akg-images:** (bl). **Bridgeman Images:** Pictures From History (cr). **Getty Images:** Print Collector (cl). **14 Getty Images:** Leemage (br). **The Art Archive:** (cl). **TopFoto.co.uk:** Roger-Viollet (cra). **15 akg-images:** Pictures from History (cr). **Alamy Stock Photo:** David Coleman (bl); Everett Collection Historical (cb). **Bridgeman Images:** Pictures from History (cla). **16-17 The Art Archive:** Kharbine-Tapabor (b). **17 Alamy Stock Photo:** Ivan Vdovin (c). **Bridgeman Images:** Pictures from History (br). **TopFoto.co.uk:** Roger-Viollet (tl). **18 Getty Images:** Leemage (c). **Rex by Shutterstock:** Universal History Archive (clb). **19 Bridgeman Images:** Pictures from

History (tr). **Getty Images:** Universal History Archive (bc). **20-21 akg-images:** Pictures From History. **21 akg-images:** picture alliance / Christoph Mohr (bc). **Getty Images:** STR (FILES) / AFP (tc). **Photoshot:** Imagebroker (crb). **22-23 Rex by Shutterstock:** Roger-Viollet (t). **22 Alamy Stock Photo:** INTERFOTO (bl). **TopFoto.co.uk:** Roger-Viollet (b). **23 TopFoto.co.uk:** Roger-Viollet (tr). **24 Bridgeman Images:** Pictures from History (tr). **Getty Images:** AFP (bc). **25 Alamy Stock Photo:** Richard Ellis (tr). **TopFoto.co.uk:** Roger-Viollet (b). **26 Bridgeman Images:** Pictures from History (ca). **Getty Images:** Howard Sochurek / The LIFE Picture Collection (br). **27 Bridgeman Images:** Bibliotheque Nationale, Paris, France / Archives Charmet. **28 Getty Images:** ullstein bild (b). **29 akg-images:** (bc). **Alamy Stock Photo:** The Art Archive (tl); Pictorial Press Ltd (tr). **30 akg-images:** (l). **31 Getty Images:** Apic (tl); AFP / Stringer (bc). **32-33 Getty Images:** Keystone-France. **34 akg-images:** Anatoliy Garanin / STF RIA Novosti (bc). **Getty Images:** Frank Scherschel (t). **35 Getty Images:** Garofalo Jack (br); Howard Sochurek (b). **36-37 Getty Images:** Bettmann. **38 Press Association Images:** AP. **39 Alamy Stock Photo:** Peter Treanor (br). **Smithsonian Institution, National Postal Museum:** (ca). **40 Getty Images:** Wilbur E. Garrett (l). **41 akg-images:** Sputnik (bc). **Bridgeman Images:** Pictures from History (crb). **Getty Images:** Carl T. Gossett Jr (tl). **42 123RF.com:** Luciano Mortula (clb). **akg-images:** Pictures From History (cra). **Alamy Stock Photo:** World History Archive (bc). **43 Getty Images:** John Dominis (t). **Press Association Images:** DANG VAN PHUOC / AP (Background). **46 Getty Images:** Bettmann (cl, cr). **Press**

Association Images: Consolidated U.s. Army / DPA (bl). **48 Getty Images:** Blank Archives (ca); Sovfoto / UIG (cl). **National Museum of American History/© Smithsonian Institution:** Kenneth E. Behring Center (cr, cb). **49 Alamy Stock Photo:** Granger Historical Picture Archive (ca). **Getty Images:** Larry Burrows (cl); PhotoQuest (bc). **50 Alamy Stock Photo:** Claudine Klodien (clb). **50-51 Alamy Stock Photo:** Granger Historical Picture Archive (b). **51 Bridgeman Images:** Pictures from History (tc). **Getty Images:** Larry Burrows (br). **52 Bridgeman Images:** Pictures from History (cla). **52-53 National Museum of American History/© Smithsonian Institution:** Kenneth E. Behring Center (b). **53 Getty Images:** Photo 12 (tc); Agence France Presse (br). **54 Alamy Stock Photo:** The Art Archive (cla, cr). **Dorling Kindersley:** Stuart Beeny (br); Vietnam Rolling Thunder (cra, crb, br/stick granade). **55 Dorling Kindersley:** Stuart Beeny (cl); Vietnam Rolling Thunder (tr, tl, cr). **56-57 Getty Images:** Sovfoto / UIG. **57 Glenn from Canada:** (tr). **Getty Images:** Cormac McCreesh (cl); James Burke (br). **58 Getty Images:** Blank Archives (tl); James Burke (br). **59 Getty Images:** STF / Staff (t). **60 Alamy Stock Photo:** Pictorial Press (r); World History Archive (clb). **61 Getty Images:** Stan Wayman (r). **Rex by Shutterstock:** CSU Archv / Everett (crb). **62 Alamy Stock Photo:** David Coleman (cl). **Getty Images:** Bettmann (bl). **63 akg-images:** Pictures From History (cra). **64 Getty Images:** Larry Burrows (crb). **National Museum of American History/© Smithsonian Institution:** Kenneth E. Behring Center (tr). **65 Getty Images:** Larry Burrows. **66-67 Getty Images:** Larry Burrows. **68 Getty Images:** Terry Fincher (b). **69 Australian War Memorial:** Image Id:REL_04044_001--1

(tl). **Getty Images:** Bettmann (br). **70 Rex by Shutterstock:** Everett Collection (t). **71 Australian War Memorial:** Image Id: ARTV09293, Unknown (tl). **Getty Images:** Larry Burrows (br). **72 Alamy Stock Photo:** Granger Historical Picture Archive (tl). **Bridgeman Images:** Pictures from History (bl). **72-73 Press Association Images:** HORST FAAS / AP (bc). **74-75 Press Association Images:** MALCOLM BROWNE / AP. **76 Alamy Stock Photo:** Granger Historical Picture Archive (bc); Hemis (tr). **77 Press Association Images:** AP (l). **78 Alamy Stock Photo:** White House Photo (bl). **Getty Images:** PhotoQuest (cra). **79 Press Association Images:** Consolidated U.s. Army / DPA (b). **80-81 Getty Images:** Bettmann (t). **80 Alamy Stock Photo:** Granger Historical Picture Archive (br). **81 Alamy Stock Photo:** Everett Collection Historical (br). **82 Rex by Shutterstock:** Courtesy Everett Collection (l). **83 Alamy Stock Photo:** The Art Archive (crb); Granger Historical Picture Archive (tl). **Getty Images:** Fairfax Media (bc). **84-85 Getty Images:** Paul Schutzer / The LIFE Picture Collection. **Press Association Images:** DANG VAN PHUOC / AP (Background). **86 Alamy Stock Photo:** ClassicStock (br). **Getty Images:** Larry Burrows / Time Magazine / The LIFE Picture Collection (cl); Co Rentmeester / The LIFE Picture Collection (cr). **88 Australian War Memorial:** Image Id:REL33848 (clb). **Getty Images:** Stuart Lutz / Gado (clb); Underwood Archives (ca). **National Air and Space Museum, Smithsonian Institution:** (br). **89 Alamy Stock Photo:** Archive Image (crb). **Getty Images:** Dick Swanson / The LIFE Images Collection (cra); Larry Burrows / The LIFE Picture Collection (clb). **National Air and Space Museum, Smithsonian Institution:** (cla). **90 Alamy Stock Photo:** Military

Images (clb). **Getty Images:** Bettmann (bl). **90-91 Getty Images:** Larry Burrows / The LIFE Picture Collection (c). **91 Press Association Images:** Henry Huet / AP (tr). **92 Bridgeman Images:** Pictures from History. **93 Getty Images:** Bettmann (br); Stuart Lutz / Gado (tc); Co Rentmeester / The LIFE Picture Collection (bl). **94-95 Getty Images:** Bettmann (b). **95 Alamy Stock Photo:** Sergii Popsuievych (br). **National Air and Space Museum, Smithsonian Institution:** (tl). **96 Alamy Stock Photo:** Ranger Images (tl); JELLE vanderwolf (crb); NASA Archive (tr). **Dreamstime.com:** Andrew Oxley (cra). **National Air and Space Museum, Smithsonian Institution:** (cla, br). **96-97 Alamy Stock Photo:** Dan Leeth (c). **97 Alamy Stock Photo:** ContributorPF-(aircraft) (crb); Antony Nettle (crb/Grumman). **Dorling Kindersley:** Flugausstellung (cra/MiG 17); Ukraine State Aviation Museum (tr); Nationaal Luchtvaart Themapark Aviodome (ca). **National Air and Space Museum, Smithsonian Institution:** (clb/GRUMMAN A-6E, clb). **U.S. Air Force:** (b). **98-99 Getty Images:** Bettmann. **99 Alamy Stock Photo:** PF-(aircraft) (bc). **Getty Images:** Pierre Mion / National Geographic (tr); Stuart Lutz / Gado (tc). **100-101 Getty Images:** Larry Burrows / Time Magazine / The LIFE Picture Collection. **102 akg-images:** Pictures From History (bl). **Press Association Images:** LEW LOWERY / AP (tr). **103 Alamy Stock Photo:** Micha Klootwijk (tc). **Getty Images:** Bettmann (b). **104-105 Press Association Images:** Rick Merron / AP (b). **105 Alamy Stock Photo:** AF archive (br). **National Museum of American History/© Smithsonian Institution:** Kenneth E. Behring Center (c). **Press Association Images:** Rick Merron / AP (tl). **106 Alamy Stock Photo:** Archive Image (cla, bc). **106-107 Press Association Images:** HORST FAAS / AP (t). **108 Getty Images:** Bettmann. **109 Australian War Memorial:** Image Id:REL33848 (tc). **National Museum of American History/© Smithsonian Institution:** Kenneth E. Behring Center (bl). **110 Getty Images:** Stuart Lutz / Gado (tr, b). **111 Getty Images:** Bettmann (tr); Science & Society Picture Library (bl). **112 Getty Images:** Bettmann (tr, bl). **113 Getty Images:** Bettmann. **114 Butler Center for Arkansas Studies:** (bc/Calendar). **Getty Images:** Nathan Benn (br). **Copyright Col. Robert Liotta:** (bl). **United States Army Women's Museum, Fort Lee, Virginia:** (cra/Plate). **The Vietnam Center and Archive, Texas Tech University:** 2117museum4410, Jerry L. Harlowe Collection (cra/Bracelet); 2117museum3234, Jerry L. Harlowe Collection (c); 2117museum3253, Jerry L. Harlowe Collection (cb); 2117museum3236, Jerry L. Harlowe Collection (fbl). **115 Australian War Memorial:** Image Id: REL27721 (br); Image Id: REL33480 (bl, bc/Lighter in box). **Getty Images:** Stuart Lutz / Gado (bc). **National Museum of American History/© Smithsonian Institution:** Kenneth E. Behring Center (tl, tr). **116-117 Getty Images:** Bettmann. **118 Alamy Stock Photo:** Everett Collection Historical (cla). **Australian War Memorial:** Image Id: REL31610 (bc). **118-119 Getty Images:** David Hume Kennerly (b). **119 Australian War Memorial:** Image Id: REL31610 (tc). **120-121 © The Board of Trustees of the Armouries:** (t). **120 Australian War Memorial:** Image Id: CUN_66_0704_VN (br). **121 Australian War Memorial:** Image Id: ART40758 (c); Image Id: REL34826 (bc). **122 Getty Images:** Dick Swanson / The LIFE Images Collection. **123 Getty Images:** Dick Swanson / The LIFE Images Collection (tc). **Press Association Images:** AP (br).

124-125 Getty Images: Bettmann (b). **125 Collection of the Smithsonian National Museum of African American History and Culture. . African American History and Culture:** (tc). **Getty Images:** STEPHEN JAFFE / AFP (cr). **US Army Quartermaster Museum:** (br). **126-127 Getty Images:** Hulton Archive. **128 US Army Quartermaster Museum:** (ca). **128-129 National Air and Space Museum, Smithsonian Institution:** (b). **129 Getty Images:** Larry Burrows / The LIFE Picture Collection (tc). **130-131 Getty Images:** Larry Burrows / The LIFE Picture Collection. **132 Alamy Stock Photo:** Flame (cl); DAVID NEWHAM (cra). **Dreamstime.com:** Jorg Hackemann (b). **133 123RF.com:** ANATOLIY L FYODOROV (tr). **Alamy Stock Photo:** Ivan Cholakov (b); Len Holsborg (crb). **National Naval Aviation Museum Collection:** (tl). **Dorling Kindersley:** Royal International Air Tattoo 2011 (c). **Getty Images:** Dennis Macdonald (clb). **134 Press Association Images:** Anonymous / AP (tr). **135 Getty Images:** Dirck Halstead / The LIFE Images Collection (tr). **Press Association Images:** AP (l). **136-137 Press Association Images:** AP. **138-139 Getty Images:** Co Rentmeester / The LIFE Picture Collection (t). **138 Rex by Shutterstock:** Sovfoto / Universal Images Group (br). **139 Getty Images:** AFP (crb). **140 Getty Images:** Larry Burrows / The LIFE Picture Collection (bl). **Wikipedia:** (cb). **140-141 The US National Archives and Records Administration:** (t). **141 Alamy Stock Photo:** Everett Collection Historical (crb). **142 Bridgeman Images:** Pictures From History. **143 Alamy Stock Photo:** The Art Archive (br). **Getty Images:** Neil Leifer / Sports Illustrated (tl). **144 Alamy Stock Photo:** Malcolm Fairman (clb). **144-145 Getty Images:** Co Rentmeester / The LIFE Picture Collection (b). **145 Dreamstime.com:** Pedro Monteiro (tc). **Getty Images:** Co Rentmeester / The LIFE Picture Collection (br). **146 Alamy Stock Photo:** Everett Collection Historical (tr). **Rex by Shutterstock:** Courtesy Everett Collection (bl). **147 Australian War Memorial:** Image: ARTV10315 (br). **Getty Images:** Dick Swanson / The LIFE Images Collection (l). **148-149 Getty Images:** Larry Burrows. **150-151 Getty Images:** STF / AFP (b). **151 Australian War Memorial:** Image Id: ARTV09308 (tc); Image Id: REL05844 (bc). **152 Alamy Stock Photo:** Military Images (cla); Stocktrek Images, Inc (cra); Stocktrek Images, Inc. (ca). **Dorling Kindersley:** Board of Trustees of the Royal Armouries (cb); Stuart Beeny (tc); Vietnam Rolling Thunder (cr, cl, cr/bullets, b); Second Guards Rifles Division (clb); The Combined Military Services Museum (CMSM) (crb). **153 Dorling Kindersley:** Vietnam Rolling Thunder (cla, tl). **Dreamstime.com:** Jorg Hackemann (ca). **National Museum of American History/© Smithsonian Institution:** Kenneth E. Behring Center (r). **154 United States Army Women's Museum, Fort Lee, Virginia:** (bc). **The Vietnam Center and Archive, Texas Tech University:** VA040590, Frederic Whitehurst Collection (cla). **155 Bridgeman Images:** Pictures From History (bl). **Getty Images:** Bettmann (t). **156-157 Alamy Stock Photo:** SPUTNIK. **158 Alamy Stock Photo:** NARA (b). **159 Dorling Kindersley:** Vietnam Rolling Thunder (b). **Getty Images:** Larry Burrows / The LIFE Picture Collection (tc). **160-161 Getty Images:** Larry Burrows / The LIFE Picture Collection. **162 Getty Images:** Stringer / AFP (cla); Fred W. McDarrah (br). **Press Association Images:** Charles Fentress Jr. / The Courier-Journal-USA TODAY Sports (cr). **163 Getty Images:** Bettmann (t). **164-165 Magnum Photos:** Marc Riboud.

166-167 Getty Images: Bettmann. **Press Association Images:** DANG VAN PHUOC / AP (Background). **168 Getty Images:** Bettmann (bl, cr, br). **170 Dorling Kindersley:** Fort Nelson (cla). **Getty Images:** Bettmann (bc). **Brown University Library:** Jerry A. Zimmer (cra). **TopFoto.co.uk:** © 2003 Credit:Topham Picturepoint (cr). **171 Getty Images:** Bettmann (clb); Larry Burrows / The LIFE Picture Collection (cla); Santi Visalli (cra); Nik Wheeler / Corbis (bc). **172 Alamy Stock Photo:** World History Archive (bl). **Dorling Kindersley:** Vietnam Rolling Thunder (tr). **Getty Images:** Stuart Lutz / Gado (cl). **173 Getty Images:** AFP / Staff (l). **174 Rex by Shutterstock:** Universal History Archive (l). **175 Alamy Stock Photo:** epa european pressphoto agency b.v. (br); Bjorn Svensson (tl). **Getty Images:** AFP / Stringer (bl). **176-177 Alamy Stock Photo:** US Marines Photo (tc). **176 Bridgeman Images:** Underwood Archives / UIG (br). **177 Alamy Stock Photo:** The Art Archive (bc). **178 Rex by Shutterstock:** Sovfoto / Universal Images Group (b). **179 Getty Images:** Bettmann (tc). **Press Association Images:** Al Chang / AP (br). **180 Getty Images:** Mondadori Portfolio (tl). **Press Association Images:** Phuc / AP (bl). **181 Alamy Stock Photo:** Military Images (tr). **Rex by Shutterstock:** Universal History Archive / Universal Images Group (bc). **182-183 Alamy Stock Photo:** Granger Historical Picture Archive. **184 Alamy Stock Photo:** Military Images (tc). **Brown University Library:** David E. Taylor (Class of 1966) (tl, bl). **National Museum of American History/© Smithsonian Institution:** Kenneth E. Behring Center (tr). **185 123RF.com:** frameangel (cl). **Alamy Stock Photo:** CNP Collection (br). **© The Board of Trustees of the Armouries:** (cb, bl). **Dorling Kindersley:** The Combined Military Services Museum (CMSM) (crb). **National Museum of American History/© Smithsonian Institution:** Kenneth E. Behring Center (c). **186 Alamy Stock Photo:** Simon Dack (bl). **Getty Images:** Express Newspapers (cra). **187 Rex by Shutterstock:** Courtesy Everett Collection. **188-189 Press Association Images:** Eddie Adams / AP. **190-191 Bridgeman Images:** Pictures from History. **191 Getty Images:** Bettmann (tr). **TopFoto.co.uk:** © 2003 Credit:Topham Picturepoint (bc). **192 Rex by Shutterstock:** Courtesy Everett Collection (tl). **192-193 Getty Images:** Bettmann (b). **193 123RF.com:** Luciano Mortula (br). **Bridgeman Images:** Pictures from History (tr). **194 Getty Images:** Buyenlarge (cl). **Brown University Library:** Jerry A. Zimmer (tr). **194-195 Getty Images:** Bettmann (b). **195 Getty Images:** Pictorial Parade / Archive Photos (tr). **196-197 Getty Images:** Bettmann. **198 Getty Images:** Universal History Archive / UIG (cla). **United States Army Women's Museum, Fort Lee, Virginia:** (bl). **198-199 Alamy Stock Photo:** Everett Collection Historical (b). **199 United States Army Women's Museum, Fort Lee, Virginia:** (tl). **200 Getty Images:** Bettmann. **201 Getty Images:** Bettmann (tr); Sovfoto / UIG (bl). **202 Bridgeman Images:** Pictures from History (br). **Getty Images:** Larry Burrows / The LIFE Picture Collection (tl). **203 Bridgeman Images:** Private Collection / Peter Newark Military Pictures (tc). **Getty Images:** Larry Burrows / Time Magazine / The LIFE Picture Collection (b). **204-205 Getty Images:** Bettmann. **206 Alamy Stock Photo:** The Art Archive (tl). **Australian War Memorial:** Image Id: RELAWM40062 (tc). **Dreamstime.com:** Alexandr Blinov (cl); Pingvin121674 (tr); Aleksandr Stepanov (br). **207 Alamy Stock Photo:** Malcolm Fairman (crb); PjrTransport

(tl); Mim Friday (cra). **Australian War Memorial:** Image Id: REL26769 (c). **Dreamstime.com:** Micha Klootwijk (cb); Meoita (bl). **208-209 Getty Images:** Bettmann (t). **208 Alamy Stock Photo:** Keystone Pictures USA (bl). **209 Alamy Stock Photo:** Keystone Pictures USA (br). **210 Alamy Stock Photo:** Granger Historical Picture Archive (clb). **Press Association Images:** Eddie Adams / AP (cra). **211 Getty Images:** Rolls Press / Popperfoto. **212 Getty Images:** Buyenlarge (tr); Time Life Pictures / USIA / National Archives / The LIFE Picture Collection (bc). **213 Getty Images:** Angelo Cozzi / Mondadori Portfolio. **214 Australian War Memorial:** Image Id: REL38058 (ca). **The Vietnam Center and Archive, Texas Tech University:** VA057073, Edgar R. McCoin Collection (bc). **215 Alamy Stock Photo:** The Art Archive (l). **Getty Images:** Larry Morris, The Washington Post (br). **216 Getty Images:** Bettmann (r); David Pollack / Corbis (tl). **217 Getty Images:** Jim Garrett / NY Daily News (tc); Santi Visalli (br). **218-219 Getty Images:** Bettmann. **Press Association Images:** DANG VAN PHUOC / AP (Background). **220 Getty Images:** Bettmann (cl, cr, br). **222 Alamy Stock Photo:** GL Archive (cl); Granger Historical Picture Archive (br). **Getty Images:** Bettmann (ca, bc). **223 Getty Images:** David J. & Janice L. Frent / Corbis (cl). **Imperial War Museum:** (cra). **National Museum of American History/© Smithsonian Institution:** Kenneth E. Behring Center (bl). **Rex by Shutterstock:** Courtesy Everett Collection (bc). **224 Getty Images:** Charles H. Phillips / The LIFE Picture Collection (tl). **224-225 Alamy Stock Photo:** Everett Collection Historical (b). **225 Press Association Images:** Bob Daugherty / AP (tr). **226 Alamy Stock Photo:** GL Archive. **227 Alamy Stock Photo:** Danita Delimont (bc); Everett Collection Historical (t); World History Archive (cr). **228 Alamy Stock Photo:** Everett Collection Historical. **229 Getty Images:** Bettmann (tl, br). **National Air and Space Museum, Smithsonian Institution:** (cra). **230 Getty Images:** Bettmann. **231 Alamy Stock Photo:** Photo by Nadia Borowski Scott / SDU-T / ZUMA Press (ca). **Getty Images:** Bettmann (clb). **Press Association Images:** AP (cr). **232 Australian War Memorial:** Image Id: RELAWM41029 (tr). **Imperial War Museum:** (bc). **233 Getty Images:** Robert Whitaker (t). **TopFoto.co.uk:** Atlas Archive © The Image Works (bc). **234 Getty Images:** Frank Zeller / AFP (tr); Larry Burrows / The LIFE Picture Collection (bl). **234-235 Getty Images:** Bettmann (b). **235 Getty Images:** Bettmann (tr). **236-237 Press Association Images:** AP. **238-239 Getty Images:** Bettmann (t). **239 Australian War Memorial:** Image Id: REL32708 (tc); Image Id: REL33515 (bc). **240-241 Getty Images:** Bettmann (b). **240 Australian War Memorial:** Image Id: REL33227 (c). **Getty Images:** Bettmann (clb). **241 Getty Images:** Bill Ray / Time & Life Pictures (cr). **242 akg-images:** (bc). **Press Association Images:** AP (tr). **243 Alamy Stock Photo:** Backyard Productions (cr). **Press Association Images:** Eddie Adams / AP (c). **244-245 Getty Images:** Bettmann. **246-247 Getty Images:** Ronald S. Haeberle / The LIFE Images Collection (t). **247 Alamy Stock Photo:** imageBROKER (br). **Getty Images:** Bettmann (tc); Stuart Lutz / Gado (cb). **248 Getty Images:** Bettmann. **249 Getty Images:** Bettmann (tc, bc). **250 Alamy Stock Photo:** ams images (cl). **250-251 Getty Images:** Alex Bowie (b). **251 © The Board of Trustees of the Armouries:** (cr). **Getty Images:** John Bulmer (tc). **252 Getty Images:** Larry Burrows / Time Magazine / The LIFE Picture Collection (cla). **252-253**

Alamy Stock Photo: Archive Image (b). **253 National Air and Space Museum, Smithsonian Institution:** (br). **254 Press Association Images:** AP. **255 Alamy Stock Photo:** Granger Historical Picture Archive (tr). **Getty Images:** Bettmann (bl). **256-257 Getty Images:** John Filo. **258 Getty Images:** Hulton Archive. **259 Press Association Images:** DANG VAN PHUOC / AP (bl); HORST FAAS / AP (tr). **260 Getty Images:** Bettmann (bl). **National Museum of American History/© Smithsonian Institution:** Kenneth E. Behring Center (tl). **260-261 U.S. Air Force:** (t). **261 Getty Images:** Alex Bowie (br). **262 Alamy Stock Photo:** The Art Archive (Toothpaste, Brush, Soap, Clothes Pegs, Matchbox and Spoon, br). **National Museum of American History/© Smithsonian Institution:** Kenneth E. Behring Center (ca, c, cr, fcr). **263 Alamy Stock Photo:** The Art Archive (tc). **Getty Images:** Gordon Chibroski / Portland Press Herald (tl, c, bl, bc). **National Museum of American History/© Smithsonian Institution:** Kenneth E. Behring Center (r). **264 Dorling Kindersley:** Vietnam Rolling Thunder (tl). **264-265 Getty Images:** Bettmann (b). **265 Alamy Stock Photo:** ZUMA Press, Inc. (tr). **266-267 Bridgeman Images:** Pictures From History. **Press Association Images:** DANG VAN PHUOC / AP (Background). **268 Getty Images:** Dirck Halstead / The LIFE Images Collection (l); Dirck Halstead / Liaison (cr); Henri Bureau / Corbis / VCG (br). **270 Alamy Stock Photo:** ITAR-TASS Photo Agency (bl). **Getty Images:** Bettmann (crb). **Press Association Images:** Josip Lee / AP (ca). **271 Dreamstime.com:** Victor Karasev (cl). **Getty Images:** Bachrach (cb); Bettmann (cra); David J. & Janice L. Frent / Corbis (crb). **272-273 Dreamstime.com:** Mikhail Starodubov (b). **272 Bridgeman Images:** Private Collection / Peter Newark Military Pictures (tr). **TopFoto.co.uk:** © 2003 Credit:Topham Picturepoint (bl). **273 Getty Images:** Sovfoto / UIG (c). **274 akg-images:** Pictures From History (ca). **274-275 Getty Images:** Keystone-France / Gamma-Keystone (b). **275 akg-images:** (crb). **Press Association Images:** NIHON DENPA NEWS / AP (tc). **276 Alamy Stock Photo:** Roberto Nistri (ca). **276-277 Press Association Images:** AP (b). **277 Getty Images:** Bettmann (tc). **278 Australian War Memorial:** Image Id: RC05477 (crb); Image Id: RELAWM40960 (tl). **Press Association Images:** AP (bc). **279 Press Association Images:** Michel Laurent / AP. **280-281 Press Association Images:** Nick Ut / AP. **282-283 Alamy Stock Photo:** Eye Ubiquitous (b). **Getty Images:** PHAN DUY / AFP (t). **283 Press Association Images:** Josip Lee / AP (br). **284 Alamy Stock Photo:** Micha Klootwijk (tr). **Australian War Memorial:** Image Id: REL16440 (bl). **Dreamstime.com:** Ronald Goncarov (clb). **284-285 Dorling Kindersley:** The Tank Museum (b). **285 akg-images:** (cla). **Alamy Stock Photo:** dpa picture alliance (cb); Evan El-Amin (tl); Stocktrek Images, Inc. (ca); Zoonar GmbH (cr); Svetlana Tikhonova (br). **Dreamstime.com:** Victor Karasev (c); Harvey Stowe (tr). **286 Press Association Images:** Nick Ut / AP (bl). **287 Getty Images:** Bettmann (tr). **Press Association Images:** AP (l). **288-289 Press Association Images:** Nick Ut / AP. **290 Getty Images:** Stuart Lutz / Gado (cl). **290-291 Getty Images:** Bettmann (b). **291 Alamy Stock Photo:** GL Archive (c). **Getty Images:** MPI / Stringer (tr). **292 Alamy Stock Photo:** Dan Leeth (bl). **Bridgeman Images:** Pictures from History (cla). **Getty Images:** Underwood Archives (br). **293 Bridgeman Images:** Pictures from History. **294 Getty Images:** David J. & Janice L. Frent / Corbis (cl). **294-295 Getty Images:** Keystone-France / Gamma-Keystone (t). **295 Getty Images:** Keystone / Hulton Archive (bl); Bettmann (br). **296 Getty Images:** Bachrach. **297 Getty Images:** Bettmann (cr); MPI (tc); China Photos (bl). **298 Bridgeman Images:** Pictures from History. **299 Getty Images:** Bettmann (crb). **U.S. Air Force:** (bl). **300 Alamy Stock Photo:** Keystone Pictures USA (b). **Getty Images:** David J. & Janice L. Frent / Corbis (tl). **301 akg-images:** (bc). **Alamy Stock Photo:** Granger Historical Picture Archive (tr). **302-303 Press Association Images:** SAL VEDER / AP. **304-305 Getty Images:** Robert Nickelsberg / The LIFE Images Collection. **Press Association Images:** DANG VAN PHUOC / AP (Background). **306 Alamy Stock Photo:** Terry Fincher.Photo Int (cr). **Press Association Images:** AP (cl). **307 Alamy Stock Photo:** dpa picture alliance (br). **308 Alamy Stock Photo:** Danita Delimont (clb). **Getty Images:** SJOBERG / AFP (br). **Press Association Images:** Anonymous / AP (ca). **308-309 Press Association Images:** Heng Sinith / AP (c). **309 Australian War Memorial:** Image Id: ARTV10379, Unknown (cla). **Getty Images:** DeAgostini (cla); Diana Walker / / Time Life Pictures (cb). **310 Getty Images:** David J. & Janice L. Frent / Corbis (cl). **Press Association Images:** JLR / AP (cra). **310-311 © The Board of Trustees of the Armouries:** (b). **311 Alamy Stock Photo:** Granger Historical Picture Archive (tc). **312 Alamy Stock Photo:** Keystone Pictures USA. **313 Getty Images:** Bettmann (t, cr). **Press Association Images:** DANG VAN PHUOC / AP (bc). **314 Alamy Stock Photo:** dpa picture alliance (bl). **U.S. Army Center of Military History:** (tr). **315 Quinn Ryan Mattingly:** (c). **Press Association Images:** Hoanh / AP (cr). **316 Alamy Stock Photo:** dpa picture alliance (bl). **316-317 Press Association Images:** AP (b). **317 Australian War Memorial:** Image Id: ARTV09304 (tc). **Press Association Images:** AP (br). **318-319 Getty Images:** Bettmann. **320 Alamy Stock Photo:** PF-(sdasm4) (bl). **320-321 Getty Images:** Dirck Halstead / The LIFE Images Collection. **321 Australian War Memorial:** Image Id: RELAWM41029 (cb). **322 Press Association Images:** Sal Veder / AP (tl). **322-323 Rex by Shutterstock:** Sipa Press (b). **323 Bridgeman Images:** Pictures From History (bc). **Getty Images:** Bettmann (t). **324-325 Getty Images:** GLOAGUEN / Gamma-Rapho (t). **325 Alamy Stock Photo:** imageBROKER (cr). **Getty Images:** GLOAGUEN / Gamma-Rapho (br). **326 Getty Images:** Roland Neveu / LightRocket (bl). **326-327 Getty Images:** SJOBERG / AFP. **327 Getty Images:** TIM PAGE / AFP (cra). **328 Bridgeman Images:** Pictures From History (cla). **Ron Quinlin, kohtang.com:** (bc). **329 Bridgeman Images:** Pictures From History (t). **National Air and Space Museum, Smithsonian Institution:** Transferred from the United States Army, Office of the Adjutant General (bc). **330 Getty Images:** Eric LAFFORGUE / Gamma-Rapho (cla). **330-331 Getty Images:** Bettmann (t). **331 Getty Images:** MARK RALSTON / AFP (crb). **332 Getty Images:** AFP (bl); DeAgostini (tr). **332-333 akg-images:** Pictures From History (b). **333 Getty Images:** Dirck Halstead / Liaison (tr). **334-335 Getty Images:** ullstein bild. **336-337 Alamy Stock Photo:** Steve Whyte (t). **337 Getty Images:** Alex Bowie (br); Universal History Archive / UIG (cra); John Bryson / The LIFE Images Collection (bl). **338-339 Getty Images:** SAEED KHAN / AFP. **340-341 Getty Images:** Jean-Claude LABBE / Gamma-Rapho (b). **341 Alamy Stock Photo:** Beren Patterson (br). **Getty Images:** Bettmann (tc). **342 Getty Images:** KHAM / AFP. **343 Alamy Stock Photo:** Mike Goldwater (tr). **Australian War Memorial:** Image Id: ARTV10379, Unknown (tl). **Getty Images:** Mak Remissa / AFP (br). **344 Getty Images:** Andrew Holbrooke / Corbis (bc). **345 Alamy Stock Photo:** mark reinstein (tc). **Getty Images:** Diana Walker / / Time Life Pictures (b). **346 Rex by Shutterstock:** Courtesy Everett Collection (tl, tc, tr, cr); © TriStar Pictures / courtesy Everett Collection (br). **347 Alamy Stock Photo:** AF archive (tc). **Battlefield Vietnam © 2004 Electronic Arts Inc.:** (br). **reprinted by permissions of The Random House Group Ltd:** (bc). **Bruce Sprigsteen- Born in the USA cover- With permission from Grubman Shire & Meiselas:** (bc/Born in the USA cover); **National Museum of American History/© Smithsonian Institution:** Kenneth E. Behring Center (bl). **Rex by Shutterstock:** Universal History Archive (tl); Moviestore Collection (tr); (c) Cannon Films / courtesy Everett Collection (cl); Universal / Everett (cr). **348-349 Peter Rice. 350-351 Alamy Stock Photo:** Mike Goldwater. Dorling Kindersley: Vietnam Rolling Thunder All tabs used in the book.

Endpapers: Thank you to everyone who submitted images for the endpapers. Other museum images supplied:

US Army Women's Museum, with thanks to Tracy Bradford, Dr. Françoise Bonnell, and Ali Kolleda. **Front endpaper:** (left-hand page) 3rd row, 3rd image; 3rd row, 5th image; 6th row, 1st image. (right-hand page) USAWM: 3rd row, 4th image; 4th row, 3rd image. **Back endpaper:** (left-hand page) 3rd row, 3rd image, (right-hand page) USAWM: 4th row, 4th image; 5th row, 1st image.

US Army Quartermaster Museum, with thanks to Luther Hanson.
Front endpaper: (left-hand page) 2nd row, 3rd image; 3rd row 2nd image, (right-hand page) 4th row, 1st image; 5th row, 4th image. **Back endpaper:** (left-hand page) 2nd row, 2nd image; 5th row, 3rd image; 6th row, 1st image, (right-hand page) 3rd row 6th image.

Collection of the Smithsonian National Museum of African American History and Culture, Gift of James E. Brown. With thanks to Doug Remley.
Front endpaper:(left-hand page) 3rd row, 4th image. **Back endpaper:** (left-hand page) 1st row, 3rd image; 5th row, 2nd image, (right-hand page) 3rd row, 4th image; 6th row, 4th image.

All other images © Dorling Kindersley. For further information see: www.dkimages.com

The publisher would like to thank the following people at the Smithsonian Institution for their kind assistance: **Kealy Gordon**, Product Development Manager; **Ellen Nanney**, Licensing Manager; **Brigid Ferraro**, Vice President, Education and Consumer Products; **Carol LeBlanc**, Senior Vice President, Education and Consumer Products; and **Chris Liedel**, President.

Thanks also to Elizabeth Taylor and Jennifer Betts at the Brown University Vietnam Veterans Archive, and to Claire Starnes for putting the editors in touch with other female veterans.

AUTHORS

David L. Anderson is Professor of History Emeritus at California State University, Monterey Bay, and a past president of the Society for Historians of American Foreign Relations. He is the author or editor of 11 books, mainly on the Vietnam War, including *The Columbia History of the Vietnam War* (2011).

Joe P. Dunn is the Charles A. Dana Professor at Converse College. His six books and more than 70 articles include his Vietnam memoir, *Desk Warrior: Memoirs of a Combat REMF* (1999). He has won numerous state and national teaching awards.

Jacob F. Field is a writer and historian, specializing in early modern English and military history. He is the author of three books, the latest of which is *D-Day By Numbers: The Facts Behind Operation Overlord.*

Jeremy Harwood worked in publishing for many years before becoming a full-time history writer. His particular interests include World War II and France's postwar battles with its colonies. Jeremy also contributed to DK's *American War of Independence.*

David Hatt studied History at Peterhouse, Cambridge. He is particularly interested in American history. David also contributed to DK's *American War of Independence.*

R.G. Grant is a history writer who has published more than 30 books, many of them about aspects of military conflict. He is the author of numerous Dorling Kindersley titles, including *Battle* (2009), *Commanders* (2010), and *World War I: The Definitive Visual History* in this series. In the 1980s, he was a contributor to the magazine *Nam!.*

Meredith H. Lair is Associate Professor of History at George Mason University, where her research and teaching focuses on war and American culture, especially in the Vietnam era. She is the author of *Armed with Abundance: Consumerism & Soldiering in the Vietnam War* (2011).

Abigail Mitchell is a graduate of Peterhouse, Cambridge and the University of Southern California. She is about to begin her PhD in American Studies and History. Abigail was an assistant editor for DK's *American War of Independence*, and an editor for both this book and *The Crime Book*, in Dorling Kindersley's Big Ideas series.

Sergeant Major (Ret) Donna Lowery was part of the first group of military women who went to Vietnam. She served in-country from January 31, 1967 to August 19, 1968. During her military career, she completed four tours as a First Sergeant, was a Senior Drill Sergeant, Personnel Sergeant, Administrative Supervisor, and the Inspector General (Ombudsman) SGM for Korea. She is the author of *Women Vietnam Veterans: Our Untold Stories.* Her contribution to this book was written with MSG (Ret) Phyllis K. Miller.

John Prados is the author of more than 30 books on Vietnam and other subjects, including Vietnam: *The History of an Unwinnable War*, 1945–1975, which was nominated for the Pulitzer Prize and won the Henry Adams Prize in American history. He is a senior fellow of the National Security Archive in Washington, D.C.

Joe Yogerst has written three books on Vietnam including the award-winning *Land of Nine Dragons* which took him to postwar Hue, Da Nang, Khe Sanh, Dien Bien Phu, and other Vietnam War locations. His writings on history, culture, and travel have appeared in 32 National Geographic books.

With thanks to everyone who submitted photos of those who served in the Vietnam War, we're sorry we're unable to include the inspiring stories that accompanied them. There are more images at the front of the book.

1ST ROW: US Army Specialist Allan Lipp (b.1942); US Army Lieutenant Bob Ford (1944–1997); Unidentified (image supplied by the National Museum of African American History and Culture); US Army Engineer Robert Lee Bellville (b.1949); US Army Specialist Ron Kroesche (b.1947). **2ND ROW:** US Army Specialist John "Jack" Rudd (1946–2003); Unidentified (image supplied by the US Army Quartermaster Museum); US Army Sergeant Allen Kashner (b.1949); US Army Specialist Claire Brisebois-Starnes (b.1944); US Army Private Alfred Vincent Spano (1945–2012); US Army Specialist Warren G. Dotson, Jr. (1947–1997). **3RD ROW:** US Army Sergeant Richard A. Rajner (b.1948); US Army Private William Klaiber (b.1946); Unidentified US Nurses (image supplied by the US Army Women's Museum); US Army Specialist Riley King (b.1944); US Marine Corps Private John Wesley Cobb (1946–1966). **4TH ROW:** US Navy Aviation Electronics Technician Herbert E. Schamp (1938–2001); US Army Specialist Richard Gilkey (b.1949); US Marine Corps Lance Corporal Thomas A. Holloran (b.1947); US Navy Petty Officer Robert Heurung (b.1948); US Army Sergeant Dennis Michael Sines (b.1948). **5TH ROW:** US Army Sergeant Vic Leneker (b.1949); Unidentified (image supplied by the National Museum of African American History and Culture); Unidentified (image supplied by the US Army Quartermaster Museum); US Navy Lieutenant Kenneth Lee Kreutzer (b.1949). **6TH ROW:** Unidentified (image supplied by the US Army Quartermaster Museum); US Army Private Dennis Jadwin (b.1947); Gary Henry Stave;